# Comrades to the End

# Comrades to the End

*The 4th SS Panzer-Grenadier Regiment*
*"Der Führer" 1938-1945*
*The History of a German-Austrian Fighting Unit*


Otto Weidinger

*Translated form the German by David Johnston*



**Schiffer Military History**
Atglen, PA

The publisher wishes to thank Mark Yerger for his assistance with this project, and George Nipe for producing the maps. "DF" insignia courtesy of Matthew Reinert of the Military History Shop.

Book Design by Robert Biondi.


Library of Congress Catalog Number: 98-84606.



Printed in the United States of America.
ISBN: 0-7643-0593-X

We are interested in hearing from authors with book ideas on military topics.

Published by Schiffer Publishing Ltd.
4880 Lower Valley Road
Atglen, PA 19310
Phone: (610) 593-1777
FAX: (610) 593-2002
E-mail: Schifferbk@aol.com.
Please write for a free catalog.
This book may be purchased from the publisher.
Please include $3.95 postage.
Try your bookstore first.

# PREFACE

I have three wishes in making this introduction to the former members of the regiment:

First congratulations that this work has succeeded as a team effort,
then the wish to pass on the author's kind words to me;
others have made great contributions!
Thirdly I would like to emphasize my personal ties with my old comrades.

The "DF" Regiment was somewhat younger than the "*Leibstandarte*", "*Deutschland*" and "*Germania*" Regiments. I was especially interested for this reason, and because the two streams of military tradition combined on a "Prussian-German" and "Austrian" foundation.

The contents of this book show better than any words that all the members of this regiment may be proud of their accomplishments to the bitter end.

Paul Hausser

# AUTHOR'S FOREWORD

This regiment history is the combined work of four regimental commanders, each of whom wrote his chapter alone or as a joint effort. Each described the regiment's actions from his point of view *at that time* as objectively as possible.

Unfortunately most of the regiment's original war diaries have been lost, which made the work especially hard. The building of the regiment history could therefore not be uniform, as the individual chapters were written under quite different circumstances. Large parts were written from memory, while for other parts personal diaries, original orders, sketch maps and maps were available.

At this point I would like to sincerely thank the former regimental commanders Georg Keppler, Otto Kumm and Sylvester Stadler for their decisive assistance. Without them it would have been impossible to produce this book.

My own chapter was written based on the personal diary entries and time table of the last regimental adjutant Georg Seegerer. I would like to express my sincere gratitude to him for making this valuable source available.

Special thanks are due to the former company commander Gert Schmager, who collected the first sources and in laborious detail work put all of the material together. Furthermore he helped enrich the book by selecting and inserting situation reports and groupings from the enemy side and our own high command from the available literature.

All maps were expertly prepared by Heinz Lindner, who undertook this painstaking work in spite of the loss of an arm in the war.

My thanks to everyone who contributed to the book with original documents, diary entries, documentary material, sketches and photographs.

It would far exceed the scope of this book to include combat reports, personal accounts and anecdotes from the companies and battalions. It is intended that these shall eventually appear as separate publications.

The four newly added registers were kindly produced by Mr. Merten and Königswinter. My special thanks to them and Walter Schallowitz for their valuable assistance.

Since the "*Der Führer*" Regiment's Second Battalion was an integral part of the SS Armored Battle Group "*Das Reich*", which fought on the Eastern Front from December 1943 until mid-April 1944, the battle group's operational history was inserted into the regiment history at the proper place.

The name "*Der Führer*", which was bestowed upon the regiment, is used in this book purely in an historical sense, because it cannot simply be erased as an historical fact. Even while the war was going on it was largely replaced in the language of the troops by the abbreviation DF, therefore it appears in the book mainly in this shortened form.

At this point I would like to honor the accomplishment of the first commanding officer of the "DF" Regiment, the then *Standartenführer* Georg Keppler, who was the actual founder of the regiment. It was he who understood how to quickly forge the officers and non-commissioned officers who were seconded from the "*Leibstandarte*", from the "*Deutschland*" Regiment and from the "*Germania*" Regiment and the young Austrian recruits into a regiment which withstood the severest tests during the war and was exemplary in its conduct.

The history of the DF Regiment gives witness to its difficult and costly actions from 1939 to 1945 in the theaters of Holland, Belgium, France, Yugoslavia, Russia, the invasion front, the *Westwall*, the Ardennes and Hungary as well as the actions in Vienna and Prague. It describes victorious offensive and defensive battles in which the regiment took part, but it also describes depressing defeats, heavy casualties, weeks-long retreats and the bitter end. The regiment's losses in killed, wounded and missing can no longer be determined, as all records were lost or fell into Allied hands. Based on the available writings, however, we can say with relative certainty that the regiment, which had an authorized strength of approximately 3,000 men, was completely bled dry three or four times and had to be completely refurbished. Based on a rough but cautious estimate, this means that the regiment suffered combat casualties of approximately 10,000 men in the years 1939 to 1945. Fatal casualties may have made up 35 to 40 percent of this total.

This book was written in memory of the dead and missing of our regiment.

It was written for the men of every rank and position who ever served, fought and bled in this regiment.

It was written to set straight the often false and malicious accounts of the war service of the *Waffen-SS* and make a contribution to a later objective writing of history.

It was written as one of the most beautiful documents of a German-Austrian fighting team and comradeship which has lasted from the war to the present day.

It was written in the awareness that this sacrificial service brought to light human values which were valid at all times and still are today and without which our youth will never be able to defend the idea of freedom if it should be called upon to do so.

Last but not least the book was written to honor the actual creator of the *Waffen-SS*, our revered *Generaloberst* (Rtd.) Paul Hausser, who to us will always remain simply "our Papa Hausser." A general staff officer in the First World War, later a *Generalleutnant* in the Reichswehr and Infantry Commander IV (Magdeburg), after leaving the army he established the *Waffen-SS* and trained, molded and raised it according to the proven fundamentals of the hundred-thousand-man-army. During the war he led units of this force at great personal risk as a division commander, as a commanding general, as commander in chief of an army and finally as commander in chief of an army group. He was twice seriously wounded while in the front lines with his soldiers.

He embodied true Prussian military tradition in that, following his conscience, he even acted against the express order of his supreme commander in order to save his divisions from certain destruction in Kharkov and preserve their fighting strength.

Thus *Generaloberst* Hausser became the greatest soldier of the *Waffen-SS* and one of the most important army commanders of the Second World War, acknowledged by both friend and foe.

And even after the end of the war he had to stand up for his force, when he appeared before the Nuremberg Tribunal as a witness for the *Waffen-SS*, testifying to this force's purely military character and defending it against the indictment's serious charges.

The war service of the regiment within the senior division of the *Waffen-SS* (the 2nd SS Panzer Division "*Das Reich*") as well as that of its sister regiment SS "*Deutschland*" and the other division units always took place as part of the German field army in purely military actions.

Wherever an operational point of main effort was formed or wherever the defense was critical, the regiment encountered the veteran panzer and panzer-grenadier divisions of the army or the tough parachute battalions of the *Luftwaffe*, with whom we cooperated very successfully.

We fought shoulder to shoulder with them all and knew that we could rely on each other. Many friendships were made which crossed the boundaries of the regiment. As well army units often fought under the regiment's command, and conversely it was itself often subordinated to army divisions.

All of this confirms the fact that the DF Regiment was a dedicated field unit and always fought in the front lines. Its history shows that the men of the front-line *Waffen-SS* divisions were nothing but soldiers ready to do their best in the service of their country and their people.

May this book also give our youth the opportunity to form their own opinion of our wartime service.

In conclusion, on behalf of my comrades at the front I would like to express to all of those former enemies we faced in open and fair combat our appreciation for their brave actions.

May the Second World War remain the last major conflict among peoples for all of history.

In this we fell as one with all upright soldiers – no matter what nation they come from – and hope that the history of this regiment, which I, its last commander, had the honor to author, will make a real contribution to truth, to peace and to reconciliation.

Otto Weidinger

# FOREWORD TO THE SECOND EDITION

The unexpectedly enthusiastic reception which the "DF" regimental history has received from former comrades of the *Waffen-SS* and the public has made it necessary to produce a second edition.

It has been supplemented with additional documents and photos and improved in many respects. Several less important documents were left out. Furthermore an index of names, places, actions and units was added.

Otto Weidinger

May the following writings by all of the regimental commanders and other contributors on the creation of our 4th Panzer-Grenadier Regiment "*Der Führer*" and its operations, which were motivated by the purest idealism, serve our comradeship forged in suffering and death.

May it also serve as a marker on the evolutionary path of our time to help truth and justice break through.

These recollections from a difficult time shall also be an unforgettable monument of selfless, sacrificial loyalty to our comrades who died believing in Germany.

Georg Keppler

# I
# The Birth of the Regiment[1]

At the end of March 1938, several days after returning from the march into Austria, *Oberführer* Georg Keppler, commander of the "*Deutschland*" Regiment's I Battalion, was ordered to form a new regiment in Austria, the third regiment of the *SS-Verfügungstruppe*. The following bases were planned for the new formation: Vienna: regimental headquarters, regimental units and I Battalion; Graz: II Battalion; Klagenfurt: III Battalion.

In order to speed up the formation and training processes, the *Leibstandarte* in Berlin and the "*Deutschland*" and "*Germania*" Regiments from Munich and Hamburg respectively were ordered to provide the new regiment with non-commissioned officers and officers. Through the cooperation of Austrian authorities at every level, at the beginning of 1938 the Radetzky Barracks in Vienna were made available for I Battalion as well as a house in the Kopfgasse for the regimental headquarters. The situation was more difficult in Graz and Klagenfurt, where there were no barracks available. As a result the hotel of the magnificently-situated Tobelbad thermal baths, southwest of Graz, were rented to serve as interim quarters for II Battalion and a school in Klagenfurt for III Battalion. From the beginning it was planned to build new barracks for all three bases and work was begun before 1938 was over. Unfortunately the regiment never occupied them. After the outbreak of war the regiment's replacement training battalion was at first quartered in the new barracks in Vienna-Schönbrunn and then at the end of 1939 moved into the new barracks in Graz-Wetzelsdorf.

Further preliminary work was the responsibility of the following officers with their working groups: *Sturmbannführer* Bittrich for I Battalion in Vienna; *Hauptsturmführer* von Scholz for II Battalion in Graz-Tobelbad; and *Sturmbannführer* Wäckerle for III Battalion in Klagenfurt.

By the beginning of May 1938 it was possible to summon the cadre personnel from the three other regiments to their new bases. Under a brilliant blue sky over the snow-covered Karawanken Mountains the regiment's commanding officer welcomed the men of the "*Germania*" Regiment from Hamburg to Klagenfurt. Their first reaction was to declare that "Hamburg is still Hamburg." Nevertheless, all these cadre personnel familiarized themselves with their new surroundings surprisingly quickly and they soon merged into an inseparable group with the young soldiers from Styria, Vienna, Tyrol, Carinthia and the Sudetenland.

The regiment recruited exclusively from volunteers; there were so many volunteers that the regiment's rapid formation was assured in spite of rigid entrance requirements. This new Austrian regiment was accepted with open arms everywhere in Austria and by all levels of society, and young men enthusiastically sought admission into its ranks. The selection and call-up of the volunteers was handled by a special office set up in Vienna under the direction of *Hauptsturmführer* Stickdorn in close cooperation with the regiment and the battalions.

In addition to basic combat training, special emphasis was placed on drill so as to allow the regiment to participate in Reich Party Day in Nuremberg in September 1938. The regiment's commanding officer expected a great psychological benefit from this participation. At the same time, however, it was intended to deal with the Austrian mentality and awaken and foster the high military abilities of the men. Consciously ignoring the specified training in the new world view, the men were reminded of the great military accomplishments of the Austrian people and army in the past. The regiment's commanding officer was convinced that emphasizing these moments was more valuable for promoting the character and military abilities of these young men than relying on the standard training regimen. Success was complete and planted the fruit-bearing seed for the outstanding military spirit that was to motivate this regiment until the last day of its existence and survive the confusion of the postwar period in close comradeship and firm friendship.

On 8 April 1939 the name "*Der Führer*" was bestowed upon the 3rd *SS Standarte* in Linz.

The regimental standard and banners were presented on Reich Party Day 1938. Growing, proud, healthy self-confidence beamed from the eyes of the young soldiers as they marched through the streets of Nuremberg to the strains of the "Prinz-Eugen March" (already wearing the regimental title on their left sleeve). Everywhere they went they were feted as the first Austrian regiment and received special acknowledgement for their exemplary discipline and deportment.

## Entry into the Sudetenland

After the return from Nuremberg the emphasis of training shifted to combat training by day and night. Shortly before the entry into the Sudetenland the army's commanding general in Vienna, *General* Kienitz, inspected the regiment in individual and unit training to the company level. The result was convincing and received full approval. Meanwhile the buildup of forces for the occupation of the Sudetenland had begun. In all haste each battalion formed three well-equipped companies with heavy weapons and assembled them, together with elements of the regimental units, in the area south of Znaim, where they were placed under the command of the army's Vienna Division under *Generalleutnant* Schubert. The chief of staff of the army's Vienna command, *Oberst* (later *Generaloberst*) Rendulic, was especially helpful in the preparation and execution of this difficult undertaking, providing most valuable support to the regiment in dealing with problems that arose.

On 1 October 1938 the "*Der Führer*" Regiment set out from its assembly area around Zwettl in Lower Austria in the direction of Znaim. Only a few days had been available for scouting purposes; intelligence concerning Czech countermeasures at the border was extremely poor. In any case their thorough preparations for the barricading of the frontier suggested that the entry would eventually run into difficulties. The news that the Czech government had ordered the peaceful evacuation of the Sudetenland was therefore all the more gratifying. As a result of this the entry proceeded without serious incident and the regiment received a boisterous welcome everywhere from the Sudeten-German population. After a brief occupation period in the Znaim area the regiment returned to its bases.

## March into Czechoslovakia

Combat and unit training was stepped up. The reorganization of the regiment from horse-drawn transport to full motorization presented not inconsiderable difficulties, in particular the accelerated training of driver instructors, technical personnel and drivers and provision of the necessary driving practice. Thanks to the cooperation and dedication of all officers, non-commissioned officers and enlisted men, the selected training objectives were met. By the beginning of March 1939 the regiment was ready for motorized operations, although it still had no experience in motorized marches and operations.

At this time the regiment was firmly integrated into the army's plan of operations. In the case of the occupation of Czechoslovakia, the regiment was to move on the city of Preßburg (present-day Bratislava) from the south and occupy it.

The regiment was ordered to assemble during the night of 14-15 March 1939 in the area around Bruck an der Leitha. The first elements of the regiment had already arrived there when the commanding officer of "*Der Führer*" was ordered to army group headquarters in Vienna. *General* Kienitz informed the commanding officer that the plan to occupy Preßburg from the south had been abandoned on account of possible strong countermeasures by the Czechs. The "*Der Führer*" Regiment now received orders to cross the Czechoslovakian border east of Gänserndorf (northeast of Vienna) at dawn on 15 March, drive through the Lesser Carpathians to Bösing (Peczinok), and there secure the Waag Valley to the south towards Preßburg and to the north roughly as far as Jablonica. One of the regiment's battalions was to be released to the army division advancing farther north. The bridge over the March east of Gänserndorf was to be checked for its ability to support the regiment's heavy vehicles beforehand.

The first thing that had to be done was halt the "*Der Führer*" Regiment's concentric march toward Bruck an der Leitha and re-deploy in the direction of Gänserndorf via Vienna. These movements, difficult enough for a motorized unit, were made extraordinarily difficult by the onset of a heavy snowstorm that covered the roads with a sheet of glassy ice. I Battalion, "*Der Führer*" Regiment was withdrawn and sent to the army division operating to the north. In spite of numerous difficulties and obstacles this regrouping proceeded without incident.

As per orders, the regiment was assembled in Gänserndorf at dawn on 15 March. Scouting produced serious reservations about the load-carrying ability of the ancient bridge over the March. But it was intact and only weakly guarded. At first the weather was favorable, but when the columns reached the foot of the Lesser Carpathians it began to snow heavily again. In the mountains themselves there was already a half-meter of new snow. In Bösing the commanding officer of the "*Der Führer*" Regiment received the report that only one of the regiment's many hundreds of vehicles had failed to arrive and that it had suffered only minor damage. The young drivers had mastered the snow-covered curves and serpentines of the Lesser Carpathians. During the afternoon hours of 15 March a radio message was sent reporting that the regiment had reached its destination.

On 17 March the Commander in Chief of the Army, *Generaloberst* von Brauchitsch, signaled that he was coming to visit the regiment. He took the long route over the Lesser Carpathians in order to express his personal appreciation. For the regiment, including I Battalion advancing farther to the north, was the only unit operating in this area of the corps to reach its assigned day's march objectives. It was a considerable achievement under difficult conditions for the young regiment inexperienced in motor transport.

## In Prague – The *Westwall* – The *Waffen-SS*

In May 1939 the "*Der Führer*" Regiment was transferred to the Groß-Born troop training grounds in Pomerania. The drive to Groß-Born took the regiment through Silesia and the Warthe District, another big experience for the young men from the lonely farms of the alpine valleys. The young soldiers' joy and amazement were great when they saw the first windmills and the first storks.

The purpose of the period at Groß-Born was the intensive reinforcement and consolidation of training. Individual and unit training, often with live firing, in cooperation with all heavy weapons resulted in a level of training comparable to that of the 100,000-man army, the *Reichswehr*. Here the foundation stone was laid for the "*Der Führer*" Regiment's later success.

Following this period, roughly at the end of June 1939, the regiment moved from Neurath to Prague to serve as the guard regiment for the Protectorate of Bohemia and Moravia. In Prague it performed guard duties at the Hradschin Castle and other important structures in the Protectorate. It was a proud military scene when each noon hour three companies marched through the streets of Prague, band playing, to relieve the watch.

While in Czechoslovakia there was a gradual return to peace and quiet, conditions in Poland were arousing concern in every German. The news of the conclusion of the German-Soviet Non-Aggression Pact on 23 August 1939 therefore had a calming effect on the regiment. Everyone counted on reason and insight to prevail, however these hopes were in vain.

On 1 September 1939 a declaration of war was passed to the Polish government. The decision of the Reich government weighed heavily on the German people, who from deepest inner conviction felt free of any guilt in this development in the state of affairs. They accepted their unavoidable fate with quiet solemnity.

The soldiers of the regiment understandably did not wish to stay in Prague, far away from the great event. And so there was a certain amount of disappointment when the regiment was ordered to remain in Prague, where it was assigned the additional task of guarding railway stations and historic buildings.

The world political situation as well as the political and military situation in Germany was further aggravated when England and France declared war on Germany. As a wise precaution, work had earlier begun to bolster the *Westwall* along Germany's border with Belgium and France. All available units not participating in the fighting in Poland were sent to the *Westwall* as a temporary measure. For the expansion of the German armed forces was not yet complete and the fortifications were far from finished. In particular the defense line lacked motorized troops to act as a mobile reserve.

In mid-September the regiment reached Waldkirch in the Black Forest after several forced marches. It was placed under the command of *General* Dollmann's army operating in the *Westwall*'s southern sector, where it was to serve as motorized reserve. The regiment's days were filled with reconnaissance, development of various intervention strategies and their assessment in map exercises, as well as familiarization with the fortifications of the *Westwall*. The regiment's excellent discipline and deportment made a lasting impression on the people of the Black Forest. Many lifelong bonds were established between young women from the Black Forest and members of the regiment.

Meanwhile the campaign in Poland had been brought to a successful conclusion. The subsequent expansion of the *Wehrmacht* incorporated the lessons learned in Poland. The first motorized infantry and panzer divisions were formed. For the "*Der Führer*" Regiment and the other regiments of the *SS-Verfügungstruppe* there now also began a new and decisive development phase: in the Reichstag it was announced that a "motorized *Waffen-SS* division" was to be formed. Used here for the first time, this term was later to have such fundamental and fateful significance!

This regimental history is not the place to go into the oft-discussed and disputed fundamental question of the advisability and necessity of the formation of the armed SS (*Waffen-SS*). However the truth will be served by the statement that the soldiers of the *Waffen-SS* and of the "*Der Führer*" Regiment in particular never considered themselves a special force or guard. All felt that they were just German soldiers. Like every soldier serving in the army, the navy and the air force, the men of the *Waffen-SS* were also conscious of their duty to people and country in those difficult times. The soldiers of the *Waffen-SS* consciously always remained outside this discussion and never saw the *Waffen-SS* as anything but a part of the German armed forces, whose organization, training, armament, pay, rations and in particular its missions in peace- and wartime were exactly the same as those of the *SS-Verfügungstruppe* and later the *Waffen-SS*. In action the divisions of the *Waffen-SS* operated exclusively under army commands, whose orders were carried out with the units of the army, whose members were looked upon as comrades and brothers in arms.

It is quite understandable that this close association and the sharing of goals and missions resulted in a strong dependence on the army. This development was not hindered by the unrealistic and unmilitary directives issued by *Reichsführer-SS* Himmler who, conscious of his slipping influence, tried to build a bridge to the *Waffen-SS*, instead it was further bolstered. How far this inner estrangement went is illustrated most impressively by the fact that in 1942-1943 Himmler proposed to Adolf Hitler that the field units of the *Waffen-SS* be removed in every respect from the SS and incorporated as the fourth branch of the armed forces. It was a proposal which, in spite of its correctness and advisability, was unfortunately not accepted. Had it been, untold misfortune and much trouble could well have been avoided.[2]

At the beginning of October 1939 the "*Der Führer*" Regiment was released from its duties in the *Westwall* and was transferred to the former Czech training grounds in the Brdy Forest east of Pilsen. The "*Der Führer*" Regiment was combined with the "*Deutschland*" and "*Germania*" Regiments, a reconnaissance battalion, a signals battalion, a combat engineer battalion, and so on, to form the *SS-Verfügungsdivision* under the then *Generalleutnant der Waffen-SS*, Paul Hausser. Formed at the same time were the division headquarters, the first *Waffen-SS* artillery regiment, division supply units and other units belonging to a division. The first division of the *Waffen-SS* had been created.

Activities at the training grounds reinforced individual training, the next generation of non-commissioned officers was trained, and most importantly larger-scale unit training was carried out. Valuable experience was gained and exchanged.

In December 1939 the *SS-Verfügungsdivision* received an order to detach one reinforced regiment to the army. The "*Der Führer*" Regiment was chosen for this task, together with an attached artillery battalion under the command of *Hauptsturmführer* Robert Erspenmüller (killed on 24 May 1940 near Aire), a company of combat engineers and a supply transport column. The reinforced "*Der Führer*" Regiment drove to the Datteln area of Westphalia, where it was quartered and placed under the command of the army's X Army Corps commanded by *General der Artillerie* Hansen. For supervisory purposes the regiment was attached to the 207th Infantry Division under *Generalleutnant* von Thiedemann.

There followed a period of tough winter training, practicing of river crossings, special training of officers through map exercises, and the conclusion of several non-commissioned officer courses within the regiment. As a result of these courses, when the campaign in the west began the "*Der Führer*" Regiment had a pool of replacement non-commissioned officers equal to three times it requirements and was able to meet all training requirements. There the regiment received its first replacements from the replacement training battalion, which at the time was stationed in the new barracks in Graz-Wetzelsdorf.

## The Western Campaign 1940

When France emerged victorious from the 1914-1918 war it believed that it could secure that position for a long time with a minimum of sacrifices. The French concept of "security" was entirely classical and found its expression in the "Maginot Line," a defense line with truly mammoth fortifications at key points.

Belgium and Holland accepted these concepts as well, so that eventually there was a continuous line of fortifications opposite Germany's western border from the Zuider-Zee to the Swiss border. Opposite them Germany, as previously mentioned, constructed the *Westwall*, not out of any feeling of insecurity, but because of its military-geographical situation and the danger of a two-front war.

When war broke out in 1939 the armies of the western states had no intention of protecting their territory by waiting behind their defensive zones, instead under their protection a buildup of forces was completed for an invasion of the German industrial region on the Rhine and the Ruhr. These intentions, of which the German command became aware of early on, inevitably prompted appropriate countermeasures.

These included deploying the reinforced "*Der Führer*" Regiment in Westphalia. Shortly before the start of the western campaign the regiment was moved out of its practice area around Datteln into the area around Bocholt, Westphalia.

10 May 1940 saw the beginning of the western campaign. Planned and executed as a "*blitz*" campaign using the most modern methods of warfare, it is and will remain unique in the history of warfare. For the reinforced "*Der Führer*" Regiment it began with the invasion of northern Holland as a unit of the 18th Army under *General der Artillerie* von Küchler, part of Army Group von Bock.

The advance by the 18th Army through Holland and Belgium triggered the Allied plan to march out of Flanders with the strong Anglo-French northern wing to meet Army Group von Bock. By doing so it helped the main German thrust on the central front achieve success.

## Operations in Holland from 10 to 14 May 1940

The alert order for the "*Der Führer*" Regiment arrived on 9 May 1940. During the night of 9-10 May the regiment moved into its assembly area around Elten, Westphalia. II Battalion, "*Der Führer*", bolstered by a platoon from the 13th Company and one from the 14th Company, was assigned to the 368th Infantry Regiment (commanded by an Austrian *Generalmajor*, a holder of the *Pour le mérite*) to serve as motorized spearhead and was readied near Anholt. At 5:35 AM on 10 May waiting assault teams crossed the Dutch border, overran the Dutch border guards and drove toward Babberik, the first attack objective. Resistance by Dutch border troops was meager, and wherever it appeared it was quickly crushed, often with just hand grenades. Removal of the numerous barricades, especially roadblocks, consumed a great deal of time. As the leading assault battalion, III Battalion, "*Der Führer*" was ordered to requisition all available bicycles and proceed to the Arnhem bridge as quickly as possible in order to prevent it from being blown. At the same time the Railway Pioneer Platoon, which had been subordinated to the 207th Infantry Division, moved off toward Arnhem. The Ijssel bridge was blown up before the platoon could reach it, however. In spite of numerous roadblocks the leading elements of III Battalion, "*Der Führer*" reached the Ijssel east of Arnhem at 7:20 AM.

At 8:30 AM III Battalion received orders to prepare for a crossing of the Ijssel. II Battalion of the *SS-Verfügungsdivision*'s artillery regiment and the attached heavy battery (11th Battery, 256th Artillery Regiment) went into position to provide supporting fire. Together with the artillery, the "*Der Führer*" Regiment's heavy weapons opened fire on enemy installations on the north side of the Ijssel, in particular Fort Westervoort, which faced the bridge. Only under this covering fire was it possible to move the anti-tank and machine-guns into the front line to place pinpoint fire on the enemy embrasures, as well as scout the most favorable crossing sites and move up and ready the inflatable boats. The potential crossing sites themselves were extremely unfavorable. Beyond the embankment the troops would have to cover approximately 300 meters of open ground to reach the water. The opposite bank of the Ijssel, which at this place was about 150 meters wide, was well protected by barbed wire entanglements. The entire area lay under heavy enemy fire from the front and the flanks.

After some of the enemy weapons had been put out of action, at 11 AM the attack was begun following a brief barrage by all weapons. In spite of the massed enemy flanking fire the leading assault teams and the combat engineers advanced determinedly. The crossing in inflatable boats was a success; the first lanes were cut in the wire on the far bank of the Ijssel at 11:15. Wave after wave followed, and by 12:15 PM the bulk of III Battalion was across the river. The brave engineers deserve recognition for their part in the crossing. After a short, but extremely sharp battle, Fort Westervoort and the enemy installations at the crossing sites were overcome, in some cases with small arms and hand grenades.

*Oberscharführer* Ludwig Kepplinger of 11th Company, in particular, distinguished himself here. Even before III Battalion crossed the river, *Oberscharführer* Kepplinger and his assault team made a daring and risky crossing of the blown Ijssel bridge and moved against Fort Westervoort. They forced the garrison to surrender, paving the way for the subsequent rapid seizure of the fort by III Battalion and making it possible for the regiment to continue to advance briskly. For this courageous and decisive act as well as for other daring actions, *Oberscharführer* Kepplinger became the first non-commissioned officer of the *Waffen-SS* to receive the Knight's Cross; he was simultaneously promoted to the rank of *Untersturmführer* for bravery in the face of the enemy. Later he was seriously wounded during the storming of the Grebbe Line. In summer 1944, by which time he had attained the rank of *Sturmbannführer*, Kepplinger failed to return from a reconnaissance mission in Normandy.

The Dutch commander of the captured Fort Westervoort asked the commander of the "*Der Führer*" Regiment, *Oberführer* Keppler, if he might keep his dagger, which had been awarded to his father in recognition of his special bravery while serving in the Dutch colonial wars. *Oberführer* Keppler granted this request.

Keppler wrote:

> *I believe I owe it to the regiment and all its members to allow these battles in Holland, in which the regiment experienced its first hard baptism of fire and created an unforgettable monument through*

*its bravery, broad space in the regimental history in memory of the survivors and in honor of our fallen comrades. When, shortly after the crossing of the Ijssel by the first elements of the regiment, the commanding general of the X Army Corps, General Hansen, and his chief of staff Oberst Gause came forward to me at the Ijssel to express his initial appreciation for the regiment's success so far, I was able to tell him that I was proud of my soldiers and would like replacements from Austria only. While the western campaign was still going on I received a letter from Austria (if I am not mistaken from Styria), a letter from the father of one of my men killed at the Ijssel. He expressed how severely the death of his son had affected him, but said that his grief had been lessened somewhat by the proud awareness that in doing so he had made a sacrifice for Germany. He went on to say, however, that my words to General Hansen (above), which a friend of his son's had heard by chance and passed on to the father, were the greatest pride for him and Austria. This letter from an Austrian father touched me deeply.*

III Battalion, "*Der Führer*", led by its commanding officer *Sturmbannführer* Hilmar Wäckerle (killed on the Eastern Front while serving as a regimental commander in the "*Wiking*" Panzer Division) made a daring advance into the city of Arnhem. Reacting energetically to quash any resistance, III Battalion quickly reached its initial objective, the west end of Arnhem.

Heavy enemy flanking fire once again interrupted ferry traffic across the fast-flowing Ijssel. Rapidly deployed assault teams quickly eliminated this threat, whereupon the first of the heavy weapons and the motorcycle company were brought across and could be sent after III Battalion. The combat engineers quickly removed mines laid beside and on the advance roads. Working tirelessly, by 4:30 PM the army bridging column subordinated to the regiment had erected an eight-ton bridge.

Meanwhile, in Arnhem III Battalion had increased its mobility with bicycles and together with 15th Company, "*Der Führer*" it advanced from Arnhem in the direction of Wageningen. Apart from several surprise barrages, especially from the difficult terrain on the right flank, III Battalion did not encounter any serious opposition until it neared Heelsum. The heavy weapons, which had been quickly sent forward by the regiment, silenced this opposition in cooperation with the companies. III Battalion encountered more stout enemy positions in Renkum. Cleverly-sited machine-gun positions at the edge of the forest west of Renkum and accurate enemy artillery fire from the Grebbe Line inflicted casualties on III Battalion, "*Der Führer*." Reconnaissance by 15th Company revealed enemy forces on the right flank near Ede and to its east. The right flank of the "*Der Führer*" Regiment was completely open as the foot-marching elements of the 207th Infantry Division were lagging behind.

At 8:30 PM all elements of the regiment, which had meanwhile crossed the military bridge near Arnhem, were assembled in the area of Renkum and east for the night of 10-11 May. So the regiment's first day of combat ended a complete success. Not only had the regiment succeeded in quickly crossing the frontier and forcing a crossing of the Ijssel, but also by the same evening all of its elements had fought their way to the outermost positions of the Grebbe Line. A statement by the general commanding Fort Westervoort, who was captured, is interesting: the Dutch Army command was firmly convinced that the Ijssel position could be held for at least three days. The "*Der Führer*" Regiment broke through the position just four hours after the arrival of the leading elements.

Dawn patrols on the morning of 11 May revealed that the enemy had abandoned his positions in the forest west of Renkum during the night. In order to screen these movements the enemy covered the area around Renkum with lively artillery fire during the night and a heavy barrage with light and heavy artillery in the early morning hours.

Advancing in developed formation, with the reinforced 15th Company in the lead, I Battalion on the right, III Battalion on the left and II Battalion bringing up the rear, the regiment attacked towards Wageningen. Once again a determined assault succeeded in driving back the enemy in quick time. Strong roadblocks and minefields delayed the entry into the city of Wangeningen. The companies fought their way through the town step by step. Resistance repeatedly flared up from houses, trees and hedges, supported by accurate artillery fire. By 11 AM the city was in the regiment's hands. Heavy enemy artillery fire fell on the city, casing numerous fires and later resulting in the almost total destruction of the city center.

Toward midday, at the west end of Wageningen, the commanding officer of the "*Der Führer*" Regiment issued the order to prepare to attack the Grebbe Position: I Battalion on the right, III Battalion on the left, boundary line the Wageningen-Grebbe road. The II Artillery Battalion went into position east of Wageningen with its observation post on the southeast boundary of the town. A request was made for a battalion of the 207th Artillery Regiment (of the 207th Infantry Division) to support the "*Der Führer*" Regiment's attack from positions east of Wageningen. II Battalion was positioned east of Wageningen as reserve battalion at the disposal of the regiment.

After the completion of preparations the regiment moved out in the directed formation with advanced left wing to attack the Grebbe Line. Contrary to information provided by spies, the forward enemy positions east of the actual defense lines on the Grebbe proved to be significantly stronger than expected. The Dutch fought extremely bravely and it was determined that they were the best Dutch colonial troops. The enemy's resistance was bolstered by numerous well-fortified fixed installations, by flexibly directed artillery fire and by the terrain. Hedgerows, trees, fences, etc, ran through the entire battlefield, limiting the field of view. The Dutch made very skillful use of the terrain, placing snipers in trees and hedgerows that were very difficult to counter. And so there began an extremely difficult and tough battle which was often decided only in hand-to-hand combat. The regiment requested another artillery battalion from the 207th Infantry Division, however it was unable to open fire until the late afternoon and even then failed to bring any significant relief. The main burden of the battle continued to be borne by the infantry. The grenadiers fought with determination and fearlessness and worked their way through the enemy position 100 meters at a time. One Dutch strongpoint after another fell. By 7 PM the point groups of III Battalion had worked their way to within 600 meters of the actual Grebbe Line. The left wing of I Battalion, which was advancing north of the road, had reached a position abeam III Battalion, while its right wing still lagged behind under heavy fire from the front and the flank. Casualties continued to mount, caused by enemy fire from the Grebbe Line and the much higher ground of the Grebbe-Berg, but mainly by the numerous snipers in trees, which together with those in the hedgerows were able to hold on in the terrain taken by the Germans for another two or three days.

After another concentration of fire, at approximately 9 PM the leading platoons of III Battalion succeeded in reaching the foot of the Grebbe-Berg. However, every attempt to force the hill that evening failed because of the heavy enemy fire. Consequently it was not possible to move the inflatable boats forward for the crossing of the Grebbe.

In view of this situation the regimental commander decided to force a crossing of the Grebbe and a breakthrough on the Grebbe-Berg during the night of 12 May under cover of darkness. Consequently II Battalion was moved up via Wageningen and Buitenwarden and positioned to the left of III Battalion in preparation for the attack. All preparations were made for the night attack. The attack was to be made by II and III Battalions against the south part of the Grebbe-Berg while I Battalion made a simultaneous feint attack against the east part of the hill north of the Wangeningen-Grebbe road.

In the end, however, this attack plan had to be abandoned at about 3 AM, because the persistent and accurate enemy defensive fire made any approach of the Grebbe by stronger forces impossible and because crossing materials could not be moved forward in the glare of the illumination flares being fired by the enemy. The commanding officer therefore ordered the bulk of II and III Battalions to pull back from the Grebbe and rest, leaving behind strong security detachments.

Even though there was no penetration of the Grebbe Line itself on 11 May, the day did end with a considerable success for the young regiment, for the battle and the drive to the Grebbe Line had been difficult and tough. That it had succeeded at all was due first of all to the selfless courage of every single enlisted man, non-commissioned officer and officer who braved the enemy fire and every danger.

The fighting on 11 May had convinced the regimental commander that an attack on the Grebbe-Berg was impossible without heavy preparatory fire by artillery. This was requested from the 207th Infantry Division during the night of 12 May and the regiment was promised three light and two heavy artillery battalions for the regiment's planned attack on the Grebbe-Berg the next morning. As a result of the late arrival of the in-part horse-drawn artillery and because of difficult sighting conditions, preparatory fire by the massed artillery, first under the artillery commander of the 207th Infantry Division later under the artillery commander of the X

Army Corps, was delayed so badly that actual fire for effect, especially on the intended points of penetration, could not be begun until approximately 2 PM.

In the meantime the regiment had deployed for the attack and its assault and combat engineer teams waited in their jump-off positions. The first assault, which was supposed to break through to the west, was to be made by III Battalion. II Battalion would follow and break through to the northwest, while I Battalion remained north of the road at the regiment's disposal, ready to immediately exploit and expand the success of II and II Battalions by driving through the bunker positions to the northwest. The regiment's initial objective was the well-constructed and fortified fort at the foot of the Grebbe-Berg on the Wageningen-Grebbe road and the strong enemy installations on both sides of the fort. The second objective was the hill of the Grebbe-Berg and the third and last for this day was the rail line east of Rhenen. With the agreement of the artillery commander the start time for the attack was set for 2:20 PM. After the final artillery barrage the assault teams of the 9th and 12th Companies moved forward, followed closely by the combat engineer teams of the 16th Company with the inflatable boats, etc. In spite of heavy fire from the enemy installations, which had not been silenced by the preparatory artillery fire, and despite the onset of enemy flanking fire, some of the leading assault teams succeeded in crossing the Grebbe in the first rush and gaining a foothold in the outer reaches of the fort. The Dutch troops manning the positions were overcome in bitter close-quarters fighting. The following elements of III Battalion began systematically fighting their way through strong and in places still-intact enemy fortifications on the Grebbe. The Dutch fought desperately but success was on our side. Here, too, this was due to the unshakable offensive spirit and the ruthless aggressiveness of the troops. Only thus was it possible to break through the forward defense line at the Grebbe and then launch the attack on the Grebbe-Berg. This was carried out by II Battalion, which had meanwhile been moved behind III Battalion and deployed on its right, and III Battalion, which continued to attack to the west. This too, especially the attack in the steep, fiercely-defended wooded terrain of the eastern part of the Grebbe-Berg, resulted in tough and bitter fighting for the companies, which irresistibly forced their way forward. The men displayed unsurpassed heroism and recklessness in these battles. At approximately 7 PM it was reported to the 207th Infantry Division that the top of the Grebbe-Berg was in the regiment's hands.

A further continuation of the attack to the west to reach the rail line east of Rhenen once again required planned preparations, as the Dutch had regrouped in a well-constructed position in the wooded terrain two kilometers east of Rhenen, which was strongly-fortified and protected by barbed-wire. Repeated attacks against this enemy position were halted by heavy defensive fire. Meanwhile I Battalion had been ordered to attack the strong bunker position at the Grebbe northeast of the Grebbe-Berg. This attack also succeeded, thanks to the determination of the assault team, which stormed one bunker after another. But this attack failed to bring any relief to the battalions attacking the Grebbe-Berg. Under heavy fire from the third enemy position on the north slope of the Grebbe-Berg, the attackers were only able to gain ground slowly. It was also necessary to move forward the heavy weapons needed by II and III Battalions to carry out the attack and repel several enemy counterattacks, which was only possible after a temporary bridge was thrown across the Grebbe to replace the destroyed lock bridge there. The regiment's combat engineers and those of 1st Company, SS Pioneer Battalion, which was subordinated to the regiment, deserve special recognition as they carried out their mission there coolly and fearlessly.

At 8 PM the commander of I Battalion, 322nd Infantry Regiment, which had been requested by the "*Der Führer*" Regiment, arrived at the Grebbe-Berg. As his battalion could be expected to arrive at approximately 10 PM, the regimental commander gave the commander of III Battalion the order on the spot to advance along the Grebbe-Rhenen road with his battalion at 10 PM and expand the bridgehead to the railway embankment due east of Rhenen, while the commander of I Battalion, 322nd Regiment was ordered to close the resulting gap between II and III Battalions with his battalion. With its commanding officer leading the way, III Battalion resumed its attack at about 11 PM. Launching a daring advance, it captured six Dutch guns in close combat with hand grenades and at about midnight reached the rail line east of Rhenen as per its orders. On the other hand I Battalion, 322nd Infantry Regiment missed its objective on account of the darkness and the difficult wooded terrain, as a result of which the gap between II and III Battalions could not be closed. In view of this situation the regiment immediately sent forward the 15th Company, however it was unable to close the gap as the Dutch had meanwhile moved strong forces back into the intervening wooded terrain. As a result significant elements of III Battalion and 15th Company "*Der Führer*" were cut off. Under the command of the twice-wounded commander of III Battalion, these cut-off elements repulsed repeated counterattacks by superior enemy forces and held their positions until the leading elements of the 322nd Regiment reached the rail line on 13 May.

During the night of 12 to 13 May the 207th Division gave instructions that the 322nd Infantry Regiment was to continue the attack from the top of the Grebbe-Berg west through Rhenen on 13 May, while the "*Der Führer*" Regiment was ordered to roll up the enemy positions at the Grebbe Line, which were bolstered by strong permanent fortifications, to the northwest.

13 May 1940. In carrying out this mission, early on 13 May the regiment attacked the enemy bunker positions on the north slope of the Grebbe-Berg and the line of hills to the northwest with I Battalion on the right and III Battalion on the left, in order to roll them up from southeast to northwest. The Dutch still put up a tough fight, but bunker after bunker and position after position fell to the fierce assaults of the attacking companies of I and II Battalions and their support weapons operating in the front lines. By approximately 11 AM roughly one and a half kilometers of the enemy position had been rolled up. The advance was then temporarily halted by the regiment, because repeated attempts by the 322nd Infantry Regiment to attack west from the Grebbe-Berg had met with no success and there were no more troops with which to close the regiment's now one and a half kilometer open flank. At about noon the 322nd Regiment attacked again, following preparatory artillery fire and the first use of Stuka dive-bombers in Holland, and gained ground to the west. Following this the "*Der Führer*" Regiment resumed its attack to roll up the Grebbe Line. By approximately 7 PM the last bunker before the flooded area was in the regiment's hands. In these battles, too, the young soldiers had distinguished themselves through their determined cold-bloodedness, storming bunkers with bayonets and hand grenades when ammunition ran low.

As the 322nd Infantry Regiment's attack on the rail line east of Rhenen bogged down again towards evening, on orders from the "*Der Führer*" Regiment II Battalion conducted strong reconnaissance toward Rhenen from the north into the enemy rear in order to take the pressure off the 322nd Infantry Regiment. Furthermore, at the request of the 207th Division the regiment's armored car platoon was placed at the disposal of the 322nd Infantry Regiment. With its help, at approximately 10 PM the 322nd Infantry Division carried forward its attack on Rhenen, which was now in flames.

14 May 1940. II Battalion, "*Der Führer*" was sent into the area ten kilometers northwest of Rhenen with orders to head off possible enemy counterattacks from the Grebbe Line near and north of Veenendal and thus secure the right flank of the 207th Infantry Division which was now advancing toward Doorn via Amerongen. This was a relatively quiet day for the regiment with only minor actions. In the evening Utrecht surrendered without a fight.

15 May 1940. At about 5 AM the regiment was placed on alert and ordered to immediately prepared for a motorized operation. The commanding general of X Army Corps, *General* Hansen, had meanwhile halted the 207th Infantry Division's advance and had ordered that as the first regiment to have broken through the Ijssel Line and the only one to have breached the Grebbe Line, the "*Der Führer*" Regiment should now also be the first regiment to carry out the further advance into Holland. Setting out from Amerongen at 10 AM, the regiment marched via Utrecht and Amsterdam to Haarlem, where it assumed responsibility for coastal defense between Ijmuiden and Zandvoort. Early on 16 May the regiment was withdrawn from the units of X Army Corps. It subsequently marched off to take on other tasks in northern France as part of the *SS-Verfügungsdivision*.

## Summary

At the Grebbe Line the SS Regiment "*Der Führer*" faced two Dutch divisions that for the most part consisted of Holland's best colonial troops. The Dutch defended themselves with determination and bravery and except for several isolated cases fought decently. It was unfair, for example, that several times white flags were raised from bunkers and afterwards our assault teams were fired on from prepared flanking positions. Dutch casualties had to have been high. The regiment took approximately 5,000 prisoners.

The conduct of every officer, non-commissioned officer and enlisted man in the battle was beyond praise. The willingness to give one's life and unshakable coolness were displayed to an extraordinary degree even in the most difficult situations. Only thus was the regiment able to achieve the great success that it did in Holland. Most of all, this success lay in the fact that because of the regiment's breakthrough alone, all of northern Holland collapsed after four days and surrendered. According to statements by several captured Dutch officers, the Dutch army command had calculated that the Grebbe Line would be defended for at least two and a half months. The regiment breached it within three days after crossing the border.

The regiment's losses in the fighting in Holland were 118 killed (including 7 officers), 231 wounded (10 officers) and 15 missing.

The most telling indication of how highly the commanding general of X Army Corps, *General* Hansen, rated the accomplishments of the regiment and its decisive success lies in the fact that when the regiment left his corps area he summoned me to The Hague, bade me farewell in a most heartfelt way, and instructed that a large part of the Iron Crosses that were available to him for his corps be given to me as an immediate gesture of his thanks for the regiment's bravery and so that I might be able to hand out the deserved decorations. I especially welcomed this proof of human and soldierly generosity because it enabled me to personally present the Iron Cross, First or Second Class to the wounded *Obersturmbannführer* Wäckerle and several other wounded members of the regiment when I visited the hospital while passing through Arnhem.

• • •

From Haarlem the regiment carried out a motorized advance via Amsterdam-Arnhem-Cleve-Venlo to Maastricht, Belgium, crossing the Meuse (Maas) for the first time near Huy and for the second time near

Givet. During the early hours of the night of 17 May 1940 the regiment found the *SS-Verfügungsdivision* near Marienbourg and was placed under the division's command again.

In the meantime the operations in the west had developed in such a way that following Army Group von Rundstedt's breakthrough of the Maginot Line with Panzer Group von Kleist, strong German armored units under *General* Guderian with air support had advanced from the Ardennes via Verdun, Sedan and Arras toward Calais and in doing so had cut off all elements of the French operational army north of this line, the Belgian Army and the entire British Expeditionary Corps and deprived them of their base of operations. The objective now was to secure the open flanks of these German armored formations and further expand the success. To achieve this all motorized units, including the *SS-Verfügungsdivision*, were moved into the front line.

During the days and nights that followed the regiment's progress was slowed by the badly clogged roads. Advancing via Hirson-Guise-north of St. Quentin and south of Arras, it then turned north through Aubigny and on 21 May reached the La Bassée-Aire area.

The French, British and Belgian units cut off and surrounded in Flanders defended themselves desperately against the German attacks now coming from the east and northeast. The Kemmelberg south of Ypres, scene of some of the most prolonged and bloody fighting of the First World War, once again proved to be a serious obstacle and the German advance ground to a halt. Consequently, on 22 May the regiment received orders to prepare to move out for an attack on the Kemmelberg from the west in order to open the way over this blood-soaked piece of ground for the German troops attacking from the east. In the end, however, there was no need for the regiment to attack, as German troops succeeded in taking the Kemmelberg from the east in the early afternoon.

Instead, on 23 May the regiment received orders to secure and hold an approximately twenty-five kilometer wide sector on the Lys and the Lys and La Bassée Canal roughly in the Armentières-Bailleul area with front facing north and northeast in the area of the XXXXI Panzer Corps commanded by *General* Reinhardt. The trapped enemy units were exerting greater pressure to the north and south, and the regiment's 9th Company had just moved into the Bailleul area to barricade the important crossings there, when it was surprised by a concentric enemy attack led by strong armored units. There was a desperate battle as the enemy tried to break through to the south. Given our weak forces, the enemy succeeded in breaking through in the first rush with about 50 tanks and a battalion of infantry. Exploiting the element of surprise of the night attack, the enemy overran the 9th Company "*Der Führer.*"

*Hauptsturmführer* Harmel, who had so distinguished himself in the fighting for the Grebbe-Berg, mastered the situation there until the commander of III Battalion "*Der Führer*", *Hauptsturmführer* Otto Kumm, was able to personally lead a counterattack by the hastily scraped-together reserves of the 9th Company supported by a machine-gun platoon from 12th Company and an anti-tank platoon from 14th Company. In barely an hour thirteen enemy tanks were destroyed in the town of St. Hilaire and approximately 400 prisoners were brought in. The bulk of the enemy tanks had not intervened in the fighting there, however, driving on in the direction of Aire instead. There they came upon the 7th Company "*Der Führer*" under the command of the brave and circumspect *Hauptsturmführer* Hans Lingner. In bitter close-quarters and street fighting the 7th Company not only succeeded in halting the enemy breakthrough, but also destroyed all the enemy tanks and captured their crews. By late morning on 24 May it was possible to report to the commanding general, who out of concern had rushed to the regiment's command post, that the enemy breakthrough attempt was a total failure. In these battles, too, the first in which enemy tanks were engaged, the bravery of the participating officers, non-commissioned officers and enlisted men earned the regiment the highest praise. Acting in a cool, calculating way, they took out the enemy tanks with direct fire or hand grenade bundles or leapt onto the steel giants, tore open hatches and panels and threw their lethal charges inside.

But the threat was not eliminated for good until the regiment attacked across the Lys near Aire on 25 May in order to establish a strong bridgehead on the north side of the Lys. It was here that the regiment encountered British troops for the first time.

Then on 27 and 28 May there was heavy fighting through the Nieppe Forest to force a crossing of the Lys Canal. While the attack made rapid progress at first, enemy resistance soon stiffened and was effectively sup-

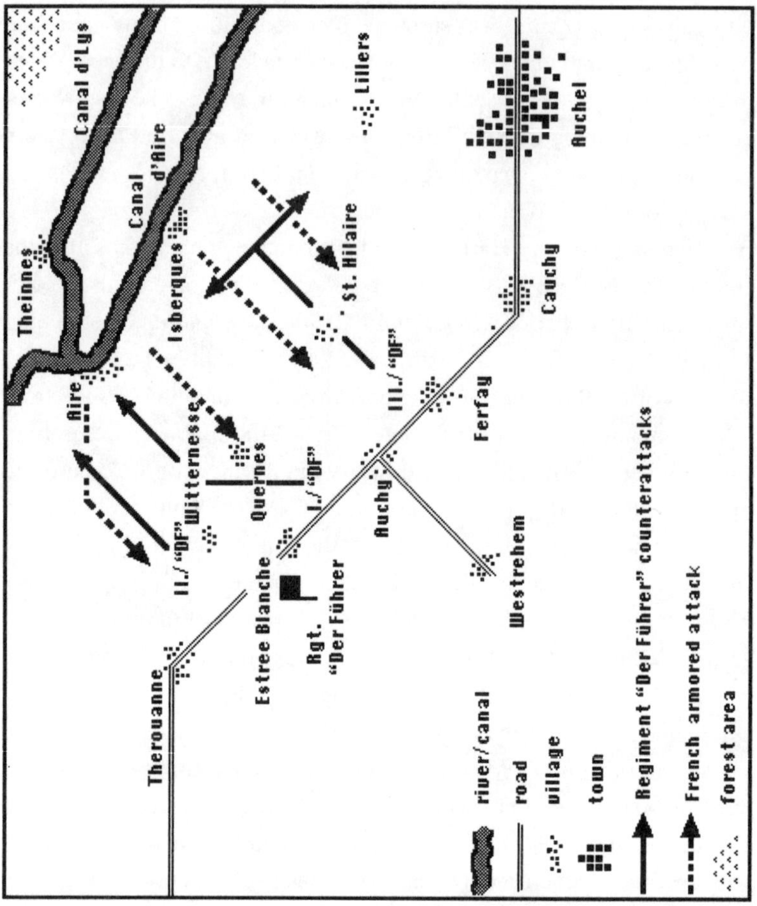


**Defense by Regiment "Der Führer" against a French armored attack that attempted to break through German lines in the Aire-St. Hilaire area on 23 April, 1940**

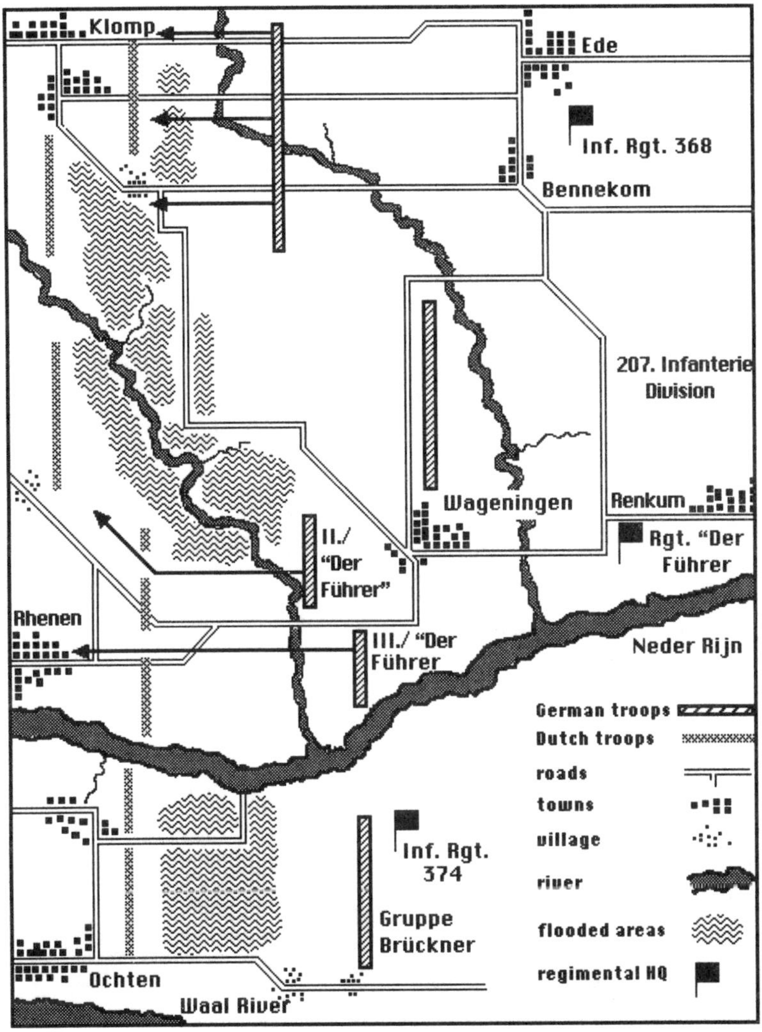


**The attack of Regiment "Der Führer" at 1600 hours, 12 May, 1940**

ported by accurate artillery fire and the complex, often swampy wooded area through which cut deep trenches. British elite troops, often standing chest-deep in the swamp, desperately defended every foot of ground and fought heroically to the end. Equally determined, the men of the regiment fought their way through meter by meter, broke the enemy resistance mainly in close combat, and in the evening were either very close to or had reached the Lys Canal. The night of 28 May was filled with tough night engagements in which the enemy, taking advantage of the lagging neighboring units (right: "Germania" Regiment, left: the army's 6th Panzer Division) tried through attacks in the open flanks to force the regiment to give up the hard-won wooded terrain. But the regiment repulsed all of these attacks. On the other hand, on 28 May an early-morning attack to force a crossing of the Lys Canal encountered such stiff resistance from the enemy, who had moved in considerable reinforcements during the night, that it failed to achieve its objective under heavy artillery fire. The regiment regrouped and in the afternoon hours of 28 May crossed the Lys

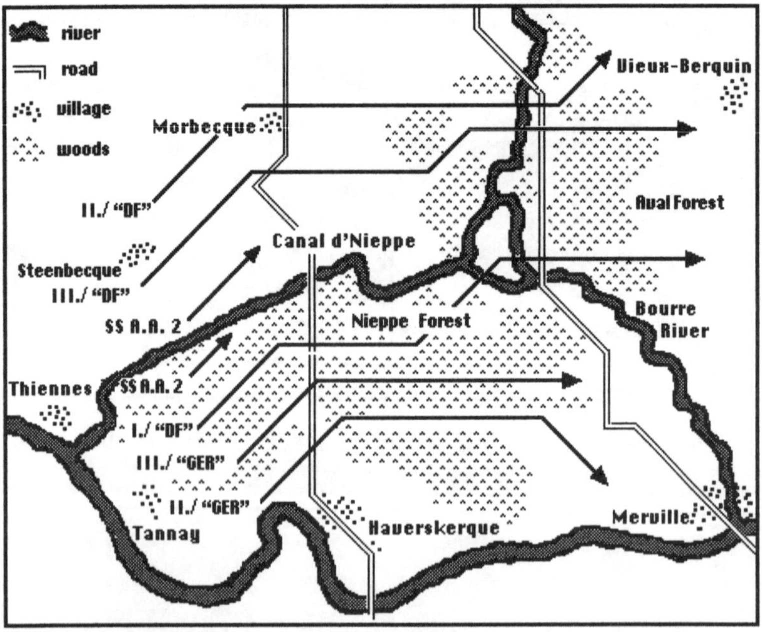


**The battle for the Nieppe Forest from 27 to 29 April, 1940 – actions of the SS-Verfügungs-Division**

Canal, however its subsequent advance was seriously hindered by heavy fighting in the difficult wooded terrain. The bitter fighting went on into the evening, and it was not until a number of enemy tanks were destroyed with the help of anti-tank guns brought across the canal that the enemy resistance weakened and finally ended in a headlong flight in the entire sector of the front. The Fôret de Nieppe was clear, the British Expeditionary Corps withdrew toward Dunkirk. The regiment followed via Hazebrouck, however it was ordered to halt in the Cassel area. From the high ground of Cassel the men saw Dunkirk lying before them, almost within reach. As a result of the inexplicable ban on a further advance, the British were able to evacuate the remains of their expeditionary corps while leaving behind all of its materiel.

As a result of the crush of German units moving toward the coast from the east and south, after several days of welcome rest, on 2 June 1940 the regiment and the SS-Verfügungsdivision were withdrawn and deployed in the area south of Arras to prepare for the attack through the Weygand Position against the rest of the French Army, which was positioned south of the area where the German forces had achieved their great breakthrough. The *SS-Verfügungsdivision* was placed under the command of the XVI Corps of von Reichenau's 6th Army. The attack began on 5 June 1940 with the *SS-Verfügungsdivision* in the second wave. The regiment crossed the Somme on 7 June and during the night of 7-8 June drove past the open enemy flank deep into the enemy's rear. The regiment was withdrawn from a developing fight against a colored French regiment and was relieved by an army regiment. The division was moved farther west to take part in the attack across the Avre toward Montdidiers-Compiègne with the "*Der Führer*" Regiment on the right and the "*Deutschland*" Regiment on the left. The regiment's initial objective was Guerbigny on the Avre. There the enemy had concentrated such powerful forces in terrain that favored the defenders that in spite of heavy fighting on 7 and 8 June and the success of the attack by the "*Deutschland*" Regiment the Avre could not be crossed. An attack planned for the 10th, involving a simultaneous flanking attack from the west by II Battalion "*Der Führer*", did not take place, as the breakthrough by Panzer Group Guderian farther east in the Champagne made it necessary to withdraw the *SS-Verfügungsdivision*, which was a mobile unit, and replace it with the army's

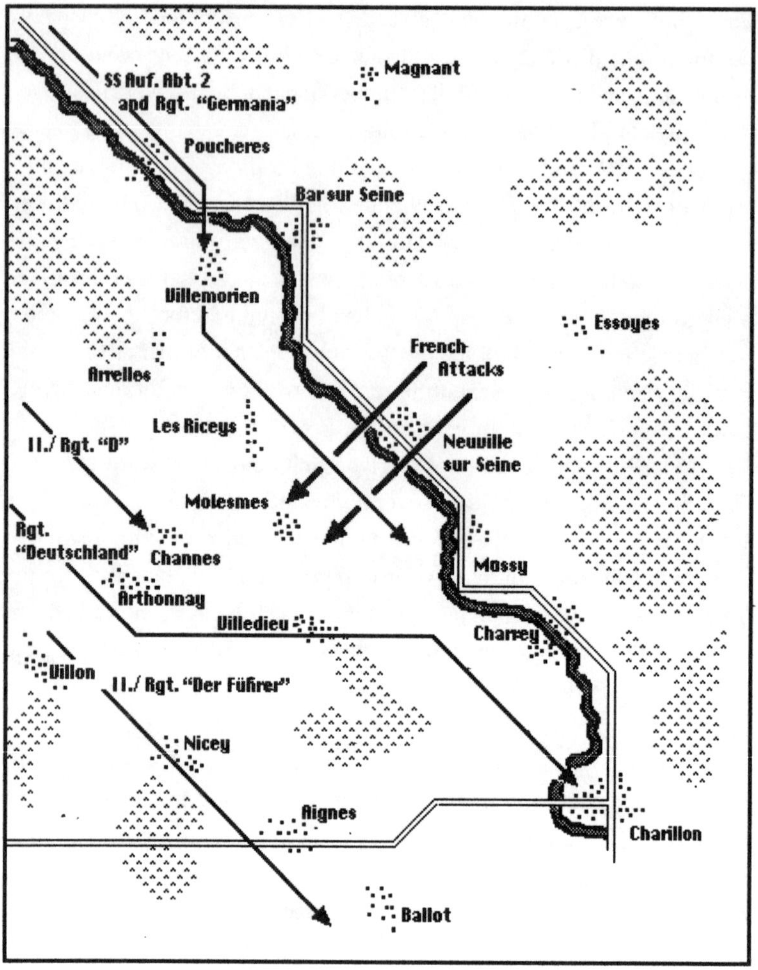


Battle on the Langres Plateau on 16 and 17 June, 1940

33rd Infantry Division in this sector. First, however, the *SS-Verfügungsdivision* was pulled back into the area north of St. Quentin, where the regiment was brought up to strength with replacement personnel from the Replacement Training Battalion.

On 13 June the SS-Verfügungsdivision was subordinated to the XIV Panzer Corps under von Wietersheim for the advance through Soissons, across the Marne near Château-Thierry and the Seine near Romilly. No one who took part in it will ever forget this march in blazing summer heat through the chalk dust of the Champagne. As well there was the lack of information on the enemy situation which necessitated strong, far-reaching reconnaissance to avoid surprise counterattacks. The first enemy resistance on 16 June south of Romilly was quickly broken. A battle near Laignes on 17 June seemed to develop more seriously. But the ability to resist of these French units, which had broken out of the Maginot Line to the west before the attack of the southern Army Group von Leeb, was already so battered that they gave up after a brief fight without, for example, committing a battalion of heavy artillery. It and a large number of prisoners and booty fell into the hands of the regiment. The regiment's last battle was fought near the village of Coulmierle-Sec, which was heavily manned by enemy troops. However, this was ended quickly with the support of several dive-bombers, and once again there was a large haul of prisoners and booty. In the midst of this battle the regiment heard the broadcast of Marshall Pétain's address to the French people in which he also announced the surrender of the French Army. The French prisoners celebrated and tried to make friends with calls of "*camarade*." There followed the advance through the western part of the Langres Plateau from Langres via Autun to Le Creusot, the old weapons forge of France.

There, too, the regiment was granted a brief rest stop. It moved out again on 21 May 1940 and in forced marches (380 kilometers was covered on the last day march) reached the internationally famous beach resort of Biarritz on the Bay of Biscay by way off Autun, Montagris, Orléans, Tours, Poitiers, Angoulême and Bordeaux. Remnants of the French Army were disarmed during the march; the numerous foreigners (British, Americans, etc) who had sought to escape the confusion of the war in the big hotels of Biarritz were surprised by the sudden arrival of the regiment but were not disturbed. The regiment's mission was to stand guard on the coast of Biscay and on the demarcation line created after the surrender which separated France into occupied and unoccupied parts. On the late evening of 26 June III Battalion "Der Führer" moved into the wild, jagged Pyrenees as far as the Spanish border, where Germany's victory over France was celebrated with Spanish soldiers. It was these unforgettable impressions, with the crashing waves of the Atlantic Ocean and the strange landscape of the Pyrenees, which, during the few days of rest and reflection, caused all the men of the regiment to fully appreciate the magnitude of the success of the Blitz campaign against France.

## Abbreviated Extracts from the War Diaries of 3rd and 6th Companies "*Der Führer*" from 9 May 1940 to 25 June 1940 (representative of all companies)

*3./DF:*

*9/5/1940 – Alert order and departure 21:20 hours with a combat strength of 3 officers, 21 non-commissioned officer and 140 grenadiers.*

*11/5/1940 – First contact with the enemy. At 10:28 Sturmmann Rainer of the 9th Squad became the company's first fatal casualty when he stepped on a mine on the Wageningen-Benneken road. In spite of heavy defensive fire 1st Platoon under Ostuf. Danz took the first enemy bunkers. Heavy artillery fire. The 3rd Platoon occupied bunker position no. 3. The Dutch defended themselves energetically, especially from positions 41, 42, 44 and 49. The enemy artillery fire increased and after the capture of bunker 43 approximately 350 prisoners were brought in. During the night all of I./DF's machine-guns were concentrated in order to provide fire support for II.DF's crossing of the lock.*

*On the first day of operations 3.DF lost Strm. Rainer, Krasser and Wagner killed as well as Grenadiers Schwammenschneider and Schäfer. Wounded were Uscha. Wille, Wippermann, Immervoll, Sturm and Schönleitner as well as Rttf. Tannich and Sturmmann Kahr. Grenadier Dirnhofer was missing.*

*13/5/1940 – I. DF readied itself in the Grebbe trench and was supposed to take positions two kilometers west of the trench. Direction of attack Horst, start of attack 12:30 hours. Preparatory Stuka attack on enemy bunkers. In spite of raising a white flag, bunker crews opened fire on 3.DF. Hstuf. Boysen-Schmidt was killed leading the company, also Uscha. Holland. Ostuf. Danz took over 3.DF and the company security for I.DF roughly near Bunker 58. Artillery fire on our positions during the night.*

*15/5/1940 – News of the surrender of the Netherlands reached the company at 22:30 hours and the same day Ostuf. Brandl took over the company.*

*18/5/1940 – Promoted to Unterscharführer for bravery in the face of the enemy and outstanding performances were: Rttf. Engelputzeder, Meindl, Kammleitner, Engel Bruckmoser, Tannich and Prankl as well as Strm. Bruckmoser.*

*23/5/1940 – Alert at 05:20: 2.DF is cut off. After scouting and preparation 3.DF attacked toward Witternesse at 12:30 and its 2nd Platoon quickly reached the north end of the village. 2nd Platoon in front of Querne and fought its way through the enemy-held village meter by meter. Rttf. Kothgasser shot in the head there and killed. I.DF continued to attack toward Aire, where 2.DF was still engaged in heavy defensive fighting. 3.DF was deployed toward Isbergues on reconnaissance, and at 19:30 the company advanced on La Roupie and dug in at the railway embankment.*

*27/5/1940 – Starting from the Canal d'Aire, 3.DF attacked across the Isbergues bridge and followed 2.DF with orders to establish contact with the left wing of "Germania." Machine-gun and rifle fire on the attack lanes from the direction of the Tanny road. 3.DF advanced rapidly and was given the Morbeque-Haverycerque road as its next objective. The Bois d'Amont was combed, and 1st Platoon advanced as far as the corner of the wood near Le Tonquet in the Bois d'Moyen. An enemy battery positioned there was attacked and put out of action.*

*28/5/1940 – Start of attack 09:20, and the company took the chapel of Le Parc. 2nd Platoon encountered enemy tanks on the Rue des Morts. Company regrouped in the Bois de Vaches. Artillery fire on the company. Members of 3.DF killed on the Rue des Morts: Uscha. Riedel, Rttf. Putz, Durinkowitz and Diessl, as well as Grenadier Klingemenn (died in Aire on 28 May 1940). Ustuf. Harms took over 3.DF after Ostuf. Brandl and*

*Danz and 13 non-commissioned officers and men were wounded there. At approximately 18:00 hours 3.DF reached Bourre Brook in the Bois d'Aval and secured positions there.*

*30/5/1940 – Obersturmführer Lex and Strm. Grüneberg were decorated with the EK II. (A. Lex was killed near Shepetovka in Russia on 11 March 1944 while serving as an Hauptsturmführer and commander of I.DF. He was among the bravest and best-loved officers of the DF Regiment. A. Lex received the Knight's Cross on 10 December 1943.)*

*5/6/1940 – Ostuf. Günster took over 3.DF and Oscha. Kraushofer became Stabsscharführer.*

*6/6/1940 – After the constant march and alert readiness of the last days, departure at 15:00: I.DF formed the advance guard. Disposition: advance guard: 1 anti-tank gun, 1 platoon I.DF, 1 platoon 4.DF, 1 platoon 13.DF, _flak platoon, 1 anti-tank gun; main unit: 1 anti-tank gun, 1 flak platoon, 1.DF, HQ 1.DF, rest of 13.DF, rest of 14.DF, 3.DF, rest of 4.DF; march route: Hendecourt-Bullecourt-Ecoust St. Mein-Mory-Ginchy-Foillères-Chaulnes-Doquescourt.*

*7/6/1940 – At approximately 12:00 hours 3.DF reached Erches and 1st Platoon cleared the village. In Guerbigny 1.DF encountered enemy troops in well-fortified positions and tried to effect a crossing of the brook. At 15:00 after regrouping, barrage by all heavy weapons on Guerbigny. 3.DF's initial objective stream bed at the east end of the village. 3.DF advanced in assault teams and with assistance from combat engineers, reached east end of Guerbigny and then the south end of the forest. The company secured there for the night without incident.*

*8/6/1940 – An assault team from the 2nd Platoon captured the fork in the road to Montdidier, and at about 07:00 the 1st Platoon broke into the village and occupied the bridge. Roadblocks were cleared by combat engineers. 12:05 continuation of the attack to the west and at approximately 15:00 attack on the Bois de Guerbigny with 2.DF left, 3.DF center and 1.DF right. The 2nd Platoon of 3.DF entered the forest and reached the road to Lignières. Enemy in strong and well-camouflaged positions. Attack gained ground only slowly. Killed in the forest fighting near Lignières from 3.DF: Uscha. Meindl, Rttf. Windgruber and Grenadier Egger, wounded were two non-commissioned officers and four men.*

*9/6/1940 – Infantry units of the army relieved 3.DF in its positions at 06:00. I.DF assembled on the Guerbigny-Bouchoir road and boarded its vehicles.*

*10/6-16/6/1940 – In blazing heat I.DF drove as part of the regimental formation through the Champagne and on 16 June reached the village of Origny-le-Sec. Battalion order from I.DF arrived at 12:00:*

*1.) Enemy is retreating in full disarray on the entire front, apparently behind the Loire. It is to be expected that the SS-Verfügungsdivision will also encounter enemy columns fleeing from the northeast on 16 June on both sides of Troyes.*

*It is the intention of the supreme command to engage the retreating enemy, cut him off from his forces in the eastern fortress area and destroy him.*

*2nd Army, left of the SS-Verfügungsdivision, will advance across a line Romilly-Troyes toward Aresse.*

*Advancing in a southeasterly direction, the von Kleist Group will prevent the enemy from escaping between Dijon and the Swiss border. XVI Army Corps left wing of Kleist Group, across a line Auxerre-Tonnerre toward Dijon. 13th Infantry Division in front of the SS-Verfügungsdivision toward Tonnerre.*

*2.) Regiment to reach the Chessy-Vanbry-Les Bordes-Le Coudre-Davrey area on 16 June.*

*3.) I.DF as March Group 5, assembly on Orvillers-St Fluoy road. March route: Beleville-Brunay-St. Pierre-St. Julien-Fontvannes-Bupey-Grand Chart-Vauchassis-Javernaut-St. Phal-Chamoy to Aeroeul. Departure at 14:30. Following battalion order from I.DF received before destination reached:*

1: *Enemy is still offering weak resistance in several villages.*

2: *SS-V-Division continue advance on 17 June with DF Rgt. right and D Rgt. Left*

3: *March route: Vilon-Maulnesse-Cruzy-le-Châtel-Nicey-Laignes.*

4: *March dispositions as before.*

5: *I.DF to be on the march road ready to march at 05:45 hours.*

*17/6/1940 – Prisoners brought in by the point during the advance. No serious resistance encountered so far. I.DF reached Nicey at approximately 10:00. I.DF is to advance to Griselles from there in order to destroy approaching enemy forces. Attack begun but broken off because enemy forces had surrendered.*

*25/6/1940 – News of the surrender of France reached 3.DF in the tent camp at Vivonne.*

## The Following extracts from the War Diary of the 6th Company "DF" Describe the Fighting in the West in 1940:

*23/5/1940 – The company was alerted by the battalion commander at about 06:00 hours. Order: Enemy has attacked from the south and fallen upon elements of the battalion (mainly train units) and II. Btl. SS-Art.-Rgt in Blessy from the rear. Enemy attack toward Blessy still being repulsed at this time. 6.DF to Blessy immediately as reinforcements.*

*The company advanced toward the west end of Blessy with the company headquarters squad, 2nd Platoon and the heavy machine-gun squad. Direction indicated by the sound of combat. A terrific firefight was in progress. The enemy had entered the south part of Blessy and had blown up several of the artillery's vehicles. We prepared to attack. Our 1st positions appeared when called. A surprise attack drove the enemy back. The enemy's losses were heavy. Our only casualty was Uscha. Kubat who received a home wound...*

*27/5/1940 – Battalion order arrived at about 17:00: 5.DF pinned down by strong enemy forces in front of the southwest part of Morbecque. 6.DF to move out at once, attack Morbecque and take the village.*

*The company moved toward the village with 1st Platoon south and 2nd Platoon north of the road to the village. 3rd Platoon had orders to attack from the south, catching the enemy in a pincer movement and splitting his fire. We were met by heavy defensive fire from machine-guns, anti-tank rifles and rifles. Enemy artillery chipped in too. Explosions and firing from every corner. After supporting fire from our heavy weapons we got up and stormed into the village.*

*Hand grenades exploded, Englishmen fell and fled. We had only one thought: into the village, we have to drive the English out. With lungs burning we reached the far side of the village. We had done it. Reports came in: Oscha. Proksch, leader of 2nd Platoon, seriously wounded, Oscha. Kaspar, leader of 3rd Platoon, killed, Uscha. Kogler wounded, Scharinger, Derler, Hofbauer, Heinze, Koller and Schreiner wounded. Prattes and Sieber killed...*

*28/5/1940 – In the Bois d'Eval: accurate enemy artillery fire. Ustuf. Heinz Werner (later commander of 10.DF and III.DF) now leader of 1st Platoon, was slightly wounded but stayed with his unit. After reaching Pt. Sec Bois we dug in. Körbisser assault team went forward on reconnaissance and returned with 80 British prisoners...*

The heroic actions of 6th Company "*Der Führer*" during the western campaign of 1940 were rewarded with fifty Iron Crosses, Second Class. Four Iron Crosses, First Class were awarded and twenty-five members of the company received the Infantry Assault Badge. Hscha. Heiger and Oscha. Egger received the War Merit Cross, 2nd Class. In the epilogue to the war diary, which all former members of 6th Company "*Der Führer*" received in 1940, the company commander, *Hauptsturmführer* Albert, wrote the following in memory of the fifteen members of the company killed in action:

> *"To you, parents and wives of our fallen comrades, this book is meant to be a simple sign of the gratitude we owe your sons for their loyal comradeship and their ultimate sacrifice.*
>
> *To you, men of the 6th Company, it shall be and remain a living memory of those proud days of combat and sacred obligation!"*

The annotation of the official report filed on 22 August 1940 said:

> *"The regiment of the Waffen-SS led by Oberführer Georg Keppler was the only regiment within an army corps to force a breakthrough of the Grebbe Line.*
>
> *The quickness of its action had far-reaching operational consequences. Oberführer Keppler, in particular, distinguished himself*

*through his bravery during reconnaissance, in preparing attacks and leading his regiment. He personally deployed III Battalion for the forced crossing of the Ijssel and the storming of the Grebbe-Berg under heavy enemy artillery fire.*

*Convinced of the decisive operational significance of the breaching of this key position, Oberführer Keppler was actively involved in seeing through this attack with his regiment and for his efforts received the Knight's Cross."*

## Occupation Time in Holland and France

On 2 July 1940 new marching orders ended the regiment's pleasant days in Biarritz, Bayonne and in the Pyrenees, which in addition to free time had provided an opportunity to overhaul weapons and equipment. On 3 July began the return march via Libourne, Angoulême, Poitiers, Tours, Orléans, Fontainbleau, Châteay-Thierry, Namur, Liège, Aachen, Mönchengladbach, Wesel, Bocholt, Deventer and Zwolle to Meppel in northern Holland. The march was edifying as in part it lead through areas known from the earlier fighting, undoubtedly stirring memories in all those who had been there. The crossing of the Reich border west of Aachen made a deep impression. The population crowded the streets and greeted the victorious regiment with enthusiasm and jubilation that went on and on. The honoraria of the city of Aachen had gathered at the border and received the regiment in such a heartfelt manner that in future it always had to schedule a brief rest stop there when passing through.

The regiment's reception was less warm in Holland, where it was stationed in the Meppel-Zwolle area on occupation duties. Some unrest and strikes in Holland had made this measure necessary, and the reception from the Dutch population was correspondingly cool and reserved. But it was not long before the disciplined, sure and modest deportment of all members of the regiment broke the ice and the initial reservedness of the Dutch was replaced by sincere friendliness. Joint cultural and social events were staged and many friendly invitations to Dutch homes followed. But not just that: many lifelong bonds were established between men of the regiment and the pretty Dutch girls.

But the primary purpose of this occupation period in Holland was again a comprehensive consolidation of the training including evaluation of all the wartime experiences in the western campaign. Non-commissioned officer courses provided the necessary replacement NCOs. At the urging of the division the regiment set up two company commander courses, which were attended by officers from the entire *Waffen-SS*. In recognition of III Battalion's outstanding performance in the western campaign, its commanding officer Hstuf. Kumm was placed in charge of the course. A new diversion was provided by exercises in which tanks and vehicles were loaded and off-loaded from transport vessels. These were carried out near Den Helder and after initial difficulties were completed with absolute safety and amazing speed. In keeping with the prevailing mood, the troops feverishly awaited a landing operation in England. English reconnaissance aircraft were extremely active and they undoubtedly followed the landing exercises with some concern. Unfortunately there was no way of knowing whether these exercises reflected the true intentions of the supreme command or whether they were merely a deception tactic.

This period in Holland was rudely interrupted when marching orders suddenly arrived in mid-December 1940. In biting cold the regiment set out as part of the *SS-Verfügungsdivision*, which had since been awarded the name "*Reich*" (later "*Das Reich*"), to drive to southern France. From Dortmund the regiment traveled the autobahn to Karlsruhe and through the snow and ice of the Vosges Mountains it reached the Langres Plateau west of Vesoul, where there were ample accommodations because of the thinning population of this area. The attitude of the population was one of absolute indifference. Generally this period in France was completely uneventful and despite initial fears it was possible to send another third of the regiment home on leave for Christmas.

Sometime in March 1941the regiment's 15th (Motorcycle) Company under *Hauptsturmführer* Fritz Klingenberg was transferred to the division, where together with the motorcycle companies of the other regiments of the division it was to be incorporated as a motorcycle battalion, a division unit. The regiment regretted the loss of this company, which had performed such useful service in the western campaign in the reconnaissance role and as a mobile combat unit.

## The Campaign in Yugoslavia

While several weeks earlier Yugoslavia had confirmed its friendship with the Berlin-Rome axis, at the beginning of 1941 that nation went over to our enemies following a coup. This surprising turn affairs led to a hasty war against Yugoslavia for which all available forces were mobilized. Thus on 6 April 1941 the "*Das Reich*" Division was suddenly and without sufficient preparation by the home service offices for the supply of fuel etc, sent from the Vesoul area in southern France across the icy Vosges mountains and the snow-covered Black Forest via Munich, Salzburg, Linz, Vienna, Budapest and Arad to Temesvar (Temeschburg), the economic and cultural center of the Banat Swabians. Everywhere the regiment marched through, in Austria, in Hungary, in Budapest, in Banat, it received a friendly welcome from the population, especially where it was of German origin, and was warmly received in its quarters west and south of Temesvar. There the regiment and the "*Das Reich*" Division were subordinated to Panzer Corps Reinhardt with the prospective mission of pacifying the Yugoslavian part of the Banat and the Batschka as far as the Danube in the direction of Belgrade. Careful reconnaissance and statements from residents revealed that the terrain planned for the regiment's advance was so swampy that vehicles were forced to use the lone, terribly poor road, which moreover had surely been mined. And so on Good Friday of 1941 the Yugoslavian border was crossed in depth on a broad front; all vehicles were left behind until the road had been cleared of mines. The regiment's objective was the village of Seleus. On its left the "*Deutschland*" Regiment advanced toward Alibunar, and on its left the army's "*Grossdeutschland*" Regiment advanced on Pancevo. Resistance was relatively light, was quickly extinguished wherever it appeared, and flared up strongly for the last time at the Theresa Canal, whose bridges were blown. Nevertheless, the advance by the companies, loaded down with weapons, ammunition and equipment, through the swampy terrain which had been transformed into a bottomless morass by steady rains before the start of the attack, was unspeakably difficult. In spite of these difficulties, in the early hours of the evening the regiment reached its objective of Seleus with all its combat gear and several skirmishes behind it, having covered almost fifty kilometers during the day.

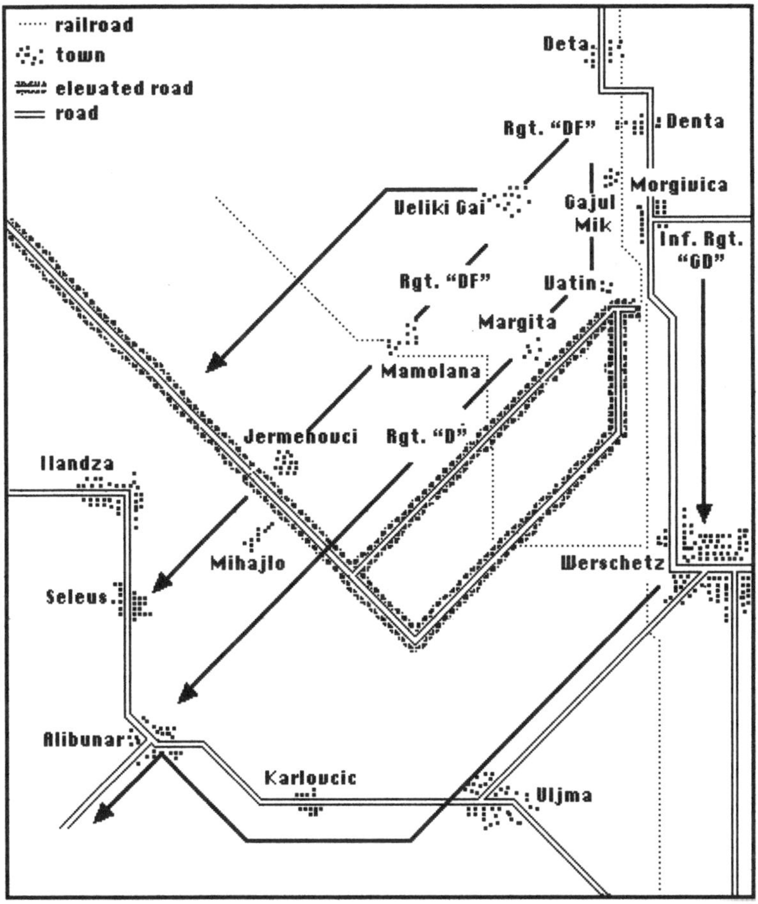


**The attack of XXXXI. Armee - Korps with SS - Division-"Reich" and Inf. Regiment "Grossdeutschland" on 11 April, 1941 from the area near Alibunar-Seleus, in the direction of Belgrade**

This marked the end of the Yugoslavian campaign for the regiment, since on the south side of the Danube German armored units were carrying out a concentric advance on Belgrade and a capture of the city from the north across the flooded Danube seemed impossible after the bridges over the river had been blown. Hauptsturmführer Klingenberg nevertheless succeeded in taking a ten-man team from his motorcycle battalion across the Danube in a motorboat, entering Belgrade and advancing to the German embassy. There he summoned the mayor and outlined the situation to him, whereupon he formally surrendered the city and fortress of Belgrade to Klingenberg. The regiment was proud that it had been Klingenberg and men of the "*Der Führer*" Regiment who had carried out this *coup de main*.

A few days later the regiment and the "*Das Reich*" Division drove via Budapest, Raab and Vienna into the Eferdingen area west of Linz, where after a thorough overhaul of training, vehicles and equipment preparations began for a new deployment.

## Appendix to Part I

The Commander in Chief Of the 18th Army — Army Headquarters, 14 May 1940

*Soldiers of the 18th Army:*

*On 10 May the troops of the army entered the Netherlands on the order of the Führer and supreme commander of the armed forces. Today a large part of the country is in our hands. Contact has been established with our airborne troops near Rotterdam across the bridges near Moerdijk.*

*The commander in chief of the army group, Generaloberst von Bock, has today expressed his thanks and appreciation to me for the army's accomplishments.*

*It gives me special pleasure and satisfaction to pass this thanks on to the troops of the 18th Army. While operations were under way I often had the opportunity to be with the fighting troops. I have been able to see for myself that every single man is prepared at the risk of his own person to do his duty. And all for Germany's greatness and freedom.*

*Now we must break the last resistance in Fortress Holland. No matter how hard the fight may be, victory will be ours.*

*Signed von Küchler*
*General der Artillerie*

The Commander in Chief of the Army Army Headquarters, 16 May 1940

Army Order

*Following the conclusion of surrender negotiations between the Dutch commander in chief and me on 15 May 1940, the entire Dutch armed forces surrendered unconditionally.*

*The war against the Netherlands is thus over.*

*We fought only against the armed forces of Holland, never against the population. I therefore expect the strictest discipline from every man. I will punish looting and excesses with all of the harshest means at my disposal.*

*Every soldier should demonstrate through his deportment and conduct that he is worthy to be a member of the German armed forces.*

*Signed von Küchler*
*General der Artillerie*

SS-V-Division Div. Command Post, 20 May 1940
Ia

Extract

*Order for the continuation of the march on 20 May 1940*

1G *Rgt. SS "Der Führer" is subordinated to the SS-V-Division. Leibstandarte SS "Adolf Hitler" leaves the division unit.*

2G *Division is to prepare for departure immediately.*

3G *March road: Givet, crossroad one kilometer south of Romédenne, Romérée, Marienbourg, road fork northwest of Couvin, Forges, Marquenoise, Hirson.*

*Subsequent march objectives by order.*

4G *March sequence:*

*March Group A: Recon. Btl., march Group B: "DF"*

*Advance detachment 15 DF; advance guard: one reinforced battalion, including Cdr. II. Art.Rgt.: battery commander and battery headquarters II. Art.Rgt.; one battery; 1. SS-Pi.-Btl.; division operations section (last march unit).*

*Main body: rgt. Less one reinforced btl.; including Rgt. HQ "DF"; KIA/WIA platoon; signals battalion,; HQ Art.Btl.; Art. Liaison platoon. At the end of the march group (in sequence): HQ Pi-Btl.; HQ Flak Btl.; Anti-tank Btl.; 1 ambulance platoon.*

*Signed Hausser*

...

SS-V-Division Div. Command post, 21 May 1940
Ia

*Division order for the continuation of the march on 21 May 1940*

1 *The SS-V-Division is subordinated to the XXXXI Army Corps.*

2 *During the night of 20-21 March the division will continue the advance via Hirson, La Capelle, Guise, Behain, Elincourt, Aubencheul without rest stops.*

*Continuation of march to Le Pave (on the St. Quentin-Cambrai road) anticipated on 21 May.*

*For the division*

*Signed Reinhardt*
*SS-Hauptsturmführer*

...

SS-V-Division Div. Command post, 23 May 1940
Ia

Extract
*Division order for 23 May 1940*

1 *Enemy forces that broke through west of La Bassée Canal destroyed. Béthune situation uncertain. Enemy attacks, especially at the boundary between V and T Divisions, cannot be ruled out.*

2 *SS "DF" is to clear further space north of the assigned boundary line with SS "G." III.DF is to move into its own combat sector. Aire bridgehead must remain in the hands of the regiment...*

...

*4. New assignments:*

...

*SS "DF" join up with the SS "G" at the rail line north of Ham, occupy defensive positions to the bend in the canal and block the canal up to but excluding Aire. The elements near Aire are temporarily subordinated to the 8th Panzer Division for the formation of a bridgehead.*

5G *Art.Cdr. will control the execution of the following artillery tasks: a) Defense in the specified line, point of main effort right, b) shift to the attack in the direction of Béthune.*

6G *Anti-tank Battalion is to be deployed with main effort on the right.*

7G *Div.C P: Auchy, northern exit. Contact by wire with SS "DF" in Matzinhem.*

*Signed Hausser*

SS-V-Division Div. Command Post, 24 May 1940
Ia

Extract
*Division order for 24-25 May 1940*

1 *Supported by the other weapons of the division, in a fast surprise advance the "Germania" Regiment has crossed the La Bassée Canal and the Lys and has successfully fought off counterattacks by enemy tanks. Elements of the 3rd Panzer Division were deployed on the division's right.*

2 *Today the Führer and Supreme Commander has ordered that there are to be no more crossings of the La Bassée Canal.*

...

*12. SS Rgt. "Der Führer" is to remain in its present area, secure the area with its front line on the La Bassée Canal and maintain contact with the 8th Panzer Division.*

*13. Code-word: Seydlitz.*

...

*16. Div. HQ: Busnes, chateau.*

*Signed Ostendorff*
*signed Hausser*
*SS-Sturmbannführer*

SS-V-Division
Div. Command Post, 26 May 1940
Ia 22:30 hours

*Order for defense during the night of 26-27 May 1940*

1 *On 26 May the SS-V-Division attacked enemy east of the La Bassée Canal and in a rapid advance has fought its way deep into the enemy positions. The enemy is in disorganized retreat toward the northeast.*

2 *During the night the division will organize for defense in its combat sector between the 3rd Pz.Div. right and the 8th Pz.Div. left.*

*Main line of resistance: La Madalerie (contact with 3rd Pz.Div.)–northeast end of Haverskerque-500 meters east of Lépinette-narrowest wood-Pont des Pendus-Kanal de la Nieppe-Château de la Motte-Le Tir Anglais (contact with 8th Pz.Div.).*

*Sector A: right boundary to exit from forest 500 m east of Lépinette. Sector commander: SS-Oberführer Demelhuber. Troops as in order of 26 May.*

*Sector B: Sector commander SS-Oberführer Keppler to the division's left boundary. Troops as in order of 26 May, as well as Recon.Btl., one flak company, 2/3rds of Anti-Tank Btl.*

*In sectors where there is contact with the enemy, contact is to be maintained through the night by forward outposts. Furthermore enemy movements on the roads before the front are to be prevented.*

3 *In Sector B reconnaissance is to be conducted to the east end of the Forêt de Nieppe, keeping watch for enemy movements in an easterly direction.*

4 *Preparations are to be made for a further advance in a northeasterly direction on 27 May.*

5 *The vehicles of the SS Rgt. "DF" are to be moved across the La Bassée Canal during the night and dispersed in the villages of Thiennes, Les Gissaux, Ft. Gassion.*

6 *The unit's ammunition stocks will be replenished during the night. As a result of supply difficulties ammunition is to be used sparingly on 27 May.*

7 *Code-word: Ziethen.*

8 *Div. HQ: Boesegehen. Lines of communication remain unchanged from 26 May.*

SS-V-Division Div. Command Post, 28 May 1940
Ia

*Order for the continuation of the attack on 28 May*

1 *No intelligence could be gathered on the enemy during the night. He appears to have withdrawn toward the northeast leaving behind rear guards.*

2 *SS-V-Division is to continue the pursuit on 28 May, 08:00 hours, clear the wooded terrain of the Forêt de Nieppe and after clearing the woods assemble at the disposal of the corps headquarters. 3rd Pz.Div. right and 8th Pz.Div. left will link up with their boundary near Vieux and continue the attack toward the northeast in front of the SS-V-Division.*

3 *Dispositions:*

...

*c) SS Rgt. "DF" with the units subordinated on 27 May. I SS "DF" attack on both sides of the Le Parc road, La rue des morts, south edge of the Bois D'Aval.*

*Objective: east end of the Bois D'Aval.*

*Recon. Btl. Support the attack by I SS "DF" with flanking fire and advances and on special order assemble at the northwest corner of the Bois Clébert (then under the direct command of the division).*

*III SS "DF" cross the canal and attack on both sides of the Château la Motte-Vieux Berquin road. Objective northeast end of the Bois D'Aval.*

4 *The units will go to the attack at 08.00 independent of one another. Crossing equipment to be taken along. The Pi.-Btl.'s flame-throwers are to be used in breaking through.*

5 *8th Pz.Div. has been informed of the attack and will establish contact with the left wing of SS "DF" near Le Tir Anglais.*

6 *Communication links remain the same as on 27 May.*

*Recon. Btl. To send operations officer to Div. CP after assembling near Bois Clébert.*

7 *Div. CP initially Boesegehen. After reaching attack objective south part of Morbecque.*

*Signed Ostendorff*
*SS-Sturmbannführer* *signed Hausser*

SS-V-Division Div. H.Q., 11 June 1940
Ia

Extract

*Preliminary order for departure of the division*

1 *Enemy in retreat before the entire front of the 6th Army. Disorganized retreat behind the Seine opposite the army's right wing. On army's left wing XXXXIV Army Corps in successful advance south of the Ourcq towards the Marne.*

*To the east of it on the army's right wing forward elements are said to have reached the Marne near Château-Thierry.*

2 *During the night of 10-11 June 1940 forward elements of 3rd and 4th Pz. Divs. of the VXI Army Corps advanced to a line Villers-Cotterêts-Hartennes in order to cross the Marne.*

3 *SS-V-Division is to be ready to march as of 11:00. Anticipate departure during the course of 11 June. The division will follow behind the center of the two panzer divisions (two march columns)*

*Signed Hausser*

...

SS-V-Division Div. H.Q., 16 June 1940
Ia

Extract

*Division order for 16 June 1940*

1 *Enemy is in full retreat before the entire front, apparently to behind the Loire.*

*It is to be expected that the SS-V-Division will also encounter retreating enemy columns from the northeast on both sides of Troyes on 16 June.*

2 *Intentions of the supreme command to engage the retreating enemy and cut off and destroy his forces in the eastern fortified area.*

*2nd Army, left of the SS-V-Division, will advance across the line Romilly-Troyes toward Auxerre.*

*Advancing southeast, the von Kleist Group will prevent the enemy from escaping between Dijon and the Swiss border; XVI Army Corps (left wing of von Kleist Group) across the line Auxerre-Tonnerre toward Dijon; 13th ID in front of the SS-V-Division toward Tonnerre.*

3 *Elements of the SS-V-Division will secure the Seine between Troyes and Romilly until the arrival of the 2nd Army.*

*Bulk of the SS-V-Division is to reach the Chessy-Cussagny-Romilly-Bouilly-Auxon area on 16 June. Any enemy crossing the Seine to the west is to be destroyed.*

4 *Security: As per verbal instructions the Seine is to be secured by SS "G" on both sides of Troyes, then north of it by SS "D" and SS "DF."*

5 *The units not employed on security duties will reach the specified area on 16 June in the following deployment:*

...

*d) march group SS "DF": Chersy-Vanlay-Les Bordes-Le Coudre-Davrey.*

*7. Advance road (Panzer Road C 2): Fontvannes-Brucey, Vauchassis,*

*Javernaut, Jeugny, Choutource. The von Kleist Group has right of way*

*over all other units. SS-V-Division behind the 13th ID.*

8 *Ready to march 16 June from 10:00 hours.*

*Departure point: Fontvannes. For Recon.Btl. leading elements at 11:00; for SS "D" leading elements at 11:45; for SS-Pi. Leading elements at 14:15; for SS "DF" leading elements at 15:15; rear-echelon units leading elements at 17:45.*

9 *Div. H.Q. Fontvannes, on the march end of rear guard SS "D."*

*Signed Ostendorf*
*signed Hausser*
*SS-Sturmbannführer*

SS-V-Division 24 June 1940, 23:30 hours

*To*
*SS Rgt. "DF"*
*Cease-fire with France begins at 01:35 hours on 25 June 1940.*

*Pasenow*

The Commander in Chief
of Army Group B H.Q., 25 June 1940

*The war with France is over!*

*In 44 days the armies of the army group have stormed and overrun the Dutch and Belgian national fortifications, forced the armies of both nations to surrender in fierce fighting, and in a bloody battle inflicted a destructive defeat on the Anglo-French armies rushing to their aid; Paris and the French coast are in our hands.*

*The number of prisoners taken by the army group has exceeded 1.5 million men, the booty in tanks, guns and weapons of all kinds is huge.*

*Shoulder to shoulder with the Luftwaffe we have achieved a victory which in history is unsurpassed in its beauty and extent.*

*The young German Army has withstood its most difficult test before the entire world, before history and before itself!*

*The suffering and disgrace that descended over our people after the World War has been extinguished by your loyalty and your bravery! The main burden of the bloody sacrifice was borne by the German Army. We intend to bear it proudly and cheerfully with full confidence in the ultimate and total victory.*

*Signed von Bock*

SS-V-Division Div. H.Q., 26 June 1940

*Extract from division order (by operations officer)*

1 *The enemy is in retreat to the south everywhere in front of the lower Loire. Still light resistance in some places, in other places no contact with the enemy.*

2 *18th Army stands in the line Agentan-Thouars-Martaize-Menclaire-Chatelrault-La Roche-Posay.*

3 *Von Kleist Group has orders to advance south between the coast and the demarcation line and reach the line Royan-Saintes-Angoulême-La Roche-Feucauld.*

*Right XV Army Corps, left XIV Army Corps.*

4 *SS-V-Division, in the center of the XIV Army Corps (right 10th and left 9th Pz.Divs.) is to reach the demarcation line in its sector with the advance detachment, with the main body the Poiters area, with one regiment Poiters.*

*7...*

*Right column: leader Oberführer Keppler*

*March group SS "DF"*

SS-V-Division Div. H.Q., 30 June 1940, 10:00 hours

*Division order*

1 *During the course of the next days the SS-V-Division will be relieved by the 1st Infantry Division and will depart to the north. Departure not before 1 July 1940.*

2 *1st Infantry Division will arrive in the SS-V-Division's area by rail beginning at noon on 29 June 1940. Headquarters, 1st Infantry Division in Dax initially.*

3 *The relief is to be prepared in direct consultation between the unit commanders of the SS-V-Division and the 1st Infantry Division as soon as the relieving unit has arrived.*

4 *Until relief the troops of the 1st Infantry Division will be quartered*

*immediately behind those of the SS-V-Division. The same quartering towns are to be used as soon as space is available. Assistance is to be given to 1st Infantry Division quartering officers.*

5 *Where quarters are not available for both units in the villages along the line of security, after relief the troops of the SS-V-Division are to assemble in front of their present quarters and in such a way that the SS "G" and the SS "D" can approach on the road along the demarcation line and the remaining troops on the Bayonne-Bordeaux road.*

6 *The reinforced 22nd Infantry Regiment will take over the sector held by SS "DF" less III Battalion and the SS-Reconnaissance Battalion.*

*1st Reconnaissance Battalion the Pyrenees border up to and including St. Jean-Pied-de-Port. Reinforced 1st Infantry Regiment the sector held by SS "D" up to but excluding Orthez.*

*Reinforced 43rd Infantry Regiment the sector held by SS "G" and Orthez.*

7 *ARKO Group to remain in its quarters until departure. II. SS Artillery Regiment to remain in firing positions southwest of Biarritz until relieved by II. AR 66 (100-mm), which is being deployed by ARKO.*

8 *Div. H.Q. as of 29 June in Biarritz, Hotel Miramar. Telephone communications with all security groups.*

*Signed Hausser*

# Operation *Barbarossa*

# War against the Soviet Union – The Beginning 22 June 1941

Three army groups were formed for the attack: in East Prussia Army Group North commanded by *Generalfeldmarschall* Ritter von Leeb; between the Pripet Marshes and Suwalki Army Group Center under *Generalfeldmarschall* von Bock; and south of the Pripet Marshes Army Group South under *Generalfeldmarschall* von Rundstedt.

Under the command of Army Group Center were Panzer Group 2 under *Generaloberst* Guderian and Panzer Group 3 under *Generaloberst* Hoth. Panzer Group 2 (Commander in Chief *Generaloberst* Guderian, chief of staff *Oberstleutnant* Baron von Liebenstein) was formed from the following units:

XXIV Panzer Corps (*General der Panzertruppen* Geyr von Schweppenburg): 3rd Panzer Division: *Generalleutnant* Model; 4th Panzer Division: *Generalmajor* von Langermann; 10th Motorized Infantry Division: *Generalmajor* von Loeper; 1st Cavalry Division: *Generalleutnant* Feldt.

XXXXVI Panzer Corps (*General der Panzertruppen* Baron von Vietinghoff): 10th Panzer Division: *Generalleutnant* Schaal; SS Motorized Infantry Division "*Reich*": *Generalleutnant* Hausser; Infantry Regiment "*Grossdeutschland*": *Generalmajor* von Stockhausen.

XXXXVII Panzer Corps (*General der Panzertruppen* Lemelsen): 17th Panzer Division: *Generalmajor* von Arnim; 18th Panzer Division: *Generalmajor* Nehring; 29th Motorized Infantry Division: *Generalmajor* von Boltenstern.

One *Gruppe* of close-support aircraft: *General* Viebig; Flak Regiment "*Hermann Göring*": *General* von Axthelm; combat engineers: *General* Bacher; signals units: *Oberst* Praun; artillery: *General* Heinemann; aerial reconnaissance: *Oberst* von Gerlach, later *Oberstleutnant* von Barsewisch. *Oberst* Mölders and his *Jagdgeschwader* (fighter wing) were responsible for air cover over Panzer Group 2's attack area.

The SS-Division "*Reich*," part of XXXXVI Panzer Corps, was initially held back as panzer group reserve. Once the bridges over the River

Bug had been freed up it was supposed to be moved up behind the left wing of the panzer corps.

## To the Dniepr

At the beginning of June the regiment was transported by rail into the Lublin area in Poland as part of the "*Das Reich*" Division – to guard the border with Russia it was said. In reality, however, a buildup was taking place there, which combined with an extensive supply organization could only mean war against Russia, a prospect which should have caused every responsible and clear-seeing German serious concern.

For in view of the overall military situation the resulting great danger of a two-front war for Germany could easily be dismissed. True, France had been overrun and lay prostrate. Beyond it, however, was Great Britain, a world power not to be underestimated for whom the defeat of Germany was a matter of life or death that became more difficult as Germany grew stronger.

It was easy to see that America's sympathies lay with the Allies and not Germany and it should have been taken into account in the German calculations as a possible future opponent. As well there was the serious dispersal of German occupation forces in France, Belgium, Holland, Denmark, Norway, the *Generalgouvernement* (Poland), in Czechoslovakia and in the Balkans, which absorbed strong military and civilian administrative forces and made them unavailable for an operation against Russia. And mixed in with all these considerations was the secret fear that the German command was insufficiently or wrongly informed about the mentality and strength of the Russian armed forces and believed that it could count on its previous luck. In any case it there seems to have been a serious underestimation of the Russians as an opponent. And so for every thinking person the Russian campaign began on 22 June 1941 as a dangerous gamble under worrying premonitions which were very soon confirmed in far greater degrees.

The date of the start of the offensive against Russia was still not known, however signs of the imminent decisions became ever clearer when individual officers from the regiment had to be detached for traffic control duties in the area of concentration southwest of Brest-Litovsk. They later described the extent of the buildup so close to the Bug.

Then suddenly, at dawn on 22 June 1941, there began a fierce barrage by guns of every caliber on the Russian positions east of the Bug. Long-range batteries pounded targets in the Russian rear, and wing after wing of German horizontal and dive bombers flew in a non-stop parade over the regiment's quarters just as the departure readiness order arrived. The fateful war against Russia had begun!

They waited impatiently for the first reports. When they came they spoke of the Russians being totally overrun at the Bug, of the successful river crossing, of the heavy fighting in and around Brest-Litovsk, and of the huge Russian losses and their headlong flight to elsewhere on the front. The developing air battles against poorly-flown Russian aircraft were watched with interest and the troops celebrated the absolute German superiority in the air. Everywhere the ground forces advanced rapidly.

The waiting lasted four days until, following the fall of Brest-Litovsk on 26 June, XXXXVI Panzer Corps was sent down the main road to Baranovichi. The regiment marched in the center of the "*Das Reich*" Division, which was in the second wave. Heavy traffic on the advance roads resulted in lengthy delays until finally the border was crossed near Brest-Litovsk. Inside the city the battle was still raging for the citadel, which was being heroically defended against all German attacks by the cadets of a Soviet officer school. Hopes for a rapid advance on the main road were in vain. It was in bad shape, overcrowded with supply and other columns, German infantry divisions marching on foot. The sides of the road were littered with a multitude of wrecked and burnt-out Russian vehicles and constantly growing columns of Russian prisoners.

But far more worse were the secondary roads which the division encountered when it was taken off the main road to guard the flank of the XXXXVI Panzer Corps in the area between the Pripet Marshes and the Baranovichi-Smolensk road. In blazing summer heat it laboriously made its way through this often swampy and mosquito-infested area via Sluzk to Swislotschi on the Beresina. Enemy resistance here was relatively minor and could usually be broken by the strong advance detachments, especially by the division's motorcycle battalion and reconnaissance battalion.

From Swislotschi the division was supposed to advance northeast on the east bank of the Beresina toward Mogilev. The only exception was the 11th Panzer-Grenadier Regiment, now part of the "*Das Reich*" Division in place of the "*Germania*" Regiment which had left the division, which had been deployed near the village of Beresino for the crossing of the Beresina. The crossing of the Beresina near Swislotschi by the bulk of the division was seriously delayed while the military bridge there was repaired. It had been blown by the Russians when the first of the division's assault guns drove across. So it was the afternoon of 6 July 1941 before the "*Der Führer*" regiment prepared to cross the Beresina bridge in second place; then it was halted by a corps order. After crossing the Beresina near Beresino, the 11th Regiment under *Obersturmbannführer* Dr. Wim Brandt had met such fierce resistance while attacking north-northeast to expand the bridgehead that it seemed that the entire advance might be halted.

The regiment received orders from the corps to move along the west bank of the Beresina, cross the river near Beresino and pursue the attack by the 11th Regiment. The military bridge near Beresino was the scene of unbelievable confusion and it was not until the corps issued an order giving the regiment absolute right of way over all other vehicles that the traffic jam sorted itself out and the regiment was able to cross to the east bank of the river that evening. At dawn on 7 July, after brief preparations, the regiment went to the attack with III Battalion under *Sturmbannführer* Kumm in the front line. After passing the most forward elements of the 11th Regiment there began a difficult battle against a stubborn enemy in dense, swampy wooded terrain. But then the Russians gave way. The subsequent fierce charge by the regiment wiped out a Russian infantry and artillery column and a number of prisoners were brought in, but then the point of III Battalion walked into a prepared ambush. The heavy enemy fire and the first appearance of flame-thrower tanks initially caused some confusion and made it necessary to regroup.

Reconnaissance revealed that the enemy, following the sole road through the swampy, primeval forest, had withdrawn east in the direction of Sabolotje. As a result when III Battalion resumed its advance it initially met no resistance. Not until early afternoon was contact again made with the enemy and resistance soon stiffened. After reconnaissance again reported strong enemy forces, the regiment was deployed from the march on both sides of the forest road in preparation for an attack, with III Battalion right and I Battalion left. As soon as the attack spearheads had worked their way through the forest they ran into a determined enemy who defended himself stubbornly in open terrain behind an embankment and received extremely effective support from his artillery – with direct fire in some cases. Prisoners identified the regiment's opponents as members of the Russian (Siberian) 100th Tank Brigade, which had earlier distinguished itself in Finland and was considered an elite unit. In view of this situation the regiment decided not to continue the attack until after planned preparations, including the employment of all heavy weapons. The artillery was moved forward and placed in position with great difficulty, while liaison officers and forward observers were sent to the battalion and company command posts.

Supported by concentrated fire from all weapons, the attack in the late afternoon hours was a complete success; however, the good training and flexible command of the Russians enabled them to withdraw farther to the east and, in spite of an immediate, vigorous pursuit by I and III Battalions, disengage.

Not until the evening did III Battalion contact the enemy again west of the village of Saosjorje; the Russians were driven back after a short, sharp battle and Saosjorje was occupied. The regiment suspended the advance on account of darkness and in view of the regiment's uncertain and totally isolated position in the Russian expanses it set up a hedgehog position in and west of Saosjorje with I and III Battalions for the night of 8-9 July. During the early evening hours the bulk of II Battalion, which had been detached to protect the trailing division headquarters, was sent back to the regiment.

At dawn on 9 July the enemy opened fire from numerous points opposite the regiment's hedgehog. After several insignificant feint attacks as a diversionary move, at 3 AM the enemy launched a heavy attack against III Battalion in Saosjorje following an even heavier artillery barrage. Vicious fighting developed in the village, which was sent up in flames, however the enemy failed to break in. The Russians, probably discouraged by the hopelessness of their advance and their heavy losses, finally abandoned their attack at about 9 AM and withdrew southeast into a wooded area southeast of Saosjorje. As per its orders, III Battalion set out to pursue with 10th Company under *Hauptsturmführer* Meyer at the point. However the enemy had so firmly entrenched himself at the forest's edge, with numerous snipers positioned in trees, that a further advance would only have been possible at the cost of heavy casualties. Consequently the edge of the forest was first systematically pounded with all available heavy weapons and artillery, including a heavy battery which was only made available after repeated requests by the division. Success was complete, the enemy resistance slackened and finally enabled III Battalion to resume its pursuit with the objective of driving the rest of the enemy into the impassable and extensive swamps to the southeast.

However, since a pursuit in this direction would have taken the regiment completely away from its direction of march to the northeast and as the primary objective continued to be to reach and cross the Dniepr as soon as possible, on orders from the division any further pursuit by the regiment at this point was halted. The retreating enemy was left to himself and the regiment was deployed for an accelerated further advance to the northeast.

Concerning these first serious battles by the regiment in Russia it must be said that the toughness, stubbornness and skill of the Russian opponent came as a surprise, but that (in contrast to several experiences in the west) in spite of his extreme fierceness and determination he fought absolutely fairly and correctly.

With II Battalion under *Sturmbannführer* Harmel in the point position and stronger security and reconnaissance, during the late morning hours of 9 July the regiment set off towards the east with Schklow on the Dniepr as its objective. After minor skirmishes with Siberian or Mongolian forces near Sabolotje in the evening, the regiment once again took up a hedgehog position for the night of 9-10 July and spent the night in the open under a rare, beautiful star-filled Russian sky.

The as yet uncompleted "Stalin Line" lay on the east bank of the Dniepr with strong bridgeheads on the west bank. On 10 July patrols by the regiment's armored car platoon under Ostuf. Schneider reported one such enemy bridgehead with a complex, wire-guarded system of trenches on Hill 215 west of Schklow. The terrain over which the regiment would have to attack was a completely open plain, visible for kilometers from

Hill 215, which was also heavily mined and therefore impassible to vehicles. Consequently from the outset the regiment committed two battalions with strong support from all heavy weapons to attack Hill 215, II Battalion right and I Battalion left. Extremely difficult fighting developed in which every foot of ground had to be fought for under heavy enemy fire. Several attempts to break into the enemy defense system on Hill 215 failed in bitter hand-to-hand fighting. Then in the evening *Oberscharführer* Blauensteiner of 5th Company finally succeeded in smashing a breach in the enemy position. Together with the following battle groups and the heavy weapons he was able to overrun seven Russian field positions, and before darkness fell this commanding and stoutly defended bridgehead was firmly in the hands of the regiment. Numerous prisoners, including many civilians, yes even women and children, who had been armed by the Russians and forced to defend the position and who had fought bravely, fell into the hands of the regiment as did a great amount of equipment.

The morning of 11 July was filled with the continued advance toward the Dniepr, the clearing of the intervening terrain of the last remnants of the enemy forces, the scouting of the most favorable place at which to cross the Dniepr and the preparations by the regiment for the attack across the river. But how great was the surprise that the heavily-fortified positions of the "Stalin Line" on the east bank of the river had been abandoned by the Russians without a fight after a heavy bombardment by our Stukas! As a result, in the afternoon hours of that very hot 11 July the regiment began the crossing of the Dniepr, which contrary to expectations was completely unopposed and proceeded smoothly.

Keppler: "While the leading elements of the regiment were still crossing I received orders by special courier to hand over the regiment and proceed as quickly as possible to Führer Headquarters near Rastenburg, East Prussia to take over the "Totenkopf" Division. The former division commander had been wounded and put out of action. This order caught me unprepared and hit me hard, for being separated from my regiment, whose officers, non-commissioned officer and enlisted men had grown near to my heart in difficult, fateful hours of combat, was unspeakably difficult for me. I passed the regiment over to the commander of III Battalion, Stubaf. Kumm, and on 12 July drove with a heavy heart back along the regiment's battle route to Lublin. Nevertheless, the entire period from April 1938 until 11 July 1941, during which I led the proud "Der Führer" Regiment in happy and difficult days and welded everyone into a tightly-knit community of fate, was and remains the most beautiful and valued memory of my long and eventful career as a soldier."

• • •

The campaign in the east had begun with unspeakable harshness. We were all firmly convinced of the necessity of this battle, all believed in our leaders and in our own strength and were in no doubt that we would emerge victorious from this confrontation.

But in spite of all the confidence, in spite of all our self-confidence, a feeling of isolation crept over us when we – following the army's armored spearheads – advanced into the endless expanses of Russia. We did not share the unfounded optimism of many who hope that they might spend Christmas 1941 at home. For us the Red Army was the big unknown, which we had to take seriously, which we could not underestimate. The goal of this struggle lay in the unforeseeable future.

In this boundless isolation of the individual the regiment became much more important to us than home had previously been; it was the community in which we all could find security and trust. And this feeling of security and trust never left us – not even in the most difficult hours and hardest battles – all of us of the "*Der Führer*" Regiment.

Otto Kumm

• • •

## II[3]

The Russians had given up the east bank of the Dniepr without a fight. While elements of my III Battalion were already crossing in inflatable boats, the regimental commander, *Brigadeführer* Keppler, informed me that I was to take over the regiment. It was not pride, but consciousness of serious responsibility, that filled me. The departure of our dashing regimental commander was militarily brief, the feeling that we probably both felt was significantly longer lasting.

At his point, in the name of all the men of the regiment I would like to express my deepest gratitude to our "old Mister Keppler" for the formation, rearing and command of this regiment. For the great humanity with which he cared for us all in a fatherly way, for his unselfish personal actions with which he inspired us and was an example.

The "*Der Führer*" Regiment still bears his face!

## Crossing of the Dniepr and Advance on Yelnya

An approximately five-kilometer-deep bridgehead was established east of the Dniepr, the foreground was cleared of straggling enemy forces and with guards posted the regiment rested. In the protection of the bridgehead the division's pioneer battalion was able to erect a military bridge and already on 13 July the vehicles could be sent across. The advance to the east was resumed in the direction of Gorki. In the march sequence the regiment followed behind the 11th Regiment.

While the 11th Regiment secured in and around Gorki (commander of the 11th Regiment Ostubaf. Dr. Brandt was killed in an air attack there), at noon on 15 July on the advance road the "*Der Führer*" Regiment received orders from the commander in chief of the panzer group, *Generaloberst* Guderian, to veer south, destroy enemy forces withdrawing east from Mogilev and then drive on towards Mislawl.

In the evening the regiment became heavily involved with strong enemy units approximately 15 kilometers north of the Mogilev-Mislawl road. The battle had to be suspended during the night due to inadequate orientation. By the morning of 16 July the enemy had withdrawn, the Mogilev-Mislawl road was reached without further enemy contact, and the advance toward Mislawl was continued with II Battalion as advance guard.

About two kilometers west of Mislawl the advance guard, which included the regimental commander and the commander of II Battalion

(Stubaf. Heinz Harmel), determined that the hills on both sides of Mislawl were held by strong tank forces. Initially it could not be made out whether they were our own or enemy tanks. The advance was continued and it was discovered that they were German tanks. A panzer battalion of the 10th Panzer Division had taken Mislawl from the northwest with orders to smash enemy columns coming from the direction of Mogilev. In spite of repeated requests by the company commanders for permission to fire at a column approaching in a cloud of dust, the battalion commander withheld the order to fire as he was uncertain whether it was a German or an enemy column.

The relief on both sides was great when the two units greeted each other in Mislawl. The mounted regiment could very easily have been shot to pieces by the more than forty tanks. The consequences could be serious when two units were not kept informed of each other's movements!

After two days of minor skirmishes around Mislawl, on 19 July the regiment resumed its advance to the northeast and rejoined the division on the Monastyrschtschino-Potschinok road. There the regiment received orders to occupy Potschinok station and the Dankovo airfield to its south. II Battalion busied itself with the destruction of an enemy artillery battalion which was placing harassing fire on the division's advance road from the south.

III Battalion (Hstuf. Hahn) had just occupied Potschinok station and I Battalion (Stubaf. Ehrath) the Dankovo airfield when the regimental commander received orders from the division commander, *Gruppenführer* Hausser, to advance towards Dorogobusch, approximately 100 kilometers northeast of Potschinok, with the regiment, less II Battalion but with the Reconnaissance Battalion (Hstuf. Mühlenkamp) and II Battalion of the artillery regiment (Stubaf. Wunder), take the city and barricade the Smolensk-Moscow highway in both directions.

The regimental commander raised doubts about this wide-ranging mission, especially since there had been no air reconnaissance for days because of bad weather and no road scouting had been carried out. However the order had been issued so irrevocably by Panzer Group Guderian that it had to be carried out without delay.

When darkness came the regiment was on the march, led by the reconnaissance battalion which was scouting the roads. The roads were bottomless and in no way corresponded with the maps, numerous small bridges were rickety and decrepit and were soon impassible. So during the night the reinforced regiment became strung out along almost the entire march route.

On the morning of 20 July the reconnaissance battalion and III Battalion came upon a well-fortified enemy position west of Dorogobusch, attacked and broke through the position in the first assault. The enemy brought up very strong reserves from the city, as a result of which the line gained had to be abandoned again and the regiment's forces withdrew to their starting position in a wood.

At the same hour the regiment received new orders: "Break off the battle for Dorogobusch, barricade the Smolensk-Yelnya road near Jaswino with all available forces against possible enemy withdrawal movements from the battle of encirclement around Smolensk." Only one bakery company was captured.

• • •

The neighboring unit on Panzer Group 2's left, Panzer Group 3 under Hoth had advanced to the Wop with the mobile units of the 12th, 19th, 20th, 7th and 17th Panzer Divisions as well as the 18th Motorized Infantry Division, bringing it into contact as well with the quickly and well built "Stalin Line." Trapped behind these advancing divisions as well as those of Panzer Group Guderian were the Soviet 20th and 16th Armies with a total of fifteen divisions and six armored formations. These enemy forces had been badly battered but nevertheless put up determined resistance.

In these days the Yelnya salient was the farthest point in the German front. This strategically extremely important jump-off point was the natural springboard for a subsequent advance on Moscow. Consequently the enemy committed all his reserves in order to reduce the Yelnya salient at all costs and recapture Smolensk. The Soviet command issued harsh orders: soldiers who left the position without orders would be shot. Officers who retreated or whose units retreated could be brought before a court martial. It was also here that the term "Guards Division" came into being. The onslaught by the German panzer divisions and motorized units absolutely had to be turned back at Yelnya.

# The Battle of the Yelnya Salient

Around Yelnya the 10th Panzer Division (Schaal) was locked in battle with far superior enemy forces.

On the morning of 22 July the division commander issued orders for the "*Reich*" Division to attack the hills east of Yelnya and subsequently defend them.

The attack was made with the "*Deutschland*" Regiment on the right (to the 10th Panzer Division) and the "*Der Führer*" Regiment on the left on the initially open left wing. The regiment reached its departure position at about noon and attacked from off the move with II Battalion on the right and I Battalion on the left. III Battalion followed echeloned to the left rear to guard the open flank. There soon developed an extraordinarily tough battle. The enemy had well-fortified positions on the lines of hills, fought with great determination and was supported by heavy artillery fire. Only through the employment of all the regiment's heavy weapons and our artillery, which employed several guns in the direct fire role, and through an enveloping attack by III Battalion from the left wing, as it possible to crush the enemy in his positions by late evening.

Once again the regiment had reached its assigned objective, but as a result of the tough fighting in the blazing heat every man of the unit was completely exhausted. Positions were established in the captured line during the night. II Battalion had its right wing at the railway embankment which ran east from Yelnya; it pushed assault teams into the village of Pronino and established contact with the "*Deutschland*" Regiment on a hill south of the rail line. II Battalion's left wing extended through a high cornfield in which lanes were tramped down for the machine-guns. The main boy of I Battalion lay in an extended gully whose only cover was provided by peat banks and piles of cut peat.

III Battalion had possession of a shallow ridge and established itself for defense in the complex, sapling-covered terrain with its front facing northeast. (Hstuf. Kempin took over III Battalion and Hstuf. Hahn the 13th Company.) The 16th Company (Hstuf. Braune) immediately began the careful laying of mine barriers, especially anti-personnel mines with tripwires. Favorable approach paths for tanks were also scouted and mined. The regiment's sole reserve was the 15th Company. The commanding officer moved the regimental command post 200 meters behind the main line of resistance into a deep rail cutting running at right angles to the front.

On 23 July at the regimental command post the division commander expressed his full appreciation for the regiment's accomplishments. Gruppenführer Hausser approved the commanding officer's plan to attack and take a commanding hill 500 meters in front of I Battalion's main line of resistance, which gave the enemy a good view of the German positions, and thus significantly improve the battalion's positions.

I Battalion took the hill in the early morning hours of 24 July and established defensive positions in the newly-won line. It would subsequently hold the position against repeated enemy attacks.

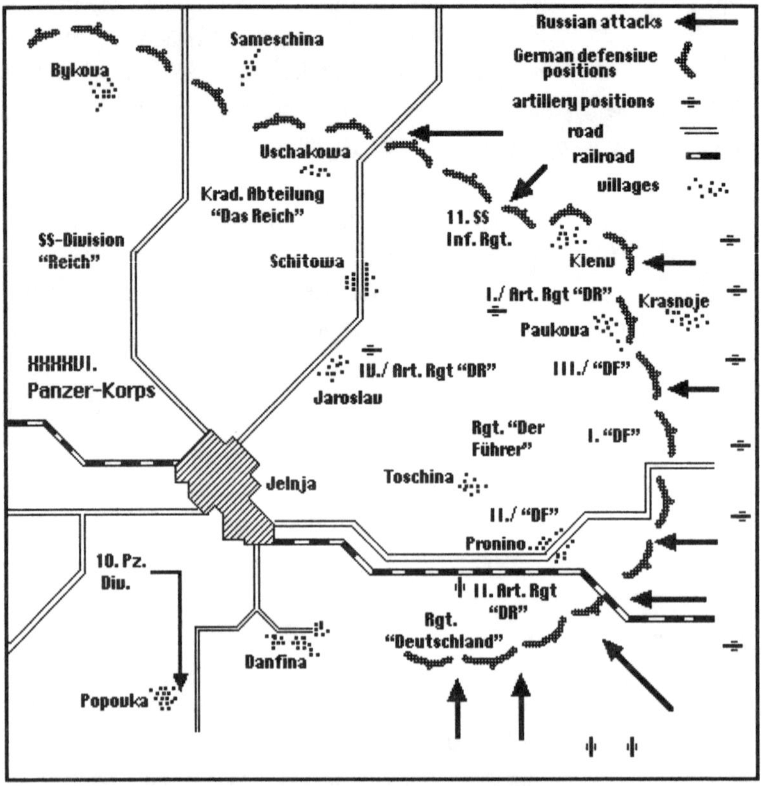


The situation from 22 July to the beginning of August, 1941

There now began for the regiment a difficult test in a defensive role, one which it withstood in heroic action: a shining example of the term "defense."

• • •

We had seen with what dash and fighting spirit our brave grenadiers from Austria and the Sudetenland stormed forward to the attack. Would this spirit also stand by them in the defense? It did, and what they achieved in the five following weeks is a glorious page in the history of the whole German Army.

The enemy launched his attacks against our positions ceaselessly, day and night, his artillery grew in strength day by day until sometimes to a true drum fire. Seven attack divisions were identified opposite the positions of the SS-Division "*Reich*." And nowhere on that wide-stretched front of the salient was a single foot of ground lost!

Day and night assault teams from the battalions probed deep into the enemy positions, frustrating numerous attack preparations and bringing back prisoners with important information.

• • •

The task of defense was made more difficult by the chronic shortage of ammunition, especially for the artillery. For the XXXXVI Panzer Corps, of which the "*Reich*" Division was a part, was at the farthest point of the entire Eastern Front during these weeks. The supply lines had become almost impossibly long.

On 31 July II Battalion was relieved by an army unit and temporarily at least was held in reserve at the disposal of the regiment. The regimental command post was moved farther north behind III Battalion where it had at its disposal a small hill from which there was an excellent view of the regiment's entire sector. It was thus possible at any time to spot an enemy attack while it was still developing and frustrate it by concentration of fire or the commitment of reserves.

The enemy deployed his T 34 type tank for the first time here. None of the tanks previously encountered by the regiment had caused the men much trouble. The grenadiers said, "We catch them in our caps!" Then suddenly ten T 34 tanks broke through the positions of I Battalion, crushed our ineffective 37-mm anti-tank guns and drove deep into the regiment's area. The men kept their nerve, however. They attacked the giants with captured Molotov Cocktails, with anti-tank mines and by pouring gasoline over them and destroyed several. The rest were knocked out in the artillery's firing position. Afterwards the tanks, some of which had burnt out, were given a close expert examination inside and out, but not without some astonishment. The opinion was unanimous: "They are going to cause us plenty of hard work!"

At the beginning of August the regiment was relieved in its former positions by units of the army (292nd Infantry Division) and was transported via the Glinka station to the land bridge between Usha and Ustrom. There it was deployed in a defensive role again with its front facing north. The tremendous battle of encirclement at Smolensk, in which according to the *Wehrmacht* communiqué more than 300,000 men were taken prisoner, was approaching its climax. It is therefore understandable that the enemy pressure to the south and southeast grew daily.

The regiment deployed III Battalion on the right and II Battalion on the left. The unit on the regiment's right here was the Infantry Regiment "*Grossdeutschland*." I Battalion had been pulled out of the line and placed at the panzer group's disposal on 12 August 1941. From these positions, too, the battalions carried out daily scouting and offensive patrols, two of which are deserving of special mention: a patrol from II Battalion passed undetected through the enemy positions, advanced approximately six kilometers into enemy territory and overran a Russian division headquarters. The patrol returned with important prisoners.

Before III Battalion's main line of resistance there was a small village. One day, after a tough fight against superior enemy forces, a motorcycle platoon from the 15th Company "*Deutschland*" was forced to abandon the village, leaving all of its vehicles behind. An assault team from III Battalion equivalent to two squads led by Uscha. Gutberlet attacked the village and drove out the enemy, who left behind numerous dead. The assault team subsequently returned safely with the motorcycles.

Especially worthy of mention in this section is the exemplary cooperation between the army's artillery commander and the regiment. The artillery commander fulfilled every request, made outstanding observations and took out numerous unpleasant enemy batteries, and effectively engaged enemy positions identified by the regiment. Unfortunately the names of this officer and his battalion are not known.

On 18 August the regiment was relieved by army units. It traveled via Glinka station, Baltutino and Potschinok to Smolensk and went into positions east of the city to rest and refit. During this brief rest period the battalions were used to help bring in the harvest on the collective farms.

During the last battles the 12th Company lost its beloved commander, *Hauptsturmführer* Hans Lederwasch.

• • •

Otto Kumm wrote:

> "I had the privilege to decorate a large number of men from the regiment with the Iron Crosses, First and Second Class in recognition of their accomplishments. An extensive commanders briefing by the division gave us a comprehensive impression of the course of the eastern campaign to date and also extinguished from the last of us any sort of optimism in assessing this campaign. We could be very proud of the accomplishments so far by the German Armed Forces, our SS-Division "Reich" and especially our regiment "DF", however the assessment of the enemy provided by the Division Ic on this occasion left no doubt as to the existing and growing strength of the Red Army."

## Battle of Encirclement at Kiev

*In spite of the overwhelming successes so far by Army Group Center, which were expressed particularly in the great haul of prisoners and booty from the battles of encirclement at Gomel and Smolensk and in the territory gained, a continuation of the advance in the direction of Moscow was initially put aside and the main effort was shifted to Army Group South. There had been much discussion concerning the wisdom of this shift of main effort, however there is no room here for comments on this theme.*

*The German plan of operations called for large elements of the Red Army, specifically the army group commanded by Marshall Budenny, to be destroyed in a large-scale battle of encirclement in the Kiev area. To this end units were taken from Army Group Center, especially Guderian's armored units (including the SS-Division* "Reich"*, the 3rd, 4th, 17th and 18th Panzer Divisions, the 10th and 29th Motorized Infantry Divisions, and the* "Grossdeutschland" *Regiment).*

*On 1 September 1941 the "Reich" Division, with the "Der* Führer" *Regiment at its head, set out for Kossowka via Smolensk, Rudja and Roslavl. On 2 September the march was continued via Mglin and Unecha toward Starodub. It rained buckets and the already pitiful roads were turned into deep morasses. Extremely great demands were placed upon the drivers. As a result of these road conditions the division became completely dispersed.*

*On 3 September there were several brief battles with the retreating enemy south of Starodub. On the evening of 3 September the regiment (without I Battalion) was in Awdejewka, far ahead of all other units of the* "Reich" *Division. South of the village elements of the 10th Motorized Infantry Division had lost considerable ground to the hard-pressing enemy in recent days.*

*Generaloberst* Guderian ordered the regiment to attack here on the morning of 4 September without waiting for the arrival of further elements of the "*Reich*" Division. During the evening of 3 September the battalions moved into the assembly area south of Awdejewka, with III Battalion on the right and II Battalion on the left. Weak enemy artillery fire fell on eastern outskirts of the village. The commander of III Battalion, Hstuf. Kempin, was wounded in a surprise barrage during the night, and with a heavy heart the commanding officer ordered the regimental adjutant, Hstuf. Linger, one of the best officers available to the regiment, to succeed him.

The attack went forward across our lines of security at 5 AM on 4 September against a strong, fiercely defending enemy. Progress was slow at first. But then II Battalion under Stubaf. Harmel smashed its way through and pursued the enemy so doggedly that the Red Army troops never succeeded in making another stand. In the late afternoon, following a surprisingly quick river crossing (Ubedy), II Battalion overran a division headquarters in its quarters. The day's balance was a large haul of prisoners and approximately twenty captured guns. III Battalion followed up to a position abreast of II Battalion. The southward advance was continued on 5 September. Large numbers of enemy troops in headlong flight in various directions were shot up by the artillery. During one such interval I Battalion rejoined the regiment, immediately assumed the point position and advanced far to the south with great elan.

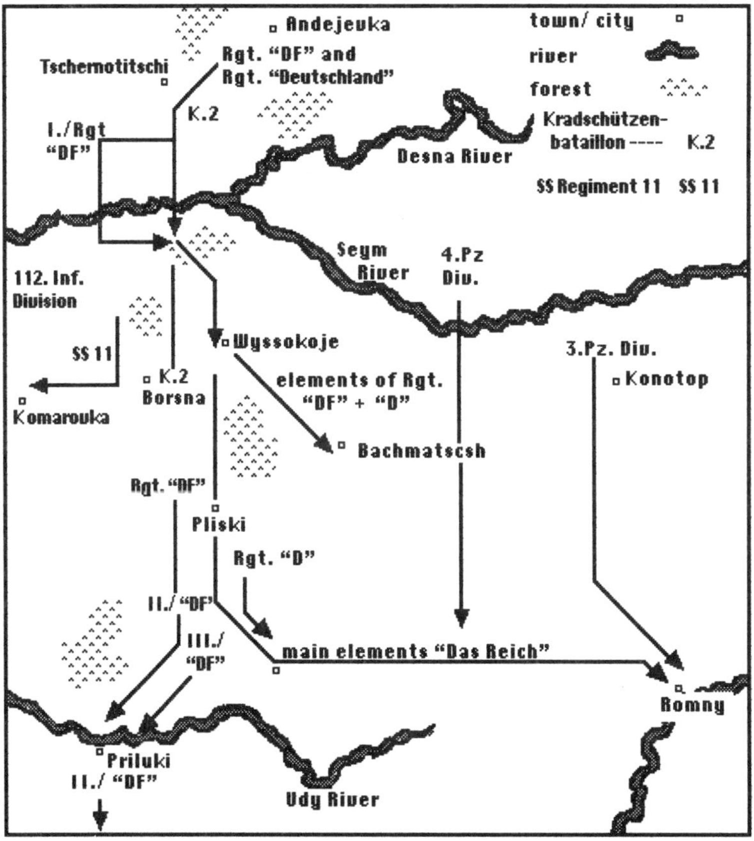


**The movements of SS-Division - "Reich" in the encirclement battle of Kiev, from 4 to 23 September, 1941**

During the advance *Generaloberst* Guderian drove along the regiment's column and greeted the troops with appreciative words. On the morning of 6 September the leading elements of the regiment were at the Desna south of Sosnitsa. I Battalion drove into an enemy column near Mjena and inflicted severe losses on it.

The enemy began to sense the start of the encirclement. On 7 September the center assault group of Panzer Group Guderian reached Konotop with the advance detachment of the 3rd Panzer Division (the Berlin Bear Division). The pocket was to be closed in the area around Romny.

Strong Russian formations withdrew across the Desna over the railway bridge near Makoshin before the 2nd Army attacking from the west. A powerful defense at the northern and eastern outskirts of Makoshin, whose backbone consisted of two armored trains, was supposed to keep this crossing over the approximately sixty-meter-wide river open for the Soviets.

The regiment attacked Makoshin from the move with the division's motorcycle battalion, which had been subordinated to it. I Battalion was still locked in a bitter struggle east of Mjena, while II and III Battalions secured east of Makoshin at the Desna. A Stuka attack on Makoshin was requested for the start of the attack at 1:30 PM. 1:30 came, no Stukas; 1:45, no Stukas; 2 PM, still no Stukas! Then, from the "*Der Führer*" Regiment's command post approximately 500 meters east of Makoshin, *Generaloberst* Guderian gave the order for the motorcycle troops to attack. Attacking fiercely, the motorcycle battalion broke into the enemy positions; an extraordinarily fierce fight developed in the village. Because of a lack of observers our artillery was only able to engage enemy targets at the edge of the village.

At 2:30 PM (the motorcycle troops had long since fought their way into the village) the Stukas came in three waves with a total of twenty-seven machines and in spite of all the signal flags and flares dropped their deadly loads into the village – onto the brave motorcycle companies!

There were frightful casualties and many curses were shouted up at the Stukas. The dive-bomber attack did have one positive result, however; the enemy armored trains were destroyed and enemy resistance in the village lessened. During this fighting the commander of the 14th Company, Ustuf. Frank (anti-tank company), and the chief of the anti-aircraft machine-gun company, Ostuf. Fritz Rentrop, led a handful of men along the eastern edge of the village and then dashed across the big railway bridge. They removed the wires leading to the demolition charges and established a foothold on the south bank of the Desna.

The enemy recognized the serious danger, for he still wanted to withdraw numerous units over this bridge. He launched a counterattack immediately, bolstered the attack from hour to hour and placed the bridge under such concentrated fire that a crossing was no longer possible. All attempts to relieve these brave men were in vain; no reinforcements could be sent to them during the day. They had to hold out alone. They dug in in the few meters of ground they had won and held the bridge, which was of inestimable value to our own plans, against all enemy attacks. Ustuf. Frank sealed this heroic battle with his death. Ostuf. Rentrop was rewarded with the Knight's Cross for this decisive act. The assault guns and the 15th Company also fought bravely.

During the night of 7 September weak elements of the motorcycle battalion were moved into the tiny "bridgehead" supported by the assault guns "*Prinz Eugen*" and "*Derfflinger*"; however, an attack from these positions held little promise of success. The regimental commander therefore decided to cross the river, with I Battalion west of and III Battalion east of the bridge, form a second bridgehead and destroy the then surrounded enemy. II Battalion was sent across approximately six kilometers to the east, attacked and took a small village on the south bank of the Desna and held it against numerous enemy attacks, thereby covering the regiment's left flank. The crossings by I and III Battalions proceeded according to plan and were completed without incident before daybreak on 8 September. I Battalion subsequently had to fight a tough battle in the complicated terrain on the south bank of the Desna, but by midmorning it reached the railway embankment south of the railway bridge. III Battalion advanced through thick fog in the valley of the Desna. Approximately three kilometers in front of it was the large village of Slobotka, sitting on a fog-free hill. Moving silently, the battalion reached the foot of the hill unseen; it then entered the village with such surprise that the enemy was unable to offer any serious resistance.

Numerous prisoners, including an artillery battalion, fell into the battalion's hands. The bridgehead was closed at the railway embankment before the morning was over and the enemy units which were surrounded as a result were completely wiped out by the motorcycle battalion and the following "*Deutschland*" Regiment.

On 9 September the "*Deutschland*" Regiment attacked south from this bridgehead with its left wing aligned with the Makoshin-Bakhmach rail line. Borzna was taken the same evening against a fiercely-resisting enemy. Then the "*Der Führer*" Regiment, led by III Battalion, continued its attack along the rail line. During the night it overtook its sister regiment "*Deutschland*" and when morning came on 10 September it was engaged in combat with far superior enemy forces, which were withdrawing to the east, at the railway junction of Bakhmach.

Contact was established with the 4th Panzer Division on the left wing. The enemy suffered severe casualties. The regiment lost one of its best and bravest officers here, the commander of 11th Company, Hstuf. Karl Ney. From Bakhmach the "*Deutschland*" Regiment initially spearheaded the attack by the "*Reich*" Division; pursuing relentlessly, it destroyed strong enemy elements. The "*Der Führer*" Regiment was moved forward sector by sector and on 15 September it rejoined the battle.

While the "*Deutschland*" Regiment, supported by assault guns and combat engineers, took the village of Jtschnja, the "*Der Führer*" Regiment was ordered to attack and take Priluki. The picture was becoming increasingly clear of the "*Reich*" Division advancing straight toward the heart of the Kiev pocket, accompanied on either side by retreating enemy armies. By the evening of 15 September the enemy had settled down again, in Matischowska and especially on the hills south of the village. II Battalion, which attacked from off the move, sustained distressing losses. The outstanding commander of the 6th Company, Hstuf. Grund, was killed here. When darkness came the battalion had to call off the attack in order to regroup.

At the same time III Battalion "*Der Führer*" was also engaged in fierce fighting at a road three kilometers to the east. On the other hand I Battalion was once again pulled out of the line at the disposal of the XXIV Panzer Corps (*General* Geyr von Schweppenburg). In spite of repeated patrols during the night, the enemy was able to withdraw unnoticed, further evidence of the high level of training and instinctively sure behavior of the Soviet officers and men.

Deployed on both sides of the road, II Battalion attacked through the abandoned positions and made rapid progress. Without further resistance II Battalion entered the north end of Priluki in the early morning hours of 16 September. The village straddled a river with a small northern part and a larger southern part stretching two to three kilometers along the river. The enemy had taken up defensive positions in the houses and gardens of the northern part. A tank platoon attacked from the west end of the village, intervening persistently in the fighting.

"Not one step back. Hold and die if necessary!" was the order given the Red Army soldiers by the Soviet high command.

Attacking from off the move, II Battalion became bogged down in the northern part of the town. Every house, every bit of garden was fiercely contested and the outcome was decided almost exclusively with hand grenades and submachine-guns. A platoon of assault guns under the command of Ostuf. Telkamp advanced with the 15th Company as far as the bridge to the southern part of the town. The bridge had been prepared for demolition beforehand, however, and the men could not prevent the enemy from blowing it.

During the night of 15-16 September III Battalion broke through an enemy position while mounted and was able to inflict considerable losses on the enemy. Continuing to attack, III Battalion reached the river a few kilometers east of II Battalion but was then pinned down by heavy fire from the southern part of the town.

Since the early morning of 16 September the regimental command post had been on a commanding hill approximately 300 meters north of the town, from which there was an excellent view of the battle area. It was possible to effectively direct our artillery from this hill and an enemy armored train was forced to retire. At approximately 9 AM the regimental commander was surprised to discover a force of enemy infantry equivalent to two battalions advancing from the northwest on a broad front toward the rear of II Battalion and the regimental command post. At the same time enemy artillery began firing on the command post. The enemy fire grew in intensity from hour to hour, while the enemy simultaneously forced his infantry attacks. The attack was stopped through the employment of every available man. Considerable help was provided by the 5th Battery under Hstuf. Johst, who engaged the attacking Russians with direct fire. However the command post was paralyzed for hours. Not until II Battalion had a firm hold on the northern part of the town down to the river was the regimental commander able to deploy the 5th Company under Hstuf. Stadler, supported by the assault guns "*York*" and "*Schill*," to counterattack to the northwest. By then, however, the new enemy was already attacking II Battalion's aid station from the rear.

5th Company truly fought magnificently in this battle. The enemy column was completely wiped out in the battle which lasted approximately two hours. About 900 dead, 30 guns, 13 tanks and 150 vehicles of all types littered the battlefield, while countless Russians drowned in the morass of the marshy river valley while trying to escape south across the river. During the night of 17 September III Battalion succeeded in crossing the river into the southern part of the town, which was burning in many places, and during the course of 17 September it fought its way west in bitter street fighting to a point just short of the bridge site. During the night of 18 September, supported by III Battalion's attack, II Battalion also crossed the river. The fierce street fighting continued throughout 18 September. But then on the evening of that day the regimental commander was able to report to the division commander from a hill south of the town: "Priluki is firmly in the hands of the regiment!"

The division commander's appreciative words were: "I am always pleased to come to the "*Der Führer*" Regiment. Everything is always in order there!"

*General* Geyr von Schweppenburg used the opportunity to advise that the pocket near Lokhvitsa had been closed, for at about 6:20 PM on 13 September a large patrol from the 6th Panzer Regiment (Panzer Group Guderian) had met the leading elements of the 6th Armored Pioneer Battalion (Panzer Group Kleist) near Lubny. The regiment was promised a well-earned day of rest.

But during the night of 19 September the regiment was alerted for a new mission and received the following order: "The enemy is moving in a newly formed corps consisting of a rifle division, a cavalry division and a tank brigade from the direction of Romny for the purpose of breaking open the pocket. Our forces there, the 10th Motorized Infantry Division, are inadequate to deal with this assault. The "*Reich*" Division, led by the "*Der Führer*" Regiment, is to proceed to Romny with all speed, attack these enemy forces through our own lines of security and destroy them."

The regiment moved out in the direction of Romny in the early morning hours of 19 September. The regimental commander drove ahead to establish contact with the security forces there and to scout the regiment's mission. From a regimental command post of the 1oth Motorized Infantry Division in the Romny church tower there was an excellent view of the terrain in which the battle would be fought. Situated on a hill, Romny was bordered by a river which ran from northeast to southwest. On the far side of the river there was a gently-sloping ridge approximately five kilometers in width, on which the units of the 10th Motorized Infantry Division had their bridgehead.

At that point there was still no sign of the enemy, however reports of the approach of the named enemy units caused minor unrest. The words "enemy tanks" already had an unpleasant effect on many units.

The battalions arrived in the early afternoon. I and III Battalions hurried across the river and readied themselves for the attack in the large bridgehead. The hills of Ssidorenkoff and the village itself were to be taken with support from assault guns. The regiment inserted II Battalion on the near side of the river approximately five kilometers to the northeast. The Russians attacked into the midst of I and III Battalions' preparations with about 30 tanks, some of them super-heavy types. The forces holding the bridgehead began to waver. With support from the assault guns "*Derfflinger*" and "*York*," which were deployed in I Battalion's attack sector, both battalions, launched a counterattack.

Effective assistance was provided by the crew of an 88-mm anti-aircraft gun in position south of the river. Displaying heroic fighting spirit, the men tackled the tanks, and those that were not destroyed by the assault guns and the anti-aircraft gun were attacked and knocked out with anti-tank mines and bundled hand grenades. An hour after the battle began, twenty-eight enemy tanks were in flames. Two of the giants managed to escape. At the same time, II Battalion attacked across the river and into a village as darkness was falling, and the companies were able to surprise and almost completely destroy an enemy cavalry regiment. Exploiting this success by II Battalion, I and III Battalions were moved up to the same level during the night of 20 September.

On the morning of 20 September the "*Deutschland*" Regiment attacked from out of the "*Der Führer*" Regiment's positions. There was bitter but successful fighting for the village of Shurawli as far as Hill 91.55. In the afternoon the "*Der Führer*" Regiment was committed again on the right of the "*Deutschland*" Regiment but met only weak resistance. At approximately 6 AM on 21 September both regiments attacked Hill 91.55 with assault gun support. After a fierce battle this commanding hill was taken from the enemy.

The "*Der Führer*" Regiment was subsequently turned south in order to attack a strong enemy force reported advancing from that direction. In the evening I and II Battalions halted in front of the village of Sackunowo, while III Battalion was left behind to guard the right flank. Reconnaissance by both battalions, during the night found the village weakly occupied by the enemy.

In the early morning hours of 23 September the regiment went to the attack without preparatory artillery fire. It passed through the village with no serious resistance and occupied a hill on the other side of Sackunowo. Then, suddenly, heavy firing flared up in the rear of both battalions involving all of the enemy's weapons. The enemy, later learned to have been in regiment strength, had camouflaged himself extremely well in houses, gardens and cornfields and was now between the battalions and the closely following regimental command post trying to attack the companies in the rear. Reacting quickly, both battalions turned and attacked Sackunowo again, this time from the south, while the heavy weapons, especially the infantry guns, intervened from the regimental command post. An extremely fierce battle developed which lasted all day long. The enemy intervened from the west with "Stalin Organs." III Battalion was later able to capture one of these weapons. By evening the battle in the village was over. The enemy left approximately 1,200 dead behind. Our losses were also considerable, however they were nowhere near those of the enemy.

The attempt by the enemy to burst the Kiev pocket in this sector had thus failed once and for all. The "*Der Führer*" Regiment had once again made a decisive contribution to the efforts of the "*Reich*" Division and played its part in making the Battle of Kiev one of the greatest victories of the entire war.

According to the *Wehrmacht* communiqué 665,000 Soviet soldiers were taken prisoner, 3,718 guns were captured or destroyed, 884 tanks were destroyed and vast quantities of war material were brought in. The commander in chief of the Soviet army group Marshall Budenny, who was relieved while the battle was still in progress, his successor Colonel-General M.P. Kirponos, and the chief of staff Lieutenant-General M.A. Purkayev were killed during a breakout attempt and the commander of the Soviet 5th Army, General Potapov, was captured. Five Soviet armies were destroyed, two armies were badly battered, one million Red Army soldiers were killed, wounded, missing or scattered. (In autumn 1941 the German eastern army consisted of twelve armies or panzer groups.) During the battle the "*Der Führer*" Regiment took more than 15,000 prisoners and captured more than 200 guns. The quantity of tanks, vehicles and other war material destroyed by it can no longer be determined.

On 24 September the regiment marched north into the Roslavl area via Itschnja, Chernigov and Gomel and was quartered around Woltschaje for several days. Replacement personnel arrived and preparations were made for the next great phase of the offensive.

## Assault on Moscow
### Code Word "Typhoon" – Attack Date: 2 October 1941

The plan of operations called for the strong enemy forces in front of Moscow to be split apart and then destroyed in the areas of Briansk and Vyazma. Once achieved, all of the forces of Army Group Center would drive on towards Moscow.

For this new operation the "*Reich*" Division was subordinated to the XXXX Panzer Corps (*General* Stumme), part of Höppner's Panzer Group 4. Its initial objective was to drive north via Roslavl, Ssburowo and Mossalsk toward Yukhnov, turn north after crossing the Oka and then close the Vyazma pocket at the Smolensk-Moscow highway near Gzhatsk.

The regiment moved off with the rest of the division on 4 October. All day long it marched northeast without contacting the enemy. The first snow fell on 6 October. On 9 October the 16th (Pioneer) Company completed a bridge over the Oka near Yukhnov. Then the regiment was deployed on the right beside the "*Deutschland*" Regiment for the subsequent attack to the north. Strong enemy groups made repeated attempts to cross the advance road to the east; there was heavy fighting and they were driven back. The commander of the assault gun battery, Hstuf. Günster, was killed near Nishnjaja-Petrjajka and was buried in Tupitschina together with two members of his crew. On the morning of 10 October heavy fighting developed south of the highway. II Battalion became bogged down while attacking across open country toward Moltschanowa. Ostuf. Holzer, commander of 7th Company, seized the initiative, personally leading an assault by his company. The company entered and soon afterwards captured the village. Patrols scouted ahead as far as the highway. All three battalions fought several more local skirmishes and in the afternoon the highway was crossed east of Gzhatsk.

The regiment temporarily went over to the defensive with fronts facing east and west. The enemy attacked from the east, from the Ssnoski area, supported by 52-ton tanks. But even these huge machines could not shake the brave men. With the help of the assault guns the enemy tanks were destroyed or forced to withdraw. The crew of the assault gun "*Lützow*" in particular distinguished itself in the recovery of the wounded.

On 11 October the attack was continued through Iwaschkowa astride the Smolensk-Moscow highway, while approximately five kilometers farther north the "*Deutschland*" Regiment attacked in the same direction along an old mail road through Stolbowo and Sujewa. While I Battalion drove through the villages of Woinowa and Kurjanowa, in the afternoon II and III Battalions were halted in front of the edge of a forest. Heavy machine-gun fire pinned the companies down. Enemy artillery began ranging in. In spite of the regiment's use of every available weapon on the forest's edge the enemy could not be silenced.

In the midst of this situation the commander of I Battalion, 7th Panzer Regiment (Hauenstein Group) of the 10th Panzer Division reported to the command post. He had sixty tanks with which to support an attack by the regiment's grenadiers. Seldom were the men so happy to see their comrades of the army as at this moment.

The tanks deployed themselves north of the road and rolled toward the edge of the forest. Approximately thirty enemy tanks emerged from the forest for a counterattack. A dramatic tank battle developed which thirty minutes later ended in total victory for the tanks of the 10th Panzer Division. The majority of the enemy tanks were left in flames, only a few escaped. Riding on the tanks, III Battalion immediately advanced farther to the east and during the night was able to break into a massive enemy position. The comradeship between the tankers of the 10th Panzer Division and the members of the regiment became ever firmer.

On 13 October the attack on the highway was continued, with III Battalion once again riding on the tanks of the 10th Panzer Division and I and II Battalions following in their own vehicles. The advance passed through the villages of Klemjatina and Rykatschowa and the Moscow defense position was reached in the afternoon.

The position was more than two kilometers deep, built in undulating terrain rising east from a stream bed. It was guarded by five tank obstacles – the stream, a line of raised obstacles, and anti-tank ditch, a barricade of iron hedgehogs, and a fishbone pattern of obstacles. In the position itself were continuous trenches, heavily wired, with excellent concrete bunkers and fighting positions. Tanks were dug in up to their turrets, while fifty emplaced flame-throwers guarded the road bridge. Beyond the position, at the edge of a forest, were more tanks and excellent observation posts for the artillery. However, the men would only become aware of all of these details during the course of the battle.

The armored spearhead halted on a hill, covered by the forest on both sides of the road. III Battalion and II Battalion which arrived soon afterward immediately sent patrols through the woods. These returned with the first reports of the extent of the positions. The regimental command post was moved forward to the hill, approximately 500 meters from the start of the position. On the later afternoon of 13 October the division commander arrived at the regimental command post and ordered reconnaissance and preparations for an attack on the morning of the 14th. Patrols were already probing the enemy. The battalion and company commanders themselves went forward to discover the most favorable places for an attack. The companies lay well-covered in the protection of the forest: right of the road was II Battalion, left III Battalion. I Battalion was another three kilometers to the rear. The enemy placed heavy harassing fire on the assembly area.

## Breaching the Moscow Defense Position

Late in the evening the division commander reappeared on the hill and informed the regimental commander that on the regiment's left the "*Deutschland*" Regiment had achieved a surprise penetration into the Moscow defense position and ordered the "*Der Führer*" Regiment's attack to go ahead that night.

Reconnaissance had revealed that the area north of the highway, III Battalion's area, offered significantly better prospects for a break-in. The regimental commander therefore moved I Battalion forward, placed it on III Battalion's left, and ordered the attached II Artillery Battalion of the Artillery Regiment "*Reich*" to also go into position to the left of the road with observers to I and III Battalions. While I and III Battalions carried out the attack, II Battalion was to guard both sides of the highway and provide supporting fire for both attacking battalions.

In a bitter man-versus-man battle, conducted almost exclusively with small arms, the assault groups of both battalions fought their way into the enemy positions, worked their way forward from trench to trench, and during the night of 14 October drove in a narrow wedge through the entire depth of the positions. Contact was established with the "*Deutschland*" Regiment. On the morning of 14 October II Battalion was moved forward with orders to roll up the enemy positions to the south from the break-in point. It was another day of tough fighting. Again and again new, well-camouflaged enemy positions and trenches appeared, some cleverly built into the back slopes of small hills. By the evening of this day of fighting the position was in the hands of the "*Der Führer*" Regiment across the highway on a width of almost four kilometers.

Even while the fighting was still in progress the brave combat engineers of the 16th Company moved forward along the highway, inspected the bridge with mine-detecting equipment and removed the mines and explosive charges under heavy enemy fire. While scouting this bridge site, approximately 300 meters forward of the regimental command post, the division commander, the venerated "Papa Hausser," was seriously wounded by tank fire. Every man, non-commissioned officer and officer was shaken by this news. The commander of the "*Deutschland*" Regiment, *Brigadeführer* Bittrich, assumed command of the "*Reich*" Division.

With the breaching of the Moscow defense position the regiment had written another glorious page in its history. It is impossible to describe in detail the heroism displayed by each assault group, by each man in this battle – it can only be said that the entire regiment was a wonderful instrument in the hands of the command.

During the night of 15 October I and III Battalions advanced farther east via Artjomki and temporarily went over to the defensive at the edge of a forest several kilometers west of Borodino. Meanwhile II Battalion mopped up the Moscow defense position further to the south.

The way was clear for the tank battalions of the 10th Panzer Division. The regiment would soon attack and fight with them again.

From 16 to 19 October the regiment continued to attack east on both sides of the highway. The enemy launched strong counterattack supported by tanks and increasingly heavy artillery fire. Even after the breaching of the Moscow defense position his fighting strength was unbroken. Near Borodino (scene of the famous Napoleonic battle) a fierce tank battle developed between the tanks of the 10th Panzer Division and Soviet T 34s. The 10th Panzer Division suffered heavy losses.

The enemy committed an increasing number of close-support aircraft in spite of the more frequent snowfalls. Each day the weather became less favorable: heavy snow showers mixed with rain; light frost during the night, temperatures above freezing during the day; the roads and the terrain were transformed into clinging mud.

The regiment's losses had by now reached such proportions that operations could only be carried out by committing the last reserves. The companies were down to 35 men on average – two platoons each made up of two extremely weak squads. But every objective given the regiment was reached, even if it required unspeakable effort.

On 21 October the Motorcycle Battalion "Reich," which had been placed under the regiment's command, drove past Mozhaysk to the south and captured the important Schelkowka crossroads, several kilometers east of the city. Mozhaysk itself was taken by the "*Deutschland*" Regiment and elements of the 10th Panzer Division on 22 October. Ten kilometers south of Mozhaysk, right beside the highway, was the large town of Borisovo. The reconnaissance battalion of the 7th Infantry Division had taken the town from the south but had been forced to abandon it again after heavy fighting. As a result the 7th Infantry Division was temporarily blocked from advancing farther.

The reinforced regiment was ordered to take Borisovo and secure the previously-mentioned crossroads with I Battalion and the motorcycle battalion. At this crossroads met the old mail road, the main road to Moscow, the highway or *rollbahn* as it was called by the German troops, and the Smolensk-Moscow rail line.

Borisovo lay on an extended ridge with natural protection in the north and south in the form of a broad river valley. The enemy had established himself in good positions on the outskirts of the town and was supported by artillery fire from the east. The regiment attacked from its readiness area with III Battalion on the right and II Battalion on the left. However,

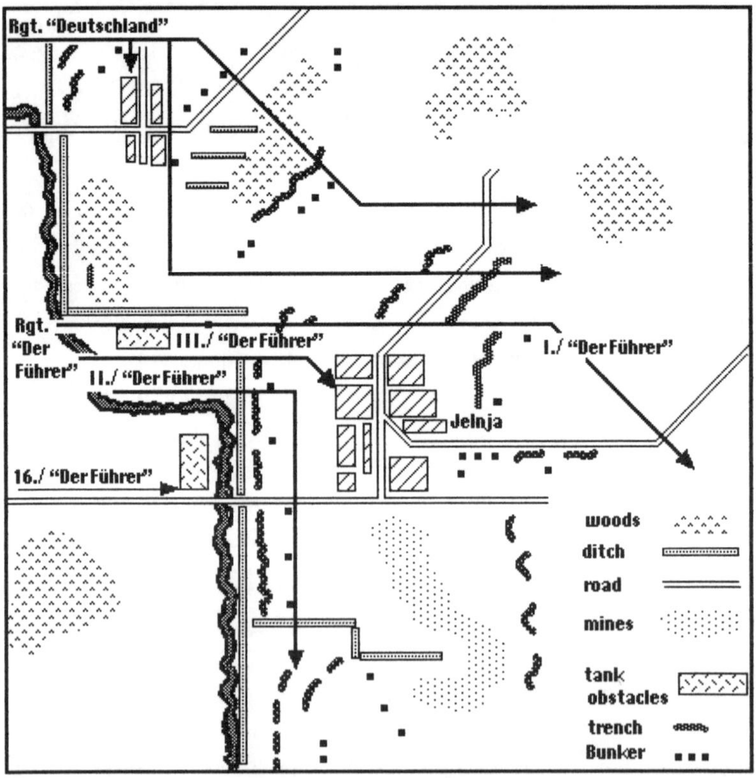


**The attack of Regiment "Der Führer" on defensive positions on both sides of the main highway at Jelna, west of Moscow**

the companies were pinned down on the floor of the valley by flanking fire and were unable to advance. II Artillery Battalion "*Reich*" under Stubaf. Adolf Wunder supported the attack, quickly recognized the focal points of the enemy defense and sharply concentrated the fire of all guns. In this way it succeeded in shooting up one strongpoint after another and then completely smashing the enemy, who was now on the move, in the town of Borisovo with the battalion's concentrated fire. Taking advantage of this artillery fire the companies entered the town and were able to establish contact with the 7th Reconnaissance Battalion to its south.

Meanwhile I Battalion and the Motorcycle Battalion, supported by assault guns, had fought an extremely tough defensive battle. The enemy had moved the 82nd Motorized Rifle Division, an elite Soviet unit, from Mongolia in order to take the important crossroads and the town of Schelkowka.

In the documentary account *Unternehmen Barbarossa*, the chronicler wrote: "When *General* Stumme was told of the battle by *Hauptmann* Kandutsch, operations officer with the Ic of the XXXX Panzer Corps, there were tears in his eyes. The 18 to 20 year olds had repulsed two Soviet battalions in close combat with spades, hand grenades and bayonets. Many of the young SS men were killed. And all were barefoot in their boots. In fifteen degrees below freezing!"

The increasing rainfalls made movements increasingly laborious. The regiment still managed to reach the major junction in the highway to Rusa and Volokolamsk approximately 25 kilometers east of Mozhaysk, but then all movement was forced to come to a temporary halt.

For fifty kilometers or more on the highway between Gzhatsk and Mozhaysk there was an endless column of vehicles bogged down to their axles – in some cases to their radiators – in the mud. Whereas before the prime movers had always been on hand to extract the vehicles, now even the half-tracked vehicles were hopelessly stuck. So the entire division was temporarily immobilized in the area of Mozhaysk and east; the men found what shelter they could and waited. Waited for winter, for the frost which would make the ground passable again.

While it is often said that the early onset of the winter of 1941 caused our first defeat before Moscow, I believe that from our experience we can say that we eagerly awaited the winter. The rain and the mud that followed had hindered us in our irresistible movements toward Moscow. The enemy used these weeks to move in fresh troops over his still intact railways, some from the Far East, and organize the defense of Moscow.

In these days the 11th Regiment of the "*Reich*" Division was disbanded and the men were assigned to the "*Deutschland*" and "*Der Führer*" Regiments. When at the beginning of November the rain let up slightly and it became colder, the "*Der Führer*" Regiment was moved across the Schapalowka crossroads from the highway north into the Rusa area. In places the Schapalowka-Rusa road was also the main line of resistance; vehicles had to cross these areas quickly under enemy artillery fire. From Rusa weak elements of the 10th Panzer Division had worked their way northeast through a wood. A corduroy road had made the muddy forest road passable. The Russians launched repeated attacks from the east, day and night, in an attempt to cut off the spearhead of the 10th Panzer Division while simultaneously pinning it down with concentric fire, especially from numerous rocket launcher batteries (Stalin Organs). The weather grew colder and snow had been falling for days. On 7 November in Staraya the regiment received orders to clear and secure the corduroy road to the east and west. Acting on information from the 10th Panzer Division that the enemy forces were weak, at first only I Battalion was committed. Two assault guns attached to the battalion, "*Blücher*" and "*Lützow*," could not be committed at first on account of the swampy terrain. I Battalion suffered heavy casualties attacking into the dense, snow-covered forest, but was able to take possession of a small hill about 500 meters south of the log road. The battalion was unable to clear the approximately three-kilometer-long forest as no heavy weapons could be moved up because the narrowness of the load road limited traffic to a single lane. The enemy even succeeded in crossing the corduroy road to the north, placing it under fire from two sides. III and then II Battalion were moved forward one after the other and employed to secure the log road. However every advance into the forest came with heavy casualties. The 3rd Company under Ostuf. Lex took very heavy casualties here.

On 12 November the regimental headquarters was moved forward through the forest to Litkino, placing it close behind the leading elements of the 10th Panzer Division. The snowfalls increased considerably and there was heavy frost during the nights.

The last major offensive against Moscow began on 17 November, by which time the cold was such that the ground was now hard frozen.

The drive by Panzer Group Guderian was made south of the city, and by the beginning of December it had reached the Rjasan area southeast of Moscow. Panzer Army Hoeppner attacked frontally from the west (the "*Reich*" Division was part of this panzer army). From the northwest Panzer Army Hoth advanced via Klim-Chimki toward the Moscow-Volga Canal.

The "*Der Führer*" Regiment was ordered to attack southeast through the forest and seize the village of Gorodishche on the far side, however in trying to carry out its mission it encountered unspeakable difficulties. A Siberian rifle division, magnificently equipped, waited in excellent positions in the forest and fought with toughness and determination. An attempt was made to smash the enemy in his forest positions through the use of one light and one heavy *Nebelwerfer* (rocket launcher) battalion. But even after this inferno of fire the attack by I and III Battalions was repulsed. The effectiveness of the *Nebelwerfer* was less than expected. The only option left to the regimental commander was to send II Battalion north around the forest and make a flanking attack on Gorodishche. This attack, which was supported by two assault guns, went forward at 11:30 AM and was a success. By the evening of 20 November the town was in the regiment's hands and the last resistance in the forest had been eliminated.

These battles at the corduroy road were among the most difficult and costly experienced by the regiment so far.

The regiment subsequently advanced through the village of Silkowo. On 22 November the regiment attacked in the Nikolskoye area. The enemy fled in disarray, leaving his heavy weapons behind. A further attack on 23 November saw the old post road and the Volokolamsk-Moscow railway embankment crossed in order to take the village of Glebowo and reach Gorki. Then the "*Deutschland*" Regiment passed through the "*Der Führer*" Regiment's positions to continue the attack. The sister regiment encountered fierce enemy resistance, however, and progress was slow. The 10th Panzer Division, which was deployed on the left of the "*Reich*" Division, moved alongside. The regiment was again sent to the attack on 25 November with orders to attack and take the city of Istra. The 15th

(Motorcycle) Company under Ostuf. Wolkerstorfer was sent to reconnoiter in the direction of Istra. Supported by the assault guns "*Prinz Eugen*" and "*York*," the motorcycle troops launched a daring raid, drove into the completely surprised enemy, seized the bridge over the Istra River and prevented it from being destroyed and subsequently established a small bridgehead. This took place in the late afternoon of 25 November.

Istra is a medium-sized city strung out along a ridge beginning approximately 500 meters east of the bridge. The small Istra River flows around the city in a half circle. On a foothill extending west to the river stood the Istra Cathedral, a complex of six large church-like buildings, the largest of which was in fact a beautiful old church. The entire complex was surrounded by a stout, five-meter-high wall. A high raised roadway led from the bridge to the outskirts of the city.

The enemy had established his defense in well-fortified positions at the foot of the hill and could sweep the broad snow-covered plain between his positions and the river with machine-gun fire. The cathedral in particular was fortified like a fortress and heavily manned. As well the Red Army troops were supported by considerable artillery fire. Farther north of the regiment a battle group of the 10th Panzer Division under *Oberstleutnant* de la Chevallerie had succeeded in taking a bridge over the Istra near Buscharowo. The brave men of the 10th Panzer Division, whose numbers had also been severely reduced (all that was left of the proud division was 28 tanks, four weak rifle battalions and ten guns), pushed the enemy toward the city from the north.

III Battalion succeeded in crossing the Istra bridge as darkness was falling on 25 November and it established a forward regimental command post in a small dugout due east of the bridge. As II Battalion was temporarily not at the regiment's disposal, II Battalion "*Deutschland*" under Hstuf. Hansmann was placed under the regiment's command. During the night III Battalion managed to break into the cathedral and the entire complex was taken in a fierce fight. However, a combined attack by I Battalion "*Der Führer*" and II Battalion "*Deutschland*" from the bridgehead on the morning of 26 November was repulsed by concentrated machine-gun fire. At noon III Battalion resumed the attack on the city from the cathedral. At the same hour the 10th Panzer Division's 69th Rifle Regiment under *Oberstleutnant* Maus intervened in the fighting in the city from the north, and by the evening of 26 November Istra was completely in our hands.

Our opponents here were the 78th Siberian Rifle Division and Manchurian units which had been brought in fresh from the Chabarowsk area with orders to hold the last keystone of the last Moscow defense position at any cost.

The main credit for this success belongs to the 15th Company under Ostuf. Wolkerstorfer and the 9th Company under Ostuf. Schober, which heroically fought their way into the cathedral. On 27 November lines of security were occupied east of Istra near Wyssokowo; these were held on 28 November in the face of increasing enemy artillery fire and air attacks.

Conditions became ever more difficult. Even though the effectiveness of the enemy units had become considerably less, numerically they

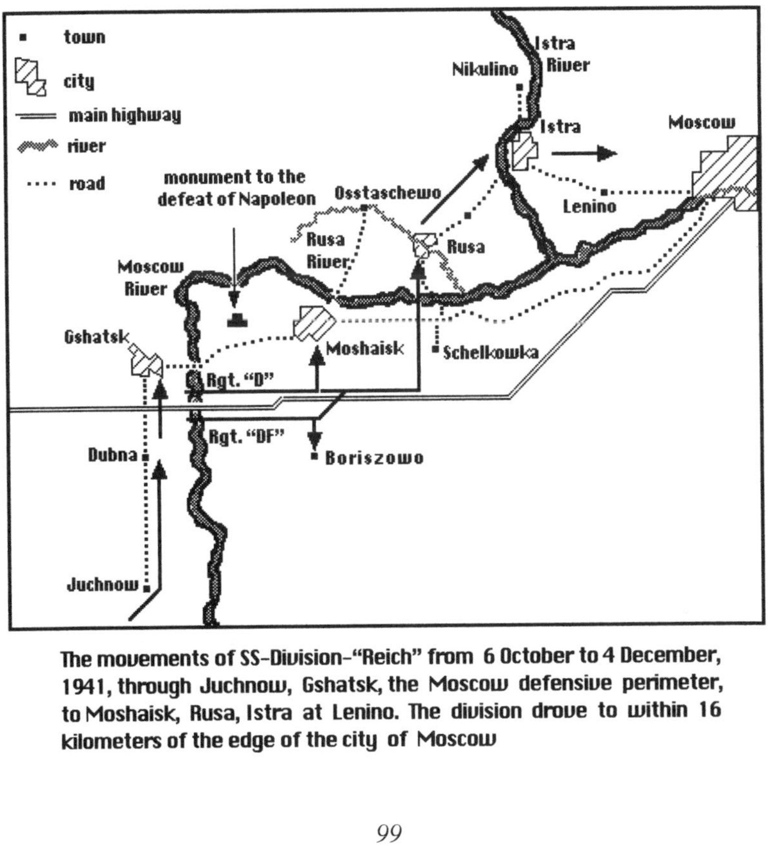


**The movements of SS-Division-"Reich" from 6 October to 4 December, 1941, through Juchnow, Gshatsk, the Moscow defensive perimeter, to Moshaisk, Rusa, Istra at Lenino. The division drove to within 16 kilometers of the edge of the city of Moscow**

were still far superior to the German divisions and had sufficient artillery of every caliber and ammunition for their heavy weapons.

"And the "Der Führer" Regiment was no longer as beautiful as a year ago!" In spite of personnel replacements from the 11th Regiment the companies on average were down to combat strengths of twenty-five men. II Battalion had to be disbanded. *Sturmbannführer* Heinz Harmel became commander of the "*Deutschland*" Regiment and the 5th, 6th, 7th and 8th Companies, veterans of many battles, were parceled out to I and III Battalions. An outstandingly successful battalion had temporarily ceased to exist. Nevertheless, it lived on in the hearts of all the men of the regiment.

Stubaf. Harmel put his heart and soul into his new duties, even though leaving the regiment was hard. He was the regiment's most meritorious battalion commander.

On 29 November the regiment resumed the attack south of the Istra-Moscow road. The temperature fell to minus thirty degrees and heavy snowstorms hindered movements. Nevertheless the regiment continued to achieve major offensive successes and advance five to six kilometers per day – and that in a very wide attack sector which could only be cleared by zigzag movements.

On 4 December the factory on the western outskirts of Lenino was taken and the same evening the companies drove through the town past the railway station on the other side. Thus a suburb approximately 17 kilometers from the outskirts of Moscow was in the regiment's hands.

The Russians threw workers militias into the battle, counterattacking with tank support. The men of the regiment were sure that they could count on the fingers of one hand the days until they would enter Moscow. The spires of the city were visible to the naked eye in the clear, cold weather. A forward 100-mm battery placed harassing fire on the city. Then orders came for the units to halt the attack where they were. The battalions went over to the defensive with III Battalion right and I Battalion left at the highway.

On 6 December came the incomprehensible order: "The attack is not to be continued! The divisions will withdraw behind the Istra and occupy winter positions there."

And Moscow was near enough to touch! Moscow – that was no question of prestige, rather it was the great railway turntable which linked all traffic in the western Soviet Union! The loss of Moscow would deprive the enemy of almost all of his potential for moving troops and supplies.

• • •

Many arguments were brought forward at the time and are brought forward especially today concerning the retreat of the German divisions before Moscow. Was it General Winter? Surely the temperatures, which reached minus 52 degrees in places, had made things difficult for the

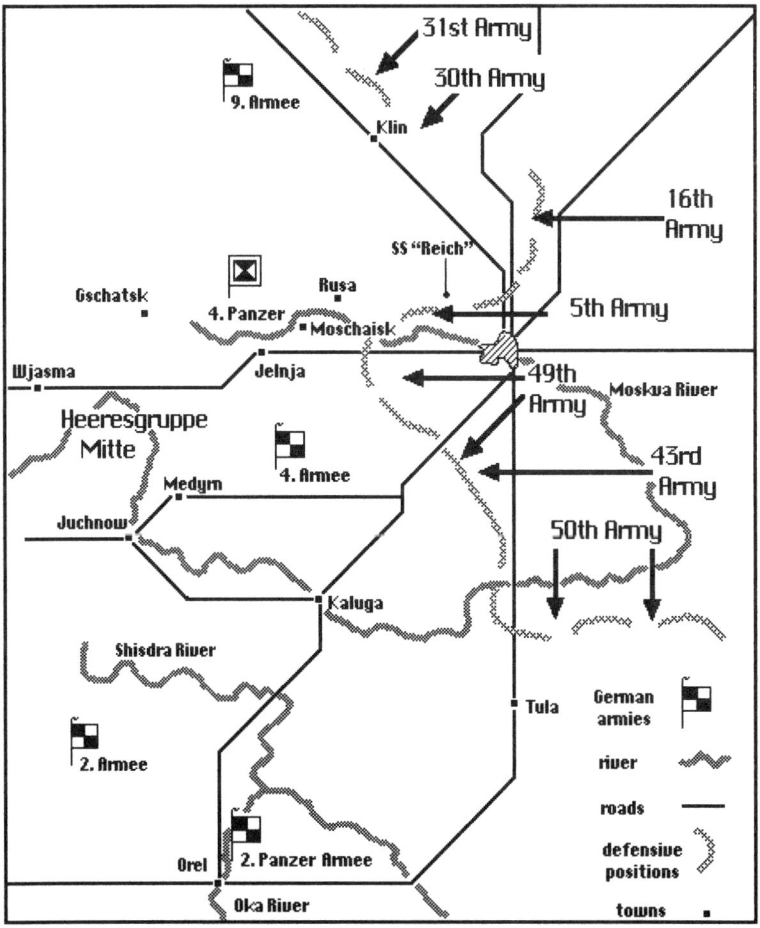


**The situation on 6 December, 1941, in front of Moscow**

German soldiers. Vehicles and weapons were not designed or prepared to function in such temperatures.

Was it the Siberian divisions? Capable and rested, equipped with white camouflage suits and the best weapons, these units unquestionably played a significant role, but not a decisive one. At Istra, for example, these units, too, were forced to retreat by the weak companies of the regiment.

Was it the Russian road system? Was it poor planning by the OKW, Führer Headquarters and the General Staff? Had they underestimated the Red Army and failed to factor in the potential sources of help, especially east of Moscow?

Why the extremely poor preparations for the winter war that was obviously coming? Was the German air force not capable of interdicting the enemy's supply lines to the front east of Moscow? Was it because of the wrecked railway system in the conquered territories? Were the locomotives prepared for winter operations or did the conversion to the western gauge cause difficulties?

Many of these arguments must surely coincide. The German frontline division undoubtedly gave their best. Months of continuous action had worn down the forces and bled the regiments white. In some cases casualties to frostbite exceeded combat losses. According to the original figures, in the period from 9 October to 5 December the "*Reich*" Division, the 10th Panzer Division and the corps units of the XXXX Panzer Corps lost 7,582 officers, non-commissioned officer and men. Total losses on the Eastern Front by 5 December were approximately 750,000 soldiers. The question arises: could a fresh force, especially one well-equipped for winter conditions, have broken the last resistance before Moscow? Even against an opponent fighting courageously and at times fanatically? It is highly probable. But let each reader form his own opinion. But now back to the "*Der Führer*" Regiment.

## Defensive Fighting between Istra and Rusa

The first decisive order to retreat took effect on 7 December. The movements began according to plan. The regiment, with one "*Der Führer*" and one "*Deutschland*" Regiment, remained in contact with the enemy as the division's rear guard. The Russians noticed the change immediately and pursued with considerable forces, particularly tanks. The men fought with steely calm, even though the great elan of the first months was gone and morale had sunk to zero. Many enemy tanks were destroyed in close combat and each attempt by the enemy to break through our thin lines was defeated.

In the book *The Great Battle before Moscow*, the Russian author A.M. Samsonov wrote of the fighting in these days:

> "General Rokossovsky's 16th Soviet Army went to the attack from the Krjukowo-Dedowsk sector and directed its main assault at Istra. The 5th Army under General Govorov, which attacked south of the 16th Army, supported the advance of Rokossovsky's army in the direction of Istra and Volokolamsk. During the fighting in the Krjukowo area, which the fascists had planned to use as the area of concentration for the final assault on the Soviet capital, the enemy defended especially stubbornly. The enemy offered fierce resistance in the Krjukowo-Kamenka-Istra area. ... Units of the 8th Guards Rifle Division 'Panfilov,' the 1st Guards Tank Brigade and other units attacked Krjukowo..."

On 10 December the regiment withdrew behind the Istra. The combat engineers of the division and of 16th (Pioneer) Company had prepared usable strongpoints. The main job, the laying out of continuous defensive positions, was begun by the men of the regiment during the night of 11 December. After the three days the position was defensively ready. On the left of the "*Reich*" Division was the 5th Panzer Division, which had arrived fresh in November. The unit on the right had crossed the Istra far to the west, leaving the "*Reich*" Division's right wing completely open. The 5th Panzer Division was in the same situation on its left wing.

After several enemy attacks against the positions of the two divisions were bloodily repulsed, he bypassed these on both sides and within a few days was able to drive far to the west. His two wings joined together in the rear and for the first time the regiment was encircled. But no one was disconcerted, so great was the regiment's confidence and its feeling of superiority even over a numerically far superior foe. Nevertheless, the enemy move had made any notion of holding the Istra position unrealistic.

So on 15 December another withdrawal to the west was ordered and begun. The regiment was once again the "*Reich*" Division's rear guard and broke contact with the enemy at midnight. Continuous snow and freezing conditions had left the roads in an unbelievably bad condition. Some of the vehicles became stuck and had to be blown up. It was a harsh blow for the men to be separated from the vehicles that had served them so long and faithfully. The regiment moved into the new line at dawn on 16 December. Following our movements closely, the enemy soon arrived. Some of his units were winter-mobile forces on skis. Fighting went on until darkness fell and the next move to the rear was made during the night of 17 December.

So the regiment withdrew via Sloboda, Liskovo, Kurova and Scherwinsky to beyond the Ruza near Borovina, fending off Russian assaults by day, by night falling back thirty to thirty-five kilometers through knee-deep snow in the icy cold.

The last, particularly tiring stretch was covered during the night of 20 December. The battalions reached the Ruza at dawn on 21 December. Some of the heavy infantry weapons were on horse-drawn sleighs; the men in their dirty snow smocks were totally exhausted. It was a scene that would move the hardest man. The enemy attacked again with strong forces while the regimental commander was discussing the deployment of forward outposts in a previously scouted line with the battalion commanders. Under these circumstances the forward outposts were forgotten and the regiment prepared for a defense west of the Ruza as quickly as possible. Apart from five or six large holes in the ground, no defensive preparations had been made in the regiment's approximately six-kilometer-wide sector. Just as the battalions were being guided into their sectors (III Battalion right, I Battalion left) the enemy broke through III Battalion. Fighting with grim fury, within half an hour the companies of III Battalion had thrown the Soviets back with heavy losses.

The initial impressions of this position, which was supposed to be the ultimate winter position, were very bad. In spite of this poor outlook the men immediately began improving the positions. Where shovels and picks failed against the hard-frozen ground, excavation was done with blasting cartridges and anti-tank mines. After three days of indescribably hard work, which was repeatedly interrupted by the need to repel enemy attacks, the regiment was ready to defend the Ruza position.

The enemy sensed that he could not break through here and reduced the level of his efforts. Only the enemy artillery grew more active, harassing the supply routes and inflicting casualties on the vehicles. Because of the deep snow the last leg to the main line of resistance could only be covered by *panye* sleigh. Severe cold and the dreaded snowstorms set in, and in a few days the country was covered in deep snow and drifting made the roads almost impassible.

So the regiment approached Christmas of 1941 – frozen pea soup, frozen bread, boot and socks almost completely worn out, supply very much in question on account of a shortage of locomotives able to operate in cold weather and huge snowdrifts on all main and secondary roads. Nevertheless, at this point the regiment finally received some winter equipment: fur-lined parkas and pants, fur-lined boots and fur coats. Transport aircraft of the *Luftwaffe* (Ju 52s) dropped extra rations for Christmas, however most landed in enemy territory.

• • •

The regimental commander, Otto Kumm, wrote of these days:

> "And yet, when I visited the men in their bunkers in the front lines on Christmas Eve, I saw everywhere the same confident determination to carry on our struggle as before. Everywhere the awareness of total superiority over this enemy. More and more the enemy sensed that his attacks against our sector of the front were costly and unsuccessful. He now limited himself to feint attacks with weak forces, kept us pinned down with artillery fire. The focal point of his attacks shifted to weaker sectors of the front. So the year 1941 ended uneventfully in the Ruza position. The heavy casualties among the administrative officers and the train units should be mentioned here. All of these men worked under the most difficult conditions and risked

their lives to supply the fighting companies within the realm of what was possible. They, too, played a part in the tremendous accomplishments and successes of the regiment in the previous weeks."

## Defensive Battle near Rzhev

In mid-January 1942 there was a planned evacuation of the Ruza position as part of a withdrawal of the main line of resistance around Gzhatsk in order to shorted the front. As a result the "*Reich*" Division was freed for new and difficult tasks.

At the beginning of 1942 the Soviets managed to break through toward the southwest between the Waldai Hills and the Volga; the bulk of the Soviet 29th Army stood in the area around Bjelyi, direction of attack toward Smolensk. Between the VI Corps in Rzhev and the XXXIII Corps on its left was a gap of approximately sixteen kilometers. The 9th Army under *Generaloberst* Model, to which the "*Reich*" Division was subordinated, planned to close the gap with attacks by both corps and then destroy the encircled enemy forces.

In a foot march the regiment fell back through Gzhatsk to Spask, where it boarded trains, and was then transported to Sychevka, fifty kilometers south of Rzhev. The "*Deutschland*" Regiment had been sent ahead in its own vehicles and was already northwest of Sychevka. The regimental commander awaited the arrival of the regiment at the division command post in Sychevka. *Generaloberst* Model issued an order to the commander of the "*Reich*" Division for him to detach one regiment from his division to VI Corps in Rzhev for the attack to close the gap in the front west of Rzhev and later defend the old breakthrough point on the Volga. The only unit that could be considered for this mission was the "*Der Führer*" Regiment, which had not been committed yet.

VI Corps planned to begin the attack on 24 January 1942 with forces of its own which were positioned behind its left wing. On 25 January it ordered the regiment to attack at dawn northwest across the line won on the 24th, reach the bend in the Volga northwest of Rzhev, and to go over to the defensive on both sides of the Volga with front to the northeast in a sector approximately six kilometers wide. At the same time other forces were to defend against the enemy forces now cut off in our rear with front to the southwest.

The battalions arrived in Rzhev at the last minute during the night of 25 January. They had been delayed by the need to retake the tracks from the enemy in several places between Sychevka and Rzhev. The battalion went straight to the attack without a rest. The enemy put up considerable resistance and the Volga was reached during the morning of 25 January. The regimental commander laid down the main line of resistance with the commanders of I Battalion (Stubaf. Fritz Ehrath) and III Battalion (Hstuf. Helmut Schulz). III Battalion was deployed right of the Volga, I Battalion left.

The Volga was frozen over and the ice was capable of supporting even heavy tanks. On the right bank of the Volga, in III Battalion's sector, was the village of Klepenino, consisting of about thirty houses. To the right of it was a broad, slightly undulating snow-covered plain. Approxi-

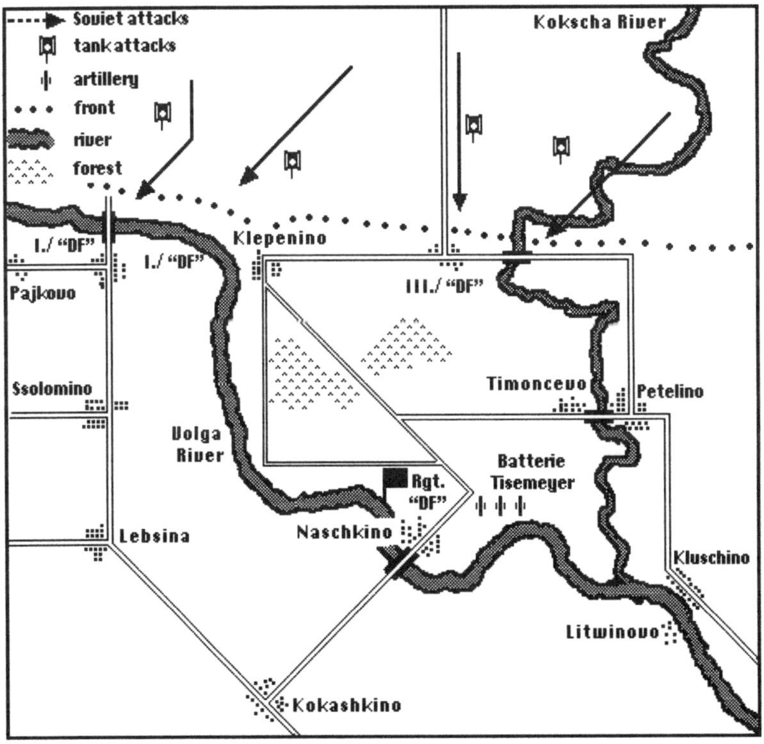


Regiment "Der Führer" at Klepenino, northwest of Rzhev, in early 1942

mately eighty meters from the main line of resistance, which ran along the northern edge of the village, began a wood which extended back to the northeast. There was another forest in the rear of the battalion approximately 600 meters deep. I Battalion's position was somewhat more favorable. There the main line of resistance ran two-hundred meters north of a forest and the position had a good field of fire and a wide view of the foreground.

The extremely weak combat strength of the regiment was cause for concern, however: two battalion, heavy weapons, headquarters and signals personnel, all together 650 men! The battalions were each down to two infantry companies and the remains of a machine-gun company, the infantry gun company to one light and one heavy platoon, the anti-tank company to two platoons of 37-mm anti-tank guns. The 15th and 16th Companies had been disbanded.

The temperature dropped from day to day and in the first days of February reached a low of minus 54 degrees!

After reaching the line the companies immediately went to work blasting holes in the frozen ground with blasting cartridges and mines. Machine-gun and rifle nests were installed in an intermediate area of one to two-hundred meters. Thus the front line was weakly manned. The defense position had no depth; the regiment had no reserves. On 26 January the commander of III Battalion, with the approval of the regimental commander, decided to advance through the forest in front of his position in order to move the main line of resistance forward to the northern edge of this small wood if possible but at least position outposts there. Surprisingly, III Battalion came upon extensive, well-manned enemy positions, the old Russian Volga position from the previous autumn.

Hstuf. Helmut Schulz had to call off the hopeless attack and he tried to withdraw his battalion into the main line of resistance as unscathed as possible. Hstuf. Schulz took a personal hand in the effort and was killed. This was a loss which could not be made good in the existing circumstances. Hstuf. Boller, formerly commander of 10th Company, took over command of the battalion. The enemy immediately attacked with strong forces but was repulsed.

The regimental command post was approximately 800 meters behind III Battalion in a small village situated fifty meters from the southern edge of the forest. Using every available means of transport, *Generaloberst* Model, the commander in chief of the 9th Army, visited the regiment once every day as this sector seemed to him to be the most endangered.

On roughly the third day, while *Generaloberst* Model was with the regiment, I Battalion brought in a prisoner with important information, a radio operator from the headquarters of the 30th Army. His statement:

Lined up on the road from Kalinin via Wissokoye to the bend in the Volga was the entire 30th Army, seven rifle and six tank divisions, with orders to carry on the attack by the 29th Army. The attack was scheduled to begin the next morning. Furthermore he told us the sequence and designations of the individual divisions, regiments and brigades.

Extremely concerned, *Generaloberst* Model left the command post. He urged the units to remain extremely vigilant even though he considered the man's statements to be exaggerated.

The attack began the next morning and exactly at the same place where the 29th Army had broken through. Traces of this were still visible on two broad roads on either side of the Volga. For three weeks the enemy attacked at this place without pause, day and night. Fortunately, however, he did not attack with the concentrated forces of the army, but instead battalion by battalion, regiment by regiment, tank brigade by tank brigade, throwing units into the battle as they arrived.

The men of the regiment held their positions against all attacks. The heroism displayed by everyone here far exceeded anything that had gone before. Each attack was repulsed with fearful losses for the enemy, often in close combat with hand grenades and bayonets. The enemy dead piled up into walls before the companies' positions.

But the worst were the attacks by the enemy tanks. Two 50-mm antitank guns were deployed with III Battalion in Klepenino, one 88-mm flak at I Battalion's command post. After several days the forward 50-mm gun was run over by several enemy tanks. The other gun went through three different crews in a short time. But this anti-tank gun kept firing until it was surrounded by about twenty knocked-out tanks which blocked its field of fire. A change of position was not possible because the gun was buried in snow to above the axles and no tractor could venture into the firing zone. So the brave grenadiers were ordered to fight off further tank attacks with mines, gasoline bombs and hand grenade bundles.

Six days later…the enemy had not achieved one penetration, even though the foremost houses of Klepenino had been burned down in the fighting.

• • •

One morning the enemy tanks appeared on the open flank of the positions manned by 10th Company. Three and sometimes four tanks positioned themselves in front of each machine-gun nest and rifle pit and fired into the company's positions from thirty to forty meters. This storm of fire lasted for half an hour, then the tanks rolled back into the wood. During the day one severely-wounded grenadier crawled through the snow to the command post of III Battalion and reported that no one was left alive in 10th Company's positions!

There was now a gap of more than one thousand meters in the regiment's main line of resistance. No reserves were available to close the gap. As a result of urgent pleas by the regimental commander to the corps, an alert company of 120 men was sent to the regiment to close the gap. This ad hoc unit consisted of drivers, cooks, tailors and cobblers under the command of pay NCOs, all worthy soldiers to be sure, but lacking in combat experience especially under these conditions.

With a heavy heart the regimental commander gave this unit the mission of closing the gap and manning the positions of 10th Company, for the regiment expected renewed enemy attacks on that very sector during the following night. And in fact the enemy did attack, beginning his assault with heavy mortar fire. The inexperienced men of the alert company lost their nerve, abandoned the positions and were shot to pieces while retreating over the open, snow-covered fields.

The corps had no more reserves to send the regiment. The enemy was now able to drive through the broad gap during the night and the next morning had strong infantry and tank forces at the south end of the forest, approximately 50 meters from the regimental command post.

The approximately eight remaining houses were prepared for defense. Deep holes were dug in the floors and embrasures were cut in the lower beams. Every man of the regimental headquarters – radio operators, runners, drivers – was now committed in order to hold this sector of the front. For three days the enemy attacked from the forest and tanks shot up the houses. But even these massed attacks were repulsed with bloody losses to the enemy. The heart and soul of the defense here was the regimental adjutant, Hstuf. Holzer, who performed as magnificently as he had when commander of the 7th and then 11th Companies. Holzer ran from man to man, instilling new will to hold on in each of them.

The regimental commander continued to press the corps, insisting that this simply unbearable situation could be changed through the commitment of reserves. His messages were answered by a visit from the chief of staff of VI Corps. Those in corps headquarters simply refused to believe what the regiment had been telling them for days. A thirty-minute visit to the regimental command post convinced him; that same evening an infantry regiment consisting of two weak battalions was dispatched with independent orders to drive the enemy out of the forest back across the main line of resistance and close the gap to the right to III Battalion (9th Company).

The attack by this regiment was under an unlucky star, however. The battalions had no sooner entered the forest when they were driven out again by an enemy counterattack. Only with difficulty did the battalion commanders and officers succeed in reassembling the decimated companies. A successful repetition of the attack was out of the question. The regimental commander was summoned to the corps and the remains of the two battalions were subordinated to the "*Der Führer*" Regiment. These companies were deployed along the Volga from Klepenino south to the regimental command post in order to prevent the enemy from crossing the river into the rear of I Battalion.

While all this was going on I Battalion and the remnants of III Battalion continued to be subjected to ongoing frontal attacks. The enemy broke into the positions of 2nd Company, which defended heroically to the last man and from which not a single man returned! In these circumstances the regimental commander decided to abandon Klepenino, which had been shot to pieces except for one house, subordinate the last nine men of III Battalion to I Battalion and withdraw I Battalion's companies to the level of that battalion's command post.

Finally the corps sent the regiment useful reinforcement in the shape of an army reconnaissance battalion under the command of *Major* Mummert, an outstanding officer. This reconnaissance battalion took over the companies manned by the regimental headquarters, resulting – at least temporarily – in a continuous main line of resistance. The regimental headquarters moved to a small village west of the Volga, just behind I Battalion. As a result the regiment's command, while still within range of the enemy's artillery and mortar fire, was no longer directly in the main line of resistance.

The enemy continued to attack without letup; his artillery fire intensified from day to day. During one attack he succeeded in crossing the Volga in the sector of the attached infantry regiment and occupying a small wood on the west bank of the river. This wood went down in the regimental history as the "Russian wood." All attempts to win back the wood, including by the "*Reich*" Division's motorcycle battalion under Hstuf. Tychsen, which had meanwhile been placed under the regiment's command, were in vain. The enemy had found such well-built positions there that he simply could not be dislodged. The enemy was pinned down, however, by a 210-mm heavy howitzer, which fired a shell into the wood every four to seven minutes. A small church hill on the west bank south of the "Russian wood" changed hands approximately ten times on this day, but in the end it was firmly in the hands of the reconnaissance battalion under *Major* Mummert.

The fighting spirit of the few remaining men of the "*Der Führer*" Regiment was unbroken. One day when the enemy attacked I Battalion's thin lines with ten tanks and infantry equivalent to a battalion, the men in their foxholes allowed themselves to be overrun by the tanks. Then they brought their weapons into position and repulsed the attack by the Red Army troops, inflicting fearful losses on them. The tanks which had broken through were knocked out in the artillery's firing positions.

Headquarters, 2nd Army compiled a battle report titled *The Winter Battle of Rzhev*. The following is an extract from that report:

> *"...through bold action, launching powerful blows, the 1st Panzer Division together with the SS-Division 'Reich,' which was moved in later, finally succeeded in cleared the area around Sychevka and thus*

*assured the supply of the critical center of Rzhev by road and rail...*

*The enemy attacks, which were continually supported by tanks and air power, reached their high point during the period 28 to 30 January 1942. These led to several dangerous penetrations and in the end could only be held as a result of the exhausted units making the ultimate sacrifice.*

*In the process the 256th Infantry Regiment, the "Der Führer" Regiment, the 413th Infantry Regiment, the 561st Anti-Tank Battalion and the anti-aircraft battle unit of II./4 and II./49 repeatedly gave examples of supreme heroism...*

*Through his almost daily flights to the front, the commander in chief (Generaloberst Model) held the fate of the army in his hand and inspired the units and command to give their all...*

*The bulk of the 29th and elements of the 39th Red Army were surrounded in the pocket and doomed to destruction. The army ordered the destruction of the surrounded enemy on the evening of 5 February... The enemy recognized the threatening situation and doubled his relief attacks against the northern front of VI Army Corps (256th Infantry Division and the "Der Führer" Regiment)... Effectively supported by tanks, artillery and aircraft, the red masses flooded in unending waves against the hard-pressed German defense front which had been in heavy combat for weeks...Entire units sacrificed themselves in the defense, inflicting unimaginable losses on the enemy, but the front held; the troops did their duty in an exemplary fashion. German heroes fought here!...*

*The decisive German success had to be paid for with the blood of German soldiers. The heavy casualties are proof of the highest willingness to serve and were particularly severe in the following units: the 86th Infantry Division, the SS-Division 'Reich' (especially the "Der Führer" Regiment and the motorcycle battalion), the 256th Infantry Division (especially the 456th Infantry Regiment), the 251st Infantry Division (especially the 459th and 471st Infantry Regiments) and the SS Cavalry Brigade..."*

*Oberstleutnant* Baron von Recum, in 1941 commander of II Battalion, 459th Infantry Regiment, 251st Infantry Division, wrote of the defensive battle near Rzhev:

"The commander of the 459th Infantry Regiment, Oberst Fischer, told me then of the heavy fighting in this sector. A neighboring unit, the remains of a Waffen-SS heavy machine-gun company, literally defended to the last man."

The regimental commander Otto Kumm wrote:

"On 17 February I received a call from our division commander, Gruppenführer Matthias Kleinheisterkamp. He informed me that the "Der Führer" Regiment was going to be relieved the next day, that the enemy in the pocket had been destroyed and that I was being awarded the Knight's Cross for the regiment's outstanding accomplishments."

With the destruction of the Soviet 29th Army the attacks against the regiment's front also stopped abruptly. On 18 February an army infantry division relieved the regiment in its positions. The regiment marched back to the command post of the "*Reich*" Division.

Thus the most difficult chapter in the history of he regiment to date came to an end. As was often the case in Russia, it had fought heroically in an almost hopeless situation and had completely carried out and completed its mission. In doing so the regiment played a decisive part in the success of the high command's plan to destroy the Soviet 29th Army and preventing the enemy from breaking through Army Group Center.

The enemy lost approximately 15,000 dead in attacks on the regiment's sector in these weeks, total losses are inestimable. Through precise knowledge of the numbering of Soviet regiments and from statements from prisoners brought in daily it was possible to determine the casualties taken by individual Soviet battalions and regiments. For this reason the regimental commander felt justified in confirming this extraordinarily high casualty figure. At the same time more than seventy enemy tanks were destroyed in the regiment's sector, which does not include those tanks which broke through and were then destroyed by other units.

The regiment was also forced to take severe losses and casualties, however. Of the 650 men who went into the battle, 150 were killed and most of the rest were wounded or put out of action with severe frostbite.

The regimental commander reported the return of the "*Der Führer*" Regiment to *Generaloberst* Model at the command post of the "*Reich*" Division: combat strength 35 men. During these battles seven battalions were subordinated to the regiment one after the other and all played a major role in the successful defense. On recommendation of the commander of the "*Der Führer*" Regiment the commander of the reconnaissance battalion, *Major* Mummert, was awarded the Knight's Cross for the heroic battle and actions of his men and for his own significant role in the defense of the regiment's sector.

Also deserving of special recognition is the outstanding cooperation between an army battery commander and the regiment. During the entire time this officer directed the fire of his guns from the front line. Every enemy concentration, every enemy attack was successfully engaged, and on order of the regimental commander all of the ammunition of his (artillery) battalion was placed at the disposal of this battery. The battery commander's name was *Oberleutnant* Tisemayer. Unfortunately the regiment number is no longer known.

An assault gun battery[4] also deserves special praise. The gunners brought the men of the regiment tangible relief through their numerous assaults against the enemy, even with their last serviceable vehicle.

The men of the "*Reich*" Assault Gun Battalion fought bravely as part of the regiment in the infantry role. After the battery lost its last assault gun on 28 January, on 1 February 32 non-commissioned officer and enlisted men were transferred to the regiment.

Concerning the conclusion of the Battle of Rzhev Otto Kumm wrote:

> *"I had just one wish: to completely reform the regiment at a training ground at home. Since the 9th Army and also Army Group Center were unable to grant this wish, on the suggestion of Generaloberst Model on 21 February I flew to Führer Headquarters in East Prussia to request permission there. But there, too, they could not make up their mind to do so. Instead they expected me to restore the regiment's operational readiness near the front in a short time after receiving 100 officers and 1,000 men as replacements.*
>
> *I argued forcefully against this unreasonable demand. For replacements of 100 officers and 1,000 men were no regiment and cer-*

*tainly no 'Der Führer' Regiment! To achieve this would require systematic indoctrination and training, but especially the continuation of a tradition achieved in the hardest fighting, which bestowed upon such a unit its high combat worth.*

*I defended my position with success! At supper I was introduced to Adolf Hitler, who immediately granted my wish. So the same evening I was able by telex to order the rest of the regiment home – first for a well-deserved leave and then in mid-March 1942: meeting place Fallingbostel training ground in the Lüneburg Heath."*

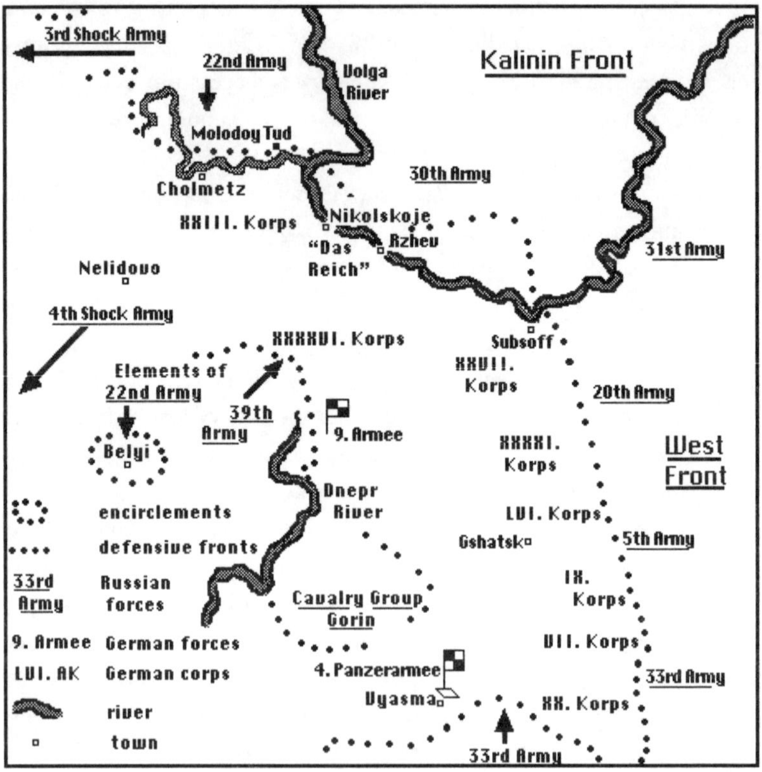


The situation on 19 February, 1942

## Reformation of the Regiment

The reformation of the Panzer-Grenadier Regiment "*Der Führer*" began in mid-March 1942 under extremely favorable circumstances. The regiment was allowed to recall all returning convalescents from the Stralsund Replacement Training Battalion and all sick and wounded officers, provided they would be fit for combat duty within the next three months, directly to the regiment. Within a short time it became apparent that a total of approximately 400 officers, non-commissioned officer and enlisted men would be returning, all of whom had seen at least part of their combat duty with the regiment and who were to form the basis of the new companies and battalions.

Transports arrived in quick succession bringing new recruits, all together about 3,000 men, eighteen to twenty years old on average. Officers were assigned to the regiment to fill any remaining gaps; some had front-line experience but the majority did not. Those men who had been sent on officer training courses shortly before the start of the campaign in Russian now returned from the *Junkerschulen* in Braunschweig and Tölz as *Oberjunker*. Following the proven routine, non-commissioned officer courses were immediately set up. As a result the most serious gaps could be filled in the foreseeable future.

Deliveries of weapons and equipment were hesitant, nevertheless, weapons training did not suffer as a result. One particularly serious bottleneck was the assignment of vehicles. Apart from the few old vehicles brought back from the east, the regiment had none. Training of drivers suffered as a result, but training as a motorized unit was completely paralyzed.

Battalion commanders were as follows: I Battalion Hstuf. Hans Opificius, II Battalion Hstuf. Sylvester Stadler, who had distinguished himself in many battles, III Battalion Stubaf. Horn, an experienced teacher and instructor from the *Junkerschule*. Hstuf. Holzer, who had proved his value as an assistant to the regimental commander in difficult times, stayed on as regimental adjutant. All of the company and platoon commander positions were filled by good men, although unfortunately one third of these lacked combat experience.

From the beginning of April 1942 the other elements of the division began arriving at the training grounds. The division, which was now designated the Panzer-Grenadier Division "*Das Reich*", was reformed by *Gruppenführer* Keppler, an officer revered by the officers and men. In keeping with the army's order of battle, the division received welcome reinforcement in the shape of a panzer battalion.

Training at the training grounds made good progress. The command of the regiment no longer had to imagine what "the real thing" would be like, instead from the very beginning training could be based on actual experience, which was invaluable in teaching the new recruits how to behave and handle their weapons in combat. The "youngsters" were enthusiastic pupils and they followed the animated, realistic descriptions given by their experienced instructors with shining eyes, energy and elan. To one day emulate them was the foremost objective of the young recruits.

At the beginning of July the regiment was transferred to northwest France ahead of the rest of the "*Das Reich*" Division and there was subordinated to *Generaloberst* Dollmann, commander in chief of the 7th Army, as operational reserve.

The regiment received its full complement of vehicles at the very last minute: I and II Battalions were once again equipped with troop transports (3-ton Opel *Blitz* trucks), while III Battalion, now an armored unit, received 3-ton armored troop carriers. The regimental units were also magnificently equipped. Concerning the allocation of vehicles, it remains to be said that this was done precisely in accordance with army regulations concerning organization and equipment. In terms of weapons and equipment the regiment was in no way different than an army panzer-grenadier regiment.

The regiment was initially quartered in the Mayenne area northwest of Le Mans. From the day of its arrival in the quartering area there began another period of significantly more intensive training at the training grounds. The regiment received a generous allotment of fuel and ammunition, due in large part to the chief of staff of the Commander in Chief West. This made it possible for unit training, which was in its initial stages, to be stepped up.

The regimental commander placed great emphasis on advanced combat practice firing and platoon, company and battalion live-fire exercises. As a result it was possible to quickly familiarize the young recruits with the suffocating effect of a firefight. Led by experienced non-commissioned officers and officers, the men worked their way to within a few meters of suspected enemy positions and bunkers, still under fire from their own machine-guns, mortars and infantry guns, before breaking in with live hand grenades. The panzer-grenadiers of III Battalion had to drive through machine-gun and rifle fire in their armored troop carriers.

The other units of the "*Das Reich*" Division arrived during the course of the summer, and exercises were continued with Panzer III and IV tanks and the artillery. It was outstanding preparation, for the companies learned to work their way forward at the leading edge of the artillery with the absolute certainty that the artillerymen and the men of the heavy infantry weapons were conscious of their great responsibility and that no shot or shell would fall among them. The experience of having one's own tanks to drive over one in a foxhole and then stopping over it removed any fear of an enemy tank doing the same thing.

One great concern of the regimental commander was that the narrow-chested youths did not fit properly into their uniforms. This shortcoming in appearance was quickly addressed, however. Even though it went against many strict regulations, many pieces of beef, pork or veal found their way into the companies' field kitchens and it was a joy to see how these extra rations were received. Anyone who was soon to go to the Eastern Front needed strength and reserves of strength.

The weeks passed at a breathtaking pace. The entire training program reached a level which could stand comparison with the outstanding prewar training in every respect. Added to this were the very significant factors of the experiences gained at the front. In keeping with its high fighting tradition the regiment was ready to take on new and difficult tasks.

On 1 October 1942 the regiment was moved into the St. Lô area and several days later into the Villers-Bocage area. The purpose of these moves was to investigate operational possibilities and practice meeting an enemy invasion. As fate would have it, this was the exact area where the regiment would fight hard battles against Allied invasion forces two years hence.

In December of the same year the regiment was transferred again, to the area south of Rennes. But the quiet time of intensive work was over. The embattled Eastern Front was calling, everyone sensed it, and the regiment was actually waiting for orders to arrive any day. The waiting ended at the beginning of January 1943. "Blitz trains" transported the "*Das Reich*" Division, once again led by the "*Der Führer*" Regiment, across France, Germany and Poland to Kiev, from where it was to drive into the Kharkov area.

While in France the Christmas violets were blooming, the area around Kiev was a vast, snow-covered plain: it was an external change fully in keeping with the change that took place in the hearts and minds of the troops.

## The Battle of Kharkov

In *West of Voronezh* the Soviet Colonel Morosov wrote:

> "In November 1942 the Soviets broke through the front of the German and allied troops. Stalingrad was outflanked on both sides and partially surrounded. A second offensive thrust there in December 1942 struck the Italian Army and completely unhinged it. The Russian units advanced on a broad front southwest in the direction of Rostov.
>
> *On 13 January the Soviet 'Voronezh Front' under Lieutenant-General Golikov, with the 40th Army (Major-General Moskalenko), the18th Independent Rifle Corps (Major-General Sykov), the 3rd Tank Army (General Rybalko) and the 7th Cavalry Corps (later the 6th Guards Cavalry Corps) under Major-General Sokolov, went to the attack south of Voronezh.*
>
> *The assigned objective was the destruction of the German XXIV Panzer Corps, the Italian Alpine Corps and the 2nd Hungarian Army. The long-range objective was to reach the Oskol, and from there jump-off positions for the recapture of Kharkov were to be taken.*

*All of these units were strongly manned, and the left neighbor of the 'Voronezh Front,' the Soviet 6th Army, was supposed to simultaneously advance from the Kantemirovka area toward Pokrovskoye and Kupyansk on the Oskol. At the same time the 'Briansk Front,' with the 13th and 38th Armies, attacked the units of the German 2nd Army positioned there and supported these plans with the objective of retaking Kursk."*

These offensive operations lasted fifteen days, after which a breach of roughly 500 kilometers had been smashed in the German front. The German and allied divisions fell back in a generally western direction wedged together and taking heavy losses.

A relief attack from the Rostov area by German armored divisions (the 6th, 17th and 23rd Panzer Divisions), the inadequately prepared 15th *Luftwaffe* Field Division, the 5th and 8th Romanian Cavalry Divisions and a weak Romanian army corps was beaten back by the enemy. This "Operation Winter Storm" under *Generaloberst* Hoth was supposed to relieve Stalingrad. But only the 6th Panzer Division was fully operational while the other two panzer divisions were extremely weak, and the fate of the German 6th Army in Stalingrad was sealed.

The SS Panzer Corps under *Generalleutnant* Paul Hausser, consisting of the SS Panzer Divisions "*Leibstandarte Adolf Hitler*," "*Das Reich*" and "*Totenkopf*", was dispatched from France too late to take part in the relief attempt.

The "*Der Führer*" Regiment initially remained a few days in Kharkov to await the arrival of the "*Das Reich*" and "*Leibstandarte*" Panzer Divisions. I Battalion, which together with elements of the regimental units, was at the head of the regiment, was directed into the Stalino-Voroshilovgrad area, where it was deployed with army divisions. As a result I Battalion was not available to the regiment for the coming battles up to the recapture of Kharkov (see: Operations by I Battalion and Battle Group Schuldt).

In the last days of January the regiment was sent forward into the Bely Kolodes-Volchansk-Velikye Burluk area and II Battalion under Hstuf. Stadler was deployed on a broad front to defend the Oskol. On the right in the Kupyansk sector was the Witt Regiment of the LAH. The extremely thin defense line could not prevent strong enemy motorized units from filtering through.

III Battalion was now also moved in to counterattack and drive the enemy back together with the 2nd Panzer Regiment of the "*Das Reich*" Division. This armored group attacked on 5 February; it succeeded in intercepting marauding enemy units in the Bely Kolodes area and inflicted heavy losses on them. On 6 February III Battalion advanced toward Oldovatka and drove the enemy back approximately ten kilometers from his positions. In following up III Battalion and the 2nd Panzer Regiment's I Battalion ran into a concentrated wall of anti-tank weapons near the village of Velikye Burluk. The panzer battalion suffered regrettable losses. The onset of darkness forced the abandonment of the battle.[5]

On 7 February III Battalion launched further relief attacks and once again the enemy was driven back. Advancing rapidly, the 10th, 11th and 12th Companies forced the Soviets back toward the northwestern end of Velikye Burluk.

9th Company advanced alone toward Gotschino and drove the enemy back. The company's heavy platoon, in particular, distinguished itself in this action: concentrating their fire from the flank, the mortars, commanded by Uscha. Posselt, and the heavy machine-gun teams under Uscha. Bieber, Hofer and Pöschel forced a breach in the enemy defense.

These energetic, lightning-quick attacks from all directions hindered the enemy's advance. However, the Oskol had to be abandoned on account of the overall situation and the division was moved behind the Donets, where it took over a new line.

By this point the previously-mentioned 6th Soviet Guards Cavalry Corps with the 210st Tank Brigade had initiated an outflanking maneuver in the direction Andrejewka-Ochotschaje-Novaya Vodolaga-Lyubotin. These enemy units succeeded in outflanking the right wing of the LAH Division. If the Soviet plan continued to succeed it would seriously threaten the Poltava-Kharkov supply road, and this enemy advance could have a detrimental effect on our own situation in the city of Kharkov. As the enemy information suggested, later confirmed by Soviet documents, the enemy was pursuing a massive pincer movement with the objective of surrounding and destroying the German forces in Kharkov.

From the Russian point of view the situation developed as follows:

"The 40th Soviet Army drove out of the Stary Oskol area via Belgorod toward Kharkov. The 69th Soviet Army attacked from Volonovka via Volchansk toward Kharkov. The 3rd Soviet Tank Army prepared to attack west from the Valuiki area. The 6th Soviet Guards Cavalry Corps was supposed to advance past Kupyansk and during the course of operations link up with units of the 40th Soviet Army west of Kharkov.

*Farther south, on 29 January the 6th Soviet Army under General Charitonov attacked in the direction of Balakleya, took Izyum on 6 February and on 8 February barricaded the Kharkov-Losovaya rail line. The area of Krasnograd-Novomoskovsk was reached against weak German security forces.*

*The units of the 1st Soviet Guards Army under General Kuznetsov carried out the main thrust west of Starobelsk toward Krasny Liman, went around Slavyansk and on 11 February took the important traffic center of Losovaya.*

*The 3rd Soviet Guards Army under General Lelyushenko was supposed to outflank Voroshilovgrad from the south. General Popov and his motorized rifle units fought in the Slavyansk-Krasnoarmeskoye area. The Soviet commander in chief of the Southwest Front wanted to advance to the Dniepr bend with his units and capture crossing points near Dnepropetrovsk and Zaporozhye.*

*South of Kharkov the Soviet Guards Cavalry Corps took the town and station of Borki with the 201st Tank Brigade and on 11 February reached the sector Msha River-Karlovka-Novaya Vodolaga."*

While the "*Das Reich*" Panzer Division was left in the sector where it was, the "*Der Führer*" Regiment was withdrawn from there and marched into the Merefa area where it was placed under the command of the LAH. In its place the "*Das Reich*" Division was sent a regiment of the LAH in order to stabilize the situation east of Kharkov to the extent possible against the enemy attacks which were being carried out in ever greater strength.

The very young regiment, which so far had been employed only in counterattacks, fighting withdrawals and defensive actions, breathed easier. It was finally going on the offensive again!

On 11 February the LAH attacked south from Merefa. On the right was the 1st Reconnaissance Battalion (Panzer-Meyer), in the center the "*Der Führer*" Regiment, which had orders to cooperate with the 1st Panzer Regiment, and on the left the Witt Regiment. The temperature hovered near minus 20 degrees and snow cover of approximately 30 centimeters hindered the movements considerably. The terrain, through which deep ravines (balkas) ran, made the use of tanks almost impossible. And so as in the past the regiment was on its own. It justified the regiment's efforts to practice working with tanks, but at the same time ensuring that every battle could be successfully concluded even without tank support.

The first two days brought fierce fighting, but great successes. Novaya Vodolaga fell on 12 February, and on the 13th III Battalion took the town and station of Borki. *Stukageschwader* 77, whose air-ground liaison officer accompanied the regiment, provided outstanding support to the battalions as they fought their way forward.

During the immediate follow-up from Borki toward Ryabushino, 9th Company became hopelessly bogged down in the deep snow which covered the terrain. The enemy immediately launched heavy attacks against the immobile company. Summoned by radio, help came hours later by way of the regiment's TKF, Ostuf. Albert Herbst, who moved in with the brave men of his repair unit and three 12-ton tank recovery vehicles and pulled free the armored troop carriers under covering fire from the company.

The regiment spent the night of 14 February in Ryabushino. The next objective was Ochotschaje, approximately ten kilometers to the south. Reconnaissance by 10th Company under Ustuf. Nickmann reported Ochotschaje occupied by the enemy. During the night the regiment, with III Battalion in the point position and II Battalion initially in reserve, moved into its starting position, a wood about 4 kilometers north of Ochotschaje, and prepared to attack. The attack was to be supported by a panzer company of the LAH and battery of the Second Battalion of the "Das R*eich*" Artillery Regiment. Advancing side by side along the Ryabushino-Ochotschaje road, the 10th and 11th Companies quickly reached the first houses of the town which lay due west of the northwards-flowing stream. The tank crews and artillerymen effectively supported the attack, expending shell after shell in direct fire. Unfortunately both soon ran out of ammunition and were lost to the main phase of the now fierce battle. 9th Company in its vehicles had worked its way to within about one kilometer of Ochotschaje with orders to break through the town and across the Berestovaya River to the south. At the moment that 9th Company moved off and showed itself on the huge open area the enemy suddenly opened up a withering defensive fire from machine-guns, anti-tank guns, mortars and tanks. The companies, especially the 9th, suffered considerable casualties. The rear elements of the companies pulled back, while the forward platoons sought cover in the houses and took up the fight.

On receiving news of this the regimental commander immediately drove to the town limits and saw that his forces were ready to give ground

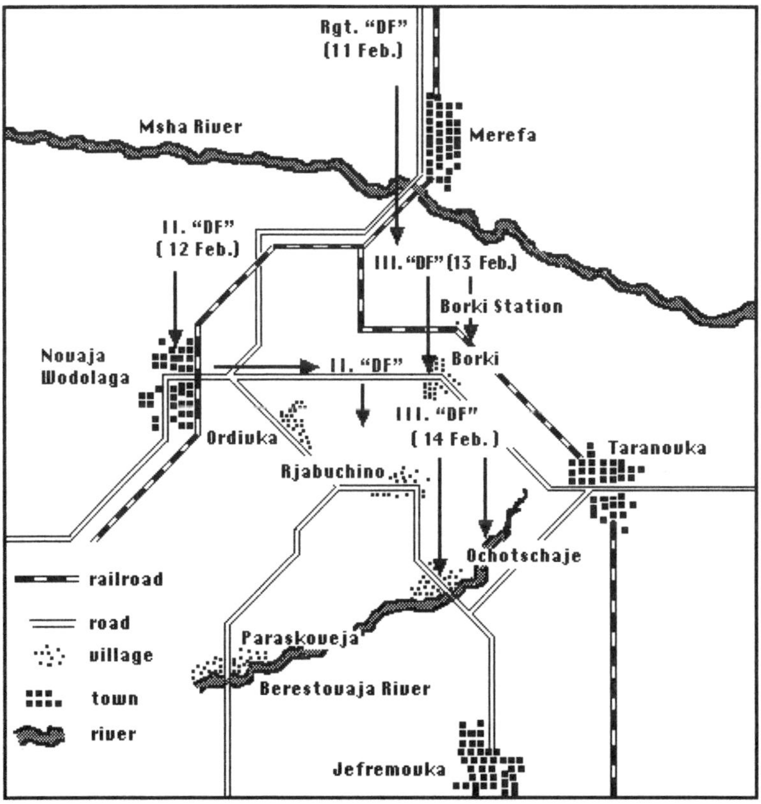


**The advance of Regiment "Der Führer" in "Leibstandarte's" area from Merefa to the south on 11 February, 1943**

against the far superior enemy. The commander of III Battalion, two company commanders and numerous officers, non-commissioned officer and men had been killed or wounded. If the battalion called off the battle in this situation, with the onset of darkness, there would be little likelihood that it would be able to mount a successful attack again. On instructions from the regimental commander, regimental adjutant Hstuf. Friedrich Holzer assumed command of III Battalion with orders begin the attack again and continue it come what may. At the same time II Battalion, riding in III Battalion's armored troop carriers, was committed from the east via Popovka toward Ochotschaje. It was determined that the enemy had positioned approximately thirty tanks as well as anti-tank guns, cleverly disguised as haystacks, in the town and was firing with every available gun. The battle went on until late into the night, but finally the enemy was forced out of Ochotschaje. Unfortunately most of the enemy tanks escaped.

The main reason for the day's success was that III Battalion had quickly regained its composure after a brief attack of weakness under heavy enemy fire and attacked again. The young men quickly regained confidence in their own strength and never lost it again.

The selfless actions of the first-aid personnel of all ranks were extraordinary in this battle; in spite of furious enemy fire the III Battalion medical officer, Hstuf. Dr. Hubert Spielberger, drove into the front lines with his men to recover the wounded.

In his book *West of Voronezh*, Soviet Colonel V.P. Morosov wrote the following of the fighting in and around Kharkov from 11 to 14 February 1943:

> "At 08:20 hours on 11 February the troops received their definitive orders to retake Kharkov. According to General Rybalko's plan, the 6th Guards Cavalry Corps was to link up with the 40th Army, block the garrison of Kharkov from the west and thus completely cut it off. An outer encircling ring was to be formed twenty-five kilometers from the inner encircling front on the line Peressetschnaja-Lyubotin-Ralkitnoye. All units received orders, not to force the fascist troops out of the city of Kharkov, but to destroy them in the city itself…

The enemy had moved in and concentrated the main forces of the SS Panzer Division 'Das Reich' and the 'Leibstandarte' from the northern Donets – at this point in time the main forces of the 'Das Reich' Division consisted of just the SS Panzer-Grenadier Regiment 'Der Führer' less its First Battalion! It launched a counterattack from the Msha River line against the cavalry units. The cavalrymen repulsed attacks on 11 February but were nevertheless forced to withdraw into the Borki-Ordivka area.

In view of the situation the commander of the Guards Cavalry Corps, General Sokolov, decided to withdraw his troops south into the Ochotschaje-Melichowka area, in order to then regroup them, make a surprise advance into the flank of the counterattacking enemy and drive into his rear into the Lyubotin area. On the morning of 13 February the cavalry units, supported by the 201st Tank Brigade, organized an all-round defense in the Ochotschaje and Melichowka areas and held a favorable position against an enemy tank grouping. On 14 February the cavalry units were involved in heavy defensive fighting in this area."

*The regiment resumed its attack on 15 February and after a few kilometers once again made contact with the enemy. But now the enemy was battered and resistance was broken in a rapid advance.*

Meanwhile the LAH's 1st Armored Reconnaissance Battalion had launched a daring advance to the south and taken the village of Bereka. There, however, it was encircled by far-superior enemy forces. II Battalion was sent toward Bereka in III Battalion's armored troop carriers and in a vigorous attack was able to break the encirclement. The enemy forces there subsequently totally wiped out by the 1st Armored Reconnaissance Battalion and II Battalion.

*On the morning of 17 February the regiment received alarming news concerning the unit on its left, the Witt Regiment of the LAH. It was being attacked in the flank from the east by strong enemy forces. The Witt Regiment had only one reinforced battalion and its situation became critical. The armored troop carriers of III Battalion were sent to the Witt Regi-*

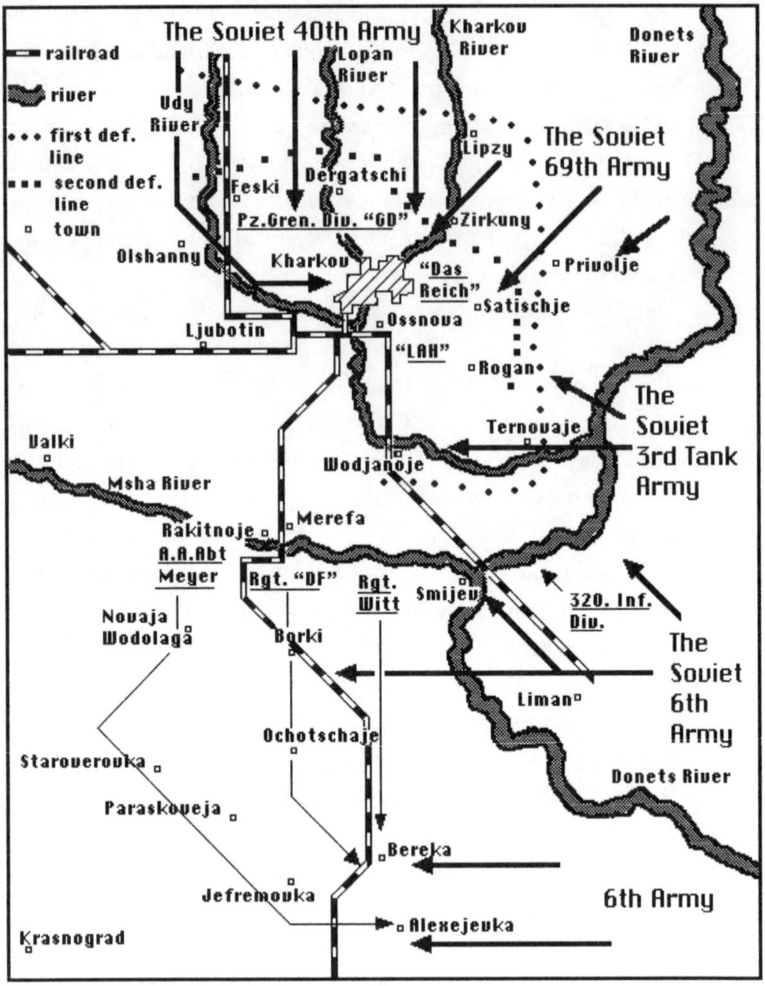


The movements of the SS-Panzer-Korps from 11 to 15 February, 1943

*ment and the battalion launched a counterattack to the east in its vehicles. This attack, too, was a complete success, and in the afternoon the Witt Regiment was able to deploy its troops in the specified defense line without serious casualties.*

*The enemy plan had been completely frustrated. The cavalry corps which was supposed to have severed the Kharkov-Poltava supply road and close the ring around Kharkov had been shattered by our much weaker forces; it was a short, sharp and successful prelude to the coming major attacks.*

*Meanwhile the situation around Kharkov had taken a dramatic turn. The relatively weak forces of the* "Das Reich" *Panzer Division were incapable of holding the thinly-stretched front east of the city for long against such superior enemy units. To the division's north, in spite of heroic efforts the* "Grossdeutschland" *Panzer Division also had to give ground and was separated from the* "Das Reich" *Panzer Division by strong enemy units. North of the city the enemy was able to begin going around the city and entered Kharkov from the north and west.*

In spite of several direct Führer orders to defend Kharkov to the last man, the commanding general of the SS Panzer Corps, Generalleutnant Hausser, decided to evacuate Kharkov, assemble his units southwest of Kharkov and make them available for a counterattack. At 12:50 PM on 15 February the commanding general gave the "Das Reich" Panzer Division the order to fight its way through to the Udy River line. He succeeded just in time in withdrawing his units, supported by tanks, through Kharkov and past the city to the southeast. At 11:30 this decision was reported to the Armeeabteilung and passed on to the Raus Corps. A new army order arrived at 4:30 PM demanding that the units defend at all costs. It was now repeated. On 16 February the rear guards of the "*Das Reich*" Panzer Division fought their way back through the city.

The "*Der Führer*" Regiment was withdrawn from the units of the "*Leibstandarte*" Panzer Division, sent to Krasnograd and once again subordinated to the "*Das Reich*" Panzer Division.

There a *Führer* order was read out to the companies. It stressed the vital significance of the coming battles and called for an unconditional effort from every man and demanded that the command carry out the orders with utmost speed. The order was not needed, however, for already the men could scarcely be restrained – finally a decisive attack.

The fact that the evacuation of Kharkov prevented one and a half powerful panzer divisions from being encircled, and enabled the defense to be conducted from a considerably shortened front was in itself a success. The decisive importance of the decision by the commanding general of the SS Panzer Corps was that it freed these units for the continuation of the attack southwards to link up with Army Group South, to which *Armeeabteilung* Lanz was subordinate following the removal of Army Group B. As a result of *General* Hausser's decision, the operational situation of *Generalfeldmarschall* von Manstein's Army Group South must have improved considerably, especially on its northern wing. Instead of a panzer corps surrounded by the enemy Army Group South now had a rested corps there with three panzer divisions.

On 19 February the "*Das Reich*" Panzer Division attacked south led by the "*Deutschland*" Regiment under Ostubaf. Harmel. The enemy (6th Soviet Army) had crossed the Kransnograd-Dnepropetrovsk road to the west with his attack spearheads. In a bold sweep the "*Deutschland*" Regiment, supported by tanks, drove into the flank of the enemy units and tore up one column after another. During the night the Orel River was crossed in Pereschtschepino. In the morning the "*Der Führer*" Regiment was moved forward; it passed through the "*Deutschland*" Regiment and continued the attack to the south. Led by the armored III Battalion, which was now under the command of Hstuf. Zens Kaiser, it drove recklessly into the enemy forces, who was on the move.

The regiment proceeded from success to success on this day, and in the early afternoon it linked up with a tossed-together group of armed forces personnel on leave holding out in Novomoskovsk. The offensive movement by the Soviet 6th Army had been thwarted; the units moving up to join it were completely shattered by the following "*Totenkopf*" Panzer Division.

From Novomoskovsk the attack was supposed to be continued east toward Pavlograd. This required a crossing of the Samara due east of Novomoskovsk. Three large railway bridges led across the widely spread out branches of the river and these were firmly in enemy hands.

During the night of 21 February II Battalion under Stubaf. Stadler was committed with orders to seize the bridges intact. II Battalion fully completed this difficult task in an exceptionally well-led attack involving the total commitment of every officer, non-commissioned officer and enlisted man. The crossing over the river was in the regiment's hands early on the morning of 21 February. II Battalion was moved into the bridgehead east of the river. The regiment had orders to continue the attack to the east. The next objective was Pavlograd (sixty kilometers away). The commanding general stressed the importance of completing this mission as expeditiously as possible and expected the regiment to be in Pavlograd in two days.

A panzer battalion (Stubaf. Tychsen) and the III Armored Artillery Battalion (Hstuf. Eichberger) were placed under the division's command for this advance. For this armored thrust the regiment organized itself into three fast battle groups, each consisting of a panzer company, a company of armored troop carriers and a battery of armored artillery. II Battalion followed at a distance in a body, providing its own security.

At 8 AM on 21 February the regiment moved out in this formation on the perfectly straight auto road, which though recently built possessed neither a foundation nor top covering, east toward Pavlograd. After a few kilometers the point vehicles encountered enemy forces; however, these were taken completely by surprise and were quickly dispersed by heavy fire.

The advance continued. Increasingly strong enemy units were encountered in the villages north and south of the road advancing in the general direction of the southwest. The new road itself did not pass through any towns. Thus it was enough for the armored columns to maintain a heavy fire to the sides with the cannon of the tanks and machine-guns and cannon of the armored troop carriers in order to advance quickly with no direct opposition.

By approximately 10 AM half the distance to Pavlograd had been covered. At 1 PM the regiment radioed requesting a Stuka attack on Pavlograd in the hope that the regiment could enter into the city as the bombs were falling. At 11:30 AM the point halted before a railway bridge which crossed the road at a height of four meters. From the railway embankment the regimental commander and the battalion commanders saw the city of Pavlograd, lying in a valley, approximately 500 meters ahead.

On the streets of the city there was a huge throng of vehicles and Russian soldiers. Pavlograd was the supply center of the Russian 6th Guards Army. 150 meters from the railway embankment there was a collective farm and there, too, a large number of Russians.

Still the regiment's armored group had not been spotted. Troops sitting in the vehicles, the long column stood ready but unable to attack, for it was impossible to say when the Stuka attack would come. The regimental commander thought back to the disaster at Makoschin.

III Armored Artillery Battalion went into position to the side of the advance road while the rifle companies and tanks spread out. Under observation by the enemy, the regiment waited for the signal to attack. Anxious quarter hours passed. Then two trucks loaded with hay came out of the city, up the road, driving toward the regiment's point. When they passed the bridge they were shot up by the tanks and immediately burst into flames. There was no reaction from the enemy.

Finally the hands showed 1 PM and the Stukas arrived. Three waves of aircraft circled over the city before diving and releasing their deadly cargoes on identified targets. The three battle groups moved off – one straight through the city, the second into the north of the city, and the third into the south of the city. The artillery battalion intensified its fire. This, together with the bombs dropped by the Stukas, which then strafed ground targets, and the cannon fire from the tanks, had a devastating effect on the city and the Red Army troops.

The enemy was completely surprised and the armored battle groups entered the city without meeting serious resistance. Where the enemy did stand and fight he was attacked forcefully and driven back by the first assault. By 4 PM the city, which was on fire almost everywhere, was in the hands of the regiment and the subordinate units. An initially immeasurable quantity of weapons, vehicles and supplies and numerous prisoners were brought in. The commanding general, *Generalleutnant* Hausser, arrived in Pavlograd before darkness fell and the regimental commander reported mission accomplished. II Battalion arrived during the early evening and a security ring was thrown up around the entire city.

The 6th Soviet Army, which had been rent asunder during its attack movement and robbed of its supply base and whose leading elements were already at the Dniepr near Zaporozhye, was completely surprised.

While the leading elements turned around and headed back toward Pavlograd, the rear elements moved closer to Pavlograd. Considerable fighting thus lay ahead.

That evening a fierce tank battle developed south of the city in which many enemy tanks, and unfortunately several of our own as well, were knocked out. The bulk of the enemy forces southwest of Pavlograd were so badly battered by the "*Deutschland*" Regiment and the 15th Infantry Division in three days of fighting that they were incapable of further attacks.

The division's motorcycle battalion advanced through Pavlograd and continued toward the east, and on 22 February it established contact with the "*Wiking*" Division fighting as part of the XXXXVIII Panzer Corps which was attacking there. Contact had thus been established with the left wing of Army Group Don.

The regiment went to the attack again on 23 February; after veering north, its initial objective was to cross the Samara near Werbki. Strong enemy forces came out to meet the attack, however the enemy had still not recovered from his surprise.

On 24 February (Werbki already lay behind the regiment) the leading companies came under fire from tanks on a hill approximately 500 meters in front of the point. To everyone's astonishment it was discovered that the tanks were ours. It took some time for both sides to realize with whom they were dealing – the tanks belonged to the armored spearhead of the "*Totenkopf*" Panzer Division. Contact had been made with the wing of the SS Panzer Corps advancing from the northwest. Fortunately the regiment suffered no casualties in this surprise encounter. The northwards attack was continued on a broad front; to the right of the regiment was the "*Deutschland*" Regiment and to its left the Baum Regiment of the "*Totenkopf*" Panzer Division.

The enemy continued to offer stubborn resistance in places. For the most part he moved in large columns, zigzagging across our direction of attack through the hilly terrain. These enemy formations were fired on with all weapons, however this delayed our own advance considerably.

The regiment's next objective was the important rail junction of Lozovaya. In the late morning hours of 25 February the regiment's point units neared the city and came under heavy fire from its southern outskirts. The city was occupied by units of the 1st Soviet Guards Army. In spite of this fire III Battalion succeeded in entering the southern part of the city with the 10th and 11th Companies as well as elements of the 12th Company and advancing as far as the railway embankment. In the evening the 9th Company advanced past these companies and deep into the city. The commander of III Battalion, Hstuf. Kaiser, accompanied 9th Company during this advance. Heavy counterattacks began, and the enemy succeeded in encircling 9th Company, which was under the command of Ustuf. Schmager.

The assault groups of II Battalion also had to fight hard in the complex terrain of factories and the rail yard. But on the evening of 25 February Lozovaya station was in the regiment's hands. Nevertheless, 9th Company had to hold out for two days until it was possible to break through the Russian encirclement. During these difficult hours a forward observer of the "*Das Reich*" Division's Second Artillery Battalion gave the 9th Company a demonstration of the artilleryman's art. He directed the fire of the batteries to within a few meters of the company's positions, giving the company necessary breathing space whenever the enemy pressed too hard. Regrettably the attack on Lozovaya cost the lives of Ustuf. Nickmann of 10th Company, a veteran of many battles, and the brave Oscha. Köck of 9th Company.

Once again the selfless actions of the medical officer of III Battalion deserve to be mentioned: with Medical Uscha. Richter, Hstuf. Dr. Spielberger courageously drove through the enemy, took on wounded of 9th Company, and fortunately in each case regained our lines under cover of darkness.

The SS Panzer Corps, which since 21 February had been under the command of Headquarters, 4th Panzer Army (*Generaloberst* Hoth) had accomplished its first mission. The enemy striking force had been robbed of its offensive strength, its main body had been forced out of the area of penetration, and it had been prevented from reaching its objectives. In these days the "*Totenkopf*" Panzer Division was struck a hard blow: the division commander, *Generalleutnant* Eicke, was shot down in his Fieseler *Storch* while on a scouting flight and was killed.

The attack was continued to the north. Following proven practice the regiment was bolstered with tanks, assault guns, anti-tank guns, anti-aircraft guns and combat engineers to become Battle Group "*Der Führer*" and fought as an independent spearhead while securing its own flanks. Here the enemy was given no opportunity to occupy continuous defense lines or carry out planned attacks. His movements were uncoordinated and obviously uninfluenced by the high command. True every village and every rise had to taken from the enemy, who fought as he withdrew, but he was no longer able to halt the rapid advance by Battle Group "*Der Führer.*"

On 28 February an enemy regrouping was in progress before the right wing of the "*Leibstandarte*" Panzer Division. The enemy withdrew two tank corps and three rifle divisions of the 3rd Soviet Army from the Lyubotin-Valki area in order to hurl them against the SS Panzer Corps. Heavy fighting broke out, which made it necessary to main close contact with the neighboring units and coordinate the advance precisely with them.

On 1 March the units of the "Das Reich" *Panzer Division* advanced to Krassnij, and on 2 March the division was north of Paraskoweja with the objective of taking the high ground around Starowerowka. On the same day XXXXVIII Panzer Corps took the village of Bereka.

On 3 March the regiment received orders to alter its direction of attack to the northwest, take the village of Yefremovka (which was known from the fighting in February), and northwest of it establish contact with the right wing of the "*Leibstandarte*" Panzer Division.

After heavy fighting, in which the enemy was attacked off the move and driven back, as darkness fell the leading elements of the regiment were approximately 1 000 meters from Yefremovka under heavy fire from enemy artillery and anti-tank guns or tanks. The village itself lay spread out from east to west on a ridge whose shallow southern slope fell off into a deep ravine.

Deployed in the front line, II Battalion took cover in the ravine. The vehicles were widely dispersed or pulled back. The regimental commander ordered the commander of II Battalion, Hstuf. Stadler, to conduct intensive scouting and, based on his judgement, either launch a surprise night attack or wait until morning and attack together with III Battalion after that unit had assembled for the attack and following a preparatory artillery barrage. Darkness fell quickly. The enemy fire subsided. Only when a patrol neared the village limits did it flare up again. The patrols were unanimous in reporting that the entire boundary of the village was defended by numerous machine-gun positions and tanks. Nevertheless the commander of II Battalion decided on a night attack, realizing that a daylight attack over the broad, snow-covered slope would result in extremely heavy casualties.

II Battalion attacked at 2 AM deployed in three attack groups accompanied by two assault guns. It was impossible to conceal the movements on the huge, snow-covered surface from the enemy. A murderous fire began, but its effect was less by the poor night visibility. The comprehensive night training given all companies proved its value here. Without significant casualties the assault groups entered the town. Using submachine-guns and hand grenades, the troops took out one machine-gun nest after another and fearlessly attacked the night-blind tanks. By dawn the large town of Yefremovka was firmly in II Battalion's hands. Our assault guns attacked at dawn, destroying tank after tank. The final tally was thirteen tanks, numerous guns, light and heavy machine-guns and several hundred prisoners. The enemy's casualties were especially heavy. By 10 AM on 4 March the town had been completely taken.

III Battalion, which was sent to follow up, drove on in a northwesterly direction through burning Yefremovka and linked up with an armored unit of the "*Totenkopf*" division. III Battalion continued its advance together with the tanks of the Meyerdress Battalion. Enemy resistance was quickly crushed wherever it flared up, and on the afternoon of the same day contact was made with the 1st Regiment of the "*Leibstandarte*" Panzer Division commanded by Staf. Theodor Wisch.

Strong enemy elements (the 15th Tank Corps of the 3rd Soviet Army) had moved to the southwest before the front of the two attacking divisions ("*Das Reich*" and "*Totenkopf*"). These elements were cut off as a result of the contact between the units of the two divisions and the "*Leibstandarte*." They were encircled here and by 5 March were completely destroyed by the "*Totenkopf*" division and the heavy weapons of the "*Das Reich*" Division. The enemy's losses in personnel were high, and a vast booty in weapons and vehicles of all types was brought in. The bulk of two tank corps and three rifle divisions could be considered destroyed. The 3rd Soviet Tank Army was decisively weakened as a result of this battle. The Berestovaya sector was in our hands.

On 6 March the SS Panzer Corps, with the "*Das Reich*" Division right, the "*Leibstandarte*" left and the "*Totenkopf*" division behind the left wing, launched an attack in a generally northerly direction from the line Ochotschaje-Krut Gorge. The two forward divisions had been assigned the Msha River line as their next objective.

Road conditions deteriorated with every kilometer. The nights were no longer cold enough to freeze solid the ground which thawed by day. The snow, which was still deep in places, alternated with mud and placed serious demands on men and machines. The enemy tried to hold every village using fresh forces. As a result progress by the regiment was halting, and because its neighbor on the right, the XXXXVIII Panzer Corps, was lagging behind far to the south it had to fight off several strong enemy attacks against its right flank. Pursuing the retreating enemy, the "*Leibstandarte*" Division succeeded in reaching the Msha River line in the initial assault. It established the first bridgehead near Bridok then advanced far to the northwest, nearing Valki.

On the morning of 7 March the regiment received an order from the commanding general to drive on across the Msha without delay and attack west past Merefa towards Lyubotin.

On the same day the Witt Regiment of the LAH took Valki in a daring attack. Simultaneously the "*Der Führer*" Regiment, with III Battalion as the right assault group and supported by assault guns and tank destroyers, advanced far to the north-northeast. The strong enemy forces in front of the units of the XXXXVIII Panzer Corps in the Rakitnoje-Merefa area were outflanked, and the regiment's objective for 7 March, the Merefa River line north of Karavan, was reached in the early afternoon after intensive enemy resistance was crushed. There the commander of III Battalion, Hstuf. Kaiser, received an air-dropped message stating that the enemy in the Korotitsch area was decamping and was withdrawing east toward the southwestern boundary of Kharkov. III Battalion, which had halted its attack, immediately restarted it with the objective of reaching the road fork north of Korotitsch.

Supported by assault guns and tank destroyers, the armored troop carriers of III Battalion raced north into the approaching twilight. 9th Company's point platoon drove straight into the midst of the surprised enemy and gained the Lyubotin-Kharkov rail line at the north end of

Korotitsch. After all of the forces of III Battalion closed ranks and a fierce night battle, on the morning of 8 March the village of Korotitsch was firmly in the regiment's hands. A strong screening force was deployed to the east.

During the course of 8 March the Wisch Regiment of the LAH stood at the western boundary of Lyubotin. The "*Der Führer*" Regiment now also attacked Lyubotin with II Battalion from the south and III Battalion from the east-southeast. While the "*Der Führer*" Regiment and the Wisch Regiment continued to battle for the city, defeating the enemy during the course of the day, a powerful battle group consisting of the Witt Regiment of the LAH drove north of the city past Lyubotin and succeeded in advancing as far as the city limits of Kharkov.

Meanwhile the "*Deutschland*" Regiment bypassed Lyubotin to the west and advanced farther north. Veering east north of the Poltava-Kharkov road, it also neared the outskirts of Kharkov. The next objective was obvious: Kharkov.

According to the war diary of the SS Panzer Corps, the following radio message was received from Headquarters, 4th Panzer Army at 12:15 PM on 9 March 1943:

*"Exploit opportunity to take Kharkov in a coup de main!"*

As described in the book *Waffen-SS in Action*, the SS Panzer Corps intended to fight its way through Kharkov while simultaneously preventing further enemy forces from being moved in from the east. To achieve this the SS Panzer Corps deployed its forces as follows: 1st Panzer Division "*Leibstandarte*" from the north and northwest, the 2nd Panzer Division "*Das Reich*" from the west on three arterial roads, the 3rd Panzer Division "*Totenkopf*" to screen to the northwest and north against the enemy forces opposite *Armeeabteilung* Kempf as well as newly brought in enemy elements.

The "*Das Reich*" Division formed two reinforced battle groups with which to complete the missions assigned to it: the "*Deutschland*" Regiment under Ostubaf. Harmel and the "*Der Führer*" Regiment under Ostubaf. Kumm. The "*Der Führer*" Regiment received orders to advance past the southern boundary of Kharkov, cross the Merefa-Kharkov road and east of this road cover the right flank of the SS Panzer Corps.

The units of the "*Leibstandarte*" and the reinforced Battle Group Harmel created favorable conditions for the break into the city, however faced with stiffening resistance at the boundary of the city they were unable to attack until their forces closed ranks. The actual attack on the city had to be postponed until 11 May.

The evening of 10 March found the SS Panzer Corps ready to break into the city: the "*Das Reich*" Panzer Division at the western boundary of the city (reinforced battle group "*Deutschland*" Regiment), a covering group with front facing southeast against the enemy forces in front of the XXXXVIII Panzer Corps (reinforced battle group "*Der Führer*" Regiment), attack forces in Ssinolizewka and west of Kuriashnoje – the Panzer Division "*Leibstandarte*" with attack groups due northwest of Alexeyevka, at the northern entrance to the city on the Belgorod road, and at the south end of Bolshaya Danilovka. The "*Totenkopf*" Division's line of security was northern section of Dergatschi-Fenski collective farm-Novaya Kultura-west of Olschany.

For the third time in this war there began a battle for the city of Kharkov. The enemy had used the previous weeks to put the city on a defensive footing. Extensive complexes of combat and anti-tank trenches had been built west and southwest of the city. The river lines and the large building complexes had been incorporated into the defense system, while in many places the streets had been barricaded or prepared for demolition.

According to Soviet writings, to defend the city the enemy had deployed the 3rd Soviet Tank Army in the city itself, the 69th Army on the western outskirts and adjacent to it in the north the 40th Army.

In spite of stubborn enemy resistance the corps succeeded in driving deep into the city, first with the LAH, then with Battle Group Harmel. Meanwhile the "*Der Führer*" Regiment fought its way through the enemy field emplacements south of the city and on the afternoon of the first day of the battle it crossed the Kharkov-Merefa road after crossing a small river. The regiment spent the night in the assigned line. On the morning of the 14th the regiment intervened in the fighting inside the city from the south. In the eastern outskirts the regiment forced a crossing of a major arterial road to the east after heavy fighting on the grounds of a locomotive factory. Contact was established there with the 1st Armored Reconnaissance Battalion (Panzer-Meyer), and the "*Das Reich*" Division's III Artillery Battalion, which was under the regiment's command, was committed to the firefight against the enemy east of the city.

Meanwhile the strong enemy force opposite the XXXXVIII Panzer Corps had stubbornly held its ground south and southeast of Kharkov in spite of the obvious threat of encirclement by the SS Panzer Corps. The opportunity presented itself to encircle and destroy these enemy units through an advance to the southeast through Rogan; however, this plan could only be realized if a road was opened through Kharkov. Given the muddy condition of the roads, the order from Headquarters, 4th Panzer Army to immediately withdraw elements of the "*Das Reich*" Division from the street battle for this purpose and direct them north around Kharkov would have meant the loss of at least twenty-four hours. Therefore elements of the "*Totenkopf*" Division were ordered to first break through to Chuguyev and hold there, while the SS Panzer Corps insisted that it complete fighting its way through the city of Kharkov before a new assignment was given the "*Das Reich*" Division. After LAH and "*Das Reich*" established contact in the northwestern part of Kharkov on the evening of 12 March, Battle Group Harmel was sent through the northern part of Kharkov to Rogan, in order to barricade the line Rogan-Wodjanoje.

The success which was in the offing for the "*Das Reich*" Division in the western part of Kharkov and which promised to ease the advance by the "*Leibstandarte*" Division had to be given up on orders from the army, in order to meet the demand to crush the enemy southeast of Kharkov.

Several kilometers east of Kharkov lay the vast grounds of the Kharkov Tractor Works, comparable in size to a small city. The enemy had dug in there with strong infantry and tank forces and was placing the eastern part of the city of Kharkov under heavy artillery fire. The tall factory buildings at the east end of the city provided excellent observation platforms for us to see into the tractor works. A unified fire plan for all artillery units was drawn up to support the regiment's attack, and the batteries began ranging fire before darkness fell on 14 March. The attack on the tractor works by the reinforced regiment was to take place on 15 March. During the night the regiment swung far to the south and marched into its readiness position by way of an airfield. At dawn on 15 March II

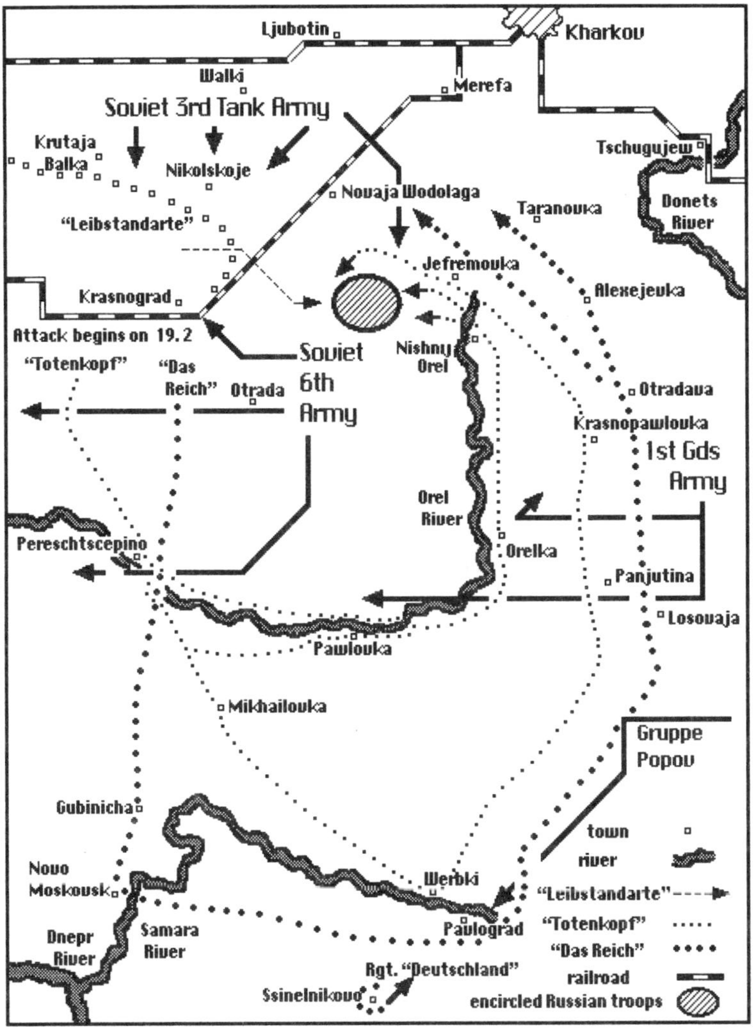


The operations of the SS-Panzer-Korps in the area between the Donets and the Dnepr Rivers, from 19 February to 4 March, 1943

Battalion of the "*Der Führer*" Regiment and II Battalion of the "*Deutschland*" Regiment (III Battalion "*Der Führer*" was fighting as part of Battle Group Harmel) were in position to attack in a workers settlement south of the tractor works.

So far the regiment's movements had been concealed from the enemy. Only through the extreme watchfulness of all officers and non-commissioned officers was it possible to avoid all unnecessary noise and light in order to preserve the element of surprise.

With the arrival of first light the artillery battalions opened fire from the west, while simultaneously the companies of the regiment left their readiness position and stormed into the complex terrain of the factory complex. Total surprise was achieved; the enemy had concentrated all his attention to the west. It was therefore some time before he turned against the attacking panzer-grenadiers. The battle that followed was an exceptionally hard one, but the tanks and assault guns provided outstanding support and helped the companies advance. Factory hall by factory hall, one complex of buildings after another was taken from the enemy, and numerous Soviet tanks were knocked out among the assembly halls. By noon time the entire huge tractor works was in the hands of the reinforced regiment. From the west armored cars of the 1st Reconnaissance Battalion pressed ahead to the factory; thus contact was established with the "Leib*standarte*" Division.

Meanwhile the battle for the city itself had ended and the decisive counterattack against the large-scale Russian winter offensive was concluded. Contact between the sectors of Army Group South had been firmly restored, while a considerable part of the Soviet offensive forces had been destroyed and the rest badly battered.

During the course of the two following days the enemy was driven back far to the north and northeast. During the night of 17 March the regiment prepared for its final attack in this phase of the conflict. Its objective was to break through enemy positions on both sides of the Kharkov-Belgorod road. Tanks of the "*Das Reich*" Division under the command of Stubaf. Tychsen were instructed to cooperate with the regiment. The attack was a smashing success. While the enemy was still quite strong in numbers and materiel, his fighting spirit had been broken as a result of the defeats in the recent weeks. With the support of the tanks the companies advanced boldly and overran the enemy positions. The road to Belgorod was cleared that same afternoon. The "*Deutschland*" Regiment and elements of the LAH were moved past the "*Der Führer*" Regiment and they continued to advance on Belgorod, which was taken the following day. On the left flank the "*Grossdeutschland*" Regiment as a loyal and selfless neighbor.

The regiment was ordered to turn east, reach the Donets and go over to the defensive on a broad front on the west bank of the river.

The Donets is extremely well suited to defense in this sector. The west bank is much higher, the river is approximately thirty meters wide and one and a half meters deep, east of the river is a wide open plain. The slightest movement by the enemy could be seen from far away. In the steep slope which drops away to the river the companies found well-built positions left from previous battles and immediately assumed a defensive posture. Quiet settled in. Only rarely did the Soviets lay down harassing fire from single guns at long range. After a few days the regiment was relieved in its positions by an army infantry regiment and was sent to Kharkov. The battalions were housed in the southeast of the city and looked forward to a period of rest and refit.

The regiment had concluded another terrific chapter in its history. Newly formed in 1942, under its veteran command it had fought admirably in these last weeks and had fully continued the tradition of the regiment. It had carried out extremely difficult missions and come through very tough battles magnificently.

In its first action from the beginning of January to mid-march 1943 the SS Panzer Corps had prevented the collapse of the entire southern sector of the Eastern Front, in the process completely destroying three enemy armies and forcing four others into headlong retreat in combination with army units. It was the last great victory in the east.

A special bulletin by the German radio network announced these great feats to the public. The "*Der Führer*" SS Panzer-Grenadier Regiment's share in these battles was so great and meaningful that every member of the regiment could be proud. When the fighting was over the regimental commander, Ostubaf. Otto Kumm, became the first member of the "*Das Reich*" Division to be awarded the Knight's Cross with Oak Leaves, while the two brave battalion commanders, Hstuf. Stadler of II

Battalion and Hstuf. Kaiser of III Battalion, received the Knight's Cross – laurels which the regiment had won for itself in these difficult battles. All of the officers and men of the regiment shared their commanders' joy in these high decorations, in which every single member of the regiment had played such a part. The decorations were announced and presented by, among many others, the division commander *Generalleutnant* Walter Krüger during a solemn ceremony in which all the units of the "*Das Reich*" Division were assembled before parked tanks and assault guns. For the regimental commander Ostubaf. Kumm it was also time to leave his proud regiment as he had been called away to serve as chief of staff in the V SS Mountain Corps.

In his memoirs he wrote:

> "I did not even have a chance to say goodbye to the regiment. During this painful separation just one thing filled me with joyful satisfaction: on my recommendation the commander of II Battalion, Stubaf. Stadler, was entrusted with the command of the regiment – a guarantee that the regiment would continue to enjoy exemplary leadership in all the battles to come."

The SS Panzer Corps's total casualties in these battles were: the "*Leibstandarte*": 167 officers, 4,373 non-commissioned officers and enlisted men killed or wounded. The "*Das Reich*" Division: 102 officers, 4,396 non-commissioned officers and enlisted men killed or wounded. The "*Totenkopf*" Division: 94 officers, 2,170 non-commissioned officers and enlisted men killed or wounded. Corps units: 2 officers, 215 non-commissioned officers and enlisted men killed or wounded.

In his personal writings *Generaloberst* Hausser wrote:

> "In examining the postwar literature it is curious that A. Heusinger, for one, never mentions the events in February and March 1943 around Kharkov in his numerous conversations in the OKH in tense situations in his book 'Order into Conflict'. Perhaps the merits and successes of the SS Panzer Corps do not fit into the book's chain of reasoning? Their importance for the supreme command is undeniable.

*In his book 'Lost Battles' Generalfeldmarschall von Manstein also makes little mention of the SS Panzer Corps. The author does not say that the main emphasis of the army rested on the shoulders of the SS Panzer Corps, since the other units had been constantly in action under difficult conditions since the relief attempt at Stalingrad at the end of 1942 and since the retreat.*

*The author mentions that during the subsequent attacks in the Kharkov area he had to intervene forcefully in order to prevent the SS Panzer Corps from moving frontally against Kharkov 'to lay it at the feet of its Führer as a symbol of victory'.*

*Naturally the SS Panzer Corps also had the desire to retake Kharkov. But its commanding general had sufficient insight to set aside this desire when the operational plans of the army group demanded it. In fact only a few days earlier it was unclear whether the corps should be turned east to attack towards Kharkov or west against the enemy facing Armeeabteilung Kempf. As for the rest, this battle developed according to the directives of the 4th Panzer Army through envelopment, without committing the SS Panzer Corps frontally. The spring weather conditions, which made the roads bottomless, did however make it necessary to quickly open the roads leading through the city."*

This view has a very peculiar ring to it and moreover contradicts the facts. In these days and hours Headquarters, 4th Panzer Army under *Generaloberst* Hoth probably had a better grasp of the situation than the army group command in the rear, as demonstrated by the radio message from Headquarters, 4th Panzer Army received by the SS Panzer Corps on 9 March 1943.

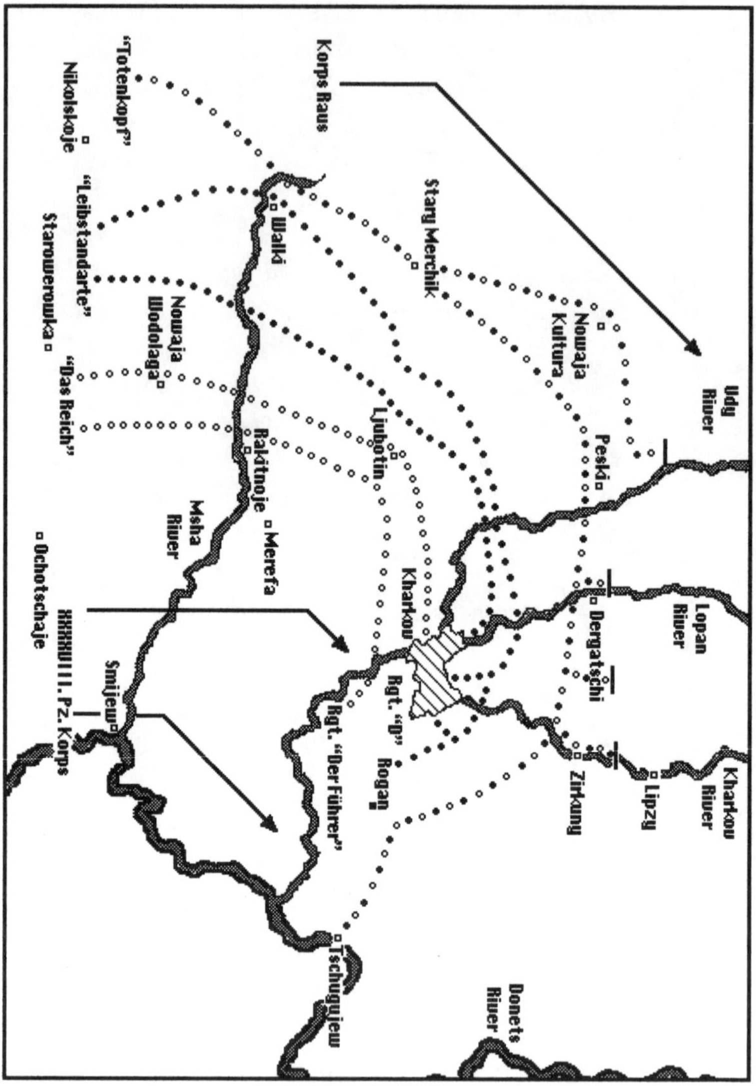


**The battles of the SS-Panzer-Korps from 7-16 March, 1943**

# Appendix to Part II

## *Generaloberst* Guderian on the *Waffen-SS*

Concentrate your forces and strike quickly! is the motto which *Generaloberst* Guderian gave the armored forces as their guiding principle. In his book *Memories of a Soldier* Guderian said of the *Waffen-SS*:

*"...The man entrusted with the task of training the future leaders of the Waffen-SS was the former army general, Hausser, formerly chief of staff of my old division at Stettin. General Hausser was a first-class officer, a brave and clever soldier and a man of outstandingly upright and honorable character. The Waffen-SS had every reason to feel gratitude to this outstanding officer...*

*...Himmler's influence saw to it that the Waffen-SS received preferential treatment in the provision or replacements and equipment. But this unfortunate fact had a negative effect on the comradeship that existed between the army and Waffen-SS units on the battlefield. I saw the "Leibstandarte" and the SS Division "Reich" in battle and later as Inspector of Armored Forces inspected numerous SS divisions, and I can sum up my impressions by saying that in my eyes these units always distinguished themselves through their discipline, comradeship and good conduct in battle. They fought shoulder to shoulder with the army panzer divisions and became – the more so the longer the war went on – like our own.*

*...Finally, however, Hitler began to distrust even those allegedly most loyal of his adherents. The fact that in march 1945 he ordered them to surrender their armbands is indicative of the degree of estrangement that by then existed between Hitler and the Waffen-SS.*

*...23 July 1941: Finally I went once again to the SS Division 'Reich' north of Yelnya. The division had brought in 1,100 prisoners the day before but had failed to advance between Yelnya and Dorogobusch. Heavy Russian bombing attacks had delayed the advance. I visited the foremost unit, the motorcycle troops under the brave Hauptsturmführer Klingenberg, in order to get a personal impression of the situation and terrain. The visit convinced me that the attack on Dorogobusch would*

*have to wait until the arrival of the Infantry Regiment "Grossdeutschland."*

*...On 6 September I visited the SS Division 'Reich' again. It was engaged in attacking the railway bridge over the Desna near Makoshin. I went to some trouble to provide air support for this. As a result of the bad roads the division was not yet assembled. On the way there I encountered a number of formations, some on the march, some resting in the woods. The excellent discipline of the troops made a first-class impression, and they loudly expressed their satisfaction at once again being part of the panzer group. The bridge was taken in the afternoon, another crossing over the Desna won.*

*On the way back we encountered units of the 1st Cavalry Division and SS units marching on foot on account of the bad roads. When I reached the division command post I gave the order to so enlarge the bridgehead over the Desna that the division could launch an attack from there toward the west bank of the Sejm in order to ease the XXIV Panzer Corps's advance across this river line."*

• • •

SS Division "Reich"
Ia Dept. Div. Command Post, 28 July 1941

Combat Report of the SS Division "Reich"
on the actions from 22 June to 28 July 1941

Within the framework of operations by Panzer Group 2 against Russia the SS Division "Reich", which was under the command of the XXXXVI Army Corps, was initially ordered to carry out traffic control in the area of the XXIV and XXXXVI Army Corps during the attack across the Bug and during the crossing of the Bug by the divisions of the first wave. The division then marched down Road 1 from 26 to 28 June with no enemy contact.

On 29 June the division was instructed to clear the area between Roads 1 and 2 of the enemy and to advance to the Beresina. While carrying out this order the division fought the following battles:

29 June: Weak enemy elements driven back by the reconnaissance battalion.

29 to 30 June: Attack by the Motorcycle Battalion and elements of the "*Deutschland*" Regiment against a Russian field position near Losza.

1 July: Advance by the Reconnaissance Battalion toward Puchowicze, minor skirmishes; attack against enemy with tanks east of P. Attack by the "*Deutschland*" Regiment along the Puchowicze-Uschi road.

2 to 3 July: Attack by the "*Deutschland*" Regiment and the Motorcycle Battalion against strong enemy west of the Beresina near Jakschziy and Perewos. Advance by the Reconnaissance Battalion toward Kolodesi, minor skirmishes.

For 4 July the division was instructed to cross the Beresina and advance toward the Dniepr.

Battles:

4 July: Crossing of the Beresina near Jakschizy and Brodez.

5 and 6 July: Advance by the reinforced "*Deutschland*" Regiment and the Reconnaissance Battalion on the Seliba-Suscha-Dolgoje road to the Druth. Battles with inferior enemy forces.

7 to 9 July: Attack by the main body of the division along the Beresino-Belawitschi toward Esmon against the 100th Russian Division, an elite unit of the Soviet Army. The 100th Division was wiped out.

10 July: Advance by the main body of the division against Schklow and heavy attack by the reinforced "*Der Führer*" Regiment against strong Russian bridgehead west of Schklow. Defensive fighting by the "*Deutschland*" Regiment west of Mogilev.

For 11 July the division was ordered to attack across the Dniepr and establish a bridgehead east of Schklow. The mission was completed with almost no fighting.

From 12 to 17 July the division advanced behind the 10th Panzer Division, while securing both flanks, by way of Jermaki, Rjasna, Mstislawl and Choslawitschi into the area around Pankovo.

Constant battles took place in these days on both flanks to free the advance road.

In Gorki the commander of the 11th Regiment, his adjutant, the regimental medical officer and a considerable part of the headquarters personnel were killed in an air attack.

On 18 and 19 July the division advanced southeast in order to capture a forward air base around Dankovo, where there are numerous airfields.

The attack to the north planned for 20 July by the reinforced "*Der Führer*" Regiment with the objective of blocking the enemy's retreat from Smolensk on the sole east-west road failed because of the difficult road conditions as well as the fact that all the forces of the XXXXVI Panzer Corps were needed in the area around Yelnya. The Reconnaissance Battalion was ordered to guard the corps' northern flank against strong enemy forces near Paszmanowa. The task of securing the southern flank near and east of Dankovo, significant because of the airfields vital to the *Luftwaffe*, was given to the Infantry Regiment "*Grossdeutschland*."

Meanwhile the area east of Yelnya, hard-won by the 10th Panzer Division, had become the objective of an attack by strong Russian units. This and the fact that the XXXXVI Panzer Corps, which had advanced far ahead, was temporarily at the end of its radius of action, made it necessary to reach a suitable position from which the Russian attacks could be repulsed and behind which it was possible to bring up replacement personnel and materiel. Furthermore the adjacent corps, which was lagging far behind, had to be given time to catch up.

The intended encirclement of the Russian army fighting near Smolensk therefore had to be postponed temporarily.

On 21 and 22 July the division was moved to Yelnya and after making brief preparations was sent to attack the strongly manned and in places heavily fortified high ground east and southeast of Yelnya. Objective was the attaining and subsequent defense of the line (1:100,000 map) Point 125.6 (eleven kilometers southeast of Yelnya), hill west of Panteloff-hill north of Krasnaya-hill at Uschakowa.

Commanders were briefed by the division commander at 5 AM on 22 July on the hill due south of the village of Yaroslavl (five kilometers northeast of Yelnya).

The attack began at 9:15 AM without preparatory artillery fire. The artillery was unable to support the attack to the degree necessary due to a shortage of ammunition. This was a serious disadvantage against the numerically superior Russian artillery. After unstoppable but costly attacks, the objective was reached during the evening in spite of constant counterattacks.

The 23rd of July was used to attack and take points of terrain important to the defense and to fortify the defense position against the expected attacks. The division's length of front was approximately 38 kilometers, to which was added a wide security front on the left wing held by the anti-aircraft fire which had to be guarded by patrols. The regiments were forced to commit all battalions and companies; only the combat engineer companies were held back as a mobile reserve for counterattacks. Given the width of front a continuous defense position was out of the question, rather the companies were dug in in the terrain in strongpoints with no depth. Large areas could only be watched over by fire from the heavy weapons.

Already during the 22nd and 23rd, air reconnaissance reported a buildup from the southeast, east and northeast against Yelnya, and the division had to expect heavy fighting. The enemy carried out probes and attacks in up to battalion strength in an attempt to gain a clear picture of our companies.

Following extremely heavy preparatory artillery fire, early on the morning of 24 July numerous regiments supported by tanks attacked on several fronts. The attacks were halted on all fronts with heavy losses to the enemy, and the enemy was forced to withdraw his infantry. Numerous tanks were knocked out.

Our air force, which was operating from forward bases around Dankovo, had to defend its airfields against enemy air and ground attacks and had almost no impact opposite the division's front. Most of the reconnaissance aircraft of the corps squadron were shot down or damaged and could not be used. Apart from reinforcement by two heavy artillery battalions, the division was on its own in a sector which would normally be held by an army. As well there were considerable difficulties in the area of ammunition supply as the road conditions were catastrophic and division, which was at the tip of the spearhead driven toward Moscow, had the longest supply lines.

From prisoner statements intelligence identified the presence of several divisions, to which new tank regiments were added daily. The artillery's observation battery identified an artillery buildup which represented an approximately five to one superiority in artillery over the SS Division "Reich."

The enemy's artillery fire led to the conclusion that the enemy had an almost limitless supply of ammunition.

On 25 July the artillery fire in several sectors increased to an intensity approaching that of the drum fire on the western front in the First World War. In five minutes 156 artillery shells of every caliber were counted landing in the sector of a single company. In several sectors the troops were unable to raise their heads from cover.

An hour-long artillery preparation was followed by attacks by regiments supported by groups of up to thirty tanks. Because of the numerous gaps in the defense front and the lack of depth of the main defensive area, the enemy achieved local breakthroughs in several places. Fierce attacks by hastily scraped together platoons drove the enemy out of the position and he was left standing before the front with heavy casualties.

But as soon as the enemy realized that his attack had been repulsed he resumed his artillery fire, and after several hours of barrage fire the enemy launched his next attack.

The enemy had almost total air superiority. Bombers and close-support aircraft attacked the infantry unhindered all day long. They were engaged only by our anti-aircraft guns, which shot down several on this and the following days. For the first time the enemy forces facing the SS Division "Reich" employed heavy tanks. The type in question was the thirty-ton T-28. The 37-mm anti-tank gun was unable to penetrate its armor. 50-mm anti-tank guns were moved up against the tanks that had broken through and chased the giants behind the front lines. But even they were unable to do anything against them. Therefore several brave men armed with bottles of gasoline leapt onto the tanks from behind, poured gasoline over them and ignited it with flare pistols. One unit had captures some Molotov Cocktails and used these successfully. A non-commissioned officer clambered onto a heavy tank, damaged a machine-gun with an axe so that it could not fire, fired his pistol through the vision slits, and subsequently set the tank on fire.

The troops fought with a determination that could not have been more fanatic. In spite of the heavy burden of the enemy artillery fire, the constant infantry and tank attacks and the gradually mounting losses, the men were enthusiastic about their success, resulting in high morale. Tackling the tanks became a sport and any tank fright was gone. Infantry attacks were answered by counterattacks. Two companies allowed the enemy to approach to within point-blank range without firing a shot; then all machine-guns opened fire at once and in the next moment both companies launched a counterattack against the enemy. The enemy battalion was put to flight and left all of its vehicles, weapons and ammunition in our hands.

The artillery, which was frequently threatened by local enemy advances, defended itself in close combat and destroyed numerous tanks at close range. As evening approached the artillery fire and infantry attacks faded away. The enemy had taken extremely heavy losses in men and materiel.

But during the night the enemy began again with intermittent artillery fire and patrol operations. Our own patrols were constantly in enemy territory, in order to prevent the troops from being surprised. Despite the over-tiredness of all the men, who had now been engaging the enemy for four days and nights with no relief, rifle at the ready and binoculars raised, there was no rest. Every man knew that the division was at the tip of our forces in Russia and held his place.

On 26 July, after the artillery fire had once again intensified and the enemy had attacked without pause, causing the regiments to constantly deploy their tiny reserves here and there to counterattack and throw the enemy out of the position, some relief was promised. A large-scale attack by heavy fighters and dive-bombers against recognized enemy artillery positions was to take place in the evening.

The troops were informed of this immediately. All breathed a sigh of relief, for our own artillery, which on the two heaviest days was restricted to eighty rounds per battery per day, was unable to provide any relief to the infantry. They were forced to look on as one enemy battery after another moved up and opened fire on our infantry.

Troubleshooters from the Signals Battalion worked constantly day and night to repair the lines, repeatedly severed by enemy fire, in order to ensure that the commanders were able to command their units. The surgeons at the medical clearing stations operated day and night, unable to take cover from the enemy bombing raids.

But in spite of their tremendous superiority on these two days the Russians were unable to gain even a foot of ground. After the conclusion of each attack the division's position was still firmly in our hands.

From 27 July the division was gradually relieved. The supply of artillery ammunition became better. Stuka and heavy fighter units attacked enemy targets identified by the infantry and artillery, and our fighters kept the airspace clear of Russian bombers at least some of the time.

Reinforcements of army artillery were moved in and it was possible to begin a systematic engagement of the enemy artillery. This had a great effect.

Nevertheless the enemy attacks continued, but as before they were unsuccessful.

By 29 July the division had been constantly engaged in heavy fighting against a numerically far-superior enemy for eight days and nevertheless the morale of the troops was outstanding. A situation map of the entire Eastern Front issued on 28 July showed the men that they were at the tip of the entire German Army, further bolstering their pride and determination.

In these eight days the division experienced the most difficult but also the most edifying days of its existence.

*Signed HAUSSER*

• • •

SS Division "Reich"     Div. Command Post, 26 July 1941,
22:00 hours
Ia     St.

> *Men of the SS Division "Reich"!*
> *Since four days ago we have been engaged in one of the decisive battles of this campaign. It has constantly demanded of every one of you the most that can be asked of a soldier.*
> *The entire German fatherland looks upon the men at the front with pride and admiration. That we have advanced farther to the east of all the divisions of the army must be an obligation to us.*

*Signed HAUSSER*

• • •

SS Division "Reich" Div. Command Post, 29 July 1941
Ia St.

Division order for 29 July 1941
*Enemy forces opposite the SS Division "Reich" consisting of five rifle divisions, two armored divisions and two motorized mechanized regiments continue to attack in battalion and regiment strength. Against these attacks the division has now held its position on a front of thirty-eight kilometers for six days.*

*Signed HAUSSER*

• • •

SS Division "Reich" Div. Command Post, 9 August 1941
Ia

Order of the Day

*On 26 June the SS Division "Reich" went to the attack as part of a panzer corps. Its path led it from the Bug near Brest-Litovsk across the Beresina and the Dniepr into the area southeast of Smolensk to Yelnya. During this time it was assigned the following missions:*

*Clearance of the complex terrain between the advance roads used by the panzer divisions; attack against field positions near Losza across the river line near Puchowicze, against bridgeheads on the Beresina and the Dniepr; destruction of strong enemy forces on the northern flank of the corps between the Beresina and Dniepr; mopping up in the rear combat zone after breakthroughs by the Russians; flanking protection to the south on the far side of the Dniepr and simultaneously to the north in the direction of Dorogobusch. Attack against strong enemy in part in prepared positions near Yelnya and finally very heavy defensive battles against a far-superior opponent (at least five divisions) with numerous tanks and very strong artillery who during the period from 23 July to 8 August tried to eliminate the easternmost corner of the Eastern Front which was held by the division. Bolstered by just one battalion from the corps reserve, the division held its position on a front of thirty-eight kilometers without yielding any ground. All penetrations were eliminated by immediate counterattack. The division thus had a decisive influence on the Battle of Smolensk. Hill 125, the projecting hill near Pantelef and Posselje, and the high-lying village of Uschakowa were hot spots which claimed numerous victims.*

*It is an indication of the division's accomplishments that its sector is now held by two and a half divisions.*

*We remember our fallen and wounded, especially the fallen unit commanders, SS-Obersturmführer Dr. Brandt of the 11th Regiment and SS-Obersturmbannführer Kersten of the Artillery Regiment's II Battalion. They will remain an example and obligation to us for all time.*

*Our best wishes go with the first commanding officer of the "Der Führer" Regiment, SS-Brigadeführer Keppler, for his new post.*

*It is impossible to mention every feat. Suffice to say that the young 11th Regiment has earned a place alongside the veteran "Deutschland" and "Der Führer" Regiments. The motorcycle battalion, the reconnaissance battalion and the assault gun battery, in part newly formed, performed extremely well under their capable commanders. The artillery showed itself to be a true sister arm to the infantry, particularly in the defensive battles, while its new survey battery passed its baptism of fire. The anti-tank gunners had numerous opportunities to successfully hunt tanks, even medium tanks. Signals battalion, combat engineers, flak battalion, military police squad and the supply troops continued to perform magnificently; several times the latter had to assume a combat role. The performance of the medical services was once again exemplary.*

*Several individual accomplishments:*

1 *Several times assault guns cleared the way for the infantry and twice were first to cross bridges. At the Beresina the Russians blew the bridge just as the assault gun of SS-Obersturmführer Telkamp was on it. The assault gun plunged approximately eight meters., SS-Hauptsturmführer Günster, the battery commander, and SS-Obersturmführer Telkamp and his crew continued the battle and distinguished themselves through their actions. The scout team of the "Deutschland" Regiment under SS-Untersturmführer von Thermann*

*also performed meritoriously here in protecting the assault guns and fighting off enemy counterattacks.*

2 *SS-Hauptscharführer Ritt and Stutzmann of the reconnaissance battalion distinguished themselves through their special circumspection and daring while serving as patrol leaders near Puchowicze and on the Smolensk-Dorogobusch road.*

3 *During the attack on the bridgehead Hill 215, SS-Oberscharführer Blauensteiner of 5.DF was the first into the enemy positions and took out seven Russian field positions with heavy weapons.*

4 *From the Battle of Yelnya: During the fight for Hill 125, using hand grenades and pistols SS-Oberscharführer Friedel of 3.DF alone covered his platoon as it went into position after the all of the platoon headquarters personnel became casualties. SS-Untersturmführer Rappl of the anti-tank battalion and his platoon destroyed a heavy 50-ton tank, two T 34 tanks and another tank; Rappl personally destroyed two tanks with hand grenade bundles and gasoline bombs. SS-Unterscharführer Rossner of 2nd Company, Anti-tank Battalion destroyed eight enemy tanks with his gun during a battle on the road to Dorogobusch. His classic, brief order: "Let them approach to fifty meters, first the leading one, then the last, then the rest!" The 6th Battery of the artillery regiment, firing in part from open positions, destroyed several enemy tanks. Battery officer was SS-Obersturmführer Stolter.*

*After heavy artillery preparation, on 24 July the enemy succeeded three times in entering the weakly-manned village of Uschakowa. The fighting strength of the defenders was seriously weakened. The situation became critical, as a further advance must threaten the entire situation of the panzer corps. The First General Staff Officer, SS-Obersturmbannführer Ostendorff, hurried to the front, personally examined the break-in points, committed the remaining heavy weapons, assault guns and later tanks, readied the last available company and personally led the counterattack. In this way he eliminated the threat on the left wing and restored the situation.*

*During these night battles the Förster Squad of the 1st Motorcycle Company provided an example of heroic fulfillment of its mission, covering the company's flank. It fought to the last man and to the last round: all of its men were found dead, rifles in position, hands on the arming cords of their grenades. Directly in front of them were sixty to eighty dead Russians!*

*Booty: 125 tanks including armored cars; 23 aircraft, including one each by the "Der Führer" Regiment and the division supply officer; 22 guns, including anti-tank and infantry guns. As well numerous machine-guns and other war materiel.*

*The battles were tough and bloody. The Russians fought with determination including close combat and employed every means of deception. Nevertheless we showed that we were far superior in the attack and in the defense. No tank, nor air attack, not even the heaviest artillery fire could frighten us.*

*The "Reich" Division can be especially proud of its accomplishments, which received the full recognition of the superior commands. We await orders for our next mission. With the men of the SS Division "Reich" they can drive the devil out of the red hell!*

*Signed HAUSSER*

• • •

SS Division "Reich" Div. Command Post, 12 September 1941

Commanding Officer

Order of the Day

1 *The Führer and Supreme Commander has awarded the Knight's Cross of the Iron Cross to Uscha. Rossner, 2nd Company, Anti-tank Battalion, for his courageous conduct while destroying several enemy tanks in the fighting in the Yelnya bend. Uscha. Rossner subsequently died of his severe wounds.*

*We lower our standards and banners before this brave man.*

2 *The Commander in Chief of the Army has sent a letter of appreciation to Ustuf. Weisenbach and Ustuf. Ehm of 14th Company "Deutschland" for successfully engaging several tanks in the Yelnya salient. Their names have been added to the "Honor Roll of the German Army."*

3 *On 1 December 1941 the division moved out of the area around Smolensk for deployment on the right wing of Panzer Group Guderian in the battle for the crossing of the Desna. Because of poor roads and frequent downpours the march placed unbelievable demands on men and equipment. The division became spread out over a period of six days.*

*Through the efforts of the reconnaissance battalion, the motorcycle battalion, the "Der Führer" Regiment and elements of the division units in particular, advancing rapidly we were able to smash the Russian units north of the Desna and capture numerous guns and a large quantity of materiel. II Battalion "Der Führer" in particular distinguished itself here through its forceful advance. The fighting for the Makoshin railway bridge, which the enemy was determined to hold at all costs, will form another glorious page in the history of the division. First to reach the bridge on 6 September were Ostuf. Rentrop of the flak battalion, Ustuf. Frank, Ustuf. Burmeister, Oscha. Ruhland, Rottf. Fredel of 14th Company "DF", then the assault guns, the 15th Company "DF" and the motorcycle battalion. Rushing forward boldly, Ostuf. Rentrop and the four men with him removed the prepared charges on the bridge, extinguished the fire that had broken out on the bridge, captured an enemy anti-tank gun and prevented the recapture of the bridge. Ustuf. Frank was killed in this action.*

*The following assault guns engaged an armored train on the south bank and together with a platoon of medium anti-tank guns disabled three armored trains on the north bank. Their early arrival enabled the motorcycle battalion to establish a small bridgehead on the south bank. The next day the motorcycle troops deployed there also bravely held the bridgehead against constant heavy artillery fire and several attacks.*

*The bridgehead was expanded considerably through the efforts of the "DF" Regiment. From it the 11th Regiment "Deutschland" and the "DF" Regiment subsequently attacked south, supported by the artillery and division troops. In an irresistible advance, including by night, the Russians south of the Desna were destroyed, the operational objective, the railway from Bakhmach to the west, was reached on 11 September, contact was established with the 4th Panzer Division and it was made possible for the left wing of the neighboring army to continue the advance south of the Desna. These marches and battles were for the most part carried out on foot. The use of motor vehicles was made extremely difficult by the bottomless roads and by the limited opportunities to move the vehicles forward on the railway embankment.*

*Commanders and troops have received the full recognition of the commanding general of the XXIV Panzer Corps, General Geyr von Schweppenburg. The advance continues.*

*Signed HAUSSER*

• • •

The Commander of Panzer Group 223 September 1941

Order of the Day

*Soldiers of the SS Division "Reich"!*

*On 1 September the division moved out of the area around Smolensk for deployment on the right wing of the panzer group in the battle for the crossing of the Desna. As a result of bad roads and frequent downpours the march placed extraordinary demands on men and equipment. The division became spread out over six days.*

*The enemy's front was breached in heavy fighting, the Desna and Seim Rivers were crossed and on 13 September the ring around the enemy east of Kiev was closed through the linking-up with a panzer group advancing from the south.*

*The commander in chief of the Russian 5th Army fell into our hands. The entire Russian southern front has been shattered. In these weeks you have once again done your duty to the full, accepted all exertions even though you have not been granted a rest since 22 June. The fighting for the Makoshin bridge will be a glorious page in the division's history.*

*I thank you for your oft-demonstrated fighting and offensive spirit. To the division, which is now leaving my area of command, best wishes for the future.*

*Signed GUDERIAN*

• • •

SS Division "Reich" Div. Command Post, 23 September 1941
Ia

Order of the Day

*After closing the big pocket east of Kiev, the "Reich" Division was quickly moved into the Romny area in order to hold Romny against a strong enemy relief attack as part of the XXIV Corps and subsequently destroy the enemy forces.*

*In carrying out this mission all units of the division once again gave their best.*

*The "DF" Regiment initially advanced together with the 41st Infantry Regiment to expand the bridgehead. Numerous enemy tanks were destroyed in this battle.*

*In the days that followed the "D" and "DF" Regiments advanced rapidly to the east and in fierce battles gained ground quickly. After destroying strong enemy elements, on the evening of 22 September the "D" Regiment entered Nedrigajloff and destroyed an enemy column. At the same time the "DF" Regiment advanced southeast in pursuit of the fleeing enemy. Enemy forces were smashed in a fierce battle on 23 September. The 11th Regiment advanced out of the right side of the bridgehead after the enemy and, advancing rapidly, took Scemjanowka. Through tireless reconnaissance, the reconnaissance battalion and the motorcycle battalion created the conditions for the successful employment of the division in the complex northern flank. While elements of the division were still in battle, the foremost regiment had already moved out again on a new mission. The demands are great.*

*Signed HAUSSER*
*Generalleutnant*

• • •

The Commander of Panzer Group 4 2 October 1941

Order of the Day

*The 2nd of October is the birthday of the late Generalfeldmarschall von Hindenburg.*

*He achieved the first great victory over the Russians and thus prevented their invasion of the Reich.*

*On his birthday we begin a new, decisive phase of operations against the last large group of Russian forces.*

*On 2 October 1941 the watchwords for Panzer Group 2 are:*

*"Hindenburg – forward – victory!"*

*Signed HOEPPNER*
*Generaloberst*

• • •

SS Division "Reich" Div. Command Post, 23 October 1941
IIa Kr./wo.

Division Order of the Day

*The SS Division "Das Reich" attacked almost without pause from 6 to 21 October 1941. We drove north from Yukhnov to Gzhatsk, with two open flanks past the east end of the Vyazma pocket. In the process strong enemy forces were beaten or destroyed and in a daring advance the objective, the Smolensk-Moscow highway, was reached. At the same time divisions of the army attacked from the west and recaptured the Yelnya positions east of Potschinok held by the division in the weeks-long defensive battle. Thus our "fallen of Yelnya were avenged," as was said in a corps order of the day issued by XXXXVI Panzer Corps. Without pausing to rest the division then advanced east on and north of the highway. The speed of this advance and the readiness for action of the officers and men, which was proved to the end, prevented the enemy from carrying out a planned buildup in and behind his Moscow defense position. Bottomless roads, snowstorms and biting cold were as much an obstacle to the division as the determined counterattacks by the numerically far-superior enemy.*

*This phase of the battle deserves to take its place alongside the previous accomplishments of the division. The success was great. All units of the division played an equal part in it.*

*We salute our fallen. Their deaths shall not have been for nothing. We remember our wounded and our best wishes go out to them.*

*One of the bravest, SS-Hauptsturmführer Günster, the commander of the assault gun battery, fell. Our division commander, SS-Obergruppenführer and General der Waffen-SS Paul Hausser, was severely wounded in the front lines. He sends his best wishes to the division for the battles to come.*

*We will once again have to prove our manhood in the next phase of our struggle. I know that I can depend on you.*

*Signed BITTRICH*

• • •

Headquarters, XXXX Panzer Corps 16 November 1941

Order of the Day

*Following the battle of encirclement at Vyazma and the breakthrough of the Moscow defense position, our advance has been halted against our will by the change in the weather which brought rain and mud.*

*Working tirelessly in the worst weather, you have created the conditions necessary for the continuation of operations. For this my thanks and appreciation.*

*The enemy has exploited this halt forced upon us and by attacking is trying to halt our advance permanently. This he has been unable to do thanks to your brave perseverance and your determined resistance in winter cold and under unfavorable conditions.*

*Now we will again go for the enemy's throat and throw the enemy to the ground once and for all, and reach the objective, Moscow, which is not far away. Forward with all strength!*

*Signed Stumme*
*General der Panzertruppen*

• • •

Headquarters, XXXX Panzer CorpsK.-H.-Qu., 27 November 1941
Abt. IIa

Order of the Day

*To the officers of III Battalion of the Panzer-Grenadier Regiment "Der Führer", of II Battalion of the "D" Regiment and the motorcycle company of the SS Regiment "DF", reinforced by assault guns, I express my special appreciation for the initiative and boldness with which you led your men in the capture of the museum bastion of Istra.*

*The same appreciation to all of the men of the above units who took part who, through their pluck, offensive spirit and outstanding bravery, played a most important role in the taking of Istra.*

*The group commander, Generaloberst Hoeppner, asked me to express his thanks and appreciation as well.*

*Signed STUMME*
*General der Panzertruppen*

• • •

Headquarters, XXXX Panzer Corps9 December 1941

Order of the Day

*Displaying the same indomitable offensive spirit with which past battles were won by the SS Division "Reich", on 8 December your men of the SS won a defensive battle against a numerically far-superior enemy who launched determined attacks from all sides using all available heavy weapons in an effort to overrun you, adding new laurels to your banners! This victory held very great significance for the operation as a whole.*

*My thanks and my appreciation for your outstanding accomplishments!*

*We lower our banners before your brave fallen comrades and we are one in certainty that despite all the difficulties with the weather and the great physical exertions and hard work associated with them, we will stand fast wherever the orders place us.*

*Signed STUMME*
*General der Panzertruppen*

• • •

SS Division "Das Reich" Div. Command Post, 11 December 1941
Ia

Order of the Day
*Men of the SS Division "Reich"!*

*In three weeks of the heaviest fighting against a determined enemy, you have, ignoring the awful cold, destroyed numerous enemy units and advanced to within a few kilometers of Moscow.*

*If our attack is now halted and we go behind the Istra into a defensive position, it does not mean that we are withdrawing before the strength of the enemy. Rather the onset of winter has caused such difficulties in conducting the war that we are moving into a winter position.*

*Signed BITTRICH*

• • •

Headquarters, XXXX Panzer Corps 13 December 1941

Order of the Day

*Today the SS-Division "Reich" leaves my area of command.*

*In a series of successful battles you have led the way from the Desna via Gzhatsk-Mozhaysk-Gorodishche-Istra-Lenino deep into the Moscow defense position.*

*I bid farewell to you with joy and pride in your success, which will go down in military history, but also with sincere sadness. I know that you will remain the men that the supreme command can rely on in any situation, no matter how difficult it may seem.*

*I wish the proud SS Division "Reich" continued success, each of you soldier's luck and a happy return home after the war is ended in victory.*

*Signed STUMME*
*General der Panzertruppen*

• • •

SS Division "Reich" Division Command Post, 21 December 1941
Commanding Officer

*Comrades!*

*In a serious hour I have been decorated with the Knight's Cross by the Führer and supreme commander.*

*You should know that I do not wear this recognition alone. I see this cross on every fighting man of the division. I wear it for the dead and for you who are still fighting.*

*Heads high, we will smash the enemy at the Ruza in order to gain time for future operations.*

*I stand in awe of the dead and your spirit of sacrifice.*

*Signed BITTRICH*
*Generalmajor*

• • •

SS Division "Reich" Division Command Post, 11 January 1942
Commanding Officer

Order of the Day

*Men of the proud SS Division "Reich"!*

*On 9 January 1942 I assumed command of the division. As a long-serving member of the division I am conscious of the honor of being allowed to lead you during the winter months. Your actions, your willingness to serve, your conduct and discipline are exemplary in the history of the Waffen-SS and the army.*

*I am certain that under my command you will continue to use all your strength to maintain and secure the success that has been achieved.*

*I am happy to pass along to you the most heartfelt greetings and best wishes of your division commander, Generalleutnant Hausser, who wishes to return to you as soon as possible.*

*With grateful reverence we remember our dead and wounded comrades.*

*Signed KLEINHEISTERKAMP*
*Generalmajor*

• • •

*"Der Führer" Regiment* *Regimental Command Post, 1 February 1942*
Commanding Officer

Order of the Day
*Men!*

*In several days of the heaviest fighting the regiment has held the front at the decisive spot and has inflicted very heavy losses on the enemy.*

*The enemy's plan, to break through at this place with four rifle divisions, a tank brigade and countless heavy weapons to free his divisions in the south, has failed.*

*The commander in chief of the 9th Army, Generaloberst Model, has reported your conduct and this success to Führer Headquarters, naming the regiment. Be proud of what you have accomplished.*

*The enemy will continue to attack, But I am firmly convinced and trust that you will also continue to fight bravely. The test we are facing here is the most difficult yet and we will see it through together. My thanks and appreciation to all of you. I have been asked to express to you the special thanks of the commander in chief of the 9th Army.*

*Signed KUMM*
*Obersturmbannführer*

## Extracts from *Wehrmacht* communiqués concerning the fighting at Kharkov

24 February 1943: Troops of the army and the *Waffen-SS* ("*Reich*" Division and "*Leibstandarte*") are continuing offensive operations against the Soviet outflanking wing between the Donets and Dniepr and are encircling strong enemy forces there.

7 March 1943: In the area south of Kharkov fast troops of the army and *Waffen-SS* ("*Das Reich*" Division, "*Leibstandarte*" and "*Totenkopf*") have broken strong resistance by the enemy and have thrown him back to the north. The encircled units of the 3rd Soviet Tank Army, consisting of elements of the 12th and 15th Tank Corps, a cavalry corps and three rifle divisions, were destroyed.

12 March 1943: Tank and infantry units of the army and *Waffen-SS* ("*Reich*" Division and "*Leibstandarte*") broke through the in-depth defensive position in front of Kharkov and entered the city from several sides.

13 March 1943: In Kharkov bitter street fighting is still going on in certain sections of the city. Troops of the *Waffen-SS* ("*Reich*" Division and "*Leibstandarte*") smashed the enemy resistance, advanced to the main railway station and occupied it.

15 March 1943: As announced by special bulletin, after days of fighting units of the *Waffen-SS* ("*Reich*" Division and "*Leibstandarte*"), effectively supported by the air force, have retaken the city of Kharkov in an enveloping attack from the north, west and south.

# III[6]

## Operations by I Battalion with the 14th (Anti-aircraft Machine-gun) Company and a Platoon of the 16th (Combat Engineer) Company in the Donets Bend area in January and February 1943

10 January 1943: I Battalion under the command of *Hauptsturmführer* Hans Opificius becomes the first unit of the regiment to entrain at Rennes, along with the 14th Company and a platoon of the 16th Company. Training, fighting spirit and equipment of the companies were excellent. The formation period in France had been put to good use. The troops exuded confidence and strength, exactly like the other battalions, even though the situation on the Eastern Front gave no cause for exaggerated optimism. The units were transported by blitz train across France (outside temperature plus 26 degrees) and Germany through Poland to Russia.

On 20 January 1943 the units detrained in Awdejewka where the outside temperature was now minus 38 degrees. On orders from the Ia of the "*Das Reich*" Panzer Division the battalion commander immediately reported to *Armeeabteilung* Fretter-Picco in Voroshilovgrad. The battalion, along with the 14th Company, the platoon from 16th Company, two batteries from the 2nd Artillery Regiment and a battery from the 2nd Flak Battalion "DR", were moved forward by road; this represented a major accomplishment on the part of the drivers, who covered the distance of 265 kilometers without serious incident.

On 22 January 1943 the battalion assembled in the Voroshilovgrad area and the next day occupied its pre-attack position in the Alexandrovka-Sabovka area.

24 January 1943 brought an unexpected change in the weather: it became warmer and started to rain. Hills 165.7 and 168.1 were attacked with tank support and the enemy was thrown back twelve kilometers. The night of 25 January saw temperatures plunge again: the thermometer now showed minus 28 degrees! The cold and an icy wind made things very difficult for the men. Casualties as a result of frostbite were considerable, and the battalion's combat strength was reduced by about 50% during this night. For as a result of the weather conditions on the previous

day the men had left some of their winter clothing in the vehicles. The forceful attack cost sweat and the rain and mild weather did the rest to soak the men to the skin. The battalion commander's decision to have parts of the battalion ride on the tanks so as to reach the objective contained in the orders was cancelled and instead the unit was ordered to hold its present positions (high plateau). Several proposals by the battalion to remain in movement, either toward the objective (patrols had not encountered the enemy) or back toward the starting position, were rejected. Not until during the night was the battalion withdrawn and relieved by two army companies. It was very regrettable that this first attack by the regimental units suffered under this unfortunate weather.

By 31 January 1943 I Battalion and the attached regimental units had reorganized themselves and were bolstered by the addition of the 30th Field Replacement Training Battalion minus headquarters and train units. At the same time the battalion was issued a 100-Watt radio station for communication with the "*Das Reich*" Division, a 105-mm gun from the army and two 50-mm anti-tank guns. A volunteer company consisting of stragglers from all elements of the armed forces formed on the initiative of *Obersturmführer* Dahl was also placed under the battalion's command. This unit would later demonstrate outstanding bravery and fighting ability.

On 28 January 1943 all of these units were combined under one command and committed to action as "Battle Group Schuldt." By 30 January all of the units had assembled in the Voroshilov area. It was learned from pilot reports that the enemy was building ice bridges over the Donets.

During the night of 1 February 1943 the Soviets then attacked in regiment strength with tank support. Launched at about 3 AM, the main thrust was directed at the small town of Voroshilov, defended by the main body of the battalion, and Petrovka to the northwest of it, defended by the reinforced 1st Company (a platoon from the 14th Company equipped with 20-mm guns on self-propelled carriages and one 50-mm anti-tank gun). The 20-mm guns and the anti-tank gun formed the backbone of the defense in Petrovka. *Rottenführer* Heider, whose anti-tank gun knocked out five enemy tanks, was awarded the Iron Cross, First Class on the battlefield and was promoted to *Unterscharführer*. The 1st Company's armorer-artificer, *Oberscharführer* Sepp Kammerer, destroyed a T 34 that had broken through with an anti-tank mine and was likewise decorated with the Iron Cross, First Class. In vain the enemy charged our positions in Voroshilov. The battalion held the defense line steadfastly against the superior enemy. The platoon from the 16th Company under the command of *Oberscharführer* Ernst von Eberstein in particular distinguished itself here. Simultaneous attacks from the left and right were repulsed by the 3rd Company under *Hauptsturmführer* Lex on the left and by *Obersturmführer* Dahl's volunteer company on the right. The enemy suffered heavy losses.

The battalion was withdrawn toward Wodjanoi during the night of 2 February. The enemy continued to press toward our positions with massed artillery and mortar fire, tanks and close-support aircraft. Despite extremely unfavorable terrain the panzer-grenadiers dug in in houses, holes and trenches and repulsed the enemy's forceful attacks. We are still grateful today for the relief and support provided by the tank crews of the army's 6th Panzer Division and the Stuka crews. During this fighting the commander of 4th Company, *Hauptsturmführer* Hocke, was killed by a direct hit on the battalion command post.

On 14 February the battalion was withdrawn from its positions. With the attached regimental units I Battalion reached the Krasnodonsky area by way of Samsonoff. In the days that followed it carried out security duties, counterattacks and attacks with limited objectives.

On 17 February rest positions were occupied in the Krasnaya Swesda area. The repair echelon of the "*Wiking*" Division generously supplied urgently needed fuel.

On 21 February the adjutant, *Obersturmführer* Pahnke, was sent to the division in the Pavlograd area with a detailed report, with the objective of having the battalion pulled out of the line and returned to the regiment.

On 23 February the battalion commander himself was ordered by radio to report to the division. The commander of 3rd Company assumed command in his absence.

Until 7 March 1943 there followed limited actions north of Debalzewo. When he returned the battalion commander brought with him orders for the reinforced I Battalion to rejoin the regiment via Pavlograd immediately. This news was well received. The march to the regiment suffered badly through a shortage of fuel. Only the organizational talents of the officers and men brought relief.

After a veritable odyssey, on 14 March the commander of the reinforced I Battalion reported his unit's return to the regimental commander. Following its reorganization into two rifle companies (Hstuf. Lex and Ostuf. Pahnke) and a heavy company (Ostuf. Rudolph) the battalion took part in the recapture of Kharkov as part of the regiment.

The story of the reinforced I Battalion in the preceding days was a tragic one. After leaving for the front as a fully capable independent unit, during this crisis-filled time the officers and men were constantly committed in the heart of the defense under unfamiliar commanders. Employed everywhere as a "flying fire-brigade," the virtually impossible was often asked – and given.

• • •

The new regimental commander "DF", Ostubaf. Sylvester Stadler, offered the following thoughts on the beginning of the period in which the regiment was under his command:

For the last time the German Army tried to regain the initiative in the east through large-scale offensive operations, however it failed to achieve a decisive success.

After subsequently launching another powerful counterattack to clear the important bridgehead on the Mius front, all available forces had to be immediately transferred to the Kharkov area to meet the major Soviet offensive under way there in order to avert the threat of breakthrough.

The pages that follow will show the degree of bravery, sacrifice, offensive spirit and steadfastness, the grim determination and hardships which these costly battles, constantly alternating between defense, counterattack and fighting retreat, to beyond the Dniepr and further into the Zhitomir combat zone demanded of all of the men of the regiment, who once again found themselves fighting at the decisive point.

It is however just an attempt, one which can surely not properly express the experience, because there are no words in our language to adequately describe the greatness of that time, the joy of success, the pride in accomplishment, the loyalty and comradeship, but also the deepest misery of despair in the difficult hours of the retreat.

For all of us who were part of this unique fighting team it was a great but also a bitter chapter in our lives!

Sylvester Stadler

# IV[7]

## "Operation Citadel"

The battles of early 1943 left a westward-projecting salient around the city of Kursk on the border between Army Group South (*Generalfeldmarschall* von Manstein) and Army Group Center (*Generalfeldmarschall* von Kluge). This salient lengthened the German front by approximately 500 kilometers and tied down considerable forces. This "open sack" was a hindrance to our operations plans in terms of supply. But even worse, the enemy could use this area as a base from which to prepare and launch attacks into the flanks of Army Groups Center and South. This enemy-held salient was to be eliminated.

"Operation Citadel" was also supposed to smash the enemy's armored reserves before they could be rested and refitted and thus regain the initiative for Germany.

The 9th Army under *Generaloberst* Model (Army Group Center) readied three panzer corps for the attack on Kursk.

Part of Army Group South, *Armeeabteilung* Kempf, consisting of the III Panzer Corps (6th, 7th and 19th Panzer Divisions and the 198th Infantry Division) under *General* Breith and the XI Army Corps (106th and 320th Infantry Divisions) under *General* Rauß, was to offensively screen the breakthrough toward Kursk east and northeast of Belgorod.

The 17th Panzer Division and the "*Wiking*" Division initially formed the army group reserve. The 4th Panzer Army under *Generaloberst* Hoth was given the job of carrying out the actual breakthrough operation toward Kursk. For this task the army had available the XXXXVIII Panzer Corps under *General* von Knobelsdorf with the 3rd and 11th Panzer Divisions, the "*Grossdeutschland*" Division and two-thirds of the 167th Infantry Division, the LII Army Corps with the 57th, 255th and 332nd Infantry Divisions, and the II SS Panzer Corps under *Generaloberst* Paul Hausser with the "*Das Reich*", "LAH" and "*Totenkopf*" Divisions as well as one-third of the 167th Infantry Division.

The start of the attack was postponed from May to July. Political considerations on the part of the senior leadership may have played a role in this. During this time the German units were refurbished and strengthened. At the beginning of July 1943 Army Group South had at its disposal over 1,000 tanks of various types (the bulk of them Panzer IIIs) and about 400 assault guns.

The 9th Army went to the attack on 5 July. The enemy responded very strongly here, and our offensive had to be halted on 11 July as a result of a massed enemy counterattack.

The enemy situation in the coming battles would reveal that at least a partial objective of the German command was reached: the destruction of the first line of Russian tank units; initial German success then forced the Russian command to employ its strategic reserves. These units were also badly battered during the course of the battle. Nevertheless the Soviet high command was able to become extremely active in this sector of the front again by early August.

## The Opposition Prior to the Start of "Operation Citadel" From *The Battle of Kursk* by Colonel I.I. Markin

*At the end of March 1943 Soviet intelligence was sure that it had identified approximately 40 German infantry and 20 panzer divisions massed in the Belgorod-Kharkov area. More specifically, the German high command had concentrated its main striking force (including the SS Panzer Divisions "Leibstandarte", "Totenkopf", "Wiking" and "Das Reich" and the Panzer Division "Grossdeutschland") in the area of Kharkov and south.*

*Based on its information the Soviet high command worked out a plan of operations for the spring and summer of 1943 to meet the expected attack on the Kursk salient and at the same time take the initiative there and on other fronts.*

*Opposite the northern wing of Army Group South (Generalfeldmarschall von Manstein) was the Soviet "Voronezh Front." It occupied a gigantic defense sector organized into five deep positions. A main defense zone had been established in the entire Kursk salient; consisting of battalion defense areas, anti-tank strong points and an intensive system of various obstacles, it extended to a depth of six kilometers. Approximately 2 500 kilometers of communications and infantry trenches were built, while far more than 30,000 rifle pits and machine-gun posts and approximately 10,000 anti-tank positions were intended to make a penetration by the German divisions more difficult. Numerous observation posts and well-camouflaged command posts were prepared, more than 430,000 mines were laid and 700 kilometers of barbed wire obstacles were built.*

*Between the individual defense sectors, which extended to depths of up to 40 kilometers, anti-tank ditches were dug and a further defense system was built. Most of the work was done at night to conceal it from the enemy. Po 2 aircraft, which were called 'duty non-commissioned officer' by the German troops and 'corn farmer' or 'vegetable gardener' by the Red Army, increased their nighttime activities.*

*The Soviet command also concentrated in this area the 2nd, 16th and 17th Air Armies, which together had more than 2,000 fighters, 800 close-support aircraft and 700 other combat aircraft.*

*The 'Voronezh Front' established a stronger defense in the direction of Oboyan (thus before the later front of the German 4th Panzer Army) and Korocha (before the later front of Armeeabteilung Kempf). Of troop concentration the author said: "The 6th Guards Army (commander in chief General Chistyakov) occupied defensive positions in the direction of Oboyan. The army's first echelon in its 64-kilometer-wide sector consisted of the 36th, 72nd, 78th and 81st Guards Rifle Divisions and the 262nd Tank Regiment. The second echelon consisted of the 15th and 73rd Guards Rifle Divisions and the 213th Rifle Division, the 148th and 167th Tank Regiments, the 27th Guards Tank Brigade and the 201st Tank Brigade.*

*The reserves of the 'Voronezh Front' consisted of the 1st Tank Army (6th Tank Corps and 3rd Mechanized Corps), the 2nd and 5th Guards Tank Corps as well as artillery and mortar troops. Large strategic reserves were also concentrated in the direction of Kursk, including the 4th and 5th Guards Armies, the 5th, 27th, 47th and 53rd Guards Tank Armies, the 4th Guards Tank Corps and the 10th Tank Corps, which occupied positions east of the Kursk salient and expanded several defense sectors, the last of which was the defense sector on the Don."*

• • •

With confirmation of his appointment as regimental commander, Stubaf. Stadler was promoted to *Obersturmbannführer*. On 22 April the regiment moved into the Dolshik-Perresetschnaja-Solotschew quartering area.

Regimental adjutant: Hstuf. Herbert Schulze; commander of I Battalion: Hstuf. Hans Opificius, commander II Battalion: Hstuf. Emil Maître, commander III Battalion: Stubaf. Zenz Kaiser.

The young replacements for the regiment were insufficiently trained when they arrived, and after some tough day and night training they were assigned to the companies. Casualties among non-commissioned officers had been especially heavy during the fighting of the winter and early spring. Consequently a non-commissioned officer training company was formed under the command of Ostuf. Werner. *Generaloberst* Hoth, commander in chief of the 4th Panzer Army, was present for the final inspection and declared that he was extremely satisfied with what he saw. Live-fire combat exercises, unit training in conjunction with all heavy weapons, with tanks and assault guns, offensive patrols, map exercises and "sand table" missions carefully prepared the units for the tasks to come.

1 July: Employing maximum camouflage, the regiment marched into the assembly area north-northeast of Belgorod and south of Jachontow. Once again "Operation Citadel" was postponed. The assembly areas were occupied for the final time during the night of 3-4 July.

At 4 AM on 5 July the "*Deutschland*" Regiment, led by III Battalion under Stubaf. Günther Wisliceny, advanced through the enemy's strong field fortifications with the rest of the "*Das Reich*" Division. The "*Deutschland*" Regiment's 10th Company under Ostuf. Schreiber reached the anti-tank ditch where it became bogged down in heavy fighting against units of the Soviet 52nd Guards Division. *Generaloberst* Hausser went to see the "*Deutschland*" Regiment's situation for himself. Supported by a *Nebelwerfer* (artillery rocket) brigade, used here for the first time, the "*Deutschland*" Regiment was able to force a further breakthrough, which made it the turn of the "*Der Führer*" Regiment to attack.

6 July: Attacking rapidly, I and II Battalions "*Der Führer*" gained ground to the north and at noontime took the small town of Lutschki. In this area the enemy had concentrated: the 51st Guards Rifle Division, the 31st Tank Corps, the 5th Guards Tank Corps, the 1st Guards Tank Bri-

gade, the 49th Tank Brigade and the 96th Tank Brigade. After the capture of Lutschki the "*Der Führer*" Regiment was regrouped and assigned to cooperate with the 2nd Panzer Regiment of the "*Das Reich*" Division.

During the early hours of the evening the regiment attacked toward Kalinin and gained ground quickly in spite of a vigorous enemy defense. An unfavorable defense line had to be occupied during the night.

Together with the division's tanks and assault guns III Battalion pressed toward Teterevino against the Soviet 52nd Guards Rifle Division and units of the 10th Tank Corps and the 183rd Rifle Division. Our attack came to a temporary halt here.

Meanwhile, according to *The Battle of Kursk* by Soviet Colonel I.I. Markin, the enemy situation was as follows:

> *Influenced by the success of the German 4th Panzer Army, the Russian command was forced to quickly move in strong reserves. The Soviet 1st Army, for example, received the 6th Tank Corps and the 3rd Mechanized Corps. The 93rd Rifle Division was moved in to guard to the east (along the rail line through Belechinino)against the breakthrough toward the north by the "Das Reich" Division. The 5th Guards Tank Corps and the 2nd Guards Tank Corps were supposed to prepare to attack east of Lutschki.*
>
> *The author wrote of the fighting on 7 July: "At daybreak the Germans succeeded in breaking through the defense by the Soviet units weakened in two days of fighting and in a narrow wedge reached the area in front of Belechinino station as well as the Teterevino area. Through their fire and short counterattacks, the 31st Tank Corps, the 5th Guards Tank Corps and rifle units of the 6th Guards Army prevented the attackers from gaining further ground. In the area west of Belechinino on the morning of 7 July the SS Panzer Divisions 'Leibstandarte' and 'Das Reich' attempted to carry the attack forward toward the Sowchos Komsomolez and Prokhorovka station. The attack was stopped by the fire and counterattacks by units of the 183rd Rifle Division and of the 5th Guards Tank Corps. The enemy subsequently altered his direction of attack and drove northwest toward the villages of Malyje Majatschki and Gresnoje. With hugely superior forces he succeeded in breaking into the defense at the eastern outskirts of the villages.*

*In order to break the strength of the German advance and prevent the further advance toward Kursk and Oboyan, the Russian high command readied elements of the 40th Army, the 6th, 10th and 2nd Tank Corps and the 2nd and 5th Guards Tank Corps, for an attack. The entire air forces were moved in as well as the bulk of the artillery of the 'Voronezh Front'."*

7 July: Tank companies of the 2nd Panzer Regiment and elements of the 2nd Armored Reconnaissance Battalion had reached the Teterevino-Lutschki II road. III Battalion attacked the rail line near Prokhorovka station with 10th Company. 10th Company's assault teams were halted by extremely heavy defensive fire. Together with the II Panzer Battalion, elements of the "*Deutschland*" Regiment and strong support by the 2nd Artillery Regiment and *Nebelwerfer* units, III Battalion attacked the railway embankment again and succeeded in driving back the enemy. The main line of resistance at that moment ran along the rail line. I and II Battalions attacked further north and drove toward Sowchos Komsomolez. Ostuf. Werner, the commander of 10th Company, was wounded during the attacks on the railway embankment and Ustuf. Krüger took over the company. Uscha. Grascher of 9th Company distinguished himself here and was awarded the Knight's Cross for his coolness in the defense and an immediate counterattack which followed. III Battalion was moved in here and was committed to an armored advance on the village of Gresnoje. Heavy enemy artillery fire. The 15th Company was deployed in the wooded terrain beside the embankment to guard the regiment's open flank and was ordered to establish contact with the elements of the 167th Infantry Division securing to the east. After the terrific heat of the previous days, during the night there was a cloudburst-like rain.

8 July: While I and II Battalions were engaged in fierce forest fighting, in the Gresnoje area III Battalion together with II Battalion of the 2nd Panzer Regiment were once again committed to an armored thrust in the direction of Kotschetowka. The forcefully executed attack succeeded and the enemy withdrew to the northwest.

The 15th Company was deployed in a defensive role between I and II Battalions. Ten T 34s subsequently attacked the company's position. The company's 50-mm anti-tank guns knocked out two of these. The assault gun battery under Ostuf Braun, which was at readiness behind the company, destroyed six tanks. One T 34 became stuck in the forest near 15th Company and was destroyed by close attack. Ustuf. Hubert Mast was killed in the attack. One tank drove through to I Battalion and was destroyed there.

In the presence of the regimental commander the 3rd Company with Hstuf. Lex of I Battalion made a daring advance and drove through to a Russian corps headquarters, capturing the Soviet general and his entire staff.

9 to 11 July: Attacks with limited objectives alternated with enemy counterattacks in the lines reached. The Soviet air force became more active. Staroshewoje was attacked. In the evening massed enemy assaults with tanks.

The following is taken from the book *The Battle of Kursk*:

> *."..not until towards evening did a group of enemy tanks succeed in breaking into Staroshewoje and threatening the rear area of the 5th Guards Tank Army, which was preparing for the counteroffensive. In order to meet this threat the commander in chief of the Voronezh Front ordered the 2nd Guards Tank Corps to undertake a counterattack from the Belchinino-Ivanovka-Vinogradovka area in the direction of Staroshewoje-Prokhorovka. At about 8:30 PM on 11 July the 25th and 26th Guards Tank Brigades counterattacked. The bitterly fought battle of movement lasted the entire night. The Soviet tank troops failed to gain ground, but through their counterattack they did hold up the enemy's advance and eliminated the danger to the 5th Tank Army."*

The panzer-grenadiers of the "*Der Führer*" Regiment and the "*Das Reich*" Division remember these engagements as the "tank battle northeast of Kalinin." The enemy repeatedly succeeded in penetrating the main line of resistance. Again and again he was driven out, even though the men of the companies were driven to the verge of desperation by the onslaught of the masses of Russian armor. Not one foot of ground was surrendered.

12 July: *Generaloberst* Hoth visited the regimental command post and after being briefed on the situation was deeply impressed by the accomplishments and morale of the regiment. He conveyed to the commanding officer, Ostubaf. Stadler, a telex from *Generalfeldmarschall* von Manstein for the regiment which was worded as follows:

> *"To the great 'DF' Regiment under the leadership of its commanding officer and its brave men my special appreciation for their accomplishments in the tank battle northeast of Kalinin. The regiment has been allocated a special contingent of 150 Iron Crosses, Second Class and 100 Iron Crosses, First Class to decorate the bravest."*

The enemy attacked with undiminished fury. During another attack in the morning two Soviet tanks broke through. The two T 34s rolled unhindered as far as 15th Company's train, where one tank rammed the company's field kitchen as its last act before being destroyed with close-range weapons. The other T 34 became bogged down and in fact was put out of action at the last minute by a 50-mm anti-tank gun which was in the rear for repairs.

This raised the number of tanks knocked out by 15th Company (motorcycle and reconnaissance company) in recent days to 14. It was relieved by elements of the 167th Infantry Division and was positioned north of Kalinin as regiment reserve.

The 5th Guards Tank Army and the 5th Guards Army continued their attacks. In the "*Das Reich*" Division's sector the enemy also committed the 2nd Tank Corps. It appeared that the tank battle had not yet reached its climax. In the woods west of Belchinino and east of Kalinin heavy enemy attacks (2nd Soviet Guards Tank Corps) alternated with immediate counterattacks by the companies of the regiment. Not until night did the sound of battle die down somewhat, heavy dark clouds brought a fierce thunderstorm. Fortunately the regiment's casualties in this defensive battle had not been very heavy.

13 to 17 July: Enemy attacks were fought off in the positions and our own forces actively conducted reconnaissance. On 14 July Ostuf. Buch was wounded during an attack on the railway embankment northeast of Kalinin. Ustuf. Schmager took over 15th Company.

17 July: On orders from the OKH the entire II SS Panzer Corps was removed from Army Group South in anticipation of employment in Italy. Army infantry units relieved the companies of the regiment in their defensive positions. The regiment assembled in the division area north of Kharkov to wait for the coming orders.

In addition to the loss of II SS Panzer Corps, Army Group South had to give up two divisions to Army Group Center and was therefore forced to abandon further attacks in the direction of Kursk and then break off the battle altogether.

To no surprise of the German command, on 17 July the enemy attacked the positions of the 6th Army (*General* Hollidt) and the 1st Panzer Army (*General* von Mackensen) in the area of the Mius and Donets front and achieved deep penetrations. "Operation Citadel" was thus brought to a final end. The enemy had thrown approximately thirty rifle divisions and more than ten tank or mechanized corps into the battle there. His losses must have been considerable.

At the request of Army Group South the II SS Panzer Corps was initially left where it was and was to be employed within the 6th Army to restore the situation there.

Travelling partly by rail and partly by road, by 30 July the regiment reached the small town of Charzyssk by way of Lozovaya and Makeyevka and then marched on to Dernowye, north of Kubitschewo.

On the previous day there the enemy had succeeded in tearing up the 6th Army's front on a width of twenty kilometers and a depth of fifteen kilometers, thus gaining a considerable bridgehead with a commanding hill position for his subsequent operations. The enemy had moved approximately sixteen rifle divisions and two mechanized corps into this bridgehead along with tank brigades and other specialized units.

## The Battle on the Mius

At 3 PM on 30 July the regimental commander arrived at the command post of the "*Das Reich*" Division and in the presence of *Generalfeldmarschall* von Manstein reported to the division commander, *Generalleutnant* Krüger, that his regiment was on its way. Several attacks on the commanding hill position had already been repulsed by the enemy with considerable losses, and consideration was already being given to halting the operation, which meant abandoning the idea of eliminating the bridgehead. During the regimental commander's report *Generalfeldmarschall* von Manstein asked in the presence of the commanding general of II SS Panzer Corps, *Generaloberst* Hausser, when the regiment would arrive. "In five to six hours," was the regimental commander's reply. This seemed too long to *Generalfeldmarschall* von Manstein and he left it to *Generalleutnant* Hausser to cancel further attack plans.

Confident in the strength of the regiment's panzer-grenadiers, however, *Generaloberst* Hausser argued that the attack should be carried out again led by the regiment. *Generalfeldmarschall* von Manstein, however, maintained that one regiment could not carry the attack where entire divisions had been repulsed. *Generaloberst* Hausser expressed the belief that after taking the high ground the offensive against the entire bridgehead would get rolling again.

This decision in assessing the overall situation was made reality by the regiment under the leadership of its commanding officer.

The commanding general offered the regimental commander every possible type of support for this attack: tanks, corps artillery, Stukas, rocket artillery and so on.

After assessing the prospective battlefield, *Generaloberst* Hausser submitted his plan of attack by telephone. Ostubaf. Stadler decided on a surprise attack during the final hours of darkness without artillery preparation and without supporting arms – except for rocket artillery, which would lay down smoke on the regiment's flanks. The regimental commander discussed every phase of the attack with his battalion commanders in the field, and the companies as well as platoons and squads were informed accordingly and issued their attack orders.

During the night the regiment's planned operation was seriously threatened when the enemy once more succeeded in breaking into the security screen and defense positions; however, the regiment's preparations behind the army units were not seriously disrupted.

On 31 July, still during the morning twilight, the rocket artillery regiment opened fire after receiving detailed instructions from the commander of the "*Der Führer*" Regiment. The rockets were right on target, forming dense walls of smoke to cover both flanks. At 4:35 AM II Battalion silently launched its attack under cover of the dense smoke and in a very short time crossed the intervening ground to a depth of about three kilometers. I Battalion, deployed next to II Battalion, made equally rapid progress and within 45 minutes the hill position was in the regiment' hands.

Taken completely by surprise, the enemy fought back desperately, however he was unable to resist the relentless attack of the panzer-grenadiers and hastily abandoned his positions.

The commander of 4th Company, Ostuf. Grieme, distinguished himself in the attack and was awarded the Knight's Cross for his decisive accomplishment.

III Battalion, committed on foot, also fought its way skillfully through the enemy positions and on 1 August attacked Hill 223.7 west of Stepanovka together with a panzer company. Ustuf. Jochen Krüger and the men of the 10th Company distinguished themselves in this operation and Krüger was later awarded the Knight's Cross.

During the morning the enemy began pounding the hill position with a fierce artillery bombardment. Concentric tank attacks were repulsed. Well protected in the excellent positions, which had earlier been strongly fortified by German troops, all of these enemy assaults were beaten off and once again the panzer-grenadiers received excellent support from the assault guns of the "*Das Reich*" Division.

Russian artillery fire knocked out wire and radio communications between the regiment's forward and rear command posts. Not until approximately 9 AM were runners able to restore contact. The important observations by the regimental commander from this hill, especially the Russian preparations to abandon the entire bridgehead, could not be immediately exploited, however. Nevertheless the attack by the II SS Panzer Corps, with the "*Das Reich*" and "*Totenkopf*" Divisions and the 3rd Panzer Division, was a smashing success, made possible only by the capture of this hill position. By the afternoon of 2 August the entire bridgehead had been taken and was firmly in the hands of the II SS Panzer Corps including the 3rd Panzer Division. Several hundred tanks, approximately 600 guns of various calibers and about 18,000 prisoners were brought in.

Headquarters, Army Group South (*Generalfeldmarschall* von Manstein) sent an appreciative telex to the "*Das Reich*" Division in which the offensive spirit and bravery of the soldiers of the "*Der Führer*" Regiment received special praise.

The *Wehrmacht* communiqué of 4 August 1943 declared:

> *"In the battle on the Mius infantry and tank units of the army and Waffen-SS under the command of Generalfeldmarschall von Manstein have frustrated repeated breakthrough attempts by strong enemy forces and in a sweeping counterattack have smashed the enemy forces which had penetrated north of Kuybischewo."*

The regiment had played a very major role in this proud success and it was undoubtedly one of the regiment's greatest accomplishments to that time. Carefully prepared, it was a classic surprise attack with minimal losses and above average tactical effects. Such an accomplishment was only possible with men possessing high fighting morale and excellent training.

Already on the afternoon of 2 August, at about 5 PM, the regiment was pulled out the positions it had reached and infantry units occupied the main line of resistance. It was entrusted to them because these units had built some of the positions themselves.

## Battles in Defense of Kharkov in August 1943 Dolshik-southeast of Bogodochow-Korotitsch

On 4 August 1943 the regiment was relieved in its newly won positions and marched into its assigned quartering area around Stalino.

Following the regiment's latest great success, which had received special acknowledgement from senior commanders and was honored and publicized in orders of the day and radio broadcasts, the morale of the panzer-grenadiers was outstanding. As well there was an unsubstantiated rumor that the regiment was to be transferred to Italy with the division. The "*Leibstandarte*" and the headquarters of the II SS Panzer Corps were already en route to Upper Italy. Advance detachments from the battalions of the "*Der Führer*" Regiment were formed and in the process of moving out.

Germany's ally Italy had already initiated cease-fire negotiations with the Allies some time earlier. Mussolini had been removed under dramatic circumstances and was then rescued by German forces. Elements of the Italian armed forces under Marshall Badoglio were in the process of openly going over to the Allies. The few German divisions in Italy were to be bolstered by the II SS Panzer Corps.

The regimental headquarters and the headquarters company entrained on 5 August, followed a few hours later by the 15th Company and elements of the 13th Company (infantry gun company under Ustuf. Lenthe). A raid by Il 2 close-support aircraft caught 13th Company unprotected, resulting in losses in personnel and equipment. The railway personnel were finally persuaded to leave and after a considerable delay the transport train departed. All of the men still believed that they were going to the "sunny south." But that was not to be the case. The train headed north!

In Novaya Bavaria, within the city of Kharkov, the regimental commander was ordered to report to *Armeeabteilung* Kempf, where he was briefed on the situation.

Signals and air reconnaissance had already revealed that the enemy was assembling armored forces in the area south of Kursk and southeast of Kharkov. A short time later, following the cancellation of "Operation Citadel," Russian tank units attacked the 4th Panzer Army's front, in particular the 167th Infantry Division of *Armeeabteilung* Kempf.

Both armies abandoned the former battleground according to plan, and finally the German divisions withdrew to the starting position of 5 July. Then on 3 August the enemy launched a major attack, tearing open a gap twelve kilometers wide against the weakened 167th and 332nd Infantry Divisions. Units of the 11th and 19th Panzer Divisions attempted to seal off the enemy incursion. On 4 August the enemy committed new units in this direction of attack. Belgorod had to be abandoned and southeast of Kharkov the Red Army might also go over to the attack at any time. Beginning north of Kharkov, by 6 August the Soviet divisions had reached the approximate line Siborovka-Solotschew-Bogoduchow-Tarrassowka-Krasnopolye.

The "dream of the trip to Italy" had thus been shattered, and the regiment took over the thankless role of "fire-brigade" in the assigned area of operations in the general line Solotschew-Bogoduchow. The enemy situation in the combat zone was totally unclear. The 2nd Armored Reconnaissance Battalion under Stubaf. Weidinger (later commander of the "*Der Führer*" Regiment) had reached Bogoduchow in a forced march and was placed under the regiment's command. Preceding the regiment, the bulk of which was still in the Stalino area or on its way by rail, the

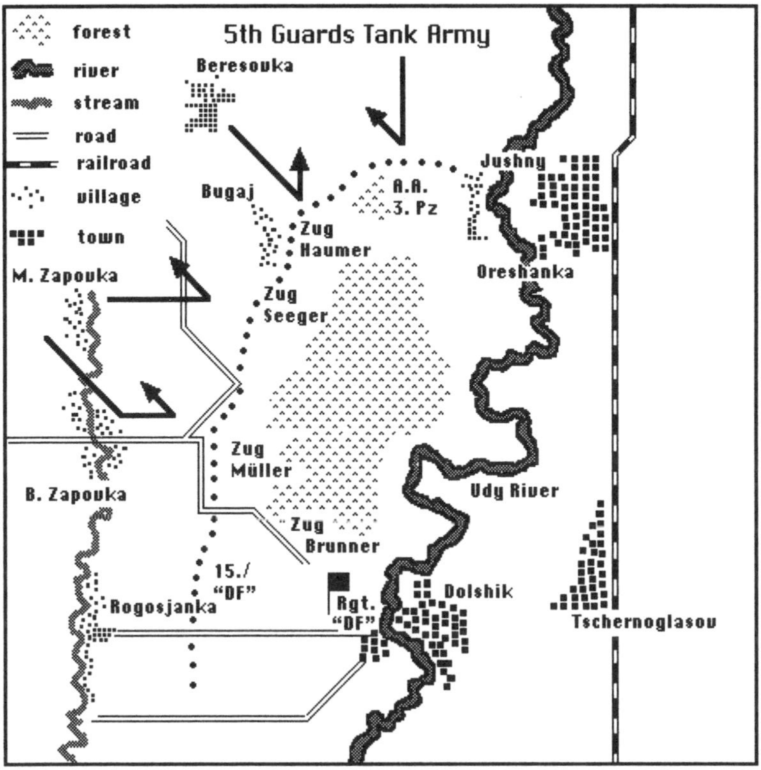


**The situation on 6 August, 1943**

1. **Zug Haumer**
2. **Zug Seeger, 1 Pak 5cm self propelled**
3. **Zug Müller, 1 Pak 5cm motorized and 3 Pak 7.5cm motorized with the Regimental Staff Company led by Hauptsturmführer Manz**
4. **Zug Brunner with 1 Pak 5cm self propelled**

regimental commander drove into the especially threatened area south of Solotschew with his headquarters and the headquarters company.

In a hastily improvised attack he succeeded in rescuing the headquarters company of the 3rd Panzer Corps (*Generaloberst* Breith) and the chief of staff, *Oberst* Merk, from a desperate defensive struggle. As a result of this the subsequent cooperation with *Oberst* Merk and his troops was especially heartfelt.

During the late morning hours of 6 August the regiment's second transport was also stopped in Novaya Bavaria, and in a forced march the motorcycle troops of the 15th Company reached the town of Dolshik, where the regimental headquarters had established a makeshift line of security. From off the move the company occupied a seven-kilometer-wide sector, which was manned strongpoint style. The headquarters company's 75-mm anti-tank gun platoon under Hscha. Manz was placed under 15th Company's command. Immediately after the company took up positions the enemy attacked, hesitantly at first but then in greater numbers. Exploiting the company's mobility, all of these attacks were repulsed. The 75-mm anti-tank platoon and 15th Company's three 50-mm anti-tank guns provided effective support. On his own initiative the regimental engineer Hstuf. Albert Herbst had outfitted two one-ton prime movers with a 50-mm cannon, boosting the company's mobile firepower enormously. During the afternoon the guns together knocked out eight tanks of various types; a shot-down Soviet reconnaissance aircraft completed the company's defensive success.

Contact was established with the unit on the right, the reconnaissance battalion of the 3rd Panzer Division, on 6 August. The left flank, to Bogoduchow, where the 2nd Armored Reconnaissance Battalion was in position, was still open, however, and no contact was made. Arriving units of the division, a combat engineer company and two companies of the "*Deutschland*" Regiment, were likewise subordinated to the "*Der Führer*" Regiment and were inserted in strongpoints on the open left flank.

The enemy repeatedly charged this makeshift and weakly manned main line of resistance. The regimental commander went to 15th Company's sector several times a day. The enemy pressure grew heavier by the hour and some anxious hours passed.

Finally, in the early morning hours of 8 August, the first unit of II Battalion "*Der Führer*", the 7th Company, arrived and was immediately deployed on the open left flank. It occupied a broad security sector and the defense had to be organized as a series of strongpoints.

In the evening the Soviets launched a surprise attack in company strength with tank support in a sector held by a squad positioned in front of a wood. After fierce resistance the squad was overrun by the Soviets. All eight men died fighting. The Soviet breakthrough was sealed off by elements of I Battalion "*Der Führer*" with the 1st Company under Hstuf. Alfred Hesselmann, which had arrived in the afternoon. The situation in the 4th Panzer Army's sector continued to be extremely serious.

According to *The Battle of Kursk* the enemy's view of the situation was as follows:

> *"At the time that the panzer divisions 'Das Reich', 'Leibstandarte' and 'Totenkopf' were engaged in offensive operations at the Mius River, the Soviet command concentrated extremely strong shock and attack formations in the Kursk salient, in order to smash the German groupings in the Belgorod-Kharkov area, isolate the railway links in the directions of Poltava-Krasnograd-Lozovaya and simultaneously barricade the roads. The subsequent long-range objective was to reach the Dniepr on a broad front.*
>
> *These missions were assigned to the 'Voronezh Front' under General Vatutin (member of the war council N.S. Krushchev), the 'Steppe Front' under General Konev and the 'Southwest Front' under General Malinovsky. The enemy had grouped in the area of Malinovka (approximately 35 kilometers southeast of Kharkov)-Volchansk-east of Belgorod-Gostischewo-Soldatskoye-Bassy: the 57th Army, the7th Guards Army, the 69th Army, the 48th Rifle Corps, the 53rd Army, the 5th Guards Army, the 6th Guards Army, the 27th Army, the 38th Army and the 40th Army. After achieving breakthrough the 1st Tank Army and the 5th Guards Tank Army were to exploit and expand the shock grouping of the 5th Guards Army. The Russian high command concentrated here seventy tanks and an artillery density of 230 guns and mortars per kilometer of front. The 2nd and 5th Air Armies had the task of clearing the airspace over the offensive.*

*On 3 August, from 5 to shortly before 8 AM, the Russian artillery opened fire with only brief pauses and increased it sector by sector into a veritable hurricane. On 5 August the 89th Guards Rifle Division and the 305th Rifle Division took Belgorod, and on the evening of 6 August the Soviet 53rd Army was near Mikoyanovka, the 5th Guards Army had reached Kasatschja-Lopan, the 5th Guards Army was in the area around Solotschew, and the Soviet 1st Tank Army had advanced to Bogoduchow.*

*If the Russian high command succeeded in bringing this wide-ranging offensive to a conclusion not only would the German units in and around Kharkov face destruction, but there would also be a danger that the entire German southern front might collapse."*

## The 2nd Armored Reconnaissance Battalion as part of the "*Der Führer*" Regiment

Meantime the 2nd Armored Reconnaissance Battalion under Stubaf. Otto Weidinger had arrived in the area southeast of Bogoduchow with all its elements. This area proved to be another focal point of the defense.

The armored spearhead of the Soviet 1st Army was nearing Bogoduchow on the evening of 6 August, and it succeeded in overrunning the weak German forces defending there. The Soviets took Bogoduchow itself on 7 August and crossed the Merla River. The Russian spearhead then continued toward the southwest.

As the defense line's sole corner bastion at first, the 2nd Armored Reconnaissance Battalion essentially had to accomplish two tasks: reconnoiter to the north and northeast as well as in a west-southwesterly direction and simultaneously establish a front to prevent the enemy from advancing farther to the southeast.

To accomplish this the 2nd Armored Reconnaissance Battalion was placed under the command of the "*Der Führer*" Regiment and the regimental commander assumed command in the now roughly forty-kilometer-wide defense sector. The 2nd Armored Reconnaissance Battalion carried out its tasks offensively, which meant that heavily armed offensive forays alternated with pure reconnaissance duties. The *Schwimmwagen* company was employed in the infantry role. Reconnaissance results were conveyed to the regimental commander and the "*Das Reich*" Division simultaneously.

The importance of the 2nd Armored Reconnaissance Battalion's defense position was underlined by the addition of units from outside the division: an army assault gun company and a panzer company with dashing officers and men. An army heavy artillery battalion, a multiple rocket launcher unit with forty-eight barrels and an army armored train also provided outstanding support in the fierce battle, which began immediately.

The armored train intervened very effectively in the fighting along the rail line to Bogoduchow, however the main burden in these days was borne by the men of the 2nd Armored Reconnaissance Battalion. The enemy achieved a penetration into the weakly manned defense lines almost daily. Nevertheless, by making every possible effort the battalion not only held the position, but with outstanding support from the assault guns was able to move the main line of resistance forward. The enemy attacked daily with undiminished fury, but by 10 August the situation here had stabilized. Russian mortar fire caused numerous casualties.

Although they had no contact with the 2nd Armored Reconnaissance Battalion, units of the "*Wiking*" Division supported the defensive battle on the right flank, and on the left flank units of the "*Totenkopf*" Division counterattacked energetically, even though they, too, had no contact with the reconnaissance battalion. Simultaneous with these attacks units of the 6th Panzer Division and the 323rd Infantry Division attacked from the 2nd Armored Reconnaissance Battalion's area, while the reconnaissance battalion itself was pulled out of the line and moved farther south. There it was again subordinated to the "*Der Führer*" Regiment in preparation for an attack in a northwesterly direction.

One feat by the 2nd Armored Reconnaissance Battalion is deserving of special mention here: without orders from the division, the commander of the reconnaissance battalion instructed Ustuf. Scheller to take two eight-wheeled armored cars in a generally west direction (roughly in the direction of Murafa-Kosjewka) through the Russian breakthrough area, establish contact with the German units on the other side, have them sketch their positions and defense lines on a map, and report by radio on enemy movements.

This foray led through the enemy's breakthrough area south of Bogoduchow. On the first day the patrol transmitted running reports on its position and the commander of the 2nd Armored Reconnaissance Battalion received important information on the enemy. Radio traffic became weaker and finally broke off completely. For two days the patrol was missing. The battalion feared that Ustuf. Scheller and his men had fallen into enemy hands. Then, unexpectedly, on the third day radio contact was restored with the eight-wheeled armored cars: "Mission accomplished, coming back."

The return was awaited with great anticipation at the command post of the 2nd Armored Reconnaissance Battalion, and when the patrol arrived safe and sound the result exceeded all expectations. Playing a cat and mouse game with Russian units the two armored cars, which were on a pure reconnaissance mission with no instructions to engage the enemy, slipped through the entire breakthrough area and came upon a corps headquarters. When Ustuf. Scheller informed the commanding general of the patrol's starting point, he looked at Scheller and his men like "spirits from another world." The corps chief of staff personally entered the situation of the troops on a map and bade farewell to Ustuf. Scheller with best wishes. The commander of the 2nd Armored Reconnaissance Battalion reported the result to the division by telephone. *Generalleutnant* Krüger was enthused by this terrific feat. For days nothing concrete had been known about the situation of the German front on the other side of the breakthrough area. Ustuf. Scheller was directed via the XI Army Corps to the III Panzer Corps, and both were extremely pleased by his great accomplishment. The army command had received extremely important information as a result of this decisive action, which had a bearing on subsequent decisions.

For this outstanding feat Ustuf. Scheller was recommended for the Iron Cross, First Class by the commander of the 2nd Armored Reconnaissance Battalion; Scheller received the decoration soon afterwards.

• • •

During the course of a straightening of the front the "Der Führer" Regiment was deployed in the line Dolshik-Point 210.6-Rogosjanka, with

I Battalion on the right (near Dolshik), II Battalion near Point 210.6 and the 15th Company in the deep open flank to the west. Massed enemy forces attacked the new defense line without letup, and the Red Army troops managed to break through at the boundary between II Battalion and the 15th Company and reach the group of houses near Point 158.2.

On hearing this alarming news the regimental commander and the crew of his armored troop carrier command vehicle "Leipzig" drove into the 15th Company's sector. The motorcycle troops were fighting off heavy enemy attacks; the Brunner Platoon, which had been held in reserve, sealed off the open flank against the broken-through enemy and the positions were held. After he was briefed on the situation by the commander of the 15th Company the regimental commander personally committed the panzer-grenadiers of II Battalion, and their quick counterattack restored the original main line of resistance.

During the night of 10 August the regiment was relieved by army units and moved into a readiness area southwest of Bogoduchow. Together with the 2nd Armored Reconnaissance Battalion the regiment attacked through Kowjagi station in the direction of Scharowka and drove the enemy back. The close bond between the regiment's panzer-grenadiers and the troops of the 2nd Armored Reconnaissance Battalion proved its worth, and in spite of intensive counterattacks the enemy was unable to make any serious incursions into the newly-won main line of resistance.

On 15 August the former commander of 1st Company, Hstuf. Hesselmann, became the regimental adjutant. Hstuf. Herbert Schulze, a veteran of many battles, took over II Battalion. The commander of III Battalion. Stubaf. Zenz Kaiser, had been wounded in the last days' fighting. The former commander of an armored reconnaissance company, Hstuf. Helmut Kämpfe, took over III Battalion. The commander of 10th Company, Ustuf. Joachim Krüger, who had taken over the company near Belgorod after Ostuf. Heinz Werner was wounded and who together with his men had played a decisive role in III Battalion's success near Teterewino (north of Kharkov), was also seriously wounded. At the request of Stubaf Kaiser, Ustuf. Krüger was promoted to *Obersturmführer* at the medical clearing station. Following his death Ostuf. Krüger was awarded the Knight's Cross for personal bravery.

Ostuf. Reinhold Scharfe, a company commander in the 2nd Armored Reconnaissance Battalion, was seriously wounded and died the same day in the field hospital.

According to *The Battle of Kharkov* the enemy saw the situation as follows:

*On 10 August, south of Bogoduchow the 1st Soviet Tank Army went to the attack again toward the south-southwest, while elements of the 5th Guards Tank Army and the 5th Guards Army deployed farther to the south in the direction of Bogoduchow from the Solotschew area. The Russian spearheads reached Scharowka and Odinnadzataja, where they encountered elements of the 'Totenkopf' Division, which resisted fiercely. On 11 August the 6th Soviet Mechanized Brigade, with support from the 1st Guards Tank Army, gained further ground and reached the village of Wyssokopolje and Kowjagi station to the east of it, severing the Poltava-Kharkov rail line.*

The author then wrote:

*"The SS Panzer Division 'Totenkopf' and the SS Panzer Division 'Das Reich' attacked simultaneously from the south and east against the 6th Mechanized Brigade and the 1st Tank Brigade.*

*At the same time the commander in chief of the 1st Soviet Tank Army reinforced his units in the area around Scharowka. Now in this area were: the 162nd Rifle Division, the 22nd Tank Brigade, and the 200th Tank Brigade of the 6th Tank Corps. During the course of the fighting the 18th and 29th Tank Corps and the 5th Guards Tank Army were also brought in.*

*Farther west the 6th Soviet Guards Army also went over to the attack and by the evening of 13 August was able to reach the approximate line of Schelestewo-Kolontajew. This army received orders to advance farther to the southwest, the 5th Guards Army was reinforced with heavy anti-tank weapons in the Bogoduchow area. As well further forces were sent to the 1st and 5th Soviet Guards Tank Armies in order to prevent a German breakthrough to the northwest into the rear of the 1st Soviet Tank Army and the 6th Guards Army."*

The regiment remained in its positions until 18 August and was subsequently relieved. Enemy activity had lessened. The regiment was to receive new missions within the "*Das Reich*" Division. Quite unexpectedly, at 2 PM on the same day orders arrived for the regiment to go into action in the Korotitsch combat zone.

The enemy situation there had developed as follows:

> *On the morning of 18 August the high command of the Steppe Front ordered the 53rd Army to resume the offensive in a generally south direction (west past Kharkov). Heavy fighting developed near Perressetschnaja and Gavrilovka. The armored spearheads of the 53rd Army succeeded in driving a wedge to Korotitsch. It was the intention of the Russian command to move south with the 53rd Army*

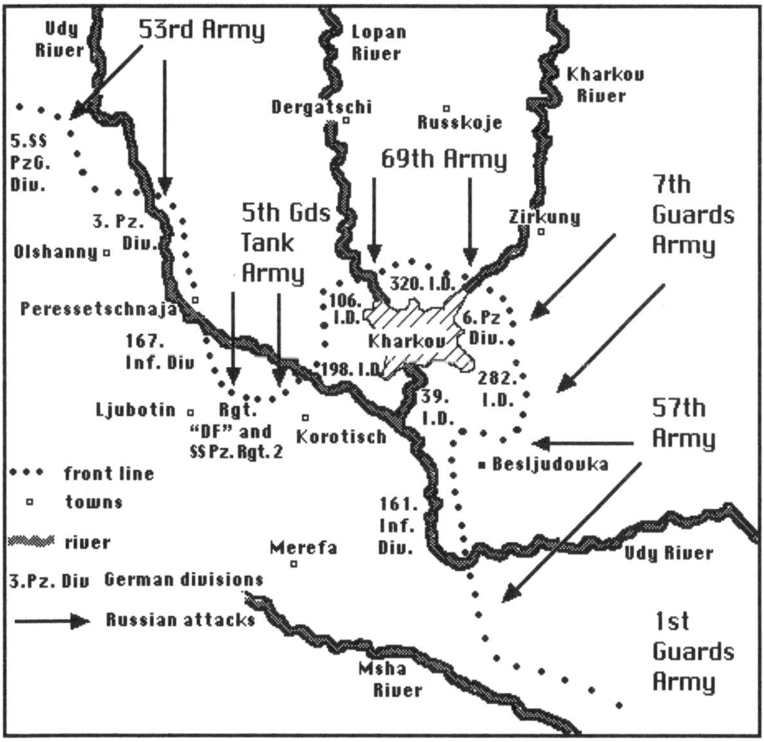


**The situation 18 August, 1943**

*west of Kharkov and drive west with the 57th Army south of Kharkov and thus complete the encirclement of the German forces in Kharkov. In order to expand the 53rd Army's initial success, beginning on 20 August the 5th Guards Tank Army was moved in with orders to take Korotitsch and thus barricade the Kharkov-Poltava rail line.*

The regiment's orders were to attack the enemy forces near Korotitsch and in view of the German troops still fighting in and around Kharkov to prevent a further breakthrough at all costs.

At this time elements of the following German units were deployed around Kharkov in a semicircle, beginning near Besljudowka: the 161st Infantry Division, the 39th Infantry Division, the 6th Panzer Division, the 282nd, 320th, 106th, 198th and 168th Infantry Divisions.

In order to reach the new combat sector the regiment had to be brought in from its previous sector 45 kilometers away. With just a few men the regimental commander hurried ahead, assuming that army infantry units were still holding in and around Korotitsch. However Korotitsch had already been abandoned by our troops. The only German soldier found there was a forward observer from an artillery battalion who was in the process of dismantling his observation post.

The small regimental detachment had reached the north end of Korotitsch when the first enemy tanks with infantry riding on them attacked. The commander went into position with his small force and himself manned a machine-gun. The enemy was halted and the forward observer was able to destroy a T 34 tank with well-directed fire.

The 15th Company arrived and with the aid of the motorcycle troops all attacks were repulsed. The enemy committed fifteen tanks, including some KV Is, followed by a battalion of infantry. Seven tanks were knocked out and the infantry were separated from their armored vehicles. The 15th Company held the position even when single tanks were able to enter the village and Red Army troops infiltrated the thin defensive lines.

The motorcycle troops' defensive struggle became increasingly difficult, heavy artillery fire pounded the main line of resistance without pause, but the 15th Company's will to hold on could not be broken. The northern part of the village remained firmly in its hands.

Finally I Battalion arrived. The enemy batteries and "Stalin Organs" once again intensified their fire and the enemy sent in wave after wave of tanks. But the "*Der Führer*" Regiment's position could not be broken.

II and III Battalions arrived and finally the required conditions existed for a counterattack. In a vigorous advance the approximately six-kilometer-wide point of penetration was closed and the main line of resistance was established at the railway embankment north of Korotitsch. The enemy moved in fresh units. The armored units of the Russian 5th Guards Army failed to achieve a breakthrough. For twelve days the regiment held its positions in this area, and wherever there was a penetration the enemy was thrown back again by immediate counterattack.

Once during these days when the enemy achieved a penetration against I Battalion, Oscha. Lainer scraped together a few men for a counterattack and mastered the critical situation. For this decisive action Oscha. Lainer of the 3rd Company was awarded the Knight's Cross.

Supported by the "*Das Reich*" Division's First and Second Panzer Battalions, the regiment fought a magnificent defensive battle. With nine Panzer IVs of his 6th Panzer Company, Hstuf. Kesten led a counterattack against sixty enemy tanks and was able to master the situation at a very critical moment. Twenty-nine enemy tanks were left knocked out and on fire. The "*Das Reich*" Division's II Panzer Battalion, which very often fought at the regiment's side, had, under the leadership of its commanding officer Stubaf. Tychsen, again provided the panzer-grenadiers with valuable help and support.

Brought in by rail, I Panzer Battalion under Stubaf. Weiß, equipped with panther tanks, also displayed great fearlessness and elan in attacks and counterattacks. Under their leadership of their commanding officer Stubaf. Kniep, the men of the assault gun battalion fought as they always did, comradely and fearless to the point of recklessness. Ostubaf. Kreutz smashed enemy tank and infantry concentrations with well-aimed fire from the batteries of the "*Das Reich*" Artillery Regiment, providing valuable assistance to the panzer-grenadiers.

But the greatest part in the "*Das Reich*" Division's success in the Korotitsch sector belonged to the panzer-grenadiers of the "*Der Führer*" Regiment. The squads and platoons held unshakably against the enemy's relentless onslaught. And if the plans of the Soviet high command failed and the enemy was denied success when the encirclement and destruction of the German troops in and around Kharkov was almost within his grasp, then it was the men of the regiment who foiled these plans!

The days in and around Korotitsch were a feat worthy to stand alongside the regiment's defensive battles at Yelnya in 1941 and Rzhev in 1942.

For his regiment's decisive actions the commanding officer, Ostubaf. Sylvester Stadler, became the 303rd German soldier to be awarded the Knight's Cross with Oak Leaves.

The *Wehrmacht* communiqué of 27 August 1943 declared:

> *"The Panzer-Grenadier Division 'Das Reich' has achieved special glory in the heavy fighting in the Kharkov area both on the attack and defense. The division alone destroyed 1,000 enemy tanks in 35 days of fighting."*

## Appendix to Part IV

Panzer-Grenadier Division "Das Reich"   Div. Command Post, 24 August 1943

Ia Ha

Division Order No. 30 (extract)

1 *Today the enemy has attacked on the right wing of the division with strong infantry and tank forces.*

*He was beaten back in the sector of the "DF" Regiment, partly in hard close-quarters combat. I express my appreciation to the regiment for its outstanding defensive success.*

*The I Panzer Battalion destroyed 53 enemy tanks on its first day in action. I express my appreciation to the battalion for this outstanding accomplishment.*

*Further strong attacks with tank support are to be expected on 24 August.*

2 *The "Das Reich" Panzer-Grenadier Division, to which the "D" Regiment has again been subordinated, is to defend the main line of resistance at present, and as soon as the enemy situation*

*permits is, in a combined attack with the 198th Infantry Division, to move the right wing forward until the angle in the corps front south of the bend in the Udy has been straightened.*

3 *New boundaries:*

*Right to the 198th Infantry Division:*

*East end of Odrynka...S of Sinolizewka.*

*Boundary line "DF" Regiment – Reconnaissance Battalion"*

*East end of Kamyschewatyja-Yvon Bogatyj-2 Kurgans, 1 km SE Arb.Hs.*

...

*Left to the 3rd Panzer Division:*

*Group of houses 800 m northwest of distillery (1 500 m S 7)-29-east end of wood northeast of 41-109*

4 *Main line of resistance:*

*North end of 12 (to be moved forward later)-north end of wood northwest of 12-27-36-182.6-wood 1 500 m south-southwest of 40-corner of wood 1 200 m east of 41.*

5 *Assignments:*

*"DF" Regiment to hold present line and prepare to advance the right wing as per special order.*

*2nd Arm.Recon.Btl. to hold present position and by holding position near 36 enable flanking tank action toward Dg. V and control of the bottom land.*

*"D" Regiment to hold and expand newly won line. In the event that the rest of the Russian group of forces ends up behind the new front near Point 182.6, they are to be destroyed on 24 August. The 2nd Panzer Regiment is to bolster the main line of resistance of the panzer-grenadiers and of 2nd Arm.Recon.Btl. by employing tanks in the front lines.*

*II Panzer Battalion to work with the "DF" Regiment and I Panzer Battalion with the Recon. Battalion and "D" Regiment.*

*Tiger company initially to "DF" Regiment. Employment with "D" Regiment anticipated in the event that enemy's point of main effort shifts.*

*An armored reserve is to be held behind the right wing so as to be able to respond to enemy breakthroughs against the neighboring unit on the right.*

*2nd Assault Gun Battalion instructed to cooperate with the 198th Infantry Division with one battery, with the "DF" Regiment with the 2nd and 3rd Batteries.*

*2nd Armored Artillery Regiment to assign II and IV Battalions and the Nebelwerfer battalion to work with the "DF" Regiment, III Battalion with the Recon. Battalion and the right wing of the "D" Regiment, I Battalion to work with the "D" Regiment.*

*Concentration of at least two battalions at a time for concentrated barrages is to be assured. One battery is to be deployed so that it can flank Dg. V from the west. Close contact is to be maintained with Artillery Commander 411. The 2nd Armored Artillery Regiment is to inform the front-line units about his battalion's observation posts in the sector. Copy of planned pauses to division.*

*2nd Armored Engineer Battalion (less 2nd Company) with a company of the "DF" Regiment under its command as counterattack reserve to mine the bottom land near Kommuna during the night and, to the extent possible, during the day and remain at the disposal of the division in the northern part of Forest 25. Report combat strength on morning of 24 August.*

*2nd Armored Flak Battalion: to regroup on 24 August in such a way that it guards the division's area of operations and can intervene in the ground fighting with the 88-mm batteries. Attempt to be made to flank along the DG V with one battery. Contact to be maintained with I./Flak 33, with which it has been instructed to cooperate.*

*2nd Armored Signals Battalion to run wire communications from new division command post to the panzer-grenadier regiments, Recon. Battalion, panzer regiment, artillery regiment, assault gun battalion, engineer battalion and flak battalion. Radio to all subordinate units.*

6 *Division command post south of 6, from noon 24 August northwest boundary of Forest 4.*

*Signed Krüger*
*Generalleutnant*

• • •

Panzer-Grenadier Division "Das Reich"
Ia Ha

Div. Command Post, 26 August 1943

Division Order No. 31 (Extract)

1 *Enemy has attacked again today. Focal point was the collective farm west of Korotitsch.*

*In an heroic struggle the men of the Panzer-Grenadier Regiment "DF", with outstanding support from elements of the 2nd Panzer Regiment and the 2nd Armored Artillery Regiment and army artillery, three times drove the enemy out of the position by counterattack. I express my special appreciation to all of the officers, noncommissioned officers and men who took part in the battle at the collective farm. They are to be made aware of this.*

2 *"Das Reich" Panzer-Grenadier Division to defend its present position, pulling out the right wing of the "DF" Regiment and replacing it with the 198th Infantry Division.*

...

5 *Relief: One battle group of the 198th Infantry Division to relieve the right wing of the "DF" Regiment during the night of 26-27 August 1943. Relief directed by regimental commander "DF." All papers concerning the position, including the mine plans, are to be handed over to the 198th Infantry Division. Timing of change of command to be determined by the regimental commander "DF." He and the new commander to report the assumption of command to division by radio or field telephone.*

*The elements of the "DF" Regiment pulled out of the line are to be positioned in the forest 2 km southwest of Korotitsch as division reserve, regrouped as per the plans of the "DF" Regiment and prepared to take over the new position on the evening of 27 August. Advance detachments to be ready by the morning of the 27th.*

*A reinforced troop from the 106th Reconnaissance Battalion is being subordinated to the "DF" Regiment to bridge the relief.*

*Relief of the right wing of the 2nd Recon.Btl. by regrouped elements of the "DF" Regiment on the evening of 27 August. The division is to submit plans for completely new regrouping, including sketch maps showing boundaries, by 08:00 on 28 August.*

*Signed Krüger*
*Generalleutnant*

• • •

Panzer-Grenadier Division "Das Reich"
Ia Ha

Div. Command Post, 26 August 1943

To
Headquarters, XI Army Corps
Ia Daily Report

1 *As in the previous days the enemy attacked the division's front with strong tank and infantry forces and attempted to force a breakthrough. There was bitter fighting all day long for the collective farm due west of Korotitsch. The collective farm changed hands three times during the course of the battle. In heavy close-quarters combat, with both sides supported by tanks, the enemy was repeatedly thrown out of the collective farm. Twenty enemy tanks were destroyed.*

*The heroic conduct of the men of the "Der Führer" Regiment is deserving of special mention. Heavily engaged almost constantly for the past four days, mainly man against man, today they made superhuman efforts in defense and attack. Today the panzer regi-*

*ment had its hardest day of combat since joining the corps. The tank battle that raged around the collective farm demanded a maximum effort.*

*Another penetration point near Kommuna was eliminated by counterattack and the former main line of resistance was restored.*

*All enemy attacks, which were made in up to battalion strength, collapsed before the division's front. According to reports received so far, thirty enemy tanks were destroyed.*

*Little own activity in the air. Enemy very active in the air. Attacks on forward line and rear area with bombs and guns.*

4 *Reconnaissance battalion 106th Infantry Division (less one reinforced troop) was positioned in the forest southwest of Korotitsch. One reinforced troop inserted into the gap between "DF" Regiment and 2nd Arm.Recon.Btl. at the west end of the collective farm and subordinated to the "DF" Regiment. It must remain in action on 27 August to bridge the relief of the "DF" Regiment.*

6 *Tank situation:*

| | | | |
|---|---|---|---|
| *Pz. III* | *4* | *Assault guns* | *16* |
| *Pz. IV* | *31* | *Anti-tank guns:* | |
| *Pz. V* | *21* | *50-mm* | *22* |
| *Pz. VI* | *6* | *75-mm* | *12* |
| *Com.Tanks* | *6* | | |

7 *Holding of Position: Relief of elements of "DF" Regiment by 108th Infantry Division and regrouping of these elements with relief of one battalion.*

8 *Sunny, warm, good visibility. Roads in good condition, very dusty.*

*The 1st General Staff Officer*
*for the division commander*
*signed SOMMER*

• • •

Panzer-Grenadier Division Div. Command Post, 17 September 1943

"Das Reich"
IIa Ob.

Order of the Day

*The Führer and Supreme Commander has awarded*
*Obersturmbannführer Stadler,*
*commander Panzer-Grenadier regiment "Der Führer"*
*the Knight's Cross of the Iron Cross with Oak Leaves as the 303rd soldier of the German Armed Services.*

*By bestowing this high decoration the Führer has acknowledged the outstanding courage and brilliant accomplishments of Obersturmbannführer Stadler and his brave "Der Führer" Panzer-Grenadier Regiment which had proved itself in countless battles and engagements in this war.*

*A special honor has been bestowed upon the regiment, as with this awarding it now has a second commander with the Oak Leaves, something of which it can be proud.*

*Moreover the entire division is proud of the acts of courage by the regiment, the most outstanding of which under its present commander took place at Kalinin, Belinichino, the Mius River line and Korotitsch.*

*It is with special pleasure that I express, on behalf of myself and all the members of the division, my congratulations to Obersturmbannführer Stadler and his brave regiment on this high decoration.*

*Signed Krüger*
*Generalleutnant*

## Fighting Withdrawal to the Dniepr near Kremenchug

On 2 September the main line of resistance was pulled back in the direction of Walki on account of the overall situation.

6-7 September: The "*Der Führer*" Regiment's strength was bolstered, making it into a very strong battle group, and it was assigned to serve as III Panzer Corps's rear guard.

In carrying out this mission the panzer-grenadiers of the "*Der Führer*" Regiment once again demonstrated their excellent fighting spirit and superior training. This planned retreat was practically a model example of "troop command" for the theme delaying resistance and retreat. Cooperation with the subordinate units functioned perfectly, a great joint effort on the part of the participating units of the "*Das Reich*" Division:

"*Der Führer*" Regiment
I Battalion, 2nd Panzer Regiment
2nd Assault Gun Battalion
2nd Armored Reconnaissance Battalion
2nd Armored Artillery Regiment including the Nebelwerfer battalion
2nd Armored Engineer Battalion

Meanwhile the 2nd Panzer Regiment and the "*Deutschland*" Regiment had been withdrawn behind the Dniepr to rest and refit.

Operations proceeded as in a "sand table exercise" from one line of resistance to the next:

Patrols of 8-wheeled armored cars from the 2nd Armored Reconnaissance Battalion, the bulk of which was employed in the infantry role, located the enemy's assembly areas. These were placed under surprise, concentric artillery barrages. Exploiting the resulting confusion, the tank crews and panzer-grenadiers of III Battalion drove into the enemy and carried through attacks with limited objectives. The success achieved in these engagements was extraordinary. Meantime the 2nd Armored Engineer Battalion had scouted and prepared a new line of resistance, which was then occupied by I and II Battalions and the main body of the 2nd Armored Reconnaissance Battalion (less the armored car company). Withdrawal of the armored elements was completed with the support of the Nebelwerfers, which laid down covering smoke. While our own armored thrusts were being carried out the artillery regiment had already scouted positions behind the new line and immediately went into firing position again. Our armored formation was taken into the new position and immediately prepared itself for the next counterattack.

This sequence repeated itself approximately every two days in almost the same rhythm and gave to all the participating men an unexpected calm and even greater self-confidence, mixed with a strong feeling of superiority over the hesitantly-pursuing Red Army, which had to accept fresh heavy blows daily and whose counterattacks always missed. This quiet self-confidence was especially valuable in the general retreat psychosis and spread to all units of the III Panzer Corps. As a result, the retreat was carried out with total order and discipline in this corps' sector.

The regiment and its subordinate units were once again honored and lauded in orders of the day and other citations. Two feats of battle by the regiment's reinforced battle group in this period are deserving of special mention:

During the fight out of the Poltava bridgehead enemy elements crossed the Dniepr ahead of our own and attacked the bridge near Poltava before the arrival of the rear guard, parts of which had been captured by the enemy.

Once again it was the gunners of the 2nd Assault Gun Battalion who determinedly halted all enemy attacks until the last vehicle of the regimental battle group had crossed the bridge. With a handful of men the battery commander of the 2nd Assault Gun Battalion fought off every attempt by the enemy to seize the bridge. In doing so Ostuf. Dr. Wolfgang Röder enabled the engineers to blow the bridge. Ostuf. Dr. Röder was decorated with the Knight's Cross for this decisive act. The engineers of the 2nd Armored Engineer Battalion blew the bridge literally at the last minute, temporarily blocking the main advance road of the Russian units. The 2nd Company of the engineer battalion under the command of Hstuf. Brosow displayed extraordinary bravery here. In one audacious night attack, engineers using flame-throwers wiped out an enemy force equivalent to two battalions that had broken through. In recognition of his actions and those of his men Hstuf. Brosow was awarded the Knight's Cross.

On 12 September the 2nd Armored Reconnaissance Battalion was in a position near Kolomak which was only semi-fortified. The terrain fell away into a hollow in the direction of the enemy and climbed toward the village of Kolomak, which sat on a hill. At approximately 2 PM there was a tank alert: 15-30-35-45-60-70-72 combat vehicles approaching, followed by masses of Russian infantry. The order issued by battalion commander

Stubaf. Weidinger: "Let the tanks roll through, engage the infantry!" He also ordered the battalion command post to allow itself to be overrun.

A radio message was sent in the clear to inform the division and at the same time request help against the tanks. The leading enemy tanks had reached the broad hollow and disappeared into its cover. In a few minutes the Soviet infantry would also disappear into this hollow – the nerves of the armored reconnaissance troops were stretched to the breaking point.

At literally the very last minute a howling noise welled up from behind and over the 2nd Armored Reconnaissance Battalion's positions: Nebelwerfer!

The salvoes fell exactly on the enemy attack lines at the precise moment when they could achieve the greatest effect. Even though the infantry had been taken out, the enemy tanks continued to roll toward the positions of the reconnaissance battalion. Muffled explosions were heard; eleven tanks had driven over mines but nevertheless kept firing. Over the telephone the commander of the 2nd Armored Reconnaissance Battalion received reports from the forward position as to when and how many enemy tanks had overrun the unit's trenches and foxholes.

On a wide front the Russian tank armada pushed on in the direction of the battalion command post. The air vibrated and the ground shook. The rattle of machine-guns rang out through the bark of enemy tank cannon. One enemy tank was already right in front of the battalion command post, aiming its gun at the entrance: the battalion staff took cover on the floor and moments of extreme tension passed. Suddenly there was a tremendous explosion and the sound of machine-gun ammunition going off! The tank was on fire, and within a short time there were fourteen T 34 tanks in flames within a small semicircle. The Russian tanks had come under accurate fire from some direction, and repeatedly one of the steel giants blew apart here and there.

A wounded Russian lieutenant crawled into the battalion command post and cried, "Everything kaput, all tanks kaput!" He was tended to and given water to drink. Clouds of black smoke rose from the burning tanks and the crews ran around their vehicles, panic stricken. The battalion dispatch rider unit disarmed and took prisoner those who were unwounded.

Suddenly our position came under machine-gun fire again – from behind! They were tanks from our division and the men in the position identified themselves as friendly by waving handkerchiefs. Hstuf. Holzer and his 1st Company of the 2nd Panzer Regiment arrived; he was amazed to find that there were still German troops in the midst of this tank graveyard and that not one foot of ground had been yielded.

Shortly before dusk the panzer company also destroyed the enemy tanks that had been disabled by mines in the forefield. Altogether there were now 72 Russian T 34 tanks sitting knocked-out before or behind our lines. Statements by prisoners revealed that the attack had been made by a Russian tank brigade, which together with a battalion of infantry was supposed to breach the German main line of resistance at this position.

The commanding officer of the 2nd Armored Reconnaissance Battalion recommended Hstuf. Friedrich Holzer for the Knight's Cross for this decisive act and the decoration was awarded on 10 December 1943. The men of the reconnaissance battalion were especially proud that they had held their position in spite of this massed tank attack and all of those who had taken part in the battle – two assault guns also took part – had their efforts acknowledged in a division order of the day. The next day the engineers completely destroyed all of the enemy tanks.

Panzer-Grenadier Division — Div. Command Post,<br>21 September 1943

"Das Reich"
Ia Ha

Division Order No. 40 (extract)

1 *The enemy has failed to seriously impede the division's withdrawal toward the Worskla River line. The initiative always remained with our troops. By establishing a bridgehead the division has made it easier for our neighbor units to disengage from the enemy.*

*The commander of the "DF" Regiment, Ostubaf. Stadler, with the troops under his command, deserve the success and the recognition for having carried out this mission with considerable losses to the enemy.*

2 *The "Das Reich" Panzer-Grenadier Division will withdraw from the Worskla position on the evening of 22 September and retire toward the K-line.*

3 *Description of the K-Line:*

*Western part of St. Ssenbary-Point 145.2 northwest of St. Ssenbary-Point 146.6-east corner of the forest 1 200 m southeast of Schewtschenki-northeast end of this forest-northeast and north end of the forest due east of Schewtschenki-north and west end of Schewtschenki-group of houses 1 400 m west of Schewtschenki-Point 134.8-group of houses 500 m south of Kalaschniki-east end of Kalaschniki.*

4 *To be deployed in the K-line:*

*Right: 425th Grenadier Regiment*
*Center: "D" Regiment*
*Left: "DF" Regiment*

*Signed Krüger*
*Generalleutnant*

The blowing of the bridge was not the end of the Battle of Poltava, however. The Red Army entered the city from the north and received help from partisans. Fierce house-to-house fighting broke out. That the German withdrawal was nevertheless able to proceed in an orderly fashion was again due to the efforts of the men of III Battalion under their commander Hstuf. Kämpfe and those of the 2nd Armored Reconnaissance Battalion under their commander Stubaf. Weidinger.

From 22 September the regiment's battle group withdrew as planned via Dobelijaki-Popovka-Brigadirovka toward Koseltschina. Forty Russian rifle divisions and twelve tank corps followed Army Group South's withdrawal toward the Dniepr. In the last days of September the enemy succeeded in moving four tank and one mechanized corps to west of the loop in the Dniepr at Kanev and dropping several parachute brigades, and in a short time these units were reinforced by eight rifle divisions and another tank corps.

As a result of this extremely threatening situation the regiment's entire battle group was pulled out of the line, rushed across the "*Generalfeldmarschall* von Reichenau Bridge" near Kremenchug and committed against the bridgehead in the Kanev area. II Battalion rushed ahead as the point unit and the 2nd Armored Reconnaissance Battalion crossed the broad river south of Kremenchug using ferries and *Schwimmwagen* amphibious vehicles.

Once again the Russian command demonstrated its speed in following up our retreating units and identifying focal points and its ability to motivate its troops to achieve outstanding feats.

On 25 September the regiment crossed the Dniepr and immediately headed north. At the same time German military and civilian columns were also crossing the river, assuming that this broad waterway together with the German troops would halt the Red Army's onslaught.

The much ballyhooed "Dniepr Position" was a bluff! There was no sign of a defense position anywhere the regiment was deployed. The river itself might present something of an obstacle – as long as it was not frozen – but improvements of natural obstacles, barbed wire emplacements, bunkers, a system of trenches and dugouts, things that would form the backbone of such a position, were almost completely missing.

In the last days of September – first days of October 1943 the regiment attacked the seven hill positions in the Dniepr loop that were already a solid part of the big Russian bridgehead. Grebeni, Juschki and Kadoma were taken from the enemy. The battalions of the regiment made further bloody sacrifices. Even detailed, well-prepared battle plans, effectively supported by the heavy weapons as always, could not change anything: the platoons and squads were steadily worn down as were the companies of the 2nd Armored Reconnaissance Battalion, which once again had to be employed in the infantry role. Near Chodoroff the reconnaissance troops and the regiment's panzer-grenadiers launched a joint attack and drove the enemy back. The commander of the reconnaissance battalion's 2nd Company, Ostuf. Walter Ehrmann, was killed in this action. The first four hill positions were taken after days of fighting, and the bridge begun by the enemy, already one third of the way across the river, now lay under accurate artillery fire.

One particularly strongly manned hill position that commanded the entire attack area proved impervious to frontal attack. The companies of II Battalion were met by fierce enemy fire when they attempted to storm the hill. The attack was tried again together with III Battalion, and the commander of 10th Company, Hstuf. Schulz, was killed. Even this joint attack, supported by heavy barrages from the 2nd Artillery Regiment, achieved no success. The enemy maintained a steady fire from snipers, machine-guns and mortars, effectively supported by artillery fire from Russian batteries which had gone into position on the east bank of the Dniepr.

It would require cunning to drive the enemy out of this position. The enemy was tied down to the front by concentrating all of the heavy machine-guns. The 15th Company then advanced through the dense undergrowth on the riverbank into the rear of the Red Army troops, climbed the approximately twenty-five-meter-high bank, broke into the enemy positions from behind under cover of twilight, achieving total surprise, and in a brief but bitter hand-to-hand struggle overpowered the enemy. The companies of II Battalion now approached frontally and occupied the hill position in the opposite direction. The daring feat by the motorcycle troops had got the regiment's attack moving again. Two more hills were taken. The enemy had one more hill in his possession, which could be seen clearly from the higher opposite bank. As our side of the river was firmly in the hands of the regiment, the enemy units there could not move. The corps and the army both urgently demanded that this last enemy position also be eliminated. In the interests of his men the commander of the "DF" Regiment rejected these demands: approximately 500 panzer-grenadiers made up the entire combat strength of the regiment's reinforced battle group. Not until the general staff officers from the army and the corps satisfied themselves of the meaninglessness of this last enemy position was the main line of resistance established by the regimental commander completely acknowledged.

9 October: Preparations in a new area against a second bridgehead in the Wesselaja-Dubrova area. In the afternoon III Battalion attacked Hill 193 east of Schtschutschinka.

12 October: The enemy achieved a breakthrough with tanks near Chodoroff. Counterattack by the regiment toward Hill 160.9 west of

Chodoroff. The 2nd Armored Reconnaissance Battalion and a panzer battalion were subordinated to the regiment for the attack. III Battalion positioned in the quartering area of Kosarowka.

10 October: Hstuf. Diekmann became regimental adjutant. All of the units subordinated to the "DF" Regiment were withdrawn and integrated into the defense line ordered by the "*Das Reich*" Division.

21 October: major attack on the "box wood." The regiment's operations officer, Ostuf. Friedrich, was wounded. The commander of the 15th Company, Ustuf. Schmager, was also put out of action. A few days later the 15th Company was disbanded and those motorcycle troops still fit for duty were combined into a platoon at the disposal of the regimental commander.

22 October: Breakthrough by enemy tanks was beaten back by a counterattack by our tanks.

26 October: The commander of the "DF" Regiment and the commander of the "*Das Reich*" Division were ordered to *Führer* Headquarters. They flew there in a courier aircraft; at *Führer* Headquarters they received the Knight's Cross with Oak Leaves from the hand of the supreme commander himself.

Subsequently *Generalleutnant* Krüger and Ostubaf. Stadler had a lengthy discussion with their supreme warlord in which they were able to describe the situation on the Eastern Front from the point of view of their units in the front lines.

They made him aware of the inadequate training of the reserves, the shortcomings in equipment and the failings in the command and pointed out the serious consequences of these errors. The two officers even went so far as to criticize the rigid holding of individual points as well as complaints and orders from *Führer* Headquarters, which often enough were out of step with the true situation at the front. They also described the catastrophic conditions and the lack of any fortifications on the Dniepr line and depicted the visible signs of disintegration of an army on the retreat. Adolf Hitler listened to their accounts with great interest.

But when, during the nightly round table session (at about 2 AM), the commander of the "*Der Führer*" Regiment openly expressed to his supreme commander the opinion that the war would be lost and all of the sacrifices by the soldiers would be in vain unless there was a fundamental change in conditions at the front soon, the shocked party around the table froze into an icy silence.

However there was no outburst from Hitler (as might have been expected). Instead he ordered the two commanders to make themselves available again the following day so that the Chief of the General Staff, *Generaloberst* Zeitzler, and the Commander in Chief of the *Luftwaffe*, *Reichsmarschall* Göring, might hear this unvarnished report personally. He insisted that the two officers speak as openly in the presence of the two men in question as they had to him.

The next day the previous evening's theme was discussed again in the presence of *Generaloberst* Zeitzler, the Chief of Staff of the *Luftwaffe* and *General* Schmundt.

It can be stated here without reservation that the fortification plans for the Dniepr position in *Führer* Headquarters in no way corresponded to the truth.

The two commanders knew from personal, on the spot experience that the anti-tank ditches and fortified positions at focal points of the defense marked on the map did not exist at all. Stadler and Krüger were also able to point out further inaccuracies in the reports received by *Führer* Headquarters concerning the Dniepr position. Even *General* Zeitzler did not hesitate to point out to Adolf Hitler several failures that had resulted from his direct intervention.

Although *Generalleutnant* Krüger and *Obersturmbannführer* Stadler were pleased to be able to give their supreme commander such an open and frank description of the situation on the Eastern Front, they were depressed to see how little of the actual fighting was known here and that they had no idea of the efforts and the state of mind of the overburdened soldiers, who were constantly in contact with the enemy.

The two commanders returned to their units full of worry for the future. An order of the day was issued in which the men of the division were given a brief account of the visit to *Führer* Headquarters.

For approximately ten days the regiment remained in the now well-fortified positions near Wessalaja-Dubrova and fought off the attacking enemy.

The *Wehrmacht* communiqué of 6 November declared:

*"The "Das Reich" Panzer-Grenadier Division has destroyed its 2,000th enemy tank since the start of the year. The division's 2nd Panzer Regiment has had a major of this success. For the battles at the side of the panzer-grenadiers, the commander of the 2nd Panzer Regiment, Ostubaf. Von Reitzenstein received the Knight's Cross, as did Ostuf. Boska of II Battalion, Ustuf. Mühleck of I Battalion, and for his courageous action near Chodoroff Hscha. Simke of II Panzer Battalion 2. The efforts of the artillery during the fighting retreat and especially at the Dniepr bridgeheads were acknowledged by the award of the Knight's Cross to Ostuf. Gast of I Battalion."*

## Offense and Defense in the Zhitomir Area 1943

On 7 November the regiment was relieved by infantry units of the 8th Army, and on orders from Army Group South the "*Das Reich*" Division was sent on a forced march in the direction of Zhitomir.

The situation of the 4th Panzer Army deployed there had become extremely threatening. The army's infantry divisions, almost all of which had been reduced to the strength of regiments, were forced to yield before the superior pressure from the enemy, and the two panzer divisions in reserve were too weak to parry the enemy assault. Kiev was evacuated after heavy fighting, otherwise the VII Army Corps fighting there would have been encircled. Not until 50 kilometers south of the city was it possible to halt the enemy. The 10th Panzer-Grenadier Division fought bravely and steadfastly there. The important rail junction of Fastov was lost, the XIII Army Corps was forced back to Zhitomir, and farther north the enemy reached Korosten. To bolster the 4th Panzer Army's front, Army Group South moved in the 3rd and 10th Panzer Divisions, the 20th Panzer-Grenadier Division, the "*Das Reich*" Division and the 198th Infantry Division at the cost of weakening the 8th Army.

A feat by the armored reconnaissance battalion must be described here, because it obtained vital intelligence information for the German command.

Oscha. Hans Siegling received orders from the division to take three 8-wheeled armored cars and drive back into the areas abandoned the previous day and to determine which villages had been occupied by the enemy. Oscha. Siegling and his armored vehicles drove at high speed into a village that had already been reached by a Russian armored spearhead. Taking advantage of the enemy's bewilderment, the three armored cars raced through the village and they managed to escape. Continuing their sortie, the armored patrol came upon a seemingly endless column of Russian heavy tanks and vehicles of every type on a major road. Oscha. Siegling coolly directed the enemy vehicles to the side and roared past the column at high speed. The radio operator steadily transmitted Siegling's observations and position reports to the division. Not a shot was fired.

The patrol spent the night hours well hidden in a haystack. During the hours of darkness Oscha. Siegling carried out further scouting with a foot patrol. He almost missed his own well-camouflaged armored cars when returning in the morning twilight! They were just about to set off on a new sortie, assuming that their commander had fallen into enemy hands. One vehicle developed engine trouble. This attracted the enemy's attention and caused him to give chase. The vehicle was started at the last minute. The chase began.

Siegling called a halt beyond a stream bed and all the fuel that could be spared was poured over the wooden bridge. As the vehicles drove away an incendiary shell was fired, igniting the gasoline. The bridge was soon in flames. This brought the first pursuit to a temporary halt. After a wild zigzag drive, which tested the drivers to the limit, Siegling and his men reached the German lines safe and sound.

A steady stream of radio traffic from the "*Das Reich*" Division provided the corps and army commands with valuable information for assessing the overall situation. Oscha. Siegling was received by the commanding general of the XXXXVIII Panzer Corps and was subsequently sent on to the commander in chief of the 4th Panzer Army. On 2 December 1943 Siegling received the Knight's Cross.

• • •

In the Fastov-Belaya Tserkov area a Tiger company of the 25th Panzer Division attached itself to the regiment; the company had just detrained, and because of the confused situation it was unable to obtain combat orders from its own division.

In the new assembly area II Battalion received instructions to establish a new line of security. A motorcycle patrol reported the southern part of the village of Kasawerowsk still free of the enemy. The enemy entered the village at the same time as II Battalion. The battalion commander, Hstuf. Herbert Schulze, sent his men to the attack from off the move. This daring thrust succeeded. The enemy was defeated, and during the course of the tough, night close-quarters battle for the houses of the village the battalion captured a Russian anti-aircraft battalion, 20 trucks, 200 prisoners and a huge quantity of war materiel.

Further rapid follow-up attacks resulted in contact being established with the 7th Panzer Division east of Zhitomir. The breakthrough to the west by the Soviet units was halted here for the time being.

Hstuf. Herbert Schulze received the Knight's Cross for this decisive deed. The rapid advance by the "DF" Regiment created the conditions necessary for Army Group South to launch its planned counterattack with the recently arrived XXXXVII Panzer Corps (*General* von Eberbach). The commanding general expressed his boundless appreciation for the bravery and nerve displayed by the men of the regiment.

As part of XXXXVII Panzer Corps, on 15 November the regiment went to the counterattack with various division units. Zhitomir was retaken during the course of this fighting and effective help was given to XIII Corps. Korosten was also recaptured.

The commander in chief of the 4th Panzer Army, *Generaloberst* Hoth, who was much loved by the men of the regiment, was relieved and his place was taken by *General* Rauss.

During the regiment's successful counterattack the panzer-grenadiers of the 25th Panzer Division fought on the unit's immediate right. This unit had been reformed in the west under *General* von Schell; when the surprise order to go into action arrived, the regiments and division units were just in the process of converting to German weapons and equipment. The division had originally been earmarked for employment in Africa. The division was hastily thrown into the pitiless eastern war and the still inexperienced units were forced to pay a high price in blood.

In the Negrebowka area the attack by the exhausted "DF" Regiment came to a halt for the time being. The panzer-grenadiers pulled themselves together again, and with the last armored troop carriers and flame-thrower tanks of III Battalion the village was taken and a line of security was established in which the 2nd Armored Reconnaissance Battalion took up position with the "DF" Regiment.

The regiment's main line of resistance, nine kilometers wide, was held, but it required a maximum effort. At this time the combat strength of the entire regiment was barely 300 men! The 2nd Armored Reconnaissance Battalion had a combat strength of forty-two men, including the officers. It had been ordered to hold a section of the main line of resistance two and a half kilometers wide! It is clear that in this situation the command had to ask the utmost of the panzer-grenadiers and reconnaissance troops.

The position was held, but luck played almost as great a role as the bravery of the small force. On one occasion an enemy force in battalion strength was charging the regiment command post when suddenly an anti-aircraft machine-gun platoon of the *Luftwaffe* happened by. Displaying exemplary comradeship, the *Luftwaffe* unit intervened and beat off the attack. The squads and platoons counterattacked immediately and brought in 300 Prisoners.

I Battalion had to be disbanded. A fresh but inexperienced battalion under Hstuf. Dr. Sayle was assigned to the regiment and took up position in the main line of resistance.

The enemy broke through at the boundary between the 2nd Armored Reconnaissance Battalion and the "DF" Regiment. The regiment's last reserve, two armored troop carriers and two flame-thrower tanks, rushed to the air of the embattled reconnaissance troops. At the same time the Russians launched a frontal attack and achieved a penetration. The commander of the 2nd Armored Reconnaissance Battalion assembled his last eight men and with them launched a counterattack. The situation was mastered once again.

The men were now simply at the end of their rope, exhausted and burnt out from the months-long fighting withdrawal, from seeing action at all the hot spots in all the big battles. The time when the brave men of the "DF" Regiment were simply not up to the tremendous demands, when they could no longer withstand the constant attacks by the Russians, seemed to have arrived. Nevertheless they kept a stiff upper lip and did their duty wherever they were sent.

The turning point came at the very last moment: the "*Leibstandarte*" Panzer Division, just arrived from Italy, was thrown into the fighting at Zhitomir and its tanks and assault guns created the necessary breathing space.

In the days before Christmas 1943 the "DF" Regiment and the 2nd Armored Reconnaissance Battalion were relieved by the panzer-grenadier regiments of the LAH. For their decisive actions and those of their courageous panzer-grenadiers during the retreat and in the Zhitomir battle zone, the commanders of III Battalion (Hstuf. Helmut Kämpfe) and I Battalion (Hstuf. Alfred Lex) were awarded the Knight's Cross. Now all of the regiment's battalion commanders wore the Knight's Cross.

Several months later the sacrificial actions of the 2nd Armored Reconnaissance Battalion in the position in the Negrebowka area were acknowledged by the awarding of the Knight's Cross to the unit's commander, Stubaf. Otto Weidinger.

The remnants of the "DF" Regiment and the 2nd Armored Reconnaissance Battalion were subsequently put aboard trains and on 24 December they departed for the training grounds at Stablack, East Prussia for a rest and refit. This was the best Christmas present of all to the sorely-tried soldiers.

## The SS Armored Battle Group "*Das Reich*" 17 December 1943 to 2 May 1944[8]

On 13 December 1943 it was announced that the "*Das Reich*" Panzer Division, which had been reduced to a fraction of its fighting strength by the wearing, months-long fighting withdrawal, was being relieved from its sector north of Zhitomir and transferred to the training grounds at Stablack in East Prussia, where it was to be brought back up to strength in preparation for new assignments.

From all of the division's remaining combat ready elements was formed the Armored Battle Group "*Das Reich*", which remained on the Eastern Front and was deployed within the army. Ostubaf. Sommer, the former Ia of the "*Das Reich*" Division (General Staff *Oberstleutnant*), was placed in command of the battle group.

The battle group's composition was as follows:

Panzer-Grenadier Regiment "*Das Reich*" under Stubaf. Hans Bissinger with I Battalion "D" under Ustuf. Hesselmann and II Battalion "DF" under Hstuf. Alfred Lex – one heavy infantry company with remaining elements of 13th and 14th Companies "D", 13th and 14th Companies "DF", one platoon from 3rd Battery, 2nd Flak Battalion (2 quadruple anti-aircraft guns) and one anti-tank platoon from 2nd Armored Reconnaissance Battalion under Ostuf. Seeger – one engineer company (two platoons from 16th Company "D" and one platoon from 16th Company "DF" under Hstuf. Schmelzer – two panzer companies from the 2nd Panzer Regiment – one artillery battalion (1 battery of heavy field howitzers, 150-mm, and two batteries of light field howitzers, 105-mm) – one reinforced reconnaissance company (one armored car platoon, two motorcycle platoons, one heavy motorcycle platoon) under Hstuf. Wulf – one rocket battalion – one flak battery – one-half of a radio company – one-half of a field telephone company – one medical company and appropriate supply units from the division. The battle group occupied positions in the Guta-Sabelotschkaja area and made preparations to spend the winter there. The battle group command post was located in Sabelotschkaja.

The "*Das Reich*" Division was loaded aboard trains for transport to the west. Also attached to the battle group was a mixed army regiment consisting of the 7th Armored Reconnaissance Battalion, 25th Armored Reconnaissance Battalion and an armored engineer battalion. Designated a special purpose regiment, it was initially led by Stubaf. Weiss, however on the same day he handed it over to the former commander of the 2nd Armored Reconnaissance Battalion, Stubaf. Otto Weidinger. Regimental adjutant was the former adjutant of the 2nd Armored Reconnaissance Battalion, Ostuf. Hans Prix. The German positions lay in a large semicircle around Zhitomir, east of the city. The northern part of the positions with front facing north was held by Battle Group "*Das Reich*."

These positions were supposed to be held for the winter at all costs. They had already been partly outfitted with earth bunkers and it had also been possible to partly house the battle group command post in earth bunkers. Things were to turn out differently, however.

The battle group was under the command of the LIX Army Corps under *General* Schulz.

## Defensive Battles East of Zhitomir

19 December 1943: An attack with limited objectives was launched to the north in order to improve our positions, parts of which lay in heavily wooded terrain. The attack was carried out with the Panzer-Grenadier Regiment "*Das Reich*" on the right and the Special Purpose Regiment on the left. The focal point of the attack was the "Lex Battalion." Hstuf. Dr. Sayle had meanwhile taken over I Battalion "*Deutschland*." The reinforced armored reconnaissance company under Hstuf. Wulf supported the attack through motorized advances on the battle group's left wing. With support from the heavy weapons the attack made good initial progress, however it later bogged down against strong enemy resistance and was called to a halt in significantly better positions. These were held in the coming days.

24 December 1943 – Christmas Eve: The Christmas gifts for the troops arrived at 5:30 AM, still in time for Christmas, and were placed in a shed in a forest glade.

At about 6 AM Russian artillery and mortars suddenly opened fire on all of the battle group's positions. This was part of a major assault on the entire front around Zhitomir. The enemy's objective was obviously to overpower the bridgehead-like German positions east of Zhitomir and take the city.

The enemy went to the attack at approximately 6:30 AM. That morning the Russians broke through almost to the battle group command post and took up position in a shed in the forest glade. The heavy field howitzer battery had to place the shed under direct fire, destroying their own Christmas presents as a result. A fine beginning to Christmas Eve!

By 9 AM the Russians had already broken into the battle group's positions at various places in the difficult wooded terrain, however these incursions were sealed off in makeshift fashion.

The men of the battle group were engaged in heavy defensive fighting all day long. Local enemy penetrations alternated with counterattacks by us, some of which involved close combat. The 25th Armored Reconnaissance Battalion's "Caesar cars" (armored troop carriers with 37-mm anti-aircraft guns) and our own heavy infantry weapons performed magnificently.

On account of the threat to our own men, the artillery could not intervene with barrage fire in this complex wooded terrain as our main line of resistance could no longer be made out. Instead it engaged enemy forces that had broken through with direct fire.

Contact with the battle group command post was cut several times, but each time it was restored through the exemplary efforts of our signals personnel. In the late afternoon the new commander of the Special Purpose Regiment, Stubaf. Weidinger, was informed by the battle group commander that the enemy was achieving serious penetrations all along the front east of Zhitomir and that the battle group was to pull back to the west during the night, but that the main road west of Zhitomir was already in Russian hands, meaning that a retreat south then along the main road was no longer possible. The last avenue of retreat was across the bridgeless Teterew.

The Special Purpose Regiment's sole reserve was the battle group's engineer company under Ostuf. Schmelzer, which had already been employed several times in counterattacks.

Toward evening Ostuf. Schmelzer reported to the commander of the Special Purpose Regiment that he had begun building a bridge across the Teterew that morning but had been forced to abandon the work as a result of the Russian attack. At his suggestion the commander dispensed with his last combat reserve and gave the order for the engineer company to leave at once and proceed with construction of the Teterew bridge with all possible speed. This order was subsequently approved by the battle group commander. At about 11 PM the signals officer Ustuf. Hentschel reported to Stubaf. Weidinger with one of the battle group's radio vehicles.

The positions were held until far into the night. Casualties were very heavy. Meantime the order to withdraw had arrived, and at about 11 PM the battle group left the positions and pulled back in the direction of Teterew.

## The Battle of the Teterew Crossing

Meantime the engineers under Ostuf. Heinrich Schmelzer had completed a major achievement: at great personal risk they built a sixty-meter-long bridge under heavy enemy artillery fire in pouring rain. The men of the train were put to work on the bridge as were all of those troops that had reached the Teterew and were waiting to cross. As per orders the bridge was rigged for demolition.

Ostuf. Schmelzer was able to report the completion of the bridge at 2:30 AM. By dawn all of the battle group's vehicles and a large part of the *Wehrmacht* units deployed in the battle zone east of Zhitomir had been fed across the bridge, thus escaping destruction at the hands of the enemy.

The Russians reached the bridge site just as the last units were preparing to cross the bridge. The men of the 16th Company defended the bridge until the last minute. Both regimental headquarters had crossed the bridge at about 3 AM. As well as the Russian mortar fire on both bridgeheads there could be heard Russian battle cries followed by the "Hurrah!" of our magnificent engineers, who counterattacked repeatedly.

The battle at the bridge became more and more dramatic. Amid the increasingly heavy mortar fire the unpleasant sound of Russian submachine-guns could be heard more frequently, a sign that the enemy infantry was already quite near. It was especially difficult to determine if and when the last German elements had crossed the bridge, therefore the bridge was kept open for stragglers for a long time.

The commander of the Special Purpose Regiment, who was responsible for blowing the bridge, issued the order to do so at 6 AM. Everyone waited tensely for the explosion, nerves were stretched to the breaking point – but there was no explosion! Then Ostuf. Schmelzer reported that an assault gun had destroyed the safety fuse of the electrical detonation system, which had been placed at the side of the road; but as a precaution he had also laid a primacord for manual detonation.

The commanding officer called the company commander imploringly: "Schmelzer, the bridge has to go up at all costs!" Anxious minutes passed, with the Russians drawing nearer all the while. By now the mortar and submachine-gun fire had become continuous. Then finally there was a huge explosion and the bridge was blown into the air. This was followed by moments of deathly silence. Only gradually did the Russian fire set in again; however, their pursuit had been halted for the time being.

Later, on the recommendation of the commander responsible for the destruction of the bridge, Ostuf. Schmelzer was awarded the Knight's Cross for his decisive action, as a result of which all of the battle group's and many army vehicles were saved from destruction and the lives of many men were saved. At the same time Schmelzer received his long overdue promotion to *Hauptsturmführer*.

## Defensive Battles North of Zhitomir

25 December 1943 – Christmas Day: Ostuf. Prix, the former adjutant of the Special Purpose Regiment, assumed command of the 25th Armored Reconnaissance Battalion (an army unit) after its commander was wounded.

The regiment withdrew toward Mininy. The Russians followed during the morning and in the evening attacked the village.

26 December: The village was held through the night and the following day. As contact had been lost with the Panzer-Grenadier Regiment "DF" on the right, the commander personally led a sortie by two cars in an attempt to establish contact with their neighbor on the right. After driving several kilometers, during which time no friendly troops were found, the vehicles turned around. A few minutes later the commander's car was fired on by a Russian machine-gun in bushes at the side of the road from point blank range. The driver cried out and the car stopped, its engine hit. In the next seconds both men jumped from the car. Fortunately the driver had received only a minor wound in the foot. The pair

zigzagged back along the road, hindered by the driver's wound. The second vehicle had driven back to the nearest rise. From there the crew provided covering fire for the pair with submachine-guns. They subsequently drove back together to the command post.

27 December: As a result of the aggressive pursuit by the Russians, especially on the battle group's left wing, the withdrawal had to be continued during the night in heavy snow showers and thick mud.

During the night of 28 December the retreat continued into the area around Studenzia. There the order reached the commander of the Special Purpose Regiment to disband the regiment and to send the battalions back to their divisions. He took over the Panzer-Grenadier Regiment "DF" in the battle group, while Stubaf. Bissinger was attached to the battle group headquarters as Ia. The regimental adjutant was Ostuf. Gerwig. *Oberführer* Heinz Lammerding took over the armored battle group, Stubaf. (Gen.Staff *Major*) Albert Stückler became Ia of the battle group. The battle group's former commander, Ostubaf. (Gen.Staff *Oberstleutnant*) Sommer, became chief of staff to *Generalleutnant* Krüger, who was already on his way west.

29 December: Studenzia was held, largely thanks to the outstanding support from our artillery. The attacking enemy suffered heavy losses.

Ostuf. Prix, who had become free as a result of the disbanding of the Special Purpose Regiment, was finally able to depart for Stablack where he was badly needed for the reformation of the 2nd Armored Reconnaissance Battalion.

## Fighting Withdrawal Southwest of Zhitomir

30 December: During the night the battle group withdrew through Zhitomir in snow and ice and on the main road via Zwiahel into the Davidovka area.

The regiment received orders to withdraw further in the early afternoon. The Russians were now only a short distance away from our positions. The commanding officer asked the battle group commander to delay disengaging from the enemy until after dark, however on account of

*SS-Oberführer Georg Keppler, the first commander of Regiment "Der Fuhrer." Awarded the Knight's Cross on August 15, 1940, as regimental commander, he ended the war as a Waffen-SS corps commander with the rank of SS-Obergruppenführer.*

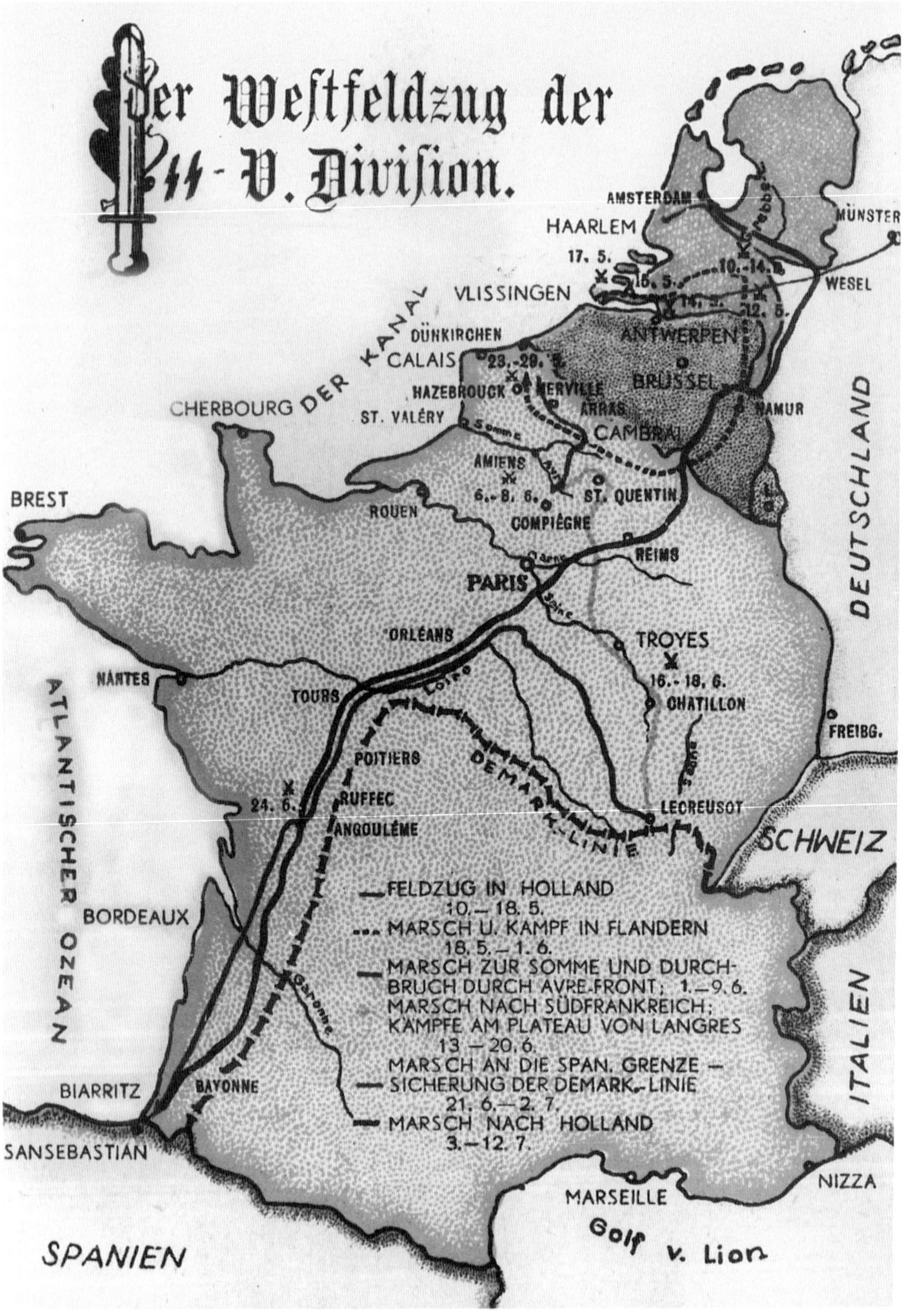


*The 1940 campaign in France was the first combat for "Der Führer" and the SS-V. Division. A wartime postcard shows the battles and movements of the offensive.*

*One of the first "Der Führer" Knight's Cross holders was Ludwig Kepplinger who was awarded the decoration on September 4, 1940. At the time of the actions resulting in the award he was an SS-Hauptscharführer with the 11th Company while in the photo he is newly promoted to SS-Untersturmführer. Kepplinger is shown above wearing a helmet on the day of the formal award presentation. Georg Keppler (with glasses wearing his Knight's Cross) and divisional commander Paul Hausser are also shown.*

*Ludwig Kepplinger after his award of the Knight's Cross and the wartime art postcard issued after the event.*

*Georg Keppler (left) with 2nd Battalion commander Heinz Harmel. Harmel later commanded Regiment "Deutschland, ending the war as an SS-Brigadeführer in command of the 10.SS-Panzer-Division "Frundsberg." He won the Knight's Cross with Oakleaves and Swords as well as the German Cross in Gold.*

*Motorcycle infantry at the start of the Russian campaign during the summer of 1941 are seen in the upper photo. Below are Otto Kumm (nearest camera) and Georg Keppler in the opening weeks of the fighting in Russia with members of the "Der Führer" regimental staff.*

Heinz Harmel (commander 2nd Battalion) explains a tactical situation while standing in his command car talking to Otto Kumm (left). In the lower photo, only the command flag tells that this ravine is, for the moment, regimental headquarters during the fast pace of combat in Russia.

*Otto Kumm as an SS-Obersturmbannführer wearing the Knight's Cross. He became the second commander of "Der Führer" and as regimental commander also won the Oakleaves. Later commander of the "Prinz Eugen" Division, he won the Swords for leadership of that unit. Kumm ended the war as an SS-Brigadeführer in command of the 1.SS-Panzer-Division "Leibstandarte" and was also awarded the German Cross in Gold for bravery. A highly respected leader and commander.*

*Sylvester Stadler as an SS-Sturmbannführer. He became the third commander of Regiment "Der Führer" when he succeeded Otto Kumm. Awarded the German Cross in Gold and Knight's Cross with Oakleaves with the regiment, he ended the war as an SS-Brigadeführer. His last command was of the 9.SS-Panzer-Division "Hohenstaufen" for which he was awarded the Swords.*

*From left discussing the tactical situation in Russia during 1943 are Karl Kreutz (later "Das Reich" commander and winner of the Oakleaves to the Knight's Cross, at the time of photo leader of the artillery regiment), Heinz Harmel (then commander of Regiment "Deutschland"), Walter Krüger (commander of "Das Reich" and Swords holder) and Sylvester Stadler (then commander of Regiment "Der Führer"). Below is Otto Weidinger (2nd from left) and Georg Seegerer (3rd from left) in Austria during the spring of 1945 with officers of "Der Führer."*

*Sylvester Stadler is shown above (left) with Paul Hausser in Russia. In the lower photo Stadler is being awarded the Oakleaves by Hitler. On the left is divisional commander Walter Krüger waiting to be awarded the same decoration and on the far right is Heinrich Himmler.*

*Otto Kumm is followed by Vincenz Kaiser while inspecting troops of "Der Führer" during reformation in 1942. Below is "Das Reich" commander Walter Krüger congratulating SS-Oberscharführer Josef Lainer on his award of the Knight's Cross (October 8, 1943) for actions as a platoon leader with the 1st Company of "Der Führer." Lainer was also awarded the Close Combat Clasp in Gold.*

*The pace in Russia was slowed by rain, mud and bitter winters.*

*A sign showing the distance to Vienna during the assault on Moscow in 1941. In the lower photo is a view of Charkow during the winter of 1943.*

*Excellent training brought success at the start of the first Russian campaign. A camouflaged armored personnel carrier moves towards the front during 1944.*

*Otto Kumm (left) with Vincenz Kaiser. Both men wear the Knight's Cross and German Cross in Gold. Kaiser was killed in 1944 as an Oakleaves winner and regimental commander with the 17.SS-Panzer-Grenadier-Division "Götz von Berlichingen." Below is the winter of 1941/1942 in Russia.*

*SS-Sturmbannführer Vincenz Kaiser wearing upper sleeve decorations for single handed destruction of enemy tanks. The lower sleeve insignia was worn by all members of "Der Führer."*

*Sylvester Stadler as an SS-Obersturmbannführer after being awarded the Knight's Cross (April 6, 1943) as commander of the 2nd Battalion.*

*Paul Hausser, the first commander of the first Waffen SS division formed and first SS corps commander. He commanded an Army Group in 1944, ending the war as an SS-Oberst-Gruppenführer and won the Knight's Cross with Oakleaves and Swords. The creator and primary influence on development of the Waffen-SS, he is respected and admired by troops of all ranks who affectionately call him "Papa Hausser."*

*Otto Weidinger, the fourth and last officer to command Regiment "Der Führer." He won the Knight's Cross and German Cross in Gold for actions as reconnaissance detachment commander with "Das Reich." After commanding Battle Group "Das Reich" in Russia, as leader of Regiment "Der Führer" he was awarded the Oakleaves in 1944 and the Swords to the Knight's Cross in 1945.*

*Above are, from left, are Walter Krüger, Josef Lainer and Sylvester Stadler in Russia during the early winter of 1943 after award of the Knight's Cross to Lainer. Below is Otto Weidinger (left) talking with divisional commander Heinz Lammerding after the return of Battle Group "Das Reich" from Russia in 1944.*

*"Der Führer" headquarters for the Jelnja battles during the first Russian campaign. Otto Kumm is 2nd from left and 3rd from left is Hans Lingner (German Cross in Gold). Regimental adjutant Friedrich Holzer, shown later in the war assigned to the Panzer Regiment wearing the Knight's Cross and German Cross in Gold in black armored troops uniform.*

*Herbert Schulze, awarded the Knight's Cross and German Cross in Gold as commander of the 2nd Battalion.*

*Alfred Lex, awarded the Knight's Cross as commander of 2nd Battalion. He was killed in Russia serving with Battle Group "Das Reich" in 1944 and also won the German Cross in Gold.*

*Joachim Krüger, awarded the Knight's Cross on June 24, 1944, after being killed as an SS-Untersturmführer serving with the 10th Company.*

*From left are Sylvester Stadler, Heinz Lammerding and Otto Weidinger in April 1944.*

*SS-Sturmbannführer Helmut Kämpfe, the much decorated commander of the 3rd Battalion. Awarded the Knight's Cross and German Cross in Gold, he was killed by partisans in June 1944.*

*SS-Sturmbannführer Otto Weidinger decorating men of "Der Führer." With him holding the decorations is regimental adjutant Georg Seegerer (German Cross in Gold). Below in early September 1944 is divisional commander Otto Baum (4th from left and winner of the Knight's Cross with Oakleaves and Swords) after awarding the Knight's Cross to "Der Führer" battalion commander Heinz Werner (5th from left). Beside Werner is Otto Weidinger.*

*SS-Sturmbannführer Heinz Werner, holder of the Knight's Cross with Oakleaves and German Cross in Gold. He ended the war commanding the 3rd Battalion of "Der Führer" and also won the Close Combat Clasp in Gold.*

*In Austria during 1945 are Georg Seegerer (left) and Otto Weidinger (2nd from left). In the lower photo is Otto Weidinger (left) with General der Infanterie Rudolf von Bünau, Battle Commander in Vienna during 1945 and holder of the Knight's Cross with Oakleaves.*

*During the bitter defensive combats at Rshew, "Der Führer" was almost totally destroyed. Only 35 men remained combat ready after the battles. But all assigned positions had been held.*

*The combats to capture Kharkov (above) in early 1943 were among the hardest fought by any Waffen-SS unit throughout the war. After the success, numerous decorations were presented. Below, "Das Reich" commander Walter Krüger (left) presents one Oakleaves and five awards of the Knight's Cross in April 1943. From left are Otto Kumm ("Der Führer" commander and first Oakleaves winner of the division), Christian Tychsen (Panzer Regiment commander, later killed in Normandy as divisional commander and awarded the Oakleaves), Karl-Heinz Worthmann (platoon leader in the 6th Panzer Company, later an Oakleaves winner who was killed in July 1943), Sylvester Stadler (2nd Battalion "Der Führer" commander), Vincenz Kaiser (3rd Battalion "Der Führer" commander), Hans Weiss (commander of the "Das Reich" Reconnaissance Detachment).*

the overall situation the idea was rejected. In this situation Hstuf. Persch, newly transferred to the battle group, took over I Battalion "D."

The withdrawal movement began while it was still light. The Russian tanks immediately tried to follow. They were repulsed by our own tanks, however. One Russian tank was knocked out. The Russian infantry attacked immediately and the situation became critical. Hstuf. Götz Persch's takeover of I Battalion "D" was complicated as a result, but by evening he had the battalion firmly in hand in spite of the withdrawal movement in the difficult, complex terrain and subsequently proved to be an excellent commander.

31 December: The enemy attacked again with tanks, once again without success. Several Russian tanks were knocked out.

On this New Year's Eve the commanding officer received word that Ostuf. Prix had been killed by tank fire while on a scouting mission in the rear area in search of broken-through enemy tanks. This represented a irreplaceable loss in military and human terms for the 2nd Armored Reconnaissance Battalion and for the regimental commander. Prix was the ideal adjutant and company commander for a reconnaissance battalion. The men of the army's 25th Reconnaissance Battalion, which Prix had commanded during his last days, were also enthusiastic about their young, aggressive battalion commander, whose ability, vim and his irrepressible humor were an inspiration to them all.

During the night of 31 December – 1 January the battle group was relieved by the 208th Infantry Division. Meantime the enemy had resumed his pursuit. Enemy artillery fire began. We marched through forests and frozen marshes to Ulyanovka.

1 January 1944: After a large-scale Russian attack at dawn the enemy broke through our left neighbor. As a result, after fighting off the attack on our own position we were forced to withdraw via Buki to Novo Rudnija.

The big picture was as follows: the Russians were advancing west and southwest with superior forces, obviously with the aim of closing the pocket around the German 1st Army in the southern sector of the Eastern Front. Russian spearheads had already passed north and south of us and advanced far to the west. Our own forces were withdrawing to the southwest and south before this superior foe.

2 January: The enemy followed up during the night and continued to attack with strong forces. The battle group was ordered to withdraw and go around the enemy penetration west of us.

After a sixteen-kilometer march through icy, snow-covered forest lanes and trackless terrain, which took us twelve hours, new positions were occupied in the Drygloff area with front facing north.

For two days the Flemish "*Langemarck*" Brigade had been fighting a fierce, costly defensive battle against a far superior enemy in the Jambol area to our west and had achieved a great defensive success. This prevented an enemy breakthrough to the south and another attempt to encircle the Armored Battle Group "*Das Reich*."

As the battle group had no contact to the left or right, the enemy succeeded in driving past our positions further to the south and southwest.

The Lex and Persch battalions were heavily engaged in defensive fighting with support from our artillery, assault guns, self-propelled guns and anti-aircraft machine-guns. The battle group's position had again become untenable and it had to withdraw again.

This fighting withdrawal, which led through the villages of Olzanka, Dazki, Burkowzy, Lichosellka and Nossiwki, lasted until 10 January. It was an especially arduous trek.

After the onset of darkness the troops disengaged from the enemy and marched all night, at times off the roads, through snow-covered terrain with drifts often knee deep, so as to occupy new positions at dawn. After a few hours the enemy appeared again. The positions had to be held all day long, often at the cost of heavy casualties, until, as per orders, a new withdrawal movement began during the coming night. This style of "fight by day, march by night" operations placed a tremendous strain on the men. They were dead tired, but every one of them knew that anyone who was left behind was lost.

At this point a word about the unit medical officers and the entire medical personnel, who, often at great personal risk, recovered the wounded, provided medical care and ensured that they were brought along with the last elements of the fighting troops, usually in *panye* wagons.

During the battle group's entire existence not a single case is known of wounded being left to the enemy. Great confidence in the medical personnel helped ensure that the fighting spirit of the troops remained high to the very last day of operations. What personal bravery, what medical skill under primitive conditions, and what improvisational ability was shown by these doctors and their medical personnel and the company medics in these months-long battles and retreats!

13 January: No significant fighting. The battle group had occupied positions on both sides of Nossiwki in a commanding sector. There was magnificent winter weather with a heavy layer of snow and frost.

## Counterattack West of Berdichev

14 January: The armored battle group of the "LAH" under the command of Stubaf. Jochen Peiper joined us. Together with it the next day our battle group launched a limited attack against the enemy in the Krasnopol-Molotschki-Stettkowzki area. The attack made good initial progress. The reinforced reconnaissance company under Hstuf. Heinrich Wulf reached and took the village of Molotschki. Peiper's armored vehicles (his armored battle group had been reduced to just a few tanks) drove far in the direction of Krasnopol until, down to just three tanks including Peiper's, they were halted before a continuous anti-tank front in the Krasnopol area.

The importance of this attack was underlined by the fact that after the attack was halted two army general staff officers went forward to Peiper to make sure that the attack was continued. However, when they saw for themselves the last three tanks and experienced the accurate anti-tank fire, demands for a resumption of the attack were dropped.

While driving to the armored reconnaissance company in Molotschki by *Schwimmwagen*, from a long way off the regimental commander spotted a group of soldiers at the northeast end of the village and assumed that they were Hstuf. Wulf's men. When he drew nearer he was fired upon – they were Russians! The driver turned the vehicle around and raced back. Another fortunate escape! After his return a telephone call to Hstuf. Wulf's command post confirmed the fact that the armored reconnaissance company was in the southern part of Molotschki, while the Russians held the northern part, through which the armored reconnaissance company had earlier carried out its attack.

Later, on orders from above, the attack troops were ordered back to their strong starting positions, and the company was able to withdraw south to the battle group's positions without loss.

15 January: The *Wehrmacht* communiqué declared:

> *"West of Berdichev regiments of the Waffen-SS counterattacked and smashed two enemy regiments, inflicting heavy casualties on the Bolsheviks."*

## Defensive Position in the Area West of Semeniwka

16 January: The battle group was relieved by elements of the "LAH" and received instructions to proceed via Semeniwka and relieve the 19th Panzer Division in its positions. The positions ran along the hills north of the line Brataloff-Grinowzy with front facing north. The width of front was twelve to fifteen kilometers, and the sector could only be very thinly manned.

The regimental commander command post was at the north end of Mal Brataloff, the Lex battalion's command post in the village itself and the Persch command post in Grinowzy.

In this sector the battle group enjoyed its first spell of quiet. The positions were improved and in places reinforced with earth bunkers.

Meantime the battle group commander, Ostubaf. Peter Sommer, was relieved by *Oberführer* Heinz Lammerding and the previous Ia Hans Bissinger by Stubaf. Albert Stückler. Stubaf. Bissinger was transferred to Berlin.

This sector was now held for four weeks (until 17 February) without major casualties. The defense was conducted offensively, in that the battalions sent patrols into the forefield daily and several times also carried out raids; these were very successful, particularly in the right sector of I Battalion "D" (Hstuf. Persch). On one occasion 35 prisoners were brought in and on another 81 enemy soldiers were captured as well as several machine-guns and mortars.

Otherwise the front remained curiously quiet. However forward observation posts did report major troop movements including tanks and guns several kilometers to the north of us on the west road through Lubar; this was not good news for us, as the Russians were obviously preparing for a new offensive far west of us.

In these days conditions alternated between mud, rain, snow and sun.

As no Russian attacks took place, the signals companies deployed listening devices in the front lines. With the help of ethnic Germans, some of whom understood Russian, enemy telephone lines were tapped and conversations overheard. These provided no noteworthy information, however, as they were mainly conversations about supply matters.

The quiet front made it possible for the men of the battle group to go in small groups to the train, where they were able to enjoy a sauna. It was the last opportunity to worry about personal hygiene for months.

On 6 February the Russian winter resumed with full fury. Deep snowdrifts hindered supply and made life extremely difficult for the food bearers, who had to bring warm rations in food containers many kilometers through the deep snow to the front lines, often sinking up to their hips.

At this point I wish to express thanks on behalf of all former members of the battle group to all of the personnel who were responsible for outfitting and feeding the battle group during this winter, and who in the course of their duties so often had to take up weapons to defend themselves.

In the past we had lost few combat and supply vehicles, however this was now to change.

As a result of supply difficulties the shortage of spare parts became more perceptible daily. In the coming marches vehicle losses due to cold and snowdrifts mounted. Losses also resulted from broken-through enemy forces firing on our train.

18 February: Quite unexpectedly, the battle group received orders to leave its current sector and proceed as quickly as possible to the Belew-Isjaslawl area, where the enemy was apparently trying to break through to the south and cut off the bulk of the 1st Army.

## Defensive Battles in the Belew-Isjaslawl Area

As withdrawing the battle group took several hours, this time the battle group headquarters hurried ahead into the new battle zone. Part of the heavy weapons followed immediately. Meantime the panzer-grenadier regiment fought its way forwards over snow-covered roads through Pischki, Ostropol and Tscherny to Staro Konstantinoff and there was immediately directed by battle group traffic control officers via Schepetowka to Belew.

The regimental commander drove ahead to Belew to ascertain the situation. There he found the battle group command post, where he reported to *Oberführer* Lammerding.

The situation was not quite clear. It was certain that the Russians were driving farther west with strong forces, with the apparent objective of veering south in the Belew-Isjaslawl area.

During the regiment's approach, which lasted several hours, the entire battle group headquarters was the only "unit" in the front line. Fortunately the enemy did not attack there in strength, instead having obviously chosen Isjaslawl as focal point.

The battle group headquarters quickly organized the defense in Belew with hastily scraped together army units and its own heavy weapons. The Russians were already feeling their way forward with patrols and raiding parties, however these were repulsed. Meanwhile the regiment was struggling forward through heavy blowing snow. Many vehicles broke down along the way, and it was only due to the fact that every one of the regiment's drivers had been issued a map of the march route prior to departure and that the repair echelons and sections worked magnificently, that almost all of the vehicles arrived the next morning.

The extremely critical situation in this sector of the front was mastered through the initiative of the battle group headquarters under *Oberführer* Lammerding. This prevented a decisive Russian thrust to the south that would have driven into the middle of the 1st Army's rear-echelon units. *Oberführer* Lammerding was later awarded the Knight's Cross for this feat.

The regiment arrived just in time to be able to intervene in the fighting. The Persch battalion was immediately committed to clear Belew, which had been strongly infiltrated by the enemy, and it fought its way into its positions north of the city.

The Lex battalion attacked Isjaslawl, already occupied by the enemy, and the battle group Ia, Stubaf. Stückler, was present for the attack. Supported by anti-aircraft machine-guns, heavy infantry guns, anti-tank guns and the artillery, which began shelling the city as the attack began, the battalion was able to retake the city after heavy fighting.

Battalion commander Hstuf. Lex, leader of the anti-aircraft machine-gun platoon Schick and *Oberscharführer* Binder all distinguished themselves in this action. Binder and Schick were seriously wounded. With just two operational 20-mm SFL 53s, Schick succeeded in bringing in 53 prisoners. In front of his position lay 33 dead. In the evening the battle group was informed that the city was firmly in our hands.

In the coming days the Lex battalion was always the scene of the hottest action; assisted by favorable terrain, the enemy was especially close to our positions there and was steadily reinforced. Everyone breathed easier when a main line of resistance was formed, even though it was no more than a line of strongpoints.

The entire battle group was engaged in fierce defensive fighting for ten days; the heavy infantry weapons, such as the *Grille* self-propelled (150-mm) guns and anti-aircraft machine-guns under Ostuf. Seegerer, the assault guns under Ostuf. Otto, the tanks and the artillery played a prominent role.

Once daily the regimental commander drove the road from Belew to Isjaslawl, parts of which were under enemy observation, to the Lex battalion. Meanwhile the battle group had come under the command of the LIX Corps.

The commanding general Schulz visited the battle group headquarters and drove forward with *Oberführer* Lammerding and the regimental commander under heavy enemy small arms fire to the Lex battalion, where he received a briefing on the situation from the battalion commander, spent some time talking with the officers and men of the battalion headquarters and passed out several cartons of cigarettes. This act by the commanding general captured the hearts of the men. In general it can be said that the battles under the command of the LIX Corps were characterized by an especially good cooperative relationship.

Situated on the hills north of Belew and Isjaslawl, our positions, sited at intervals of 400 to 800 meters according to the terrain, commanded the forefield and through accurate fire simulated a strong defense position eleven kilometers wide. The anti-aircraft machine-guns, in particular, made repeated changes of position under cover and commanded the entire sector.

Supplied from a German ammunition depot on the northern edge of Belew, for the first time the anti-tank guns were able to expend ammunition lavishly and fired at every Russian tank and truck that appeared on the road from the north.

The *Grille* self-propelled guns (150-mm), which at Isjaslawl were deployed in expertly camouflaged positions far to the front amid the houses, smashed every Russian concentration or assembly with extremely accurate pinpoint fire.

The enemy's fighting strength, which grew daily, and his determination in assaulting our positions showed clearly just how great the danger of an enemy breakthrough to the south was here.

## Defensive Success in the Staro Konstantinov Battle Zone

4 March: Totally unexpectedly, the regiment received orders to withdraw via Tschepzy in the direction of Staro Konstantinov.

As the Russians were already pressing toward Staro Konstantinov with strong forces from the southeast and were steadily gaining ground, the entire Belew-Isjaslawl battle zone obviously had to be evacuated quickly in order to avoid encirclement.

The result was that on 7 and 8 March all of the units deployed in this area converged from all sides on the Schepetovka-Staro Konstantinov road and almost completely blocked it. The regiment's column sat on the road trapped and immobile for many hours while the enemy drew nearer.

On 7 March the Russians carried out seven air attacks on Staro Konstantinov's north bridge; thanks to the outstanding defense mounted by the anti-aircraft machine-guns and the quadruple flak no hits were scored on the bridge.

Finally, on 8 March, the regimental commander covered the last stretch to Staro Konstantinov on foot in order to establish contact with the battle group headquarters. All of the city streets were completely blocked. *Oberführer* Lammerding personally directed traffic at the main intersection. From him the regimental commander learned that he was to take over the battle group effective immediately as the battle group headquarters had orders to leave that day for transport to the division to take part in its reformation. *Oberführer* Lammerding had received orders to assume command of the "*Das Reich*" Division.

A short time later the regimental commander received a summary from the battle group's Ia, Stubaf. Stückler, according to which part of the battle group's remaining troops, some of which were engaged in combat, were stuck in traffic kilometers away. The two battalions of the Panzer-Grenadier Regiment "*Das Reich*" were combined into one battalion under the command of Hstuf. Lex, while the battalion headquarters of I Battalion "D" and Hstuf. Persch returned to the division.

When the traffic jam gradually began to sort itself out the old battalion headquarters departed. Taking over the battle group in this ticklish situation proved to be extremely difficult.

From positions on the hills north of Staro Konstantinov the Lex battalion inflicted heavy losses on the approaching enemy with assistance from the anti-aircraft machine-guns (commanded by Rosenzweig and Schulz). The two *Grille* self-propelled guns, positioned right in the ammunition dump, kept the approaching enemy under continuous, pinpoint fire. Ustuf. Wolf repulsed an attack on the village of Sasslutsch with two anti-aircraft machine-guns.

Effective at once the battle group was placed under the command of the 19th Panzer Division under *General* Källner, all of whose armored elements were already in combat southeast of Staro Konstantinov with the Russians who were already pressing toward the city from the southeast.

Using the few remaining prime movers, the new battle group commander laboriously drove past the blocked columns to the forward command post of the 19th Panzer Division, which was located on a hill southeast of the city in armored troop carriers. There he reported to *General* Källner to place the battle group under his command. However, since not a single unit was as yet available due to the clogged roads, the greeting was rather frosty.

The commander asked for his orders and had the sector that the battle group was to occupy as quickly as possible entered on the map. It was on the right of the positions held by the 19th Panzer Division. However the battle group commander also requested and received orders from the division commander to the city's military commander to the effect that effective at once the Armored Battle Group "*Das Reich*" had priority over all other units and that he was to use all available officers to clear the streets for the battle group.

The battle group's operation officer, Ostuf. Buchwald, took these instructions to the city's military commander with the commanding officer's advisory that the city could not be held unless the battle group was allowed to proceed as quickly as possible to its positions.

In fact the streets were cleared in a relatively short time. All of the battle group's officers played a major role in this. Soon afterwards Hstuf. Lex arrived at the head of his battalion at the command post, which had meanwhile been set up right beside the road at the south end of the city, and received his new mission orders. The battalion was reinforced by anti-aircraft machine-guns, *Grille* self-propelled guns and anti-tank guns and immediately moved into its position on the previously open wing of the 19th Panzer Division.

Meantime the traffic jam in the city had eased further, and one by one the battalion and unit commanders checked in at the command post, were informed of the change in command of the battle group and received their new combat orders. The new defense position was set surprisingly quickly and contact was established with the 19th Panzer Division.

On the evening of the same day the battle group, which was considerably smaller after the calling away of the headquarters, was firmly in the hands of the commanding officer.

The very next night the Russians achieved a penetration in the 19th Panzer Division's sector; at the request of *General* Källner the Lex battalion launched an immediate counterattack. The attack, with two assault guns and two anti-aircraft machine-guns under the personal command of Hstuf. Lex, eliminated the enemy penetration.

In the early morning hours the commander of the 19th Panzer Division personally called the battle group commander, expressed his pleasure at the quick occupation of the position and thanked him warmly for the comradely assistance provided by the Lex battalion in eliminating the enemy penetration in his division's sector.

The ice was broken, and in the coming days of combat a very successful association was forged between the battle group and the 19th Panzer Division.

9 March: The Lex battalion achieved several significant defensive successes, all of which were marked by truly excellent cooperation on the part of all the heavy weapons. Three to four Russian attacks were repulsed here in the concentrated fire of all weapons.

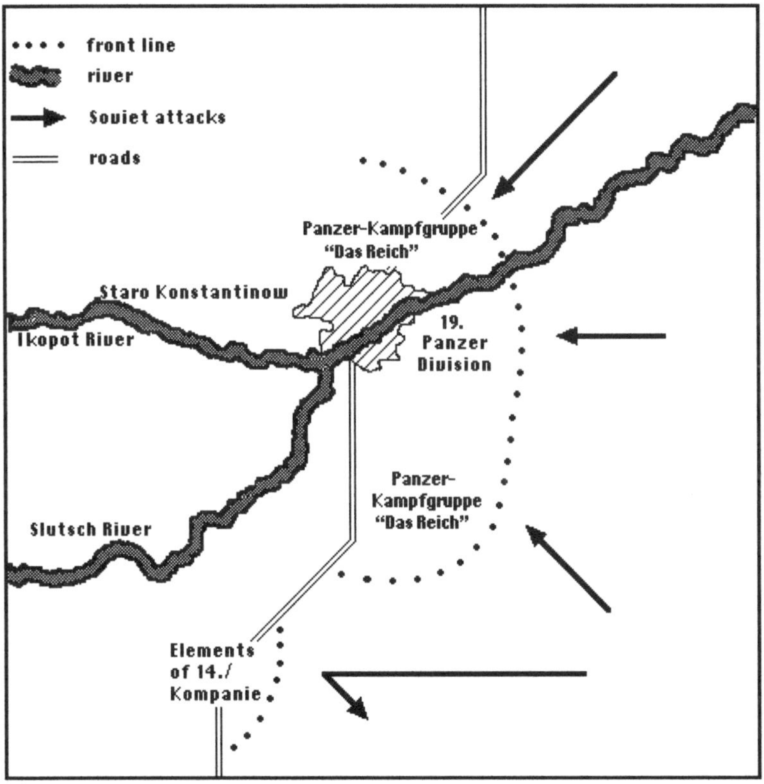


**Actions of Panzer-Kampfgruppe "Das Reich" from 4 to 9 March, 1944**

Meantime an anti-tank platoon with two 75-mm was still in the munitions dump at the northern boundary of the city and fired the 314 high-explosive shells it found there at the attacking enemy, which pressed forward over the hills into the city. Through their outstandingly accurate fire these two guns alone achieved a great defensive success, causing the enemy to cease his attacks altogether by day and only feel his way forward cautiously by night.

The train of the 14th (Heavy) Company had moved into Matrunki south of the city the previous night. There, with the two anti-aircraft machine-guns under Dahnke and Henne, it fought off an attack by two enemy companies that had broken through. The enemy units were obviously under orders to sever the supply and later retreat road to Proskurov. So the first action by the shrunken battle group in the Staro Konstantinov area was a convincing success, with defensive victories in the north, southeast and south of the city in the 19th Panzer Division's area of operations.

## Counterattacks South of Staro Konstantinov

10 March: In spite of these defensive successes, as a result of a deterioration in the overall situation the order came to withdraw south on the main road in the direction of Proskurov. Here, too, serious traffic tie-ups developed.

The battle group reached the crossing over the Bushok and was subjected to enemy air attacks all day. There were no losses, however, as the Russian aircraft made very inaccurate approaches and their aim was poor.

11 March: The battle group fought off enemy attacks from the east toward the main road.

## Hstuf. Lex: Killed in Action

On this day the battle group was struck a heavy blow: supported by assault guns, heavy infantry guns and anti-aircraft machine-guns, the Lex battalion attacked the town of Petschiski, east of the main road. While standing on an assault gun briefing the battalion, Lex was shot in the head by a Russian sniper and killed. An outstanding unit leader, wearer of the Knight's Cross, who was always the soul of the battle in his battalion, had met a soldier's death. He left behind a painful gap. The entire division mourned him, and while issuing orders at the command post of the 19th Panzer Division *General* Källner paid his respects in the presence of all unit commanders to this outstanding officer, whom he had learned to value highly as a soldier since their first day of working together. The battle group commander placed the Lex battalion under the temporary command of Ostuf. Eckert.

12 March: Several days earlier the repair echelons of all units had gone to Proskurov, where there were several larger tank workshop and weapons repair companies, and worked without pause to repair the broken-down and recovered vehicles and weapons.

It was thanks to these repair echelons that we were still so operationally ready after three months of winter operations under the most difficult conditions, in difficult defensive battles and fighting retreats, with no deliveries of replacement equipment. The actions of Hstuf. Herbst, Ustuf. Rötzer, Annewanter, Buchwald, Lösch and Wimmer were especially praiseworthy.

14 March: Thanks to their work the 14th Company, for example, was once again able to field five anti-aircraft machine-guns on self-propelled carriages, one quadruple flak on an eight-ton prime mover, two *Grille* self-propelled guns and two 75-mm anti-tank guns. This company also had in service five heavy prime movers for use as supply vehicles.

The 14th Company's weapons formed the backbone of the battle group. The tremendous effect of the self-propelled 20-mm anti-aircraft guns against enemy infantry (especially using high-explosive ammunition) and the *Grille* with their 150-mm infantry guns on self-propelled carriages soon became known through the corps and army divisions in the entire combat area and they were very highly regarded as support weapons.

Our infantry received outstanding support during these difficult winter battles thanks to the excellent command of these weapons in action by the company commander Ostuf. Georg Seeger. As a result the company played a particularly important role in the successes achieved in this sector of the front. Finally, Hstuf. Sepp Unterkofler took command of the Lex battalion.

## Counterattack North of Proskurov

16 March: Heavy fighting northeast of Proskurov. Together with the 19th Panzer Division, the battle group carried out a counterattack with tanks against a large wood east of the main road. The battle group placed all twelve of its serviceable armored vehicles at the disposal of the 19th Panzer Division so that an armored point of main effort could be formed on the left wing together with the tanks of the panzer division, while it carried out a pure infantry attack on the right wing. The success was complete. In a short time the wood was in our hands. Eight enemy tanks were destroyed. One of the battle group's tank commanders, who drove far ahead of the rest of the field in his Panther, succeeded in knocking out the first super-heavy "Stalin tank with long-barreled gun." The battle group's infantry cleared the wood of the enemy. The huge enemy tank was examined and then blown up. The successful tank commander was awarded the Iron Cross, First Class on the spot by *General* Källner.

17 March: After considerable tie-ups directly north of Proskurov there was a major withdrawal movement to Lissa Gorka by way of Proskurov, Lesnewo and Golowskowo.

18 March: The battle group left the formation of the 19th Panzer Division. Its commanding officer was given a warm farewell by *General* Källner and receives a truck full of goods for the men of the battle group. These were distributed when it reached its destination and were the cause of much joy.

The battle group was placed under the direct command of the XXIV Panzer Corps commanded by *General der Panzertruppen* Nehring.

During the preceding battles, on 7 March Uscha. Erich Seeliger, a platoon leader in the 11th Company of the Panzer-Grenadier Regiment "DF", had distinguished himself through conspicuous bravery and was named in the Honor Roll of the German Army. Seeliger died a soldier's death in this action.

19 March: Motorized march in heavy blowing snow farther east via Deraschnia-Wolkowinzy-Sloboda-Serbinowszy to Ssewerinowka. From there an attack toward Korostowzy was carried out. Hstuf. Unterkofler received a serious neck wound and Ostuf. Eckert took over the battalion again.

## Battle for Bar

20 March: Between the battle group's positions to the east and the city of Bar lay a large wood west of Mankowce. On orders from the panzer corps, during the late afternoon the battle group was to withdraw west through the wood toward Bar, in order to occupy new positions at the eastern and southeastern boundaries of the city.

During the afternoon, however, from the command post Russian infantry was observed entering the wood in growing numbers. Thus the Russians were already between the battle group and its trains in Bar.

Since a withdrawal to the west through the wood must lead to a night forest battle with casualties and great command difficulties, with the added threat of an attack by the enemy from his former positions, the battle group commander decided that as he had no communications with the panzer corps he would first withdraw north across the Row, skirt the entire wooded area and reach the city from the north by way of Tokariwka, Studowzy, Annoniwka and Popiwka.

The night march went as planned with no enemy contact and no casualties. Immediately after reaching the city the battle group made its way to the eastern and southeastern outskirts and encountered the enemy in the last houses.

After making brief preparations the battle group attacked and drove the enemy out of the town back toward the hills east of the city. Then it occupied its assigned positions.

The battle group was finally reunited with its trains. It had accomplished its mission while avoiding a costly forest battle and was still completely intact. The command post was initially located in the north of Bar.

22 March: The battle group commander was requested by the XXIV Panzer Corps to provide written justification for his unauthorized changing of the withdrawal order and for bypassing the enemy-occupied wood. This was submitted during the course of the day. In it the battle group commander stated that he bore full responsibility for the decision and would do the same thing again in a similar situation, because by doing so he had avoided unnecessary casualties and command difficulties and had completed his mission with the least possible losses. As the preconditions for the original withdrawal order had fundamentally changed and the battle

group had no contact with the corps, he had been forced to act independently. Only in this way was the battle group's combat strength preserved. This brought the affair to an end.

The battalion attacked the town of Pilazine with the Kleinert, Hinz and Dahnken anti-aircraft machine-guns and took it.

## The Traveling Pocket

23 March: A report was received stating that the main road to the south was already in enemy hands and that to our west the Russians had broken through to the south. Consequently the pocket around the 1st Panzer Army under *General* Hube, to which the Armored Battle Group "*Das Reich*" belonged, had probably been closed, or at the least communications had been severed with the remaining front and the rear.

From Hstuf. Count Seiffert, who came to the battle group from the Reich by way of the 1st Panzer Army, we learned that the army was being supplied by the *Luftwaffe* and that the wounded were regularly being flown out to Breslau. He brought with him maps that were valuable to us, but on which we found something in particular was missing.

The plan of action for the 1st Panzer Army was as follows: each day the still relatively potent panzer and panzer-grenadier divisions were to attack toward the west or southwest, while the units whose strength had been seriously reduced, which included our battle group, were to hold their positions on the eastern front as well as the northern and southern fronts through the day until nightfall and then during the night withdraw the same number of kilometers as the attacking units had gained on the pocket's western front during the day.

This new and simple style of fighting resulted in the creation of the "traveling pocket," which each day moved a good piece closer to the new front to be established in the west. It was, however, extremely arduous for the units, especially for those on the southern, northern and eastern fronts; for it meant nothing less than these units fighting a defensive action on the three fronts all day and then having to march all night in snow and cold or in thawing weather in muck and filth, so as to go into position again at dawn and, as soon as the Russians caught up, fight all day again.

The troops scarcely had any opportunity to sleep, and keeping the men awake in the positions or during rest stops became a problem faced by all officers and unit leaders. It often happened that the men (for the most part ethnic Germans from Hungary and Romania) simply toppled over asleep or crawled off into a haystack to finally get some sleep.

It required all the efforts and watchfulness of the officers and the non-commissioned officers to rouse the men and get them going again. The excessive physical exertions and the constant overtiredness often made many completely apathetic. In one case a young company commander, who had tried in vain to get a soldier to resume marching, finally saw no other way to save the man than to draw his pistol. He threatened to use the weapon if the man did not immediately get up and accompany the rest. The exhausted man stood up and said apathetically, "Then shoot me and get it over with!" With the help of some of his comrades who had interrupted their march, after a brief rest during which he regained a little of his strength the soldier was finally convinced to carry on.

On another occasion a man who had crawled into a hayloft to sleep was overlooked when his unit departed. He subsequently had to be reported as missing.

Casualties grew daily. The winter clothing of many men hung down in tatters and in many places the red stuffing of the insulated vests was visible. The state of the men's footwear deteriorated. The last haircuts and last shaves lay far in the past. On the other hand they were still being relatively well supplied with ammunition and food. The battle group supply organization, which was outside the pocket, was also called in at the last minute. On those occasions when no food arrived the soldiers had to live off the land.

Increasingly the units replaced their lost vehicles with the brave and hardy *panye* ponies, and soon we were jokingly calling our panzer battle group the "*panye* battle group."

So for us these weeks-long defensive battles and fighting withdrawals in the "traveling pocket" were the most strenuous and hardest mission of this winter. Of the three-thousand men the battle group had at its formation there was approximately one-thousand left.

24 March: After days of snow and ice there was now an onset of thawing conditions. Fuel and ammunition ran low and on orders were

"rationed." The mud made things increasingly difficult for us. The situation became more uncertain day by day. We met the enemy everywhere. We were never sure when we reached a village on a night march whether or not it had already been reached by the enemy.

## Fighting Withdrawals and Retreats Southwest of Bar

24 March: The command post was moved into the city of Bar. Away from the highway secondary roads were scouted which had not yet been taken by the enemy. The battle group was removed from its direct subordination to the XXIV Panzer Corps and was placed under the command of the 101st Light Infantry Division commanded by *Generalleutnant* Vogel.

Since there were contradicting reports concerning the barricading of the highway to the southwest and as many vehicles had passed this stretch of road without meeting the enemy, another attempt was made to bring the battle group's wheeled vehicles down the highway through to Novo Uszycha under the command of the signals officer, Ostuf. Hentschel. Meanwhile the battle group, with its remaining tracked vehicles, proceeded on foot off the highway, in part through extremely difficult terrain, and reached the village of Kosariwka, which contrary to our expectations was not occupied by the enemy.

Contact with the vehicle column was at first maintained with a backpack radio; however, during the night contact was lost, which made us fear the worst.

During this night march the battle group commander noticed that the ethnic Germans, of which the battle group was largely made up, were conversing among themselves in Romanian.

During the second half of the night the commander drove ahead in one of the battle group's prime movers to the command post of the 101st Light Infantry Division and reported to the division commander. During a briefing on the enemy situation by the Ia, a special missions officer came in and rather excitedly reported that the Russians were approaching from the northwest. A marching column and Russian words had been heard. He had already ordered two machine-guns into position.

The battle group commander stepped in at once. He had the man show him on the map from which direction the enemy was coming, and it immediately became clear to him that this "enemy" could only be his approaching battle group. He explained to the division commander and the Ia and this explanation caused general amusement. The Romanian being spoken by our ethnic Germans had been taken for Russian. No one had wondered that the commanding officer had just come down the same road on which the supposed enemy was now approaching, which was typical of the generally uncertain situation at that time. The Russians could appear from any direction! One almost had the uneasy feeling that the big pocket was about to break up into several small ones. We were just lucky that the Russians were obviously just as unsure of the situation as we were.

The senior command ordered that during each night march security groups had to remain in contact with the enemy for at least two to three hours to cover the retreat. This order was only carried out one time, however. The security group in question never returned and had to be reported missing, although the exact route of retreat and march destination were known to it. These men probably fell asleep from over-exhaustion and were overrun by the pursuing Russians or they missed the retreat road. Consequently in all subsequent withdrawal movements the leaving of security groups in contact with the enemy was dispensed with and this had no ill effects on the retreat.

The next day, 25 March, the signals officer, Ostuf. Hentschel, reached our battle group on foot with the remaining drivers of our wheeled vehicles. He also brought a Panzer IV tank and four or five wounded with him and made the following report:

> "While returning with the vehicles the task had fallen to the signals men to try to get the valuable radio vehicles out of Bar to safety with the other remaining vehicles south on the highway.
>
> At midnight Bar was already supposed to have been in the main line of resistance and all vehicles were also to have been evacuated by then. At 2 AM we were still stuck in a mass of vehicles inside the city. Not until morning did some movement come to the column. We were able to leave the city. More or less out of control, cars, trucks,

prime movers and especially *panye* wagons tried to get away to the southwest. At about 8 AM all movement on the highway halted. We could hear shooting and an explosion. The battle group's signals officer went forward on foot along the stationary column. The Russians had severed the highway, which was crossed by a rail line in front of a rise. The enemy had dug in on the railway embankment, partly in overturned freight cars. The highway was fired on by anti-tank guns and mortars. An 18-ton prime mover blazed fiercely, next to it a car. A *Luftwaffe* major – a Knight's Cross wearer – lay dead beside it. The leading vehicles had all been abandoned. The drivers and passengers had taken cover in a wood beside the road. Many were already talking about surrendering. However, when they heard that all of the battle group's vehicles were in the column they cleared the road, and our eight-wheeled armored car took the point, even though it was armed with just one machine-gun. The signals men, including our battle group medical officer Dr. Fuchs, took rifles in hand and worked their way forward next to the highway.

Also in the battle group's column was a Panzer IV tank under the command of Hstuf. Burmester. The signals officer had this tank drive off the highway to the right toward the embankment. A battery of light field howitzers supported us with direct fire on the embankment. In this way we were able to fight our way over the railway embankment. However, the intersection of highway and rail line remained under heavy fire. Scarcely had our tank crossed the railway embankment on the highway when the vehicle column began moving again panic-like. We dashed across the dangerous area with our vehicles and almost al reached a hill in front of a village. We heard a wild firefight. No more vehicles could be seen on the road leading from the village. We wanted to go around this village, as it was already late afternoon, and turned onto a relatively solid secondary road. It became ever worse, however. Soon the first vehicles got stuck. We tried to pull them out of the mud with the Panzer IV. Our evasive maneuver did not go unnoticed by the Russians, however. We came under fire, and more and more vehicles became stuck. The first radio vehicle (Kfz. 17) was shot up.

With a heavy heart the signals officer was forced to decide to abandon the immobilized and under fire vehicles. The most important documents were transferred to the Panzer IV, which also took on board our four or five wounded and Dr. Fuchs. It was especially hard for us when we placed the magnetic anti-tank hollow charges on our eight-wheeled radio car. The Horch car belonging to the battle group commander was also lost here. We carried on on foot and reached the battle group the same night. Oñ the highway we picked up a German armed forces woman auxiliary who had been left behind in the hospital in Proskurov."

Thus our entire valuable motor pool had been destroyed in a single night. The loss of the radio car and our battle group artillery hit us especially hard.

All of our personal belongings, from the battle group commander down to the youngest soldier of the headquarters, were also lost. Now we owned only what was on our backs.

25 March: The battle group marched through Daschkowzy-Wonkowzy; there were isolated skirmishes with Russian reconnaissance units. We arrived on literally our last drops of fuel. But miraculously during the night *Rottenführer* Ziegele arrived with a vehicle full of fuel.

26 March: We marched via Sinkoff to Strichowzy with occasional minor contacts with the enemy. Our last *Grille* had to be blown up on account of radiator damage and a fractured cooling fan shaft. Thus our last infantry gun on a self-propelled carriage, whose 150-mm shells had so often provided us such effective supported on offense and defense as the "ordinary soldier's artillery," had been lost.

27 March: An attempt to reach our assigned objective, the village of Ruda-Gortschitschanskaja, by way of Gortschitschanskaja failed, as the Russians had already occupied the place. But we discovered a gap near Ivankowzy through which we marched west before attacking from the west and reaching and occupying the assigned position.

## Battles North of Kamenets Podolsk

At 3 AM on 28 March the battle group launched an attack east along the highway through Sscibory to Marschozizy. The Russians had dug in on Hill 296.6 on the highway and it had to be taken if we were to reach our assigned positions in Ruda Gortschitschanskaja. The only support available to the infantry was three anti-aircraft machine-guns. In close-quarters fighting, after three counterattacks by the enemy, the battle group was able to force him to withdraw.

29 March: Ruda Gortschitschanskaja was reached, and several enemy attacks on the village were repulsed. Heavy weapons, such as artillery, flak, assault guns and tanks were becoming scarcer. Because of a shortage of fuel and lack of vital replacement parts, one vehicle after another, one valuable weapon after another, had to be blown up.

Meanwhile we were subordinated to the 168th Infantry Division. The entire division had just a single car for the division commander and had received practically no fuel – and of course the battle group received none either. It was the beginning of a catastrophe for all our vehicles, and in spite of all of our resourcefulness and temporary measures there was nothing we could do to avert it.

At night we could see the navigation lights of the steady stream of German aircraft landing and taking off at Kamenets Podolsk; in spite of anti-aircraft fire they performed their admirable mission of supplying the pocket with food and ammunition. The empty Ju 52s evacuated the wounded who were brought to the airfield from all directions, thus relieving the surrounded army of a serious worry and responsibility. A truly great accomplishment by our air force! During the night the battle group withdrew via Donajewzy and Mogilevka to Muschkotinzy, where another continuous defense line was established.

30 March: Continued retreat, withdrew via Worobiowka, Slobotka and Schatawa to Makoff.

Winter returned with all its fury and the hardships became even greater. Roads could no longer be seen in the snowstorm. The tracks left by the marching column disappeared in the snowdrifts in seconds. The battle group struggled through often knee-deep snow.

The calm, undemanding *panye* horses became our men's most faithful helpers, hauling the *panye* wagons loaded with weapons and ammunition, carrying exhausted men, and most importantly transporting our wounded to the new position or the nearest medical clearing station, if in fact we knew where there was one. If one had seen the battle group marching past, one would have immediately thought of Napoleon's soldiers during the retreat from Moscow through the Russian ice and snow desert of Russia.

31 March: With the onset of darkness the battle group withdrew further to the south, in the process crossing the forward airfield near Kamenets Podolsk, where there were still several Ju 52s waiting for wounded. These were the last aircraft to reach the pocket in spite of the snowstorm and the anti-aircraft fire, as the airfield had to be abandoned a short time later.

A tempting thought, that these aircraft would be landing at Breslau two hours later! But the battle group stamped on through the snowstorm past the still empty aircraft and continued toward the south. The march lasted all night and passed through Ziolkowze, Pudlowze and Dolzek before Sariza was reached on the morning of 1 April.

On this night the fuel finally ran out for most of the vehicles and the commanding officer was forced to give the bitter order to blow up the bulk of the vehicles before crossing the Smotritsch. Only the most vital combat vehicles for weapons and ammunition were permitted to go on – insofar as the fuel situation permitted.

The vehicles, which were drawn up around the crossing site in a semicircle, were blown up with a heavy heart, and the blazing, widely-visible graveyard of the battle group's vehicles was a sad and depressing sight. Each vehicle with the men's few possessions had become to them a small piece of home. As a result of outstanding maintenance and the truly excellent work of the repair echelons, so far we had always succeeded in freeing vehicles which became frozen in, mired in mud or stuck in the snowdrifts; and now they had to be blown up, not because of mechanical defects or other technical problems, but because of a lack of fuel! Assets of tremendous valuable were destroyed in a very short time. When the order was given to destroy the vehicles, the commanding officer made the personal papers of the members of the battle group the special responsibility of the senior non-commissioned officers of the companies.

2 April: All day long the battle group struggled through an icy snowstorm, finally reaching Rychta, and attacked and took the village of Fridowze.

3 April: Several of the remaining vehicles became bogged down during the march to Kudrynze. Prime movers were employed in an attempt to at least keep the last self-propelled carriages operational. But the last quadruple flak on a self-propelled carriage and a 20-mm gun on a self-propelled carriage had to be blown up because of motor and transmission damage.

4 April: The retreat continued through Zalesie to Germanovka. The Russian reached a part of the village before us and had to be driven out by counterattack. Then the companies went into position at the outskirts of the village. The division command post of the 168th Infantry Division was also located in Germanovka.

In contrast to all the previous Russian villages this village had an almost German look about it. The houses (stone) were neatly whitewashed. The inhabitants were a fine blonde breed, and Germanovka, as its name suggests, is obviously of Germanic, not Slavic, origin – perhaps a remnant from the campaign of Charles XII of Sweden.

The battle group command post was set up in a large stone house where preparations were just being made for a wedding. The inhabitants of the house, like all the people there, were very communicative and courteous, even though they in no way "fraternized" with the enemy and did not ingratiate themselves. We were extremely impressed by the neatness of these people and the cleanliness of the village. As well, the sun shone for the first time again over the broad fields of snow.

## Russian Demands for Surrender

In the late morning two German soldiers came toward our position at the outskirts of the village from the northeast and demanded to be taken to the command post. They had no weapons or belts and stated that they had been taken prisoner. A Russian officer had ordered them to go to the German positions in Germanovka and give to the officer in command there a letter in German from the Russian commanding general to the commanding officer of the 168th Infantry Division demanding that he cease fighting.

The contents of the letter were roughly as follows:

> *"The pocket around the 1st Panzer Army has been permanently closed. Your struggle against the vastly superior Russian forces is hopeless! For you there is no escape. Give up! You have fought honorably. You will therefore also be treated honorably by us as prisoners and will be released to go home as soon as the war is over! Any further fighting is senseless and will only result in unnecessary casualties! Put an end to the war at last! Become prisoners of war! Insightful German officers, united in the national Committee for a Free Germany, have taken this step before you. This letter will serve as identification for you and all of the units under your command when you cross the Russian lines. Lay down your weapons and come to us! We will not shoot at you."*

We could only smile. Nevertheless the commander drove to see *Oberst* Landau and gave the letter to him. He, too, was amazed by this primitive demand for surrender. Then he placed the letter in the files. The two soldiers were placed in the care of the 168th Infantry Division.

In spite of many desperate situations in the pocket the 1st Panzer Army did not give up, and the iron determination of all the German units to hold on was rewarded a short time later.

## Withdrawal Movements at the Triangle of National Boundaries: Russia-Romania-Poland

5 April: Moved out at 5 AM in freezing cold. Our route led via Krzywcze and Gorne to Korolovka. From the 168th Infantry Division we received gasoline containers which had just been dropped by the *Luftwaffe*; 80 liters of fuel, enough for our vehicles to drive several more kilometers. For a brief time our route took us through Romanian territory.

The battle group had fought its way out of Germanovka to Wolkowzw at dawn and created the preconditions for a continuation of the march. In these days our drivers came up with the oddest idea for obtaining fuel. Every vehicle abandoned beside the road or in the villages was carefully examined for fuel, and if any was present it was carefully siphoned into a canister. And so our tracked vehicles were kept moving.

6 April: The battle group's route led via Stratkowze, Wysuzka and Bilze to Olexinze.

7 April: We reached the village of Scypowce. The sun shone again and winter was obviously coming to an end.

## In Galicia

Only minor changes of position. It was Easter Sunday. The battle group took up quarters in a Galician village. The command post was housed in a school. To our astonishment the teacher spoke fluent German. He invited us to visit him in the evening and generously shared with us his Easter cake; these were baked in large quantities here as Easter was the biggest holiday of the year. This was an unexpected pleasure for us after months of deprivation. On the wall hung a picture of Emperor Franz Josef and beside a picture of the entire imperial family. We learned that the Galician teacher had learned German at the time of the Danube monarchy and he spoke it amazingly well after so long a time. When we asked why he still had pictures of the emperor and his family hanging in his home, he began enthusiastically to tell us about those times, which he must have experienced as a very young man.

He said, "You know, the period when Galicia still belonged to the Austro-Hungarian monarchy was our golden age. We were worth something, were treated decently and got something for our money." And then he spent the entire night reveling in the good old days.

This experience moved us deeply and we felt a great respect for this amazing political accomplishment on the part of the Danube monarchy that 26 years after the collapse of the Austro-Hungarian Empire in this land, which was always regarded as its stepchild and to whose godforsaken garrisons so many imperial officers had been sent as punishment, the shining period of the Danube monarchy was still talked about so enthusiastically, and that in spite of all the voices that had passed over this land since, pictures of the emperor and the imperial princes still hung in the parlors as reminders of the good old days.

As we learned the next day, our men received an extremely hospitable reception from all of the families, and everywhere they found picture from the time of the emperor.

## The German Counterattack to Open the Pocket

9 April, Easter Sunday: The battle group departed at dawn and reached the village of Chartanowze by way of Hinkowze. The battle group had been ordered to assemble in this area as LIX Corps reserve.

After reaching its destination the battle group's signals platoon, contrary to previous practice, laid down telephone lines to the 168th Infantry Division. The very first conversation with the Ia brought good news. The gist of what he said was as follows:

> "I believe that the sun is shining on us again. We have just received word that the II SS Panzer Corps, under the command of *Generaloberst* Hausser with the '*Hohenstaufen*' and '*Frundsberg*' Divisions and the attached 100th Light Infantry Division, coming from France, has detrained further to the west and is presently attacking toward the east in order to link up with the 1st Army's pocket. This link-up may take place in the Buczacz area before today is over.
>
> This morning the first lone truck driving from Lemberg (Lvov) got through to the army without contacting the enemy."

When the commanding officer expressed his joy and mentioned that he had served in *Generaloberst* Hausser's staff for several months and that that he knew many of the commanders in the two SS divisions well, there was also great joy on the other end of the line.

Once again, as so often in war, yesterday's hopeless situation had changed abruptly. But the fighting was not yet over.

The *Wehrmacht* communiqué of 9 April 1944 stated:

> *"In the Kamenets Podolsk area a powerful German battle group consisting of units of the army and the Waffen-SS under the command of General Hube has frustrated attempts by superior enemy forces to encircle it after 14 days of heavy fighting. The fiercely resisting units were overrun after a bitter struggle and contact was established with the army and Waffen-SS relief force attacking from the west."*

While the communiqué merely speaks of "frustrating the encirclement," the situation was such that all contact with the west was severed for fourteen days.

10 April: In the Torskie area units of the 1st Infantry Division were relieved by the battle group, whose strength had been reduced to that of a battalion reinforced by heavy weapons.

## Decisive Counterattack Northeast of Worwolince-Slone

On this day the battle group was once again placed under the command of the LIX Corps under *General* Schulz. The corps chief of staff, *Oberst* von Natzmer, came to the battle group command post in person to brief the commanding officer on the situation.

The battle group had already received orders to withdraw further to the west in the coming night. This order was rescinded as a result of a serious crisis facing the corps and new orders arrived for a difficult mission.

11 April: The Russians launched a surprise attack with two rifle divisions supported by strong tank, mortar and anti-tank units and took the very commanding Hill 347 northeast of Worwolince station. From there they commanded the entire valley of Slone and Tluste Miasto. The enemy already had moved artillery into position in large numbers, and from the strong, accurate fire it was obvious that he was in possession of excellent observation posts.

The commanding hill had to be restored to German hands, otherwise the corps's withdrawal through the valley would have turned into a catastrophe under the concentrated fire of the enemy artillery and the pursuing Russian units.

Once again the battle group had been selected for a difficult mission. It was placed under the command of the 75th Infantry Division and in the late afternoon marched into the assembly area at Worwolince. The village itself was under heavy artillery fire. The commanding officer reported to division commander *General* Beuckemann, who demonstrated his coolness by playing cards with several officers of his staff until the arrival of the battle group.

A shell struck the house just as the commanding officer went up to the division command post, blowing a large hole in the roof – right above the card players. Stones flew, the mortar rained down, but otherwise nothing happened. The general's comment: "Unfriendly people! Then we will just have to retire to another corner of the parlor."

The commanding officer reported his battle group present and ready to accept orders. The division headquarters was obviously expecting a fully operational "armored battle group" with heavy weapons, tanks and so on. A short time later the battle group marched past the division command post.

When the general saw the shabby, cocky-looking men, who were transporting their heavy weapons on panye wagons or were themselves sitting on peasant horses with old ropes for stirrups, he just shook his head and the humorous name "SS panye battle group" was heard once again.

The trains had been combed once again – everyone who could be spared had to be sent into the line in order to bolster the badly depleted battalion for this difficult attack across open terrain.

The battle group made its preparations during the night of 12-13 April. The attack was supported by the artillery of the 75th Infantry Division and by two assault guns from the 300th Assault Gun Brigade's 1st Company. The fire support from the two self-propelled 20-mm anti-aircraft guns was therefore especially valuable. While Ostuf. Eckert led the battalion, Hstuf. Count Seiffert, newly transferred to us, took over a company made up of tankers, artillerymen and train personnel.

Everyone knew that this attack was decisive for the days to come. The pocket's eastern front could not be allowed to collapse at the last minute while on the western front contact was being established with the II SS Panzer Corps attacking from the west.

At dawn the battle group, deployed in depth on a wide front, moved out under covering fire from all heavy weapons against an opponent far superior in men and weapons and after a fierce struggle retook Hill 347. Losses were heavy, however. Several anti-tank guns were captured or destroyed as well as a large number of machine-guns and small arms.

An officer from the headquarters of the 75th Infantry Division watched the entire attack through a binocular telescope; when it was over he called the commander of the battle group and enthusiastically expressed his admiration for this spirited attack. He said:

> "The only times I have seen an attack like this was by storm troops in the First World War and at the beginning of this war. Your men are magnificent soldiers. I would never have believed that such a thing was still possible at this stage of the war."

In spite of heavy casualties the hill was held against numerous enemy counterattacks until the evening of 13 April. Once the battle group was temporarily forced off the hill by a concentrated barrage from all of the enemy's heavy weapons, but an immediate counterattack restored it to our hands. Unfortunately this last and especially heavy attack resulted in casualties of about 40 dead and approximately twice as many wounded.

Hstuf. Count Seiffert, a young and dashing artilleryman who led a decisive infantry attack by his men, died a soldier's death here.

## A Lull

In the late afternoon an order was received stating that the battle group was to withdraw from Hill 347 after darkness set in and that it was initially to be stationed in a village near the front, where it was to have a brief period to recuperate as corps reserve.

The commander and his small staff waited for the last elements of the units leaving the front and said goodbye to the commander of the 75th Infantry Division, since effective immediately the battle group was directly subordinate to the corps.

At this point one special feat from the recent battles has to be mentioned. It was accomplished by the signals men in the battalions and in the battle group under the command of Ostuf. Hentschel. They had set up and maintained communications within the battle group during the past months, even under the most difficult conditions and in crisis situations. Great flexibility, independent action, improvisation and every possible type of stopgap measure enabled them to perform this considerable feat.

Deserving of special mention are the trouble shooters, who always operated alone with their comrades, day and night, in icy cold and snowstorms, in rain and mud; probably more than anyone else, they suffered from the loneliness and isolation of the Russian winter.

14 April: Not until late in the night did the battle group reach the quartering area and thus for the first time in a long time rest and a chance for some proper sleep. Everyone lay in the deep sleep of exhaustion until late morning. Subsequent to this orders were issued for the men to wash, shave, get their hair cut, clean their weapons and put their kit in order.

## The Battle Group is Pulled Out of the Line

The commanding officer was awakened from his noon nap by the operations officer, Ostuf. Nietschke; he brought the following completely unexpected and scarcely believable order from the corps:

> "Order has just been received from the Army High Command that the SS Armored Battle Group '*Das Reich*' is to be withdrawn from the Eastern Front immediately and is to be transported by rail to the "*Das Reich*" Division in France for reorganization."

At first we looked at each other speechless and could not believe it; for we had long ago given up any hope of getting out of Russia, and the men said openly that we slowly but surely were all going to be "used up." The commanding officer was immediately ordered to the chief of staff, *Oberst* von Natzmer; there he received confirmation of the report and was given further details.

The entraining station was Halicz, approximately eighty kilometers away from our current quarters. It had to be reached on foot.

It is strange how quickly situations change in war. Yesterday still involved in the fiercest fighting – and today the order to leave the Russian Front! Naturally there was great joy when the commanding officer officially informed the officers of the battle group of this happy news following his return from corps.

15 April: Unfortunately our joy was mixed with a drop of bitterness, as the last intact or repaired self-propelled carriages mounting four anti-aircraft machine-guns and all of the remaining operational heavy weapons which the men had been able to retain during this weeks-long fighting retreat had to be turned over to LIX Corps before departure. Of course in the existing situation the Eastern Front could not afford to give up any weapons.

The handover of the self-propelled carriages by the crews almost reminded one of a funeral. It was hard for them to take leave of the anti-aircraft machine-guns, which had enabled them and the battle group to get this far.

In the afternoon various decorations were handed out on our recommendation.

A little later *General* Schulz personally came to the battle group and thanked the officers, non-commissioned officers and men for their outstanding performance while serving in his corps and expressed regret that he was losing this ideal "fire-brigade." He said a heartfelt goodbye to each officer with a handshake and wished us continued soldier's luck.

In spite of all our joy we were sad to say goodbye to this brave, outstanding general and his chief of staff, *Oberst* von Natzmer, with whom the battle group had enjoyed an excellent relationship.

Thus the battle group's tour of duty had come to an end. During this winter its men had fought their way over approximately 900 kilometers, travelling under the most difficult conditions, much of it on foot in freezing cold, in snowstorms and through the spring mud. Having left all of its combat capable elements behind on the Eastern Front in this battle group, the "*Das Reich*" Division had thus also made its contribution to this winter campaign of 1943-44.

## March to the Entraining Station at Halicz

Hstuf. Herbst was placed in charge of preparations for entraining at Halicz. At approximately 5 PM we received the order to depart the next morning. But as the march route passed quite near the front near Buczacz, the battalion commander, Ostuf. Eckert, asked in the name of his officers for permission to depart during the night. The destination was Halicz, where the battle group was to be entrained.

The battle group moved out at 11 PM. The companies, "batteries" and tank crews marched on foot, rode in horse-drawn vehicles, or rode on horseback with their sick and wounded all night long (for the first time with no pressure from the enemy) maintaining perfect march discipline. The commander and his small staff stayed behind to see to the handing over of weapons and equipment.

16 April: At dawn the commander followed in one of the battle group's prime movers after obtaining from LIX Corps a special allotment of Iron Crosses, First and Second Class for the special accomplishments by the battle group.

On the way there was no sign left of the marching battle group. Not until the commanding officer drove through Buczacz did Ostuf. Eckert step out of a house and report to him that the battle group had already reached its first day's objective and had moved into quarters. Thirty-five kilometers had already been covered! At the same time he asked that the battle group might continue on immediately and naturally this request was granted.

The commanding officer drove ahead to Halicz, to where he had sent an advance detachment under the command of a special missions officer the day before in order to take charge of preparations for the transport by rail.

On 17 April, with all preparations proceeding smoothly, the commanding officer returned to the battle group. He allowed the battle group, approaching at a steady pace with its *panye* wagons and horses, to pass by him once again. Everywhere he saw smiling faces and high spirits – an unforgettable picture. The hardships that lay behind us were already half forgotten.

We later learned that the name of Hscharf. Hans Gödecker, platoon leader in the headquarters company of the SS Panzer-Grenadier Regiment "*Das Reich*", was entered in the Honor Roll of the German Army on this day.

18 April: In Halicz all remaining weapons, equipment and prime movers were handed over to the LIX Corps and the panye horses to the horse collection sites, from where they would serve the newly-arriving infantry units as welcome comrades in arms during their march to the stabilizing front. A steady stream of stragglers from the pocket arrived at the straggler assembly points, however there was not a single member of the battle group among them. Here they were fed, reequipped and put together in new combat companies.

At noon the commanding officer drove to the command post of the II SS Panzer Corps. He was received by *Generaloberst* Hausser and reported the departure of his battle group. The general extended his hospitality to the commanding officer, who outlined the battle group's operations.

"Papa" Hausser related that two days earlier he had been standing beside the road to Halicz near Buczacz when he saw a body of men approaching from the east at a steady pace – a very rare sight during the breakup of a pocket, where one saw so many stragglers. He asked who it was. But before he could get an answer the leader of the march group came up to him and reported: "SS Armored Battle Group 'Das Reich' en route to the entraining station in Halicz!" He was very happy to meet a unit from his old "*Das Reich*" Division here, especially one whose deportment after these heavy battles did the division proud. The farewell was heartfelt – especially for the many acquaintances in the corps headquarters.

It was a special kind of experience to once again drive through the rear area of an intact corps with its entire supply organization including corps hospital, bakery and butcher company, repair section and so on.

19 April: Rest day. All of the waiting mail, all of our rations and uniforms that had not reached us in the pocket, was now handed out in one go, and for the first time after long, hard months the men had a good time. In the afternoon a big closing parade was held, during which the special allotment of decorations was issued and the commanding officer

once again lauded the battle group's accomplishments and expressed his gratitude.

A telex was sent to the "*Das Reich*" Division informing it of our return.

## The Battle Group's Departure

20 April: The battle group entrained, with a single train sufficing to accommodate it. The signals officer had procured and set up another army radio receiver, and at 9 AM the train slowly set off on its eight-day trip to France to the solemn strains of the overture from *Tannhäuser*. The first leg of the trip took the train through Chorodoff and Lemberg (Lvov).

21 April: The battle group was deloused in Przemsyl. On the way we passed long trains heading the other way, transporting new assault guns and tanks to the front, and we rolled west with the reassuring feeling that the front which we had just left was stabilizing and being reinforced.

Hungarian *Honved* units equipped with magnificent horses were also being transported in the direction of the front. Based on our experience we were very skeptical that the Hungarian thoroughbreds were the right thing for the war of attrition in the east.

## Through Germany

22 April: The train passed Oderberg and Oppeln for Breslau, where the battle group was fed by the Red Cross at the train station. Notification of the death of Hstuf. Count Seiffert was also posted here. His relatives lived in Breslau.

23 April: The journey continued through Leipzig, Naumburg and Erfurt. Everyone was in high spirits about this trip through Germany. It was spring and the land lay before us in beautiful sunshine. We did, however, get our first impression of the destruction of German cities by the Allied air forces. The sight of the ruins put us in a pensive mood.

24 April: In magnificent weather the journey continued through Frankfurt, Kaiserslautern and Saarburg.

For the first time we saw huge formations of enemy bombers, glinting in the sun and approaching with a sonorous drone, completely unopposed by the German defenses as they made their way to their targets. We clenched our fists in impotent rage and were shocked by this turn of affairs.

25 April: Continued through Besançon to Lyon. The battle group was deloused again. On 26 April we reached Avignon.

## Return to the Division

27 April: Finally the train rolled into its destination station in Toulouse. Marching music sprang up and we saw the regimental band of the SS Regiment "*Deutschland*", which was on hand to welcome us. The regimental commander Ostubaf. Günther Wisliceny was also there and he warmly welcomed the commanding officer and the battle group.

From him the commanding officer learned that he was being awarded the Knight's Cross for his actions as commander of the 2nd Armored Reconnaissance Battalion "*Das Reich*" near Negrebovka.

While the battle group marched into the prepared barracks complex, the commanding officer drove to the division command post in Montauban, where he was warmly welcomed by the new division commander, *SS-Brigadeführer* and *Generalmajor* Lammerding, from whom he had taken over the battle group in Staro Konstantinov, and officially reported the return of the battle group. At the same time the division commander officially presented him with the Knight's Cross. This was followed by a celebration to mark the award and the return of the battle group.

28 April: In the late morning the entire battle group assembled in open square formation in the barracks courtyard and was greeted by the division commander. He thanked all of the officers, non-commissioned officers and men for their outstanding accomplishments, which had already been expressed in the awarding of numerous Iron Crosses, First and Second Class, and congratulated the battle group's commanding officer on receiving the Knight's Cross.

In his answering speech the commanding officer said that he would of course also wear this high decoration, which had been awarded him at the very end of the battle group's existence, as a decoration for the great accomplishments of the entire battle group, even though the Knight's Cross had been awarded for his service with the reconnaissance battalion.

## Disbandment of the Battle Group

The winding-up and disbandment of the battle group took place between 28 April and 2 May 1944, and the members of the battle group were sent back to their old units. Soon afterward the "Russia survivors" went on a well-deserved home leave in order to recover from the extraordinary hardships of the Russian winter. Of the approximately 3,000 men of the battle group at the time of the handover 800 returned to the division. It must also be taken into consideration, however, that when units were combined as a result of the shrinking of the battle group the headquarters which were freed up as a result were immediately sent west to the division to take part in its reorganization and that many of the wounded returned to the division following their release from hospital.

Great services were also performed by the battle group's engineer, Hstuf. Herbst, during the increasingly difficult transports to the west as well as in the general sphere of spares procurement and vehicle maintenance, for which he was decorated with the German Cross in Silver.

None of the members of the battle group will ever forget the hardships of these months-long defensive battles and fighting withdrawals, a time in which the battle group was entirely on its own and was continually forced to fight under unfamiliar commands with constantly changing subordinations.

This account was therefore not just written as a chapter in the history of the regiment, but instead is also intended to be a lasting memory of all of the men of the SS Armored Battle Group "*Das Reich*" and an expression of our gratitude.

## Appendix to Part V

Extracts from *Wehrmacht* Communiqués:

*15 January 1944: Units of the Waffen-SS counterattacked west of Berdichev, smashing two enemy regiments and inflicting heavy casualties on the Bolsheviks.*

*28 February 1944: Army troops and forces of the Waffen-SS counterattacked near Jampol and drove back the enemy.*

• • •

SS-Panzer-Grenadier Regiment
"Das Reich" Regimental Command Post,
19 February 1944, 5:15 PM

Ia Ge/Bo

Regimental Order

*For the continuation of the regiment's march on 20/2/1944*

1 *Enemy information: None. The battle group expects that the regiment will continue its march expeditiously with all means at its disposal.*

2 *SS Panzer-Grenadier Regiment "Das Reich" will continue its march on 20/2/1944 with all units and will initially reach Staro Konstantinov.*

3 *March objective: Staro Konstantinov. March route: Pischki – Ostropol-Tscherna-Staro Konstantinov. Probable march distance: 35 kilometers.*

4 *Departure point: Junction of Oshariwka-Pischki road and highway to Ostropol.*

5 *March order and departure times: Depart Pischki: 7 AM: regimental operations section and headquarters company, 14th Company. 8 AM: II Battalion. 9 AM: III Battalion.*

6 *Combat Train I to accompany the battalions, Combat Train I of the regimental headquarters to be ready to go in Ostropol at 7:15 AM and integrate itself.*

7 *Signals communications: radio. The regiment is to report its position hourly.*

8 *Regimental command post: Until 7 AM on 20/2/1944 in Oshariwka. After arrival in Staro Konstantinov: center of town.*

9 *The battalions are to ensure that every driver and every non-commissioned officer is familiar with the march route. As well, to the extent possible all entrenching tools are to be taken from the villages.*

*Signed Weidinger*
*SS-Sturmbannführer*
*And regimental commander*

• • •

75th Infantry Division — Division Command Post, 14 April 1944

Commanding Officer

*To the*
*Commander of the battle group of the SS Panzer Division "Das Reich"*
*Sturmbannführer Weidinger*

*The SS Battle Group "Das Reich" was subordinated to the division on 12 and 13 April 1944.*

*That day the enemy attacked the division's defense front with the bulk of two rifle divisions supported by tanks and strong mortar and anti-tank units. The important Hill 347, northeast of Worwolince station, was lost.*

*Moving out from Slone, the SS Battle Group "Das Reich" under the command of Sturmbannführer Weidinger with support from I Battalion, 300th Assault Gun Brigade launched a resolute counterattack against an enemy far superior in personnel and weapons and retook the hill. In the process several anti-tank guns and a large number of machine-guns and small arms were captured or destroyed.*

*In spite of heavy casualties the hill was held against numerous enemy attacks until the evening of 13 April. Even when the battle group was temporarily forced off the hill by concentrated fire from all the enemy's weapons, an immediate counterattack restored the vital hill to our hands.*

*The "Das Reich" Battle Group played an outstanding role in the division's defensive success through its resolutely executed attacks and its determined holding-on in the defense.*

*The division expresses its special gratitude and appreciation to the battle group for its excellent cooperation and outstanding willingness to serve. The division's best wishes go with its comrades of the Waffen-SS in their subsequent actions.*

*Signed Gerwig*
*signed Beuckemann*
*SS-Obersturmführer* *Generalleutnant*
*and adjutant* *and division*
*commander*

• • •

168th Infantry Division Division Command Post, 15 April 1944

Commanding Officer

Division Order of the Day

*Today the SS Battle Group "Das Reich" leaves the division formation. Under the division's command since 21 March 1944, the battle group, under the leadership of its proven and willing commander Sturmbannführer Weidinger, has made a significant contribution to the division's great success in the difficult, weeks-long rear-guard actions in the encirclement area of Kamenets-Podolsk.*

*To the commander of the battle group and to all officers, non-commissioned officers and men I express my gratitude and my appreciation for their actions as part of the 168th Infantry Division.*

*I wish you similar success and continued soldier's luck in the battles to come.*

| | |
|---|---|
| *Signed Gerwig* | *signed Landau* |
| *SS-Obersturmführer* | *Oberst and* |
| *and adjutant* | *acting division* |
| | *commander* |

• • •

1st Panzer Army Army Headquarters

Army Order of the Day

*The encircling ring of strong enemy forces has been breached!*

*On 23/3 the Russians were on the verge of bringing to a victorious conclusion a battle of destruction the equal of Cannae, Sedan and Tannenberg.*

*After achieving a breakthrough against our neighbor, from the east and west he had completed a double envelopment of the 1st Panzer Army north and south of the Dnestr and was attacking the army's eastern and northern fronts constantly with his infantry masses. The Russians were so certain of their victory, believed so strongly that our only choices were flight to the south or surrender, that they committed some of their forces to continue their operations to Romania.*

*Against any other opponent the Russians would have been right. But the German 1st Panzer Army, its communications severed, surrounded on all sides, a broad river with only a single crossing in its rear, stood firm like a rock. And when the order was given the army attacked, inadequately supplied at first, in spite of great terrain and weather difficulties.*

*The surrounding enemy was himself encircled, shattered, driven back and cut off from his communications. He now had elements turn back from the south bank of the Dnestr and began a pursuit in the north, but it availed him nothing.*

*The panzer and infantry divisions poured into the stunned enemy like a torrent and smashed his troops and plan of operations.*

*The accomplishments of the troops and command were unparalleled.*

*Officers, non-commissioned officers and men of all arms gave their best and their utmost, whether they served in the breakthrough spearheads, rear guards or flanking cover.*

*The count so far of enemy equipment destroyed or captured: 358 tanks, 190 guns, 29 assault guns, 4 self-propelled guns, 2 ATCC, 57 anti-tank rifles, 174 machine-guns and numerous small arms.*

*And as an especially beautiful side of this glorious page in the history of the 1st Panzer Army, all of our wounded were taken along and saved in a display of selfless comradeship. The Luftwaffe, in cooperation with the army supply agencies, contributing to the success of the operation by dropping supplies under the most difficult conditions, displaying an admirable willingness to serve.*

*On 6/4, after completing the breakthrough and far west of the original encirclement front, contact was made with the approaching forces of the Waffen-SS.*

*The 1st Panzer Army is free again and with the bulk of its forces is ready to strike further hard blows against the enemy, who lost this battle and with it a decisive success, wherever it is ordered to do so.*

*Long live Germany!*

*Signed Hube*
*General der Panzertruppen*

# Reorganization of the Regiment in Southern France 1944
## And the March to the Invasion Front[9]

## Organization of the 4th SS Panzer-Grenadier Regiment "*Der Führer*"

Regimental headquarters and headquarters company: signals platoon and motorcycle scout platoon.

I Battalion: battalion headquarters and signals platoon – 1st, 2nd and 3rd Companies (panzer-grenadier companies), 4th Company (heavy company).

III Battalion Armored: battalion headquarters and signals platoon – 9th, 10th and 11th Companies (armored troop carrier companies), 12th Company (heavy company in armored troop carriers).

I Battalion "D": attached to the "DF" Regiment – battalion headquarters and signals platoon – 1st, 2nd and 3rd Companies (panzer-grenadier companies), 4th Company (heavy company).

13th Company: infantry gun company: one platoon self-propelled guns, two platoons towed guns.

14th Company: anti-aircraft machine-gun company: two platoons each with four self-propelled carriages mounting 20-mm guns, one platoon with four towed 20-mm guns.

15th Company: motorcycle and reconnaissance company: two motorcycle platoons, one heavy motorcycle platoon (heavy machine-gun) on motorcycles with sidecars (*B-Krad*).

16th Company: combat engineer company: three engineer platoons, one armored troop carrier flame-thrower platoon with three flame-thrower half-tracks.

Combat train – supply train – baggage trains I and II.

II Battalion, which was not yet operational, at first stayed behind in the Montabaur area and was attached to the "*Deutschland*" Panzer-Grenadier Regiment.

## Preparations

Following the withdrawal of the unit headquarters and battle-weary units of the "*Das Reich*" Division from the Zhitomir area of Eastern Front in December 1943, and after a stay of approximately four weeks at the Stablack training grounds in East Prussia, the regiment was moved with the rest of the division into the area around Bordeaux for rest, training and reorganization. Later it was transferred into the Toulouse-Montauban area.

The transfer to the west also served the purpose of strengthening the German presence in France, to help maintain peace and order and, looking ahead, to help defend against the invasion that was sure to come, with only the location and date still not known.

II Battalion with the 13th and 14th Companies had stayed behind on the Eastern Front as part of the "*Das Reich*" Battle Group, which comprised all still combat-ready units of the division. It did not rejoin the regiment until after the return of the battle group at the end of April, following difficult and costly fighting retreats in the winter of 1943-44.

The regiment was stationed in the Moissac-Montauban quartering area, as follows: regimental headquarters and regimental units in Moissac, I Battalion in Valence d'Agent, II Battalion in Castelsarrasin, III Battalion in Montauban.

Like all of the other units of the "*Das Reich*" Division, the regiment had been seriously weakened by the months-long, wearing battles in Russian and required a complete overhaul, including officers, non-commissioned officers and men, as well as vehicles, weapons and equipment.

Most of the personnel replacements had arrived by the beginning of May 1944. They were made up mostly of Alsatians and ethnic Germans and members of other states. Approximately fourteen different nationalities were identified among the young replacements assigned to the regiment.

Only a small minority were volunteers, all the rest had been conscripted. There could be no more talk of the cream of the crop. The unit's inner structure had to suffer as a result, and this was soon reflected in the form of desertions from every unit of the regiment.

In this context it must be stated that the employment of Alsatians in a combat role in the west was a mistake, as their ties to France through upbringing and family were much too close. Several Alsatians later stated before a military court in Bordeaux that after deserting from the German Army they had disappeared into the *maquis* or had voluntarily surrendered to the British or Americans.

The lowering of the quality of personnel replacements was also reflected in a rise in military and criminal offenses, as a result of which the division court was forced to impose harsh sentences.

Because of the very strained supply situation, deliveries of vehicles, weapons and equipment were hesitant and marked by long delays; consequently the regiment was inadequately equipped for long periods during the training periods.

The allocation of fuel for the training of new drivers and for motorized exercises was extremely limited, which obviously had a very limiting effect on training.

The young replacement troops arrived with totally inadequate basic infantry training, and this had to be supplemented before squad, company and unit training could be started. As a result of this the restoration of the regiment's operational readiness was a slow and incomplete process. Nevertheless, several large exercises and inspections by army generals, including Inspector of Armored Forces *Generaloberst* Guderian, were completed to the extreme satisfaction of both sides.

Sturmbannführer Adolf Diekmann commanded I Battalion, which joined the regiment in autumn 1943. On the day of the invasion it was still not yet fully operational in terms of equipment.

II Battalion under its veteran commander Stubaf. Schulz was completely reorganized in France. The return of the battalion's core, which was still deployed in the east with the Battle Group "*Das Reich*", could no longer be counted on. Thus the senior, battle-tested officers, non-commissioned officers and men who returned with the remnants of the old II Battalion and the battle group were all the more welcome. Nevertheless, since this battalion left the most to be desired in terms of vehicles, weapons and equipment – the battle group having returned without vehicles and equipment – when the invasion came it had to remain behind as not yet operational. It followed the regiment to the invasion front several weeks later. In relatively good shape in terms of veteran squad and platoon leaders, the battalion survived for many more months through the sparing and clever use of personnel.

III (Armored) Battalion under its veteran commander and armored troop carrier specialist Stubaf. Kämpfe became fully operational just prior to the start of the invasion as a result of the timely arrival of new armored troop carriers. Until the arrival of II Battalion at the front it formed the actual core of the regiment.

A four-week non-commissioned officer course under Ustuf. Gerhard Schmager went a long way toward alleviating the serious shortage of non-commissioned officers.

The 13th (infantry gun) and 14th (anti-aircraft machine-gun) Companies under Ostuf. Erich Lenthe and Hstuf. Friedrich Hermann respectively were two-thirds equipped with guns and anti-aircraft machine-guns and operational.

The 15th (motorcycle) Company had been reformed from the motorcycle platoon of the regimental headquarters a short time before and was still in training. It went into action with two platoons.

The 16th (engineer) Company under Ostuf. Ernst von Eberstein was fully operational with three engineer platoons and one flame-thrower platoon (three flame-thrower half-tracks).

The French resistance movement became more active throughout the entire training period, especially after April. This movement (the *maquis*) was obviously controlled by the Allies from the other side of the Channel, at least according to guidelines developed there. The individual camp commanders usually executed practical command.

There was soon an increase in ambushes of German soldiers and acts of sabotage of all kinds, such as setting fires, robberies and the blowing of bridges and railroads. This "war in civilian clothing" resulted in considerable personnel and materiel losses, and it gradually developed into a palpable threat to the German occupation authorities as the following examples show:

In February 1944 the *Major* of the *Wehrmacht* Order Police was wounded in the hands by terrorists near Pontarlier south of Sâone and was then killed with a bullet in the base of the skull.

On 10 May 1944 three German railway workers were killed in Decazeville, also shot in the head.

On 6 June 1944 a German soldier was killed in Capdenac, with a bullet to the base of the skull.

On 1 June 1944 several German soldiers and two German railway workers were found shot in Figeac (Toulouse region).

At the same time sixteen cadets from the *Luftwaffe* ground combat school at La Courtine were attacked at the Mussidan (Dordogne) station and fourteen were killed; their bodies were horribly mutilated and desecrated.[10]

The regiment was placed on alert several times in May 1944 on orders from the division and the high command. It conducted several operations against the *maquisards*. This resulted in a return to quiet and order on the surface, however the resistance movement continued to grow underground.

According to Defense Situation No. 6 of the 2nd Panzer Division "*Das Reich*" dated 27 May 1944, confirmed sources indicated that the resistance movement was currently in a state of total mobilization and all groups (armed and unarmed alike) had received their operational orders. It was clear that after the start of the invasion the enemy command would drop trained forces in an attempt to take firmer control of the resistance groups and coordinate their efforts with military operations.

The *maquis* bands consisted of armed terrorists who carried out robberies, acts of sabotage and ambushes. Many *maquisards* lived undetected among the population; some were forced laborers who had escaped.

The chiefs, who provided money and arms, lived outside the camp; private operators fed and equipped the camp, which housed six men. There were, however, camps of twelve, eighteen and in isolated cases twenty-four or more men.

Regular supply drops by British aircraft supplemented the stocks of weapons and ammunition; indeed the entire organization of the French resistance was almost exclusively in British hands. Only in rare cases did weapons come from French or Italian army stores. The terrorists were forbidden to leave the camp alone under penalty of death.

As the Allied bombing campaign against German cities intensified, with correspondingly heavy civilian casualties, the emotional strain on the fighting troops also grew. Almost daily some member of the regiment received news telling of the total destruction of his home, the tragic death of his wife and children, parents or siblings. Those affected returned from home leave shaken and depressed.

After the invasion began all leaves were cancelled in order to avoid lowering the units' fighting strength; meanwhile the bombing terror against German cities became ever more pitiless and cruel. As a result everyone suffered to an increasing degree from nagging uncertainty about the fate of relatives.

These constant inner stresses were increased even further by the *maquisards*' guerilla war, which was not fought according to the terms of The Hague Land Warfare Convention and which constantly threatened the security of all. Every comrade lost in this unsoldierly and dastardly way fed the growing bitterness within the regiment. The years-long struggle against Bolshevism in Russia had also taken a considerable toll on the men's mental strength.

This mental state of the men must be taken into consideration in assessing the combat performance of the regiment on the invasion front, in order to judge fairly its all-out effort in spite of all hindrances in the final year of the war.

## March to the Invasion Front

6 June 1944: During the morning the division passed on the following situation report to the regiment: "Since the early morning hours the invasion has been under way on the Channel Coast. Action in Normandy is to be expected. Come to march readiness."

7 June: March preparations were concluded during the course of the day. In the afternoon a division order arrived for action in the Limoges area, where several army units had been surrounded by the *maquisards*. For the regiment this meant providing its own transport. All non-operational units of the division, including II Battalion "DF", remained where they were at first under the command of the commanding officer of the "*Deutschland*" Regiment, Ostubaf. Wisliceny. They would be moved up to the invasion front at a later date. During the night of 7-8 June the

regiment's units moved from their quarters on the advance road to a position near the departure point.

8 June: In the early morning hours the regiment and elements of the signals battalion set off as the first march group down National Road 20 via Cahors, Souillac, Brive and Uzerche toward Limoges.

Since the 2nd Armored Reconnaissance Battalion, which as advance detachment was supposed to precede the regiment, could not move off on time, the regiment at first marched at the division point in the following formation: 15th Company, regimental headquarters and signals platoon, 16th Company, 14th Company, 13th Company, III Battalion (Armored), I Battalion.

Behind the regiment came the artillery regiment and division headquarters as the second march group.

March group three consisted of I Battalion "D" with the assault gun and flak battalions.

The march, which was interrupted by a lengthy rest stop at about midday, proceeded according to plan until the afternoon. In every town through which the regiment passed, the German military commander had already taken security measures in the form of roadblocks on the side streets and barriers in front of the town headquarters. A peculiar tension hung in the air. The families of the town headquarters, which had been totally isolated in bandit territory since the start of the invasion, welcomed the panzer division with a sigh of relief. There was still no sign of the resistance movement. In beautiful summer weather the march was continued into the early hours of the afternoon.

As the division's flank was not secured, I Battalion was diverted from the march road west between Cahors and Souillac, and it marched as the regiment's left side column down National Roads 701 and 703 to secure the left flank in the direction of Limoges.

Since departure the regimental commander had driven in the regiment's point position. At about 5 PM the situation became tenser. The behavior of the civilian population was more reserved. In some places the villages appeared deserted.

The regimental commander ordered a motorcycle platoon from the 15th Company under Ustuf. Josef Winkler to the point; then, suddenly, shots were heard. The platoon had come upon a guarded roadblock beyond a curve in the road. Fire was returned immediately. Elements of the 2nd Armored Reconnaissance Battalion, which had arrived in the meantime, also joined in the battle. After the terrorists had been overpowered, the area of the group of houses was searched and the roadblock was removed. In the distance several armed civilians fled into the forest. In the next village a shed was burning, probably a signal to other resistance groups. The cluster of farms called Noailles lay approximately eight kilometers south of Brive.

The march resumed with the 2nd Armored Reconnaissance Battalion in the point position. Later another unmanned roadblock was cleared away.

At approximately 7 PM the head of the regiment reached Brive. The commanding officer was briefed by the local commander and learned that a *Wehrmacht* unit, III Battalion, 95th security Regiment, was completely encircled by *maquis* forces in Tulle.

On orders from the division the reconnaissance battalion was diverted toward Tulle. The division operations section likewise headed there. After Brive III Battalion assumed the point position in the march group and at about 8 PM, following a rest stop, resumed the advance toward Limoges. Several unguarded felled trees had to be cleared away en route.

The division, which was now under the command of the LXVI Army Corps (Clermont-Ferrand), established radio contact with the corps and during the night received orders to reconnoiter in the Brive-Tulle area and establish contact with the German detachments based there, as the corps no longer had contact with them.

In a radio broadcast the Allied High Command declared the entire French resistance movement to be a regular part of the internal French armed forces. For the first time in warfare an attempt was made to legalize a guerilla-style war against a regular army. This one-sided declaration was not sufficient to do so, but if following this declaration the partisans had abided by the terms of the Hague Land Warfare Convention, the one-sidedness of the declaration could have been remedied. These terms of the Land Warfare Convention were: responsible command, identification by uniform or armband, open carrying of weapons and adherence to the usages of war with regard to wounded, prisoners and civilians. The regimental commander was prepared to treat partisans who abided by these rules as regular soldiers.

9 June: At approximately 2 AM the head of the march group reached Limoges, where the regimental commander immediately sought out the local commander and received a briefing on the situation around Limoges.

The regiment was greeted with general relief. All the Germans in the city hoped that it would stay for as long as possible. The offices in Limoges had been cut of from the outside world for two days. No vehicles had got out through the *maquisards*' roadblocks or into the city from the outside. There was talk that the *maquis* was about to launch a concentric attack against the city.

The regimental command post was set up in the Hotel "Centrale" in the center of the city. The regimental commander briefed the battalion and company commanders on their quartering areas.

The regimental headquarters and the regimental units took up quarters in Limoges. I Battalion moved into the area north and northwest of Limoges, with the battalion command post in St. Junien. III Battalion was assigned the area around St. Léonhard de Noblat east of Limoges, and I Battalion "D", which was subordinated to the "DF" Regiment when the march ended, was quartered in the Pierre Buffiére area. III Battalion moved into its quartering area at dawn.

I Battalion encountered numerous obstacles and following a tiring journey did not arrive in Limoges until the late morning; after being briefed it marched on into its quartering area. During its security march on the left flank the battalion had had to engage in several fierce firefights. Its route took it through Gourdon, Payrac, Groleyac, Carsac, Calviac, Carlux and Peyrillac, where it rejoined National Road 20.

I Battalion had suffered its first casualties. Numerous obstacles of felled trees had been removed. The commanding officer, Stubaf. Diekmann, made a harried and overtaxed impression.

The assignments given the battalions and regimental units were:

Reconnaissance and if necessary combat missions for individual companies or ad hoc battle groups in the area of Limoges to establish contact with the various German agencies in the affected quartering areas, which – if necessary – were to be freed. Any *maquis* camps that were found were to be destroyed.

III (Armored) Battalion "DF" under *Sturmbannführer* Helmut Kämpfe was ordered to reach the city of Guéret located approximately 60 kilometers northeast of its quartering area and free the garrison there which was encircled by *maquisards*.

Radio communications with the various units was impossible on account of the considerable distances to the battalions and the very hilly, wooded terrain, consequently these had to operate independently according to their missions. Since lone dispatch riders or vehicles could no longer reach their destinations on account of *maquis* ambushes, contact could only be maintained by heavily armed special missions officers in armored troop carriers or convoys of several vehicles. As a result the regiment received only sparse reports.

During the night of 9-10 June III Battalion's medical officer, Ostuf. Dr. Müller, arrived at the regimental command post with several men in an armored troop carrier with bad news: "Stubaf. Kämpfe has fallen into the hands of the terrorists." He then went on to describe the events of 9 June as they affected III Battalion. His report follows:

Guéret had been occupied by the maquisards on 7 June and the entire *Wehrmacht* staff of the local commander was taken prisoner. On 8 June a German army unit, which came from the direction of Montluçon, tried to liberate the city but was halted by fierce resistance.

On 9 June the attack was resumed from the east, now with air support, while III Battalion advanced on Guéret from the opposite direction.

The battalion had moved out in the early morning. During the midmorning, prior to reaching the city, the point encountered one or two trucks with armed Frenchmen riding on the cabs heading in the opposite direction on a twisting section of road in a heavily-wooded area. Having obviously underestimated the strength of the approaching column, these opened fire. The squad leader in the first armored vehicles was seriously wounded in the head. The leading vehicles immediately opened fire with all weapons. Tragically, it turned out that the occupants of the trucks were German (female auxiliaries, army officers and officials and several soldiers) who were being taken west from the city, which was being relieved from the east. One or two Germans were killed; a French woman in the service of the Germans was wounded. The remaining wounded escaped serious injury and several others were not hurt.

When the leading elements of the battalion reached the outskirts of Guéret the town was already in the hands of German troops again.

By sundown the battalion had assembled in a small town before Guéret. The wounded French woman was delivered to a hospital there. Stubaf. Kämpfe instructed Ostuf. Dr. Müller to drive the wounded to the train in the quartering area. Müller drove ahead in an armored troop carrier; then at about 8 PM Stubaf. Kämpfe, driving alone in his Talbot, overtook him, waved and roared away.

He had driven ahead of the march column in order to express his tanks to the mayor of a village on the march road for having a destroyed bridge repaired during the course of the day.

Twenty minutes later, by which time dusk had fallen, Dr. Müller found his commanding officer's empty car, its engine running and doors open, sitting on the road at the edge of the forest. An empty submachine-gun magazine lay under the car. There was no sign of a battle or traces of blood.

The battalion point arrived about ten minutes later. Ostuf. Weihrauch, who was driving in the lead position, immediately ordered the woods combed in spite of the failing light and sent Ostuf. Dr. Müller to report what had happened to the regiment in Limoges. There was no radio communication. All of the searching was in vain. Kämpfe remained missing.

Dr. Müller subsequently drove back to the battalion and Ostuf. Heinrich Manz temporarily took over command of III Battalion.

The news of the capture of the outstanding and generally liked commander caused great excitement and bitterness in the entire regiment. Kämpfe's disappearance was a serious loss to the regiment in military and human terms. Every unit that could be contacted was immediately informed of what had happened and was instructed to conduct inquiries in its quartering area. None produced any result, however.

During the late hours of the evening, at about 10 PM, Stubaf. Weidinger drove to Tulle escorted by a motorcycle from 15th Company. He had orders from the regimental commander to report the incident and also convey a report on the situation in Limoges and important supply reports. Weidinger arrived at approximately 3 AM after an uneventful drive. The trip was necessary because radio could not bridge the approximately 130 kilometers between Limoges and Tulle.

On the way he met trucks of the division carrying French labor service workers. As Stubaf. Weidinger learned, they had been arrested on suspicion of having made common cause with the *maquisards*. It was an entire battalion of about 400 men with a major in command and three other officers as company commanders. After their arrival in Limoges they were turned over to the regiment. Since all available men of the regimental headquarters were employed elsewhere, they were guarded by soldiers of the local commander.

At division headquarters in Tulle Stubaf. Weidinger learned of the events of the previous day and of the terrible fate of the German town garrison.

## The Events in Tulle

When the 2nd Reconnaissance Battalion retook the city of Tulle on 9 June it discovered the bodies of forty German soldiers of III Battalion, 95th Security Regiment with their skulls smashed in and eyes put out.

According to eyewitness reports the rebels, which included Poles, Spanish communists and even four Russians, drove over still living German soldiers with heavy trucks and mutilated them beyond recognition. Women in company with the terrorists defiled the bodies. Several of the dead had to be buried as unknown, as unbelievable facial mutilations made identification impossible. One of the dead was found to have had holes bored through both heels and a rope passed through the holes. He had obviously been dragged to his death in this way. Many of the dead were found to have been shot through the soles of the feet as many as six times. Two French priests later stated before the Standing High Military Court that as well ten or twelve German soldiers had been shot against the wall of the Tulle cemetery.[11]

This execution was carried out on 7 June by partisans, even though the priest who was present pointed out the irregularity of the act.

The mutilated bodies that had been found were examined by the surgeon Dr. Roschmann of the division medical company and by the security battalion's medical officer. The mutilations were identified and photographed by the Ic, Hstuf. Kovatsch. The report was passed on by the division to the LXVI Army Corps as a special incident.

Ninety-eight *maquisards*, who were picked out of the captured men with the help of the population and identified as terrorists (most were not from the village), were subsequently hanged. A French priest administered the last rites. Afterward the French labor battalion was employed to bury the hanged men in the cemetery in Tulle.

It was later learned that another 62 German soldiers who had fallen into the hands of the maquisards, including medics and railway workers, had been shot by the rebels in a wood near Naves (10 kilometers north of Tulle) on 9 or 10 June 1944.

Therefore in the Tulle area alone German losses through the illegal fighting methods of the *maquisards* amounted to at least 114 soldiers killed while prisoners, not counting those men killed or wounded in the encounter with the reconnaissance battalion and the German railway workers killed at the station.

In the opinion of the German command authorities and based on statements by the local French authorities of the prefecture and mayor's office, who had helped in picking out the suspects, the terrorists in Tulle were communist bands consisting mainly of Spanish and French communists and they ultimately were responsible for what had happened in Tulle.

Therefore the German side also called upon the civilian population of Tulle to loyally assist in effectively combating the "common enemy", namely the communist bands.

The official report by the French authorities on the executions in Tulle before the international military court at Nuremberg delivered by the French prosecutor stated that:

> "On 7 June a large group of guerrillas attacked the German security forces and following a battle which lasted into the afternoon succeeded in taking control of the majority of the city...
>
> At about 8 PM on the same day strong German armored units rushing to the aid of the garrison entered the city, which was hastily evacuated by the terrorists.
>
> The troops that had recaptured Tulle decided on make reprisals. The French internal forces, which had taken the city, had withdrawn.
>
> The Germans were unable to take any prisoners and reprisals were made against the civilian population..."

This official French report makes absolutely no mention of the fact that 40 German soldiers of III Battalion, 95th Security Regiment had holed up in a school when the guerrillas took the city. The guerrillas called upon the soldiers to lay down their weapons and surrender and promised them their lives and decent treatment. Believing these promises the soldiers put down their weapons and came out of the school with hands raised as a gesture of surrender. As soon as they had left the building they were fired on by the terrorists, who disregarded the promise they had made, and as described above were bestially mistreated, mutilated and desecrated in unbelievable ways. Several bodies had had their sex organs cut off and stuffed in their mouths, while others had been defiled with human feces. That is how they were found by the arriving German troops.

As well the bodies of 10 to 12 other disarmed soldiers from the same battalion were found at the cemetery wall; according to statements made by the French priest Espinasse they had been shot there by the terrorists *after their capture*.

How would French troops and command authorities have acted if the roles had been reversed? The answer is not difficult: exactly the same or more rigorously!

Interestingly even the official French report speaks of guerrillas (in the translation). But guerrillas do not enjoy the protection of the Hague Land Warfare Convention. Elsewhere the report speaks of terrorists (translation), and only later in the report do they receive the designation "the French internal armed forces." At this time, in a move unique in the history of warfare, the Allied High Command had flatly declared the French *maquisards*, the majority of whom were Spanish Reds or French communists and who were outside the Hague Land Warfare Convention, to be "internal French armed forces," even though the maquisards wore no common external insignia, carried concealed weapons and fought mainly from ambush in the German area of operations and the marshalling area for the defense against the invasion then in progress. However the German troops who retook Tulle had no inkling of this coup by the Allied military command.

Furthermore this was a clear breach of the German-French ceasefire agreement of 1940, which was still in effect, according to which resistance against the German occupying power was threatened with a resumption of hostilities.

At the time the German command authorities felt certain that the terrorists had not withdrawn from Tulle, but had instead disappeared into the civilian population. Therefore they, or the majority of them, still had to be inside the city and the German troops had failed to take prisoners because the terrorists had chosen not to fight. The terrorists, the majority of whom were probably not locals, therefore had to be picked out of the male civilian population with the help of the local authorities such as the mayor, the director of the munitions factory and others. And so it happened.

The statement by the then mayor, Colonel Bouty (Page 34), that the Ic of the Kowatsch Division had told him that "the German authorities had decided to hang 120 *suspects*," proves that those executed were considered partisans and not hostages.

The local secretary of the prefecture, la Roche, declared in his statement (Page 44) that:

> "The SS Captain appeared late in the afternoon and informed the prefecture that 120 *terrorists* (his own characterization) had been sentenced to death by hanging on orders from his superiors, who were stationed far from Tulle."

The choice of hanging as the method of execution was probably chosen because of the vile actions of the terrorists in killing with bestial sadism and cruelty an enemy who had surrendered based on a promise of fair treatment then mutilating and desecrating the bodies. In doing so they had placed themselves outside the rules of war and of humanity. Consequently in the German view the military form of execution by shooting was out of the question.

Since the German command was convinced that the terrorists were still in the city hiding out among the civilian population, obviously all of the male residents of Tulle without exception were assembled on a factory courtyard because all were suspects at first. Apparently they were there divided into three groups, probably one of German sympathizers, one of absolutely neutral residents and one of non-residents, who were picked out with the help of the local authorities. This latter group must have contained all of the terrorists still in Tulle but disguised as civilians.

But a number of persons were released from this group on the word of the mayor and factory director who were certain that they were not terrorists. Finally there were left 120 terrorists, who after careful selection with the help of leading personalities of Tulle could only be terrorists or their accomplices. Of these 98 were hanged.

That there was indeed objective cause to assume that some of the citizens of Tulle were cooperating with the terrorists or were terrorized by them, as was claimed many times by the population, is revealed on Page 43 of the statement:[12]

> "We were then asked about the possible presence of any *maquis*, and although there were about 30 in the city at the time we of course did not say this."

At the request of the elderly bishop of Tulle, who was given an audience at the division headquarters, the terrorists were given spiritual succor before they were hanged and were promised a Christian burial, which took place in the cemetery.

Everyone can understand that the French population supported the partisans, who were fighting for the freedom of France. But one cannot deny understanding to those who took steps to defend the lives of the soldiers entrusted to them against the unmilitary and vile fighting methods of the terrorists.

It is impossible to be sympathetic, however, when the French authorities remain silent about the cause of the reprisals, namely the mutilation of the murdered German soldiers, and when three decades later they respond to one of the authors regarding the German accusation that they did not testify truthfully: "One forgets that this 'evidence' is the report that the *prefect requested* in order to send it to the *Vichy* authorities...and actually so that a protest might be made to the *occupation authorities*." Following the liberation of Tulle in late summer 1944 the French authorities executed 98 German prisoners as a reprisal; none of these men had had anything at all to do with the events in Tulle in June 1944.

## Ostuf. Gerlach's Report

10 June: At approximately 6 AM Stubaf. Weidinger arrived back in Limoges with the motorcycle platoon without incident.

Meanwhile the investigation into the disappearance of Kämpfe was in full swing. In the early morning hours a member of the dispatch rider section found Stubaf. Kämpfe's personal papers in the city on the main street near the regimental command post and turned them over to the regiment. From this it was concluded that Kämpfe had been transported by the *maquisards* by car through Limoges to another place. It was therefore to be assumed that he was still alive and that he had been able to throw this symbol from the car during the drive through the city.

In the early hours of the morning Ostuf. Karl Gerlach, special missions officer of the "*Das Reich*" Assault Gun Battalion, arrived at the regimental command post completely exhausted and dressed only in his under clothes and reported his experiences to the regimental commander. It is best that we let him describe in his own words what happened to him on 9 June; the following is the statement given by him to a German lawyer for the Oradour trial:

> *"Coming from the south of France, the regiment arrived in Limoges during the night of 8-9 June 1944.*
>
> *On the morning of 9 June in Limoges I received from regimental commander Stadler orders for the assault gun battalion to take up quarters in the Nieul area. Referring to a map he briefed me and warned me about the resistance fighters active in this area.*
>
> *I subsequently drove to Nieul with six men in three cars. We established quarters there; but as they were inadequate, following the map we drove into the neighboring town. My car was faster than the other two vehicles; I was therefore soon forced to stop and, as they had not followed me, turn around in order to find them again.*
>
> *After driving a short distance, on the open road I was suddenly stopped by a truck in which I saw military uniforms. At first I thought they were friendly, for we had been told that there were French in militia uniforms fighting on our side. Before I could give it any more thought, much less make use of my submachine-gun, seven or eight*

*uniformed men jumped out of the truck, pointed their weapons at us and approached my car shouting 'hands up!'*

*They hauled my driver and me from the car, ripped our uniforms from our bodies and said while making unmistakable gestures: 'SS! Finished right now!*

*We had only our underclothes on. Dressed like this, we were shoved by them off the road down into some bushes. I was sure that they were going to shoot us, therefore I tried to speak again and explain myself, first to the leader, a tall slim man, early thirties, in military uniform. But he didn't seem to understand me and just kept saying: 'No SS! SS finished!' I therefore spoke to a younger man who spoke relatively good German, apparently an Alsatian, who appeared to feel sorry for us. But that also did no good. I then declared that I was the division operations officer and that I could provide important information if I was brought before a maquis leader. That seemed to make an impression on the Alsatian; he translated this for his leader. The latter looked at me and said something that I did not understand.*

*My driver and I were dragged back to the car, where we had to climb in again and were placed under guard. Then we drove off. After a while I saw road signs and was able to get my bearings. Then came a sign at the entrance to a village; it read: Oradour-sur-Glane. Then we stopped on the main street of Oradour-sur-Glane. We were forced to get out. We were surrounded by maquis and many curious onlookers. I saw numerous uniformed persons, including women wearing yellow leather jackets and steel helmets. The attitude of the population became more threatening from minute to minute. A man in uniform therefore had us brought back to the truck. I saw ropes being brought out of a shed next to a bakery on Oradour-sur-Glane's main street. My driver and I were fetched from the truck again and tied up with the ropes. We were bound in such a way that both of our arms were tied behind our backs; as well the knots were secured with wire. We stood like that for about three-quarters of an hour. Then French civilians came riding up on a tandem bicycle. They spoke to the people. Then we had to climb into the car again.*

*The men who had captured us also climbed into the car; they remained with us as guards. We drove away from Oradour-sur-Glane, following the tandem bicycle that led the way, continually giving signals from 100 meters ahead. On the way we halted for the first time in front of a house, on the front of which there was a telephone sign. From there the two civilians on the tandem bicycle made a call. They returned to the truck and explained something to the leader of the guard detail in French, which we did not understand.*

*We then turned left off the main road into an uninhabited area. After driving another three or four kilometers we were dropped off at an outguard. The ropes were removed and we were given something to eat. Meanwhile the truck with the guard detail drove away; it returned about two or three hours later. After we had been tied up again we had to climb back into the truck.*

*We drove about eight to ten kilometers to a forest lane, at the corner of which there stood a marker stone that said '6.5 km to Bellac.' We turned off the road in this forest lane and after about 300 meters came upon a French truck marked with the Tricolor.*

*Here we were dragged from the truck again and mistreated in the cruelest way. They dragged us to a young maquis, apparently the commander of the post. He wore a blue uniform.*

*We were not interrogated; he merely screamed at us: 'SS no interrogation, kaput at once!' The young Alsatian, one of the men guarding us, tried to make objections, but he was coarsely rebuffed by the commander. The commander now called over several Frenchmen who were also wearing blue uniforms and, as far as I could tell from gestures and movements, gave them the order take us into the woods and shoot us. My driver recognized the situation quite clearly and struggled, refusing to go along. Enraged, the Frenchmen standing around us fell upon him. I used this moment to run into the nearby forest and bushes. I ran as fast as I could for my life was at stake. I heard shots; I turned around and saw my driver fall. I plunged onwards, seeking protection behind trees and bushes. They followed and shouted after me, several shots passed my head. I constantly changed direction, and through these deceptions and under cover of twilight I succeeded in escaping.*

*As I had studied the map well before leaving Limoges, I knew that I had to reach the Bellac-Limoges rail line. This I did and the next morning, on 10 June, I arrived at the Limoges command post.*

*I reported to my regimental commander Stadler and described what had happened. He told me that I had not been the only one who had been attacked and kidnapped the day before. He told me about the commander of the "Der Führer" Regiment's III Battalion, a man named Kämpfe, who had not yet returned and had probably been killed. The regimental commander ordered me to get some sleep as we had some long marches ahead of us.*

*When I got up the commander of I Battalion "Der Führer", Diekmann, had me show him on the map the place where I was captured and the way to the spot where my driver was shot. Soon afterwards he set out with the 3rd Company under the command of Hauptmann Kahn, destination Oradour-sur-Glane..."*

During the course of the morning the commander of I Battalion, Stubaf. Adolf Diekmann, came to the regiment in an agitated state and reported the following:

In St. Junien two French civilians had come to him and informed him that a high-ranking German officer was being held prisoner by the *maquisards* in the village of Oradour-sur-Glane. As part of a celebration he was to be publicly executed and burned the same day. The entire population of Oradour-sur-Glane was working with the maquis and there was a senior maquis headquarters in the village.

At about the same time the SD office in Limoges informed the regiment that according to intelligence from their French operatives there was a senior maquis command post in Oradour-sur-Glane.

Stubaf. Diekmann therefore immediately asked the regimental commander for permission to take a company there in order to free the captive. In his opinion it could only be Stubaf. Kämpfe, a close personal friend.

The regimental commander thereupon informed Diekmann of the events in the same village of Oradour-sur-Glane from the previous day and immediately gave his approval for this operation, however with additional instructions that if, contrary to expectations, Kämpfe was not found,

Stubaf. Diekmann was to bring back captured maquis leaders if at all possible. He intended to use the prisoners to negotiate with the resistance movement for Kämpfe's release.

Ostuf. Gerlach, who was still with the regiment, was summoned and gave Diekmann detailed directions using a map.

It has often been claimed by the French that Oradour-sur-Glane had been confused with another Oradour. However, according to Ostuf. Gerlach's statement, based on the facts as described any confusion was out of the question. Diekmann then drove off.

At this point it must be stated emphatically, as the former Ostubaf. Weidinger testified in his deposition to the Standing High Military Court in Bordeaux, that no order was ever issued by the regimental commander Staf. Stadler, by the "*Das Reich*" Division, by any other office of the German Army or by the police to carry out mass executions in Oradour-sur-Glane and to burn the village to the ground as was at first claimed by the French.

There was, however, a standing order from the Commander in Chief West, which stated that houses in which weapons were found were to be burned down immediately. And in its order of the day on 8 June 1944 the LXVI Reserve Army Corps, to which the "*Das Reich*" Division was subordinate, had, on instructions from the *Wehrmacht* operations staff, called for "extreme harshness and ruthlessness" in the battle against the bandits:

> "In order to restore peace and security the harshest measures must be employed to terrorize the inhabitants of this constantly infested area until they finally lose their desire to accept these resistance groups and allow themselves to be ruled by them, and as a cautionary example for the entire population. Ruthless harshness is vital in this critical hour in order to eliminate the danger in the rear of the fighting troops and avoid greater sacrifices in blood among the troops and the civilian population."

All day long it was impossible to establish radio communication with Stubaf. Diekmann on account of the terrain and the distance.

During the late morning the O3 of the division, Ostuf. Dr. Walter Wache, came to the regiment to assist the regimental commander in the investigations into the disappearance of Kämpfe, which went on all day.

At the same time Stubaf. Weidinger, who was at regimental headquarters for familiarization, established contact with the commander of the Limoges security police in order to exchange intelligence on the enemy and to ask him to make available to the regimental commander a *maquis* leader in the custody of the security police.

Ostubaf, Meier of the security police agreed to this at once and also promised to release fifteen more maquisards in the event that Kämpfe was given back.

The maquis leader in question was brought to the regimental command post. Acting as interpreter, the O3 told him that he would be given his freedom in exchange for a promise to immediately contact his headquarters and tell them that fifteen more maquisards would be released as soon as Kämpfe was returned alive.

The regimental commander had also asked the administrative officer how much money could be made available to support this operation. The later replied with a sum of 35,000 Reichsmarks. The sum was promised as an additional reward for Kämpfe's release in order to give the offer more weight.

Having known Stadler personally for years, the author, who was a witness to this conversation, was absolutely certain that the commanding officer would keep his promise.

In these days the commanding officer tried everything to get Kämpfe back while avoiding unnecessary bloodshed. He had even, contrary to military practice, used money in an attempt to bring the negotiations to a successful conclusion.

The maquis leader declared himself in agreement with the offer and was therefore taken by car to the outskirts of Limoges, where he was set free at the last German sentry post. He called back in the evening and reported that he had not yet found his headquarters. Then nothing more was heard of him.

Not until much later, namely during the trial in Bordeaux (January to March 1953), was it learned that the negotiator had reached his maquisard headquarters and had passed on his offer. At the Oradour trial Canou stated that he had turned Kämpfe over to "his chief." As Canou was a member of the St. Léonhard *maquis*, his chief was a certain Guingouin, to whom we will have to come back. Canou's statement at Bordeaux was printed in *Le Monde* on 25-26 January 1953:

> "The Germans, declared M. Canou, seemed to be especially fond of Major Kämpfe; for they tried to obtain his release amicably, offering to exchange him for 30 resistance men being held in Limoges. Nothing came of it."

It turned out that *Standartenführer* Stadler's exchange officer had been received but not accepted by the *maquis* leader. This leads to the inevitable question as to whether it was even still possible to exchange Kämpfe at noon on 10 June, or to put it bluntly, whether he was still alive.

Toward noon Ostuf. Dr. Müller came to Limoges again with two armored troop carriers and brought the female auxiliaries, officers, officials and soldiers who had been freed the previous evening to the regimental command post. The female auxiliaries complained a great deal about the vile and cynical treatment they received from the *maquisards* during their captivity in Guéret.

Since the division's hospital was en route to Normandy and not operating, the man with the head wound had to be taken to the French hospital in Limoges, where in spite of an operation by a French doctor he died the same day.

Late in the afternoon of this day Stubaf. Diekmann returned to the regiment and reported roughly the following to the regimental commander:

The company had encountered resistance in Oradour the bodies of several executed German soldiers were found. (Source: Stückler report. Agrees with the results of the court martial investigation.) It then occupied the village and immediately conducted an intensive search of the houses. Unfortunately this failed to turn up Kämpfe, however large quantities of weapons and ammunition were found. He had therefore had shot all the men of the village, who were surely *maquisards*.

The women and children were locked up in a church while all this was going on. Then the village was set on fire, as a result of which the ammunition that was stored in almost every house went up. The burning of the village resulted in fire spreading to the church, where ammunition had also been hidden in the roof. The church burned down very rapidly and the women and children lost their lives.

Staf. Stadler was extremely shocked by this report and shaken to the core he said to Stubaf. Diekmann:

> "Diekmann, this may end up costing you dearly! I am going to ask the division court at once for a court martial investigation against you. I cannot allow the regiment to be charged with something like this!"

Furthermore he was angry over the fact that Diekmann had not carried out his order to bring back captured *maquis* leaders in the event that Kämpfe was not found. Deeply upset, he dismissed Diekmann, instructing him to file a detailed report. Diekmann did not defend himself, instead he obviously trusted in the court martial investigation.

Staf. Stadler reported the happenings in Oradour-sur-Glane to the division commander, *Brigadeführer* Lammerding, as soon as he arrived and asked for a court martial investigation against Diekmann. Lammerding promised to initiate one as soon as the combat situation permitted.

There were many more encounters, ambushes and casualties. Only in the quartering area of I Battalion, "*Deutschland*" Regiment was there complete peace.

Following the incidents in Oradour and Tulle the Ic intercepted a radio message sent by a senior *maquis* headquarters calling for a cessation of the struggle against the Germans until the "*Das Reich*" Division had left central France. Resistance was senseless in view of the great sacrifices that had been demanded at Oradour and Tulle. These sacrifices were out of all proportion to the successes achieved.

Another enemy transmission was intercepted stating that *Sturmbannführer* Kämpfe had been shot as a reprisal for the destruction of Oradour.

Not until much later, when the defensive battles in Normandy had been under way for some time, did the division receive by way of the military commander of France a complaint from the French prefecture of Limoges concerning the events at Oradour. The regiment and division were obliged to reply to the charge. This was the first known French version of the events at Oradour, according to which the town's entire population had been killed.

For the sake of completeness, however, it must be stated here that while in the military prison in Bordeaux members of the German security police told the author that the entire French resistance movement had suffered such a shock from Tulle and Oradour that they were incapable of action for weeks. It was for this reason alone that the German occupation troops in southwestern France (a total of 30,000 men) were able to link up with the German divisions withdrawing from Normandy without interference from the *maquisards*. Without this shock effect on the maquis, German losses through resistance action would have been much greater.

The files of the Bordeaux Senior Military Court (examining magistrate Lesieur) have the following to say about the Kämpfe affair:

> *"Major Kämpfe, the commander of III Battalion, risked driving ahead of the march column in a car in the twilight. Abeam the town of La Bussière, in the district of St. Léonhard de Noblat, he was capture by several maquisards, including Sergeant Canou.*
>
> *Major Kämpfe was taken to the neighboring district of Cheyssous. His capture was to serve as the pretext for a whole series of reprisals.*
>
> *III Battalion was following approximately ten minutes behind its commander. After the abandoned car was found the Germans, who were accompanied by several militia people, searched the houses of the village and took reprisals.*
>
> *As for Major Kämpfe, he was executed by the maquisards as a consequence of the bloodbath in Oradour-sur-Glane."*

This version is not the only one, however. There were "witnesses" who stated that Kämpfe was shot while trying to escape, while some others date the shooting of Kämpfe as 11 June 1944 and still others long after that. The location of Kämpfe's grave was not given. French doctors who offered to exhume the body were threatened.

During the course of 11 June a division order was received calling for the march to the invasion front to go ahead on 12 June.

Under these circumstances Staf. Stadler decided to set free the French labor battalion, which was still being held prisoner, as there was no evidence of cooperation with the *maquisards* and the battalion made a very disciplined and military impression. The only condition was that the entire battalion was to be confined to a barracks until after the regiment's departure so as not to make it too easy for it to join up with the terrorists.

On behalf of the regimental commander, Stubaf. Weidinger met in the office of the commander of the security police with the leader of the French militia in Limoges and informed him of the regimental commander's plans.

The latter was pleasantly surprised and declared that he was deeply moved by the generosity of the German commander, who, as he put it, had given a part of the French youth another opportunity to prove itself for the true France.

At about three in the afternoon on the same day the regimental commander himself officially released the entire battalion from captivity. The release took place in a formal fashion with a brief speech by the regimental commander, with the labor battalion's chaplain, an Alsatian, acting as interpreter.

The militia leader, who had immediately made a barracks available, thanked the commanding officer in moving words, and the French labor service personnel, who had expected a long period of captivity, were extremely surprised and impressed by their sudden release.

Subsequently the entire battalion, led by its officers, moved unescorted into the waiting barracks in the middle of the *maquis*-surrounded city.

The march by an entire French battalion at this critical time made a great impression on the French population. News of this event was broadcast the same day by the press and local radio.

Elements of III Battalion carried out one more operation, to round up an armed French military police unit which had gone over to the maquisards. The approach of the German troops was obviously observed and reported by the civilian population. When the battalion reached the forest camp it was only able to capture one or two Frenchmen and free a few German soldiers. The bulk of the military police unit had escaped.

The regiment spent the rest of the day preparing for the upcoming march.

The court martial investigation, which began following the arrival in Normandy, revealed that *Sturmbannführer* Diekmann had found the bodies of "executed German soldiers" in Oradour, as the division Ia stated for the defense at Nuremberg in 1949. Division commander Lammerding has since died and his papers reveal that he made himself solely responsible to the Federal German government for the Oradour trial in Bordeaux. However, the federal government, represented by the then Legal Protection Office of the foreign office, rejected *General* Lammerding's position then and later. This posture was directly linked to discussions by the legal protection office with the French prosecutors, who had promised that all of those convicted in the Oradour trial would be released forthwith.

As far as the result of the court martial investigation, *General* Lammerding revealed in his papers what the federal German government had known during the trial:

Among the dead, Diekmann had found at the entrance to Oradour the charred remains of a German medical unit. The wounded had been tied up with the drivers in the cab, where they were burned to death. Lammerding gave evidence of this act after the war; however, this, too, was overlooked by the federal German government.

Without minimizing the sacrifice of the innocent population of Oradour, especially the women and children, these new facts provide a different perspective on Diekmann's decision to burn down the village and shoot the men.

After the war the events in Oradour-sur-Glane were investigated in depth by the Standing Senior Military Court in Bordeaux and dealt with in a major trial.

Accused were the battalion commander Stubaf. Diekmann, the company commander and the entire 3rd Company "*Der Führer*." The men of this company, the majority of whom had been found in British captivity, were handed over by the British to the French and taken to Bordeaux. At first there were eight Germans and one Alsatian (a volunteer), a very small number as the vast majority of the company's personnel had been killed or wounded during the company's first action in Normandy (in the Noyer area). Other members of the company, all from Alsace, did not arrive until later.

Oradour began occupying a prominent place in Allied war propaganda against Germany soon after the "*Das Reich*" Division's departure for the invasion front. Every Allied radio station called out the name of Oradour as a disgrace to all Germans worldwide.

Diekmann's action stood in stark contrast to the position of the regimental commander, who at the same time was striving to negotiate with the maquisards, who in the German view were criminal terrorists, in order to secure Kämpfe's release. His humane conduct was further illustrated by the release of the French labor battalion.

As a result of the facts revealed in the papers left behind by Lammerding, however, Diekmann's decision must now be seen in a different light.

The fact that Diekmann went beyond the orders of his regimental commander and made his own decision can no longer be interpreted as excess. First, it must be stated that Diekmann wanted to free his friend Kämpfe and had orders as to how to do so. Having failed to find Kämpfe and taken no hostages, Diekmann must have come to the conclusion that Kämpfe was no longer alive and could not be freed.

As a result of this new situation, which was not foreseen in his orders, Diekmann reached his own decision, which, as a staff officer, he was not only entitled but was also obliged to do, especially as their was no communication with the regiment. Of course this was on his own responsibility. In assessing the situation Diekmann had to take into consideration the standing order from the Commander in Chief West and the corps special order. Witnesses stated that Diekmann did not reach this decision easily.

Since his actions were in total contradiction to the order of his regimental commander, he had to provide a legal justification for this independent decision one way or another. He seemed to have been clear on this and that is also shown by the behavior of Stadler, who immediately requested a court martial investigation. That Diekmann and Stadler made no further statements because of their differing views probably lay in the nature of the matter and in the effort to now leave the decision to the division court.

Consequently neither the command of the "*Der Führer*" Regiment nor that of the "*Das Reich*" Division can be blamed for the destruction of

Oradour, nor can any other German agency or the leadership of the Reich.

Why the 3rd Company under Diekmann's command went to Oradour-sur-Glane was described in detail. Furthermore, interrogation of the then Ostuf. Gerlach made clear:

1 that the village of Oradour-sur-Glane was in the hands of the *maquisards*,
2 that the entire population was on the side of the *maquisards*, as it assumed an increasingly hostile posture toward the two Germans,
3 that women also appeared there as active members of the *maquis* wearing steel helmets and leather jackets,
4 that orders from a high-ranking *maquis* headquarters came to Oradour-sur-Glane (civilians on tandem bicycle) and were immediately carried out,
5 that a confusion of Oradour-sur-Glane with another village of the same name is out of the question.

It was not true, as a French propaganda tract about Oradour claimed, that in retaliation for German losses caused by the *maquisards* a high-ranking German police officer held a pencil over a map and dropped it, whereupon the point stuck in the village of Oradour. He is then alleged to have ordered the destruction of the village and the extermination of the population. The author justifiably characterized this description to the interpreter of the military court in Bordeaux, Mr. Daniel, as blatant war propaganda, devoid of any truth.

Questioning of Diekmann and various other members of 3rd Company by the judge of the "*Das Reich*" Division began immediately at the first opportunity, when the division had reached its destination Normandy and was at a state of constant readiness. But these inquiries were interrupted by the battle in Normandy, in which the division was involved. As a result they were submitted by the division commander, who was seriously wounded a short time later, the Ia and the court officer. They are mentioned in part above.

During the course of the interrogations by the division commander Diekmann learned that the enemy radio had reported that *Sturmbannführer* Kämpfe had been shot on account of the "massacre of Oradour," for which he was held responsible. This report must have placed Diekmann in a serious moral dilemma. If this report was true, then instead of freeing his friend he had been responsible for his death; and the burning down of the village also probably seemed more questionable to him in view of the deaths of the women and children. Diekmann probably sought death as a result, for according to eyewitness statements he stood up in the midst of extremely heavy fire without a helmet, wearing only a forage cap, until he was fatally wounded by a shell splinter. The commander of 3rd Company, Hstuf. Erich-Otto Kahn, was also seriously wounded (loss of an arm), and the unit had such heavy casualties in dead and wounded that two-thirds of the company was put out of action. After the fighting at Noyers it was no longer operational. The regiment and the division saw no rest for many months in the heavy fighting that followed. Consequently the judicial investigation could not be continued, especially since the only man responsible, Diekmann, against whom the investigation was exclusively directed, had been killed, and the officer who carried out his orders, Hstuf. Kahn, had been seriously wounded and was no longer available for questioning.

During the inquiries at Bordeaux the court faced a dilemma, in that one third of the 3rd Company consisted of men from Alsace conscripted into the *Waffen-SS* and that it had been a platoon of Alsatians which was deployed at the church in Oradour.

Since France had never recognized the reincorporation of Alsace into the Reich under international law, these Alsatians were Frenchmen who had fought on the side of the enemy and taken part in the action at Oradour as men under orders. What a tragedy for these men!

Another problem was the fact that certain of these Alsatians had become members of the French Army after the war, had served at the front in Indochina for several years as non-commissioned officers and wore French decorations for bravery. One day they, too, were brought to Bordeaux – in French uniforms.

Soon afterward, however, there was a sharp reaction in Alsace. Alsatian deputies in the National Assembly declared categorically that unless all Alsatians who had been conscripted into the *Waffen-SS* were set free immediately, there would be grave political consequences in Alsace.

How sensitively France reacted in this matter is shown by the fact that these Alsatians (with the exception of the one who had volunteered for the *Waffen-SS*) were freed a short time later. This was gratifying to the Alsatians, but in human and legal terms it was a crass injustice to their German comrades of the 3rd Company, since they had been conscripted into the *Waffen-SS* just like the Alsatians. Difficulties arose from the fact that approximately half of the Germans in pretrial detention had not yet reached the age of eighteen when the act took place – and consequently were not criminally responsible.

In Bordeaux the author questioned the men of the 3rd Company about Stubaf. Diekmann's state of mind in Oradour. They stated unanimously that he had paced up and down the village street with an expression of cold, grim determination, so edgy and tense that no one could have dared refuse to obey his orders. These men were thus acting under binding orders.

How cruel is war, that it forces young, blameless men, still not criminally responsible, into this devilish pincers of moral dilemma and binding orders, from which there is practically no escape. None of them would ever encounter such a frightful situation in civilian life.

As far as the setting on fire of Oradour is concerned, it appears that the "Sperrle order", according to which all buildings used by the *maquisards* as quarters or to conceal weapons and ammunition were to be burned down, played a part in Diekmann's decision.

In both the Sperrle Order and the order issued by the corps special emphasis was placed on quick and independent action. The Sperrle Order even went so far as to say: "In view of the present situation there can be no grounds for punishment for excessively harsh measures." What this meant was: take harsh measures first, then report.

In any case French sources reveal that Diekmann initially adhered closely to his orders. He had, after the townspeople had been assembled in the marketplace, first demanded that the mayor furnish hostages. The mayor, Dr. Desourteaux, refused. Then, according to the French sources, Diekmann walked with him to the mayor's office, which was located at the northern exit from the village. When he returned from there about thirty minutes later, Diekmann, before he gave the order to shoot the men in the barns, looked "so tense and grim" as the men of 3rd Company described in Bordeaux. This was underlined by the statement of a female witness, Madame Taillandier of Paris, who was present in Oradour at the time of the events in question. *Le Monde* wrote of her testimony on 28 January 1953:

> "The SS men seized her, but they had to let her go again, no one knows exactly why. Even she herself does not know. She simply stated that she was from Paris and the word caused an officer to relent. But another declared, 'They killed one of our German officers here. Therefore everyone is now being put up against the wall'."

This statement suggests that during the half-hour that he was away with the mayor, Diekmann reached the conclusion that *Sturmbannführer* Kämpfe, whom he was supposed to rescue, was no longer alive.

The men of the 3rd Company told the author that during the burning of Oradour hidden ammunition exploded in almost every house. This, and the statement by Ostuf. Gerlach, proves that Oradour was a resistance base.

The worst was the tragic deaths of the women and children, who were drawn into this disastrous situation and subsequently lost their lives in the church. Their sad fate will always be deeply regretted.

For internal political reasons the French court also applied two standards in the passing of sentences:

The big Oradour trial was played out from 13 January until 12 March 1953, or for eight weeks, before the Higher Military Court in Bordeaux and the eyes of the world press. The Alsatians who had been set free also had to appear. One Alsatian and one German were sentenced to death in absentia. The German company members received sentences of eight to twelve years hard labor. The Alsatian company members received between four and eight years forced labor. The sentences of the Alsatians were suspended. One German was cleared.

Several months later the sentences of the two men condemned to death in absentia were reduced to life imprisonment and later to lengthy jail terms. They, too, were released after several years.

Thus the German side atoned for the events at Oradour.

In December 1944 the former senior resistance leader of the communist *Francs-Tireurs-et-Partisans* in the Limousin region and most recently mayor of Limoges, Georges Guingouin, was arrested for more than one hundred cases of mass murder committed against his fellow countrymen during the "liberation" in 1944. Guingouin had already been kicked out of the Communist Party on 19 November 1952 as a "renegade." But he was the man under whose leadership the Limousin region was supposed to become an independent Soviet republic – a situation that placed General de Gaulle in considerable political difficulties. Guingouin's chief of staff was Jean Chaintron, member of the central committee of the Communist Party of France. Guingouin had made eliminated enemies in droves, and he had also had persons who knew his secret killed long afterward. He is one of the most sinister figures of the resistance, and it was gratifying that this movement at least tried to clean itself up before Guingouin discretely disappeared into a mental clinic.

Guingouin was also the leader of the St. Léonhard maquis, whose ranks also included Sergeant Canou. It was he who captured *Sturmbannführer* Kämpfe and – as he later testified in court – had passed him on to his "chief." Kämpfe was thus in the hands of Guingouin. What that means becomes clear when one reads in the 15 January 1954 issue of Le Monde that it was Guingouin who, acting on orders from the central committee of the French Communist Party, attacked the towns of Tulle, Guéret and Limoges in June 1944. What happened in Tulle is known. It was the same thing that went on in Guéret before Kämpfe's battalion arrived there. And when the Stadler march group reached Limoges it was already an isolated city with an assault by the *maquisards* expected at any minute.

The partisan headquarters had been reported in Oradour-sur-Glane, and the Oradour area was the sole possibility in the Limousin region for assembling and launching further maquis actions – by 9 June everything else had already been occupied by units of the "*Das Reich*" Division.

The finding of Kämpfe's pay book in Limoges points from the scene of his capture east of Limoges to the opposite side, namely to Oradour. One can imagine the fate that Kämpfe met at the hands of Guingouin when one reads in the 4 March 1954 issue of *Le Monde* what the socialist deputy Montalat of the *Département* of Corrèze said of Guingouin's crimes against his French countrymen: "...ugly and vicious crimes which terrorized the population."

In summing up it must be said that in its war against the German occupying power the Maquis acted contrary to the German-French Cease-fire Agreement of 1940, broke the "Hague Land Warfare Convention" and seriously violated the Geneva Convention in the treatment of German prisoners.

The German Army had no interest in waging a war against Frenchmen; rather its focus was repulsing the Allied invasion of Normandy. Its actions against the *maquisards* were always no more than reactions to the crimes of the *maquisards* against German soldiers and civilians.[13]

• • •

12 June 1944: All investigations into the disappearance of Stubaf. Kämpfe proved fruitless. At 6 AM the regiment, positioned at the front of the division, which marched on two roads, resumed the march to the invasion front on National Road 147 via Bellac-Portiers and then on National Road 10 via Tours to Clère. On the way the units were subjected to numerous fighter-bomber attacks.

Hstuf. Heinz Werner, the former regimental adjutant, had assumed command of the shrunken II Battalion. Ostuf. Seeger became regimental adjutant. March sequence: 15th Company, regimental headquarters and signals platoon, III Battalion, 14th Company, 13th Company, I Battalion, train, 16th Company.

13 June: From Clère the march was continued only by night because of the mounting fighter-bomber attacks. 7 PM departure via La Flêche to Chateau Bourgon south of Domfront.

14 June: In the morning the regimental headquarters' column was hit by heavy fighter-bomber attack before the last vehicles could be dispersed. Sixteen vehicles burned out. Fortunately there were no casualties.

Staf. Stadler received news that effective immediately he had been appointed commander of the 9th SS Panzer Division "*Hohenstaufen*."

• • •

The last commander of the "*Der Führer*" Regiment placed the following thoughts at the beginning of the chapter of the regiment's history described by him:

The victory fanfares had long since faded away. The war had become more pitiless and cruel. We were no longer fighting to win. The western Allies prepared for the decisive blow against Germany. On the Eastern Front our efforts were devoted toward a slow fighting withdrawal toward the German frontiers before the constantly growing strength of the enemy armies. The bitterest of all for us front-line soldiers was the fact that the homeland could no longer be protected by the German front. Germany groaned under the mounting and destructive bombing terror, which claimed the lives of countless men, women and children. The time of costly fighting withdrawals and depressing retreats, without any hope for a turn for the better, had begun and gave the German people and its soldiers no peace until the unconditional surrender.

The final stage of the "*Der Führer*" Regiment's path also led through this most difficult part of the war, forged into an indissoluble fighting team and community of fate to the bitter end.

Otto Weidinger

## VII

14 June 1944: Stubaf. Weidinger assumed command of the "*Der Führer*" Regiment. At 8 PM it resumed its march via Domfront to La Ferrière.

15 June: The regiment was placed under the command of the army's 2nd Panzer Division; however, a relief in the division area ordered for 11 PM was cancelled. Regimental command post: Château de Brécy. Staf. Stadler left the regiment. Night march to Jurques.

16 June: Entire day spent under cover against enemy aircraft in the Jurques area.

17 June: At 11 PM marched into the division's assigned quartering area southeast of St. Lô. Arrived before dawn.

The regiment remained in the St. Lô quartering area from 17 to 26 June. Orders were issued for meticulous camouflage to prevent being seen from the air and wide dispersal of vehicles, camouflaging of headquarters air and ground, no march movements with vehicles by day and limiting of all movements, even by individual men, to an absolute minimum by day.

St. Lô was no-man's-land and had been destroyed by Allied air attacks. With the "Omaha bridgehead" the enemy (US forces) had established a deep beachhead whose southern boundary extended almost to the city of St. Lô.

The British had three large beachheads in the Caen-Bayeux and between Arromanches and Riva Bella established the bridgeheads Gold, Juno and Sword.

Field Marshall Montgomery's troops from Canada and the motherland assaulted the positions of the 12th SS Panzer Division following an unimaginable drum fire from guns of every caliber.

The Sherman tanks approached the German anti-tank positions in waves, turned against the panzer-grenadiers, who knew how to defend themselves against this mighty war machine. The Tiger tanks with their 88-mm guns created the only breathing spaces. Whenever these tanks appeared the Shermans had no chance.

On 13 June Hstuf. Michael Wittmann inflicted a crushing defeat on the British 22nd Armoured Brigade of the 7th Armoured Division with just one Tiger. When it was all over 25 armored vehicles, including a number of Cromwell tanks, were in flames. Hstuf. Wittmann's handful of Tigers faced the famous 8th Hussars, the 1st Armoured Regiment and the 5th Artillery Battalion as well as elements of the 1st Infantry Brigade: nevertheless the then Hstuf. Wittmann (LAH) won the battle at Villers-Bocage.

The Odon River had once again become a key defense point. According to the plans of Headquarters, 7th Army, German panzer divisions were to drive north from the area of Villers-Bocage in a concentric night attack, taking the enemy in the flank and driving him back. The 2nd SS Panzer Division "*Das Reich*" was army group reserve and was ordered to a state of constant alert readiness.

## Action Southwest of Caen in the Noyers Area

26 June: During the course of the day the "*Der Führer*" Regiment received an order from the 2nd SS Panzer Division "*Das Reich*" worded approximately as follows:

> "Enemy – English 11th Armoured Division – has crossed the Odon on the Villers-Bocage-Caen road with armored forces and is pushing deep into the front of the 12th SS Panzer Division 'Hitler-Jugend', apparently with the goal of taking the commanding Hill 112.
>
> *Effective immediately the 'DF' Regiment, without III and II Battalions (latter still in former Montabaun quartering area) but with the attached I Battalion 'Deutschland', is placed under the command of the army's 2nd Panzer Division. Initial objective Jurques by night march. There report to 2nd Panzer Division and receive further orders.*
>
> *Command post 2nd Panzer Division: La Ferrière (?). Departure 9 PM. Probable action in area southeast of Caen as part of counterattack against enemy forces which have broken through."*

At 9 PM the regiment and the forces under its command moved out. March road Tessy s. V.-Montbertrand-St. Martin-St. Pére-Jurques. March formation and sequence: 15th Company (motorcycles and reconnaissance), regimental headquarters "DF" and signals platoon, 16th Company (engineers), 14th Company (anti-aircraft), 13th Company (infantry gun), I Battalion "DF", I Battalion "*Deutschland*."

Arrival in Jurques at approximately 12 AM. The regimental commander immediately reported to the Ia of the 2nd Panzer Division and was briefed on the situation as follows:

> "Yesterday was the heaviest day of fighting so far by the I SS Panzer Corps in the sector of the 12th SS Panzer Division and the Panz*er-Lehrdivision.* Tremendous amounts of materiel employed by the British. Enemy – 11th Armoured Division – has already crossed the Villers-Bocage-Caen road with tanks. Expect a continuation of the enemy attempts to break through in the coming morning. Command post of the *Panzer-Lehrdivision*: Mons, approximately ten kilometers northeast of Villers-Bocage, north of the road to Caen. Our attack to begin at dawn. Further orders from the *Panzer-Lehrdivision*."

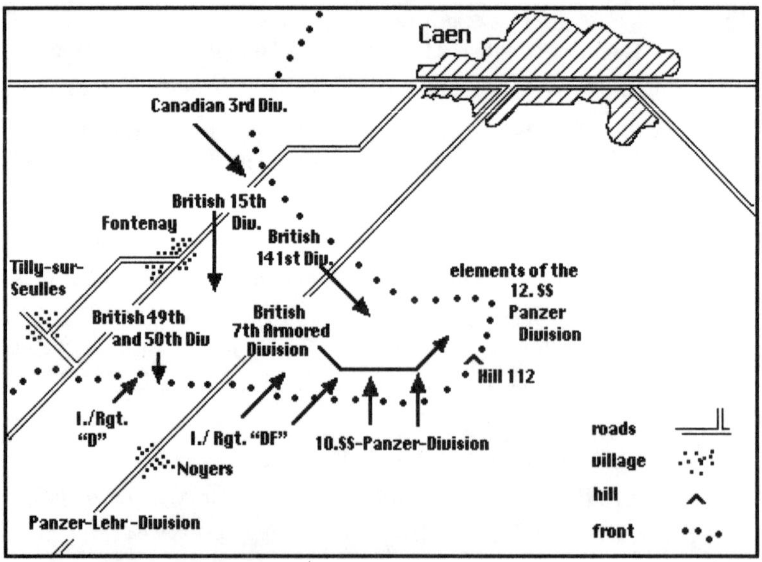


**Counterattack by Kampfgruppe "Der Führer" at Noyers, end of June, 1944**

27 June: The "DF" Regiment resumed its march to Villers-Bocage at about 1:30 AM and arrived in the area south of Mons at dawn. The front was still relatively quiet. Harassing fire was falling on both sides of the road to Caen. Total uncertainty as to the situation. The regimental commander reported to *Generalleutnant* Bayerlein at the command post of the *Panzer-Lehrdivision* and was briefed on the situation. Large gaps loomed in front of the division. Heavy losses had been suffered by day. The situation east and northeast of Noyers was completely uncertain. As a temporary measure engineers guarded the gaps in the front. The armored cars of the reconnaissance battalion maintained loose contact with the adjoining units in the form of contact patrols. Permanent contact with the adjoining units had been lost and due to a shortage of forces could not be restored. In *Generalleutnant* Bayerlein's view a daylight attack along the Villers-Bocage-Caen road to seal off the enemy penetration was out of the question. In any case, it appeared much more important to stabilize the front and restore cohesion before the enemy resumed his attempts to break through.

The regiment was ordered to restore the situation in the sector approximately one kilometer east, northeast and north of Noyers, occupy positions and establish contact with the adjoining units, elements of the 12th SS Panzer Division on the right and of the *Panzer-Lehrdivision* on the left.

The regiment's boundary with the 12th SS Panzer Division on the right: Villers-Bocage-Caen road; on the left with the Panzer-Lehrdivision: Noyers church-Tessel-Bretteville church-west end of Fontenay le Pesnel. During the course of the midmorning the regiment was to submit a sketch map illustrating the positions it had occupied. The regiment occupied its assigned positions under heavy artillery fire, suffering its first casualties in the process.

Deployed were: right I Battalion "DF", left I Battalion "D." Boundary line: Noyers-Cheux road, road to I Battalion "D." The 13th Infantry Gun Company supported the battalions' defensive effort from positions in the Noyers area, with one platoon assigned to work with each battalion. The 14th Anti-aircraft Machine-gun Company subordinated one platoon to each battalion. The 15th Motorcycle and Reconnaissance Company formed the counterattack reserve north of Noyers and scouted potential combat areas in both battalion areas. The 16th Engineer Company scouted possibilities for enhancing natural obstacles in the regiment's sector and potential combat areas in both battalion areas as counterattack reserve. Communications: telephone and radio to the battalions. Regimental command post: farm on the northern outskirts of Noyers.

Loose contact was established with the *Panzer-Lehrdivision* during the course of the midmorning. Patrols established contact with the 12th SS Panzer Division. Permanent contact on both sides could not be established. No significant enemy attacks. Own patrols in the forefield. Enemy probing attacks, especially against I Battalion, were repulsed. No sign of our air force. During the night harassing fire by enemy artillery.

28 June: At dawn enemy attacks began on the regiment's entire front. The enemy achieved several penetrations against I Battalion "DF" and I Battalion "D", however these were eliminated by immediate counterattacks. The enemy attacks were well supported by sharply concentrated artillery fire. I Battalion "DF" also received flanking fire from the previous area of penetration to the east. Casualties were heavy. Contact between the two battalions was severed. The 15th Company closed the gap.

The heavy fighting continued all day long. The enemy appeared to growing in strength steadily. There were heavy barrages on Noyers and the regimental command post. Little sign of our own artillery. In the evening hours and during the night very heavy caliber enemy guns (naval artillery) intervened in the fighting.

29 June: The early morning saw the start of the counterattack by the II SS Panzer Corps in a northeast direction from the area to the southeast of Villers-Bocage with: 10th SS Panzer Division "*Frundsberg*" under *Brigadeführer* Harmel to the right of the regiment south of the Villers-Bocage-Caen road, and; the 9th SS Panzer Division "*Hohenstaufen*" under *Brigadeführer* Stadler left of the regiment in the *Panzer-Lehrdivision*'s area. The OKW had withdrawn the 9th and 10th SS Panzer Divisions from the fierce defensive struggle in the east and had deployed it at this focal point of the defense on the invasion front.

These units, like the 1st SS Panzer Division "LAH" positioned farther east, were in no way at full combat strength. Nevertheless, it was the opinion in *Führer* Headquarters that these SS panzer divisions, hardened in battle in the east, would bring about a change in the precarious situation there.

The objective of the counterattack by the SS Panzer Corps was to destroy the British forces which had made a deep penetration to the south and seal off the penetration. For the attack the regiment was placed under the command of the 10th SS Panzer Division, and it was supposed to join the attack by the two panzer divisions when their leading elements were abreast of the regiment.

This decisive counterattack, which had neither the massed support of our air force or our artillery, which alone could have promised success, was halted abreast of our positions by the concentrated fire of the enemy artillery, which pounded the attacking divisions almost without pause. Against this tremendous expenditure of materiel by the enemy the attack objective could not be reached; however, at least an almost completely continuous front was established. In this action the officers in command of the units encountered for the first time previously unknown difficulties.

The terrain was extremely complex. Dense hedgerows passed through the regiment's sector at intervals of approximately 100 meters. There was nowhere in the regiment's sector from where one had an overview of the terrain. Because of the tremendous artillery barrage wire communications were almost always out. Extraordinary demands were made of the troubleshooting teams, medics, runners, radio operators and special missions officers. Casualties among these groups were extremely heavy. Scarcely any of them was left uninjured in this action.

As a result of lack of communication with the battalions and because of the uncertainty of contact by runner, the command was almost always in a state of uncertainty as to the real situation in the entire sector.

A direct hit on a side building of the regimental commander by a heavy artillery shell killed ten people. Most of the dispatch rider section, several signals men and one war correspondent were dead. The heavy casualties at the front also continued.

Tight control over the units engaged was impossible in this situation. The situation remained uncertain and complex all day long.

With the help of observer aircraft, which hung in the sky all day long completely undisturbed, the enemy artillery fired at every prominent point of terrain, and the barrages became more intense and more frequent.

Consequently the units and formations were senselessly pounded to pieces before they could employ their infantry forces effectively. It was a one-sided battle of materiel on a scale never before experienced.

In the late afternoon the O1 of the 10th SS Panzer Division contacted the regiment. The division commander, *Brigadeführer* Stadler (former commander of the "DF" Regiment) had been wounded. Staf. Thomas Müller was leading the division at present. He, too, visited the regiment.

The division was now being led almost exclusively through the use of special-missions officers, since the telephone lines were almost always out and absolute radio silence had been ordered. All units were visibly nervous about using their radios. The enemy artillery was supposedly coupled with fast acting radio direction finders and could open fire on a functioning radio stations within minutes. The regimental commander therefore issued the following order to all radio operators: "Everyone in the field of fire take full cover – this applies to the radio operators as well!"

This never caused the regiment any difficulties. It employed only seasoned officers as special-missions officers. They had to memorize all division orders, in addition to written orders, and had instructions to avoid at all costs allowing the written orders to fall into enemy hands in dangerous situations or because of the almost always-complicated situation. This procedure proved extremely effective in the invasion front battles that followed.

30 June: Futile attempts to get the attack moving again. Each attempt saw the enemy artillery fire rise to hurricane force and smash the squads and platoons.

The heavy casualties resulted in the appearance of fresh gaps in the front. The 9th and 10th SS Panzer Divisions simply could advance no farther. Three British divisions were pressing against the regiment's left flank and against the unit on the left, the *Panzer-Lehrdivision*: the 2nd Armoured Division and the 49th and 50th Infantry Divisions, some of Field Marshall Montgomery's elite units.

In the afternoon the commander of I Battalion, Stubaf. Adolf Diekmann, was killed by shell splinters in front of his command post north of Noyers. The death of the commander, who had been the soul of the resistance, resulted in a crisis. I Battalion's front threatened to collapse. Toward evening the regimental command post was in the front line and a short time later four British tanks appeared before the command post. Flame-throwers of the 16th Company led by the company commander, Ostuf. von Eberstein, brought rapid relief. The enemy tanks were put out of action and their crews, which included a British battalion commander, a major, were taken prisoner. After a brief interrogation they were sent to the rear.

While I Battalion, which had been badly battered as a result of direct action at the enemy's break-in point, reorganized itself during the night, the brave engineers of 16th Company secured the sector. Three days of almost constant enemy artillery fire on the break-in point from the north and from flanking positions to the east, had caused I Battalion to have the highest rate of loss in the regiment.

In the early morning hours of 1 July, at approximately 3 AM, one last attempt was to be made to eliminate the deep enemy penetration through a large-scale night attack.

The "*Hohenstaufen*" Panzer Regiment was to attack in the "DF" Regiment's sector and arrived in this area after darkness fell. A conference of all unit commanders taking part in the attack took place at the "*Der Führer*" Regiment's command post. The commanding officer of the "*Hohenstaufen*" Panzer Regiment, Ostubaf. Woith, was at the "*Hohenstaufen*" Panzer Division and was supposed to bring the attack order with him. When he failed to arrive, the regimental commander immediately drove to his command post where he learned that Ostubaf, Woith had been seriously wounded in an artillery barrage. As a result there was total uncertainty as to the start time for the attack. The "*Hohenstaufen*" Panzer Regiment found the terrain in the regiment's sector unsuitable for tanks and it was pulled back during the night.

Later orders came that the attack was to take place at 6 AM. The regiment's companies moved off at 6 AM and advanced rapidly. The panzer-grenadiers were certain that they could reach the attack objective, but then the attack by the "*Hohenstaufen*" Panzer Division was stopped. The squads that had advanced the farthest were forced to disengage from the enemy in daylight and consequently casualties were heavy. The weak 3rd Company, which had advanced particularly far under the command of the very young Ustuf. Klar, suffered heavy losses.

The British followed up at once. Their advance was blocked, but some of the wounded panzer-grenadiers of 3rd Company were taken prisoner. The 1st (Ostuf. Kurt Scholz) and 2nd (Ostuf. Werner Schwarz) Companies stabilized the situation. Ustuf. Klar was reported missing.

British attacks were repulsed all day long, but the last attempt to restore this decisive sector of the front through an attack had failed. In the afternoon the regimental commander held preliminary discussions at the command post of the "*Hohenstaufen*" Division for the withdrawal of the regiment.

2 July: The positions were held. The commanding general of the 7th Army, *Generaloberst* Dollmann, died of a heart attack. *Generaloberst* Paul Hausser, the former commander of the SS Division "*Das Reich*", assumed command of the 7th Army as commander in chief in these critical days and weeks. The regiment was happy and very proud that "our old Papa Hausser", who was loved and respected by panzer-grenadiers and officers alike, had taken over this important post.

I Battalion of the "*Deutschland*" Regiment under its outstanding commander Hstuf. Schuster, who was killed several days later, had fought especially bravely in recent days. In spite of heavy losses the battalion had held its positions, sometimes in close combat using spades, submachine-guns and hand grenades. The commander of 1st Company "D", Ostuf. Grohmann, especially distinguished himself and was subsequently awarded the Knight's Cross.

At 3 PM the "*Der Führer*" Regiment was relieved in its positions by units of the 277th Infantry Division and was pulled out of the line. The regiment's subordination to the *Panzer-Lehrdivision* was lifted and part of this division moved into the St. Lô area.

The regiment marched to Jurques. The regimental commander had driven ahead to the command post of the 2nd SS Panzer Division "*Das Reich*." There he described the unit's experiences in its first action on the invasion front to the commander in chief of the 7th Army, *Generaloberst* Hausser, who happened to be present, and the division commander, *Generalmajor* Lammerding.

I Battalion, which was temporarily unfit for combat because of the heavy casualties it had suffered, remained in the train area for a near-front refurbishment with men from the field replacement training battalion. Hstuf. Meisenbacher assumed command of the battalion.

In five days the battalions and companies deployed in the regiment's sector had lost an average of 40% of their combat strength. I Battalion's losses were 60%! The regiment, with the attached I Battalion, "*Deutschland*" Regiment and without its II and III Battalions, had sustained 846 casualties in its first action.

3 July: March into the area of the 2nd SS Panzer Division "*Das Reich*" at Pont Bellenger and Couverts.

## Action at La-Haye-de-Puits

4 July: At about 8 PM the regiment received marching orders from the division. Direction of march northwest. The regiment became a battle group and once again temporarily left the formation of the 2nd SS Panzer Division "*Das Reich.*" Assigned to the regiment were: the 2nd Armored Reconnaissance Battalion "*Das Reich*", 2nd Assault Gun Battalion "*Das Reich*", and II Battalion, 2nd Artillery Regiment "*Das Reich.*"

Available from the "*Der Führer*" Regiment were: III Battalion, 14th Company, 15th Company (still only one motorcycle platoon strong), and 16th Company.

Not operational, but undergoing near-front refurbishment, was I Battalion. Not available because it had not yet arrived from the former Montabaun quartering area was II Battalion "DF" under Stubaf. Herbert Schulze.

After reaching the area of operations at La-Haye-de-Puits the "DF" Battle Group was placed under the command of the 353rd Infantry Division. The division commander was *Generalleutnant* Mahlmann.

5 July: Night march by the battle group via Ville-Boudon, St. Aubin du Perron, Catelinais and Perriers to Lessay.

Not until the area east of La-Haye-de-Puits was III Battalion of the "*Deutschland*" Regiment subordinated to the "*Der Führer*" Regiment.

The "DF" Battle Group reached the open country near Perriers at dawn and initially marched to Lessay. Immediately the first enemy fighter-bomber attacks began. While the battle group took cover against air attack, the regimental commander drove ahead and reported to *Generalleutnant* Mahlmann at the 353rd Infantry Division's command post. He was briefed on the situation as follows: the enemy (3rd, 9th and 30th US divisions) was exerting pressure on both sides of La-Haye-de-Puits and was trying to outflank the city (an important road junction) on both sides and after gaining the road to Lessay advance deep into the French interior.

The "DF" Battle Group's orders: the battle group was to be deployed in the 353rd Infantry Division's sector to support that badly weakened division with the task of preventing at all costs an outflanking of the road junction of La-Haye-de-Puits.

To achieve this the regimental commander deployed his units as follows: on the right III Battalion "D" at the north end of the Fôret de Mont-Castre. Center 2nd Armored Reconnaissance Battalion on the ridge between Fôret de Mont-Castre and La-Haye-de-Puits. Left III Battalion "DF" in the sector north of Montgardon west-southwest of La-Haye-de-Puits.

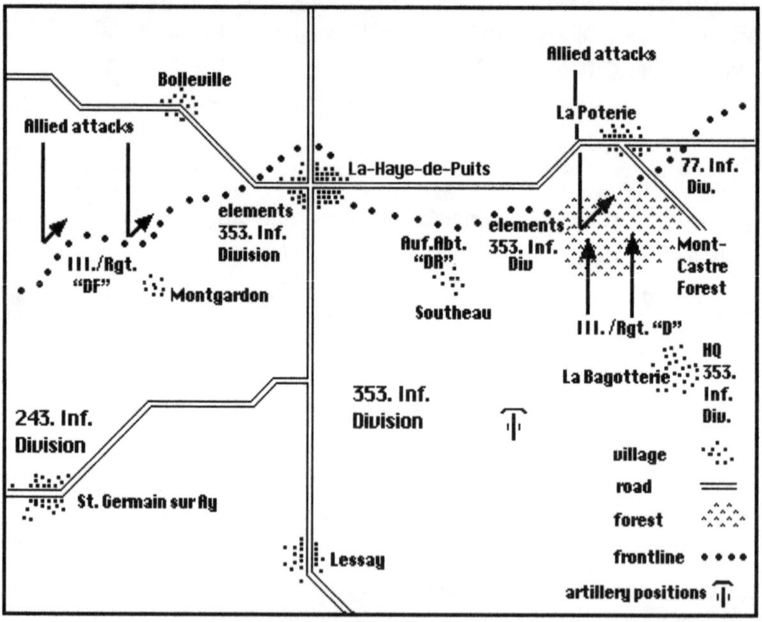


**Kampfgruppe "Der Führer" in defensive actions on both sides of the town of La-Haye-de-Puits- early in July, 1944**

The action was conducted battle group style, which means that there was no solid contact between the three units involved. Each battalion occupied a sector approximately two kilometers wide.

The 2nd Assault Gun Battalion remained in Mobec as mobile reserve and scouted operational possibilities, especially in the sector held by III Battalion "DF." II Battalion of the 2nd Artillery Regiment went into position in the Vesley-Laulne area in such a way that it could effectively support the defensive effort by the 2nd Armored Reconnaissance Battalion and III Battalion "D" and was instructed to cooperate with both units. The 14th Company "DF" attached one platoon each to III Battalion "DF" and the 2nd Armored Reconnaissance Battalion. The 16th Company "DF" scouted possible sites at which to block the roads coming from the enemy side and remained at the disposal of the regimental commander as counterattack reserve.

In the individual sectors contact was to be established with the elements of the 353rd Infantry Division there and the defensive battle was to be waged jointly.

Communications: Radio – medical clearing station: Lessay – command post "*Der Führer*" Regiment: at the express wish of the 353rd Infantry Division was set up only several hundred meters from the division command post west of La Bigotterie for the purpose of maintaining continuous wire communications with this division. The positions of the "DF" Battle Group had to be occupied quickly.

Meantime the activities of the enemy fighter-bombers had increased even further, and the units had great difficulty moving into their positions. The commander of the "DF" Battle Group therefore issued the following order to the units under his command:

"The battalions are to send forward scouting parties to precisely mark the companies' approach routes. Traffic-control officers will see to it that the units 'work their way forward in leaps and bounds' into the position in their vehicles one after the other, taking advantage of lulls in fighter-bomber activity over the advance road."

This procedure was equally time-consuming and nerve-wracking, and it took almost the entire day before the units finally succeeded in occupying their sectors. Even the headquarters of the "*Der Führer*" Battle Group had great difficulty reaching its command post.

6 July: Heavy enemy artillery fire on the entire sector and heavy pressure on our positions, which continued in the following three days. The commander of the 2nd Assault Gun Battalion, Hstuf. Dr. Röder, was wounded.

7 July: Heavy enemy attacks by Canadian troops alternated with immediate counterattacks by us, especially in the Bois de Tave-Prairie.

8 July: The enemy artillery fire intensified again and alternated with fierce enemy attacks. The enemy tried stubbornly to outflank La-Haye-de-Puits. The focal point of the defensive effort clearly lay west of La-Haye-de-Puits with III Battalion under the command of Hstuf. Heinz Werner.

This brave battalion experienced the heaviest fighting. Every attack was repulsed, often in bitter close-quarters fighting. In the course of one day alone III Battalion fought off eleven attacks, nine of them by immediate counterattack. Deep penetrations against the units on the right and left (elements of the 353rd Infantry Division) were sealed off with hastily pulled together forces. This battle exacted a heavy toll. Through its unshakable steadfastness, III Battalion, effectively committed by the squad and platoon leaders and company commanders, prevented the enemy from outflanking La-Haye-de-Puits. The soul of the resistance by the panzer-grenadiers was their commanding officer, Hstuf. Heinz Werner.

In the afternoon the commander of the 2nd Armored Reconnaissance Battalion, Hstuf. Wulf, was seriously wounded.

In his book on the invasion titled *Sie kommen!* ("They're Coming!"), Paul Carell wrote:

> "This forest of Mont-Castre (La-Haye-de-Puits) occupies a special place in the histories of the 353rd Infantry Division and the 15th Parachute Regiment under Oberst Gröschke: as a bloody battlefield..."

The "*Der Führer*" Battle Group and its attached units played a very decisive part in repulsing the massed enemy attacks. The panzer-grenadiers of III Battalion have fond memories of the brave 353rd Engineer Battalion commanded by *Hauptmann* Pillmann, which through its selfless actions held its positions as a good neighbor.

9 July: After darkness fell the battle group was relieved by elements of the 24th, 77th and 353rd Infantry Divisions. The battle group's subordinate status to the 353rd Infantry Division was lifted.

## Defense Position near Perriers

10 July: At 4 PM the commanding officer received orders in Montcuit for action in the area northeast of Perriers, on both sides of the road to Carentan, abreast of Raids. The enemy was pressing hard from the direction of Carentan on both sides of the road to Perriers.

The regiment once again came under the command of the 2nd SS Panzer Division "*Das Reich*." The 2nd Armored Reconnaissance Battalion and III Battalion, "*Deutschland*" Regiment remained attached to the regiment, while I and II Battalions were still not available. Deployment was, from left to right: 2nd Armored Reconnaissance Battalion, III Battalion "D", III Battalion "DF." Area covered by the units: approximately 1.5 kilometers. The 13th Company "DF" went into position southeast of Raids in such a way as to be able to effectively support the defensive effort by the 2nd Armored Reconnaissance Battalion and III Battalion "D." The entire 14th Company "DF" went into position in the sector held by III Battalion "DF" in order to provide effective anti-aircraft defense in the battalion area. 16th Company "DF" reconnoitered a second and third line, which were to be hastily bolstered. The 2nd Panzer Regiment assumed responsibility for anti-tank defense in the entire sector of the "*Der Führer*" Regiment and worked closely with the panzer-grenadiers. The 2nd Artillery Regiment was assigned to work closely with the "DF" Regiment and all of its resources supported the "DF" Regiment's operations. Adjoining units: on the right the 17th SS Panzer-Grenadier Division "*Götz von Berlichingen*", left the 5th Parachute Engineer Battalion (*Oberstleutnant* von der Heydte). Communications: field telephones and radio. Medical clearing station: La Renaudiere.

10 to 13 July: Heavy enemy attacks and raids with tank support were repulsed, counterattacks sealed off or eliminated local penetrations. The positions were expanded and fortified.

Enemy tanks, usually three or four vehicles at a time, fired minutes-long barrages at identified infantry positions, expending a tremendous amount of ammunition and forcing the panzer-grenadiers to take cover. Under this tremendous supporting fire assault teams worked their way up to our positions and were suddenly in the German trenches and rifle pits. This almost always resulted in fierce close-quarters actions. On one occasion, following a local counterattack a rifle pit was reoccupied in which lay the bodies of one German and two British soldiers.

In this position the "*Der Führer*" Regiment enjoyed perfectly ideal cooperation with all units of the 2nd SS Panzer Division "*Das Reich.*" The regiment received outstanding support, especially from the 2nd Artillery Regiment commanded by Staf. Karl Kreutz.

Staf. Kreutz had all of the batteries, rocket launchers and even heavy howitzers in this area placed under his command, virtually doubling the 2nd Artillery Regiment's strength. Thanks to efficient organization there was, for the first time, sufficient ammunition on hand, and through an exemplary, strictly controlled central fire control enemy the artillery was able to immediately smash attacks against every sector of the main line of resistance. In particularly difficult situations Staf. Kreutz concentrated the fire of all batteries of the reinforced 2nd Artillery Regiment under one fire control. Almost every attack preparation by the enemy was disrupted, often as soon as it began.

Neither before or subsequently did the regiment ever experience better support from the artillery. As a result, the bond of comradeship between the panzer-grenadiers and the artillerymen became even stronger.

It was the same with the men of the 2nd Panzer Regiment. The crews of the tanks gave their best as they fought side by side with the panzer-grenadiers. They fought off the numerically superior enemy tank forces with grimness and determination, and the tank crews courageously launched counterattack after counterattack in response to dangerous situations.

Without the outstanding support of the artillerymen and tank crews it would not have been possible for the regiment to hold these positions for fifteen days against a vastly superior foe.

13 to 15 July: The defensive fighting went on unabated. The 16th Company and other available forces stepped up work to complete the second and third lines.

16 July: The enemy had worked his way to within 50 to 100 meters of our positions and had dug in there. Approximately 200 meters to the rear the enemy had strong, continuous lines of security in well-built positions. The artillery battle had become much quieter during the day. In the sector of the 2nd Armored Reconnaissance Battalion commanded by Hstuf. Resch, three enemy reconnaissance advances, in part supported by tanks and artillery, were repulsed. III Battalion "D" beat back an enemy assault team. The 2nd Artillery Regiment placed accurate shellfire on enemy troop concentrations in front of the sector held by III Battalion "DF."

All signs pointed to an intensified resumption of the enemy attacks. The forces on the right, elements of the 17th SS Division, were engaged in heavy fighting and the situation there was uncertain in places. The regimental commander personally established contact with his opposite number on the right. Advance detachments of I Battalion "DF" arrived. The battalion had completed its hasty refurbishment.

17 July: During the night the enemy pulled back approximately 200 meters. Heavy vehicular traffic was spotted behind the enemy front. At about 6 PM the enemy launched an attack against the 2nd Armored Reconnaissance Battalion's sector without significant artillery support and was immediately beaten back. Simultaneously there were heavy fighter-bomber attacks against the positions of the 17th SS Division and the enemy also fired smoke shells. After heavy artillery preparation at approximately 7 PM the enemy attacked the forces on our right toward the southwest. The situation was uncertain. We received news that Field Marshall Rommel had been seriously wounded in a strafing attack.

III Battalion "D" was relieved by I Battalion "DF." In the meantime the "*Deutschland*" Regiment had arrived from the Toulouse area. Advance detachments and the first units of II Battalion "DF" also arrived from the south of France.

A direct artillery hit on the command post's telephone exchange resulted in dead and wounded.

18 July: The 2nd Armored Reconnaissance Battalion was relieved by II Battalion commanded by Hstuf. Herbert Schulze. Thus for the first time in a long while the "*Der Führer*" Regiment was complete and deployed in the main line of resistance with all of its battalions. The 2nd Armored Reconnaissance Battalion and the regimental units occupied the second line. Consequently there was an adequate reserve available.

19 July: Heavy, extremely well directed barrages by our artillery on recognized assembly areas before the main line of resistance. In the evening the regiment's operations officer brought the following news: enemy (elements of the US 29th Division) has succeeded in entering the city of St. Lô. Remaining units of the 30th Fast Brigade fighting desperately for every street against a superior enemy.

20 July: A fierce thunderstorm transformed the positions into a sticky morass. Nature raged, and hail, lightning and thunder temporarily brought the fighting to a halt except for several successful offensive patrols by us.

• • •

"Assassination attempt against Adolf Hitler!" The news went through the companies like lightning.

The heavy artillery fire, which had not let up in spite of the storm, gave the panzer-grenadiers and their officers little chance to clarify the causes and significance of the assassination attempt. To all normal thinking soldiers at the front it was incomprehensible that German officers should want to do away with their supreme commander in the midst of this fateful battle of our people. Enemy fighter-bombers, artillery and tanks dictated our thoughts and actions. The soldiers of the "*Der Führer*" Panzer-Grenadier Regiment had absolute faith in their immediate leadership.

21 July: A fighter-bomber made a low-level attack on the 14th Company's positions and Hstuf. Herrmann, the company commander, died a soldier's death. The fighter-bomber was shot down by our guns as if flew away.

22 July: During the evening hours the enemy, supported by tanks and artillery fire, broke into III Battalion's front near Le Closet almost at the boundary with the 6th Parachute Regiment. The penetration reached a depth of one kilometer and a width of about two kilometers. An immediate counterattack by III Battalion with assistance from tanks of the 2nd Panzer Regiment was a smashing success: by approximately 9:30 PM were had reoccupied our positions and brought in about 300 prisoners, including a lieutenant-colonel and eleven other officers.

23 July: At 6:15 PM an enemy patrol in platoon strength, supported

by eight tanks, felt its way toward II Battalion's sector. Using captured maps and information gained from prisoners, the enemy was striving to roll up the Raids position from the northwest.

24 July: Employing numerous bomber squadrons in waves of attacks from dawn to dusk, the Americans forced the decisive breakthrough at and to the west of St. Lô. 2,000 bombers had transformed the sector held by the *Panzer-Lehrdivision* and the 13th and 15th Parachute Regiments into a "lunar landscape" and shattered the previously mentioned units.

25 July: The enemy achieved another breakthrough against the elements of the 91st Air-landing Division farther to the west and the 243rd Infantry Division in the Lessay area. Cooperation with the paratroopers (commander Hptm. von der Heydte) was outstanding.

26 July: After a forty-five-minute barrage from all his heavy weapons, the enemy attacked the forces on our left, units of the 6th Parachute Regiment, in battalion strength. A total of thirteen attacks with tank support were beaten off under the concentrated fire of all our weapons. The 2nd Artillery Regiment scattered a concentration of tanks with mounted infantry opposite the regiment's sector.

After fifteen days of successful defense the main line of resistance, the water line, was still firmly in the hands of the regiment.

On the evening of 26 July an unexpected order was received for the regiment to withdraw with the division toward the "Yellow Line", a scouted but undeveloped position just five kilometers south of Perriers. This move was made in order to escape the threat of encirclement resulting from the enemy breakthroughs at St. Lô and Lessay.

The regiment disengaged from the enemy after darkness fell. It had fought a classic defensive battle in the position near Raids and the old maxim had been confirmed: "A unit is always most effective when it fights as a complete unit under its own command."

The 2nd SS Panzer Division "*Das Reich*" had taken considerable losses; however, the intentions of the enemy (the American VIII Corps), to break through the regiment's positions, had foundered on the unshakable defensive will of the panzer-grenadiers. The division commander, *Brigadeführer* Lammerding, was wounded. The commander of the 2nd SS Panzer Regiment, Ostubaf. Christian Tychsen, assumed temporary command of the division.

## Withdrawal Movements between Perriers and Mortain

27 July: During the night of 26-27 July the "*Der Führer*" Regiment occupied its directed sector in the "Yellow Line", which ran in a generally east-west direction approximately five kilometers south of Perriers.

Since the unit which was to hold the line on the left, the 91st Airlanding Division, had not arrived yet, the regiment had to extend its own line to the left to a point west of the main Lessay-Coutances road. On the regiment's right was the 17th SS Panzer-Grenadier Division "*Götz von Berlichingen.*"

28 July: The regiment had just occupied the positions, when at about 3 AM it received orders to withdraw to the line Savigny-Cambernon-northeast boundary of Coutances. Since the regiment could not reach the new line until dawn, the companies suffered badly from constant attacks by American fighter-bombers. Because of the heavy losses of the recent days and weeks the new position was very thinly manned. In places the enemy was already in the positions of the new main line of resistance and had to be attacked and driven out. The enemy attacked again but was repulsed. The left flank was open. The 243rd Infantry Division was supposed to be west of Coutances. Nevertheless, renewed attacks were likewise beaten off. The "*Der Führer*" Regiment's command post was in Courcy.

Heavy enemy attacks from the northeast, from the area of Martigny and farther east, were reported. The enemy's total command of the air made it impossible to disengage from the enemy during the day. A group of enemy forces drove past the regiment's right flank in the area of the 17th SS Panzer-Grenadier Division, apparently with the objective of reaching Granville. The threat of encirclement which this move posed to the German divisions farther north was obvious. During the course of the day enemy armored spearheads were reported approximately ten kilometers behind the regiment's positions in the area of St. Denis le Gast. The "*Das Reich*" Division's command post in Trelly was attacked by enemy tanks. In the afternoon the division commander, Ostubaf. Christian Tychsen, was killed there. SS-*Standartenführer* Otto Baum, commander of the "*Götz von Berlichingen*" Division, temporarily also assumed command of the "*Das Reich*" Division.

During the night of 29 July a division order was received for a withdrawal to the line on both sides of Percy. The route there was left to the discretion of the regimental commander.

Stubaf. Weidinger therefore decided to swing through Granville by night with the entire regiment, including the attached III Battalion "D", through the then still open but steadily shrinking gap, escape the looming encirclement and arrive by the following morning in time to occupy the new line on both sides of Percy.

This withdrawal order, which was delivered by special missions officer, was partly rescinded by division shortly before the regiment was to leave its positions. The division Ia, Stubaf. Stückler, telephoned the commanding officer and gave to him the order that on instructions from above the regiment, together with the infantry division and the paratroopers of the 6th Regiment, was to drive southeast through the enemy forces, which had meanwhile advanced farther, to the new sector at Percy.

The regimental commander's pleas to withdraw this order were denied. Reference was made to the express order from the 7th Army and the necessity to "take along" the infantry divisions in particular in the attack.

The consequences of this order were obvious to the commanding officer: complete clogging of the march roads, general confusion at night, associated command difficulties, late arrival in the new sector, the danger of casualties to fighter-bomber attack at dawn.

The commanding officer reluctantly issued this order to his battalions. During the march radio contact was maintained between the regiment and the battalions, which now fought their way through in the direction of Percy on the march roads directed by the division.

In order to at least have the heavy infantry weapons, the engineer company and the means of command occupy the new position on time and prepare the arrival position for the battalions which would arrive the next morning, the regimental headquarters "DF" together with the 13th, 14th and 16th Companies carried out the original plan. They passed through the gap, which was still there, unbothered by the enemy by way of Granville, Beauchamps and La Mancellerie and reached the directed sector without losses and, more importantly, on time.

In the morning the regimental commander went to the division command post in Colombe to receive a more detailed briefing. The new officer in command of the division, Staf. Baum, and his staff had taken the same route as the headquarters and regimental units.

The battalions of the "*Der Führer*" Regiment sent regular radio messages during the night. As foreseen by the regimental commander, the clogged roads were a particular source of problems.

The regiment's motorcycle platoon was immediately sent into the forefield in patrols to secure the sector, and the 16th Company temporarily assumed responsibility for guarding the sector. The 13th and 14th Companies immediately went into position with their guns in order to cover the area in front of the new main line of resistance and more importantly to be ready to fire when the battalions arrived. II Battalion of the 2nd Artillery Regiment, which on order of the regimental commander had joined the regimental units during the night as a result of which it arrived intact and ready for action, likewise went into position immediately to support the coming defensive battle.

Not until the afternoon did the battalions arrive in the sector, scattered and having suffered heavy losses in men, weapons and vehicles to American fighter-bombers. Completely exhausted and actually not ready for operations, the panzer-grenadiers nevertheless occupied the directed positions.

The losses suffered by the 2nd SS Panzer Division "*Das Reich*" as a result of this order were extremely high: armored vehicles and guns of the 2nd Artillery Regiment were shot up by the fighter-bombers. The division's 2nd Flak Battalion was completely lost. It was only because the enemy continued to advance southwest parallel to the sector that the regiment's position did not come under serious attack on this day.

29 July: The battalions' positions were moved approximately one kilometer to the north.

30 July: Deployed in the new defense line were: from the right, II, III and I Battalions. On the regiment's right was the "*Deutschland*" Regiment and farther to the right the remaining units of the *Panzer-Lehrdivision*. Units of the American 2nd Armored Division were identified opposite the sector. At 9 PM there was a change of position to the Clementiere area.

31 July: Heavy enemy attacks on the regiment's sector all day long. Deployed were: from the left, I, II and III Battalions. On the left once

again was the 17th SS Panzer-Grenadier Division. On the right the "*Deutschland*" Regiment. During the night of 1 August change of position into the Basliere sector. Enemy armored spearheads reached the city of Avranches. In the evening change of position to Mesnil Chlichamp.

2 August: No enemy contact. On 3 August the position was moved back again into the Le Boshenard area.

On 4 August the enemy broke through against the units on the regiment's right and left.

The enemy expanded the western breakthrough and marched south along the coast road. The way into Brittany was open to the enemy. Fighting a mobile battle, he screened his eastern flank with strong forces in the line St. Sever-Mortain-Mayenne.

5 August: Change of position to St. Clement east of Mortain.

## Counterattack at Mortain

6 August: The regiment reached the area northeast of Mortain in the late morning. Briefing by the division on plans for a decisive attack dubbed "Operation Liège." Several panzer and motorized divisions were to attack west toward Avranches and reach the coast with the objective of severing the supply lines of the enemy forces that had broken through to the south near Avranches and encircling them. The 1st SS Panzer Division "LAH" with 100 new Panther tanks was to form the attack's main striking force. The German air force was to commit one-thousand fighters to clear the air for these operations. Overall command of the operation lay in the hands of the XXXXVII Panzer Corps under *General* Baron von Funk. The offensive group consisted of the 2nd SS Panzer Division "*Das Reich*", a battle group from the 17th SS Panzer-Grenadier Division "*Götz von Berlichingen*" under Ostubaf. Fick, the 2nd Panzer Division under *General* von Lüttwitz and the 116th Panzer Division (Greyhound Division) under *General* Count Schwerin.

The same night the regiment completed its attack preparations and moved into its assembly area northeast of Mortain. The attack was spearheaded by III (Armored) Battalion with four assault guns under Hstuf. Dr. Roeder; behind it was II Battalion and the 16th Company. On the regiment's right were elements of the 1st SS Panzer Division "LAH." On the left (between the "*Der Führer*" and "*Deutschland*" Regiments) was Battle Group Fick with orders to take the enemy-held Hill 317. Already encircled, the enemy there was being supplied by air. Most of the materiel dropped fell into German hands.

The "*Der Führer*" Regiment's orders were: maintaining contact with the 1st SS Panzer Division advancing further north, drive north past Mortain and carry the attack forward in the direction of Avranches. Spearheading the "*Das Reich*" Division's attack was the "*Deutschland*" Regiment with attached 2nd Armored Reconnaissance Battalion. The "*Deutschland*" Regiment was to swing south, enter Mortain and subsequently advance down the Mortain-St. Hilaire road. The 2nd Panzer Regiment was sent to the "*Deutschland*" Regiment.

At 10 PM the "*Der Führer*" Regiment moved out of its assembly area and ran into the still incomplete movement by the "LAH." The panzers of the "LAH" had absolute advance priority over every other unit. As a result of this halt at the crossroads due north of Mortain the regiment lost valuable time. Finally the armored troop carriers of III Battalion and the assault guns could start their engines and drive past Mortain to the north. According to information from the division, only Mortain itself and Hill 317 east of the city were strongly defended by the enemy. At the present time only light resistance was to be expected on both sides of Mortain. Behind III Battalion's point company (9th Company under Ostuf. Harald Scholz) came the regimental headquarters together with headquarters, III Battalion.

At the eastern end of the cluster of houses called L'Abbaye Blanche the point came under heavy fire from three sides and was forced to dismount. Casualties were taken. Sitting in well-camouflaged positions, the enemy, units of the American 30th Division, halted the regiment's mounted attack with a tremendous expenditure of ammunition.

As usual, the enemy's Thunderbolt fighter-bombers and other rocket-firing aircraft had commanded the skies since daybreak, plunging like vultures on the attacking columns. Two assault guns were hit by rockets and burned out. III Battalion brought in fifteen prisoners. These rescued the wounded crews of the burning assault guns and brought them to the casualty collection point; exceptional behavior by the recently-captured Canadians.

For hours the platoon, company, battalion and regiment command post was located in a house in the main line of resistance. The cluster of houses lay under heavy mortar fire. When a shell struck the roof of the house, tables were pushed together and the various staffs took cover beneath them for additional protection against shell splinters.

In the midst of this inferno someone suddenly began playing a folksong on a harmonica, and in a display of gallows humor everyone joined in the melody singing. One song after another rang out in the hellish din of bursting shells.

Just as the men began singing "Oh, you wonderful German Rhine," the door opened and a tall Canadian prisoner pushed his way in seeking protection from his countrymen's mortar fire. The Canadian, who was wounded, listened to the Germans singing in the midst of the din of battle, shook his head and murmured: "The war is a merry thing!"

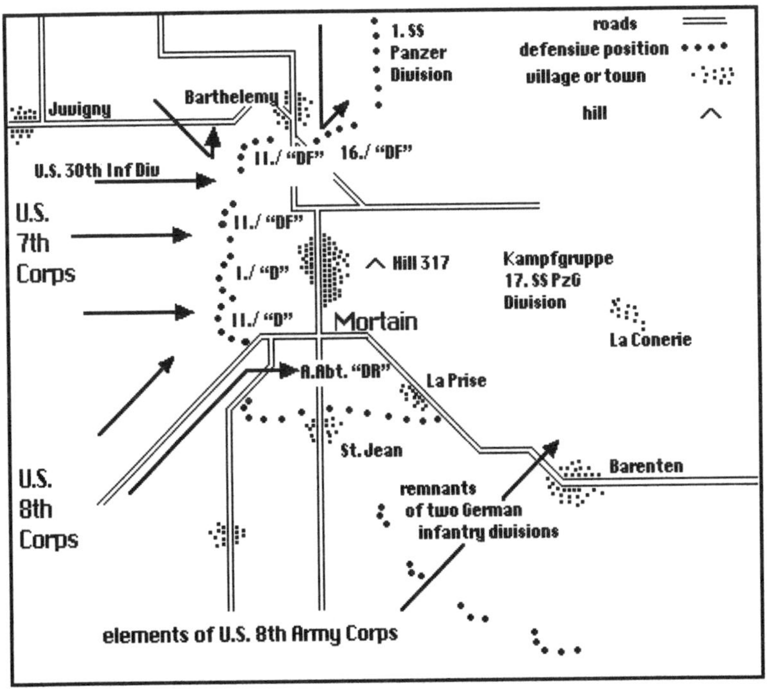


The attack upon Mortain – Situation on 10 August, 1944

Not until a pause in the firing in the afternoon was it possible for the units to spread out.

In the early afternoon the division ordered the attack halted. After darkness fell the regiment went over to the defensive.

On 8 August the regiment was in position with II Battalion to the right of the road and III Battalion to the left. The 16th Company was inserted on the right wing of II Battalion, because there was no contact with the unit on the regiment's right, the "LAH." III Battalion was able to establish contact with I Battalion "Deuts*chland*." Continued enemy activity in the air, artillery and mortar fire on the positions.

9 August: In midmorning the enemy pressed out of the Juvigny area toward the sector held by the "*Der Führer*" Regiment. The threat from the right flank, where units of the 1st SS "LAH" should have been, was already becoming obvious.

10 August: Several attacks by tanks belonging to units of the US 3rd Armored Division, especially from the northeast and north, were halted. Individual enemy tanks that broke through were taken out in close combat. Our own casualties were considerable.

11 August: Coming from the north, the enemy drove into the regiment's flank with tank support. Under artillery fire and continuous strafing attacks, our positions west of the Mortain-St. Barthelmy road had to be pulled back. There the regiment finally made contact with the SS "LAH" on the right. At about 11 PM the positions were withdrawn again as part of a move by the 2nd SS Panzer Division "*Das Reich*." The regimental command post was located in St. Clement.

"Operation Liège" had failed.

For the first time a strong concentric land attack had been brought to a halt exclusively through air power. Three-hundred German fighters had taken off from bases in the Paris area as planned to support the attacking panzer units, but British and American fighters engaged the German wings in fierce combats as soon as they had taken off. As a result not a single fighter unit was able to reach the Mortain-Avranches combat zone.

With the tank and assault gun crews of other units, the panzer-grenadiers of the "*Der Führer*" and "*Deutschland*" Regiments also lost faith in the German air force, which was simply no longer capable of dealing with the enemy's tremendous superiority in the air. *General der Flieger*

Bülowius had been unable to keep his promise to the commander in chief of the 7th Army, *Generaloberst* Hausser, "to keep the airspace above the attacking panzer divisions clear."

On the enemy side the entire American VIII Corps under General Bradley was mustered to eliminate the deadly threat to the deeply advancing American units. As a result of the efforts of the enemy air force, the German attack had collapsed forty-eight hours after it began.

12 August: At approximately 8 PM the "*Der Führer*" Regiment marched into the La Mde. Aube area.

13 August: At 9 PM began the big withdrawal movement by way of La Fresne-Foret-Yvrandes-Fromentel to Montreuil.

14 August: At daybreak the regiment arrived in the Montreuil area. Enemy fighter-bomber activity did not permit any movement by day. March was resumed at 8:30 PM by way of Menil-Occagnes, northwest of Argentan.

15 August: All roads were completely clogged during the night. At about 9 PM the regiment marched via Bailleul and Tournay to Chateau St. Lambert. South of our advance road American armored forces were driving east and southeast against negligible opposition, while to the north the British were halted and in places even forced back in a big defensive battle near Falaise.

16 August: On orders from division a battle group was formed to seal off an enemy breakthrough north of Thrun. Under the command of Stubaf. Krag, commander of the 2nd Armored Reconnaissance Battalion, II Battalion and the 2nd Assault Gun Battalion were committed in a clearing counterattack. The battle group succeeded in reversing a threatening situation. The regiment moved to the Orville area.

In the Falaise-Argentan area a great battle of encirclement by the Allied forces against the German 7th Army was under way. The huge pocket was obviously supposed to be closed by the British from the north and the Americans from the south in the area southwest of Vimoutiers.

As per orders, the 2nd SS Panzer Division "*Das Reich*" and its units escaped the pocket at the very last minute.

## The Opening of the Falaise Pocket
### 17 to 21 August 1944

17 August: In the evening hours march by way of Survie to Orville.

19 August: Following Battle Group Krag's breakout from the Falaise Pocket, II Battalion returned to the regiment.

20 August: In the afternoon the regiment received a division order worded roughly as follows:

> *"In a major battle of encirclement, the Enemy has surrounded the bulk of the 7th Army in the Thrun-Chambois-Falaise-Argentan area. On 21 August the 'Das Reich' Division, which is avoiding the encirclement as per orders or has already broken out of the pocket with some units, will attack from the Les Moulins-Mardilly area to open the pocket.*
>
> *Moving out at dawn, the regiment, together with the remaining units of the 2nd Panzer Regiment 'Das Reich', will attack toward Chambois by way of Roiville-Fresnay-Le Samson-Champosoult-Mont Ormel in order to open the pocket. The 'Hohenstaufen' Reconnaissance Battalion will secure the right flank. On the left: 2nd Reconnaissance Battalion 'Das Reich'."*

After darkness fell the regiment marched via Le Sap into the assembly area at Les Moulins.

21 August: Echeloned in depth, the regiment went to the attack at approximately 6 AM. III Battalion led the attack with the remaining units of the 2nd Panzer Regiment. Behind came II Battalion, which simultaneously screened the left flank. The regimental headquarters followed directly behind the attacking units of III Battalion.

For hours the units passed shot up horse-drawn and motorized columns; they had apparently fallen victim to fighter-bomber attack after breaking out of the pocket and heading east. The attack made rapid progress. Stragglers from the big pocket, alone and in groups, were taken in by the leading units of III Battalion and were directed to the rear. They were often unarmed and had obviously been through a tremendous mental and physical ordeal. They were therefore extremely glad to meet up with the attacking regiment; the attack itself was not hindered by the enemy air force, which was obviously concentrating on destroying the German forces trapped inside the pocket.

Enemy artillery fire began at approximately 8 AM. Weak resistance was broken. At 9 AM III Battalion encountered strong enemy forces and the artillery fire, bolstered by mortar and rifle fire, increased in intensity. III Battalion sustained casualties.

II Battalion was deployed in the forest south of the advance road with its front facing south to guard the left flank. Not until the afternoon was loose contact established with the "*Hohenstaufen*" reconnaissance battalion on the right. Strong patrols maintained contact with the 2nd Reconnaissance Battalion "*Das Reich*", which was advancing south of the regiment.

In spite of concentrated fire on III Battalion an increasing number of German soldiers came out of the pocket in large and small groups; after a brief rest at the regimental command post they were directed to the east. Units of the Polish 1st Armoured Division harried the regiment from the southwest. At the point of his III Battalion, Hstuf. Werner, the battalion commander, personally briefed the commander of a Panther tank on the situation. The crew of this tank succeeded in knocking out twelve enemy tanks in rapid succession; the enemy vehicles were in position on a hill with their broadside facing the Panther and were firing into the diminishing pocket. The success of this tank had contributed significantly to the success of the attack so far. The panzer-grenadiers of III Battalion would never forget this effective support. At about 10 AM the division commander, *Oberführer* Baum, appeared at the regimental command post for a briefing on the situation.

Ever larger groups of German soldiers were spotted in the forefield, striving to cross the open terrain to reach the foremost units of the regiment. Now and then a combat vehicle, most belonging to the parachute troops, would approach at maximum speed from the direction of Chambois and pass through III Battalion's lines. The tension of the past hours was visible in the faces of these men, and they were proud to have brought their weapons and equipment out of the hellish pocket.

With artillery and tank support, at midday III Battalion resumed the attack and, ignoring threats to its flanks from the north and south, reached the ridge approximately 1 200 meters southwest of Champosoult.

The pocket had been opened!

From then until the afternoon an unbroken flow of soldiers of the 7th Army streamed east on the Champosoult-Orville road. These elements were almost all on foot. Vehicles and heavy weapons remained inside the pocket, either knocked out by the concentrated enemy fire, abandoned or blown up by their owners.

By about midday the commander in chief of the 7th Army, *Generaloberst* Paul Hausser, had still not reached the regiment's foremost units. Many had seen him. The companies of III Battalion received orders to "keep a special look-out for the army commander in chief."

After its attack had succeeded, the regiment reported to the "*Das Reich*" Panzer Division:

> "Pocket opened near Champosoult. Contact established with surrounded units, which are streaming east out of the pocket. Regiment requests field police to control traffic to the 'DF' command post."

On receiving this report the division called for the attack to be continued toward Chambois, as per the original order.

In the opinion of the regiment, however, this order had been overtaken by the events of the last hours. If this order were carried out the enemy would be able to close the pocket again behind the regiment and the regiment's principal task, to keep the pocket open, would be unfeasible. The regimental commander put forward this view to the division. Nevertheless the division insisted that the attack be continued in the direction of Chambois.

In view of the overall situation, especially as it affected III Battalion, the commanding officer could not carry out this order and left the regiment in its existing positions. From there, in spite of constant threats and attacks from north and south, it succeeded in keeping the pocket open until 4 PM. By then the last elements of the surrounded forces had left the pocket in the regiment's sector.

In the afternoon an officer reported that he had seen the commander in chief of the 7th Army directly in front of the regiment's positions. III Battalion was immediately ordered to send an assault team to get the commander in chief out. A subsequent report made this mission unnecessary, as the commander in chief had gone back into the pocket, allegedly to establish a new line of resistance. Gener*aloberst* Hausser reached the German lines in the 2nd Reconnaissance Battalion's sector with a serious facial wound.

Two commanding generals, three division commanders, several regimental commanders and approximately 300 officers came out of the pocket on foot with the soldiers.

At the regimental command post these officers issued their first orders for the assembly of their units. The regiment tended to the arriving wounded as best it could and saw to it that they were evacuated quickly. The main task was channeling the forces streaming out of the pocket away as quickly as possible. With the help of the military police, who had been deployed in the meantime, this proceeded quickly and smoothly.

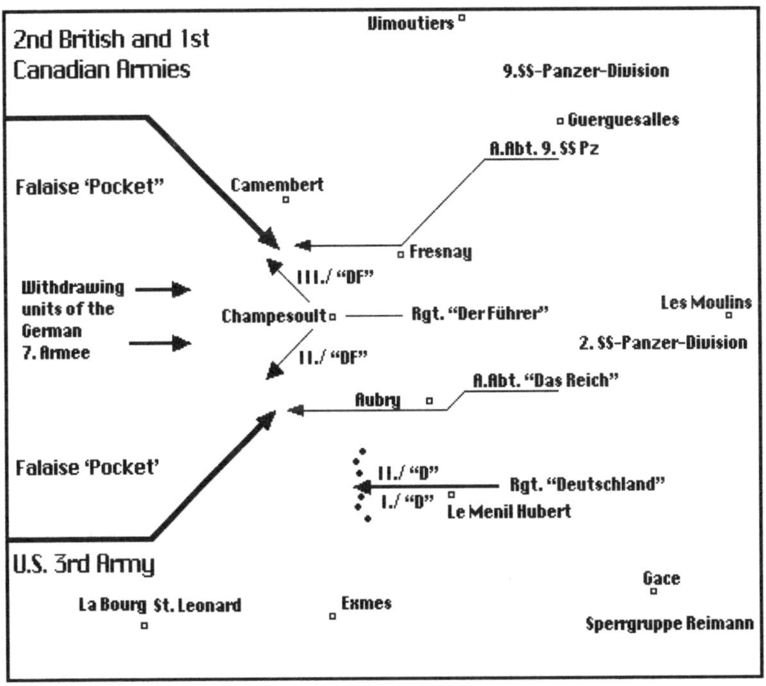


The counterattack on the mouth of the Falaise Pocket on 20-21 August, 1944

The regiment made available its last ambulance for the wounded commander of the "*Leibstandarte*", *Brigadeführer* Wisch.

The troops spoke of a "Stalingrad in Normandy": approximately 50,000 soldiers got out, but 10,000 dead and approximately 40,000 prisoners remained behind.

According to cautious estimates by regimental adjutant Ostuf. Seegerer and the adjutant of III Battalion, Ostuf. Schmager, approximately 8,000 to 10,000 German soldiers passed through the regiment's lines in these hours.

10th Company in particular distinguished itself in this battle. Together with their company commander Ostuf. Manz, the men of the company were the heart and soul of the resistance, and together with the radio operators and runners of Headquarters, III Battalion they stubbornly held the main break-in point open.

The "*Deutschland*" Regiment and the 2nd Reconnaissance Battalion also succeeded in maintaining contact with the surrounded forces.

As per orders, at 4 PM the regiment evacuated its positions after it had become apparent that no more stragglers were going to arrive. The regiment first withdrew to Fresnay. At approximately 10 PM the regiment marched via Roiville and Pontchardon to Avesnes.

## Defense Position south of Rouen and the Crossing of the Seine

25 August: Enemy armored forces pursuing the German forces withdrawing to the northeast were advancing down the Brionne-Rouen road. The possibility of yet getting all of the German divisions and units across the Seine was deteriorating from hour to hour since most of the bridges had been destroyed and the concentrations of troops and vehicles at the crossing points were under continuous air attack.

The regiment's mission:

> *Occupy positions south of the Forét de la Londe, roughly following the Bourgtheroulde-Elbeuf road, and keep the loop in the Seine near Rouen open for the crossing of the German units for at least*

> *forty-eight hours by screening to the south. Powerful armored patrols are to be deployed to the south with orders to delay the enemy armored spearheads' approaching the Seine so as to gain time for the crossing.*

Deployed were: right III Battalion (Hstuf. Werner), center II Battalion (Hstuf. Schulzer), left I Battalion (Hstuf. Meisenbacher). Adjacent units: on the right a army division (number not known), on the left the "*Deutschland*" Regiment, which had orders to retake Elbeuf, which had been occupied by the enemy.

Powerful patrols from II and III Battalions were in contact with the enemy all day; they determined that the enemy had not pushed as hard toward the loop in the Seine as toward Elbeuf, surely because of the bridge there. I Battalion, which was hindered throughout the entire operation by lack of transport, remained in positions west of Elbeuf.

26 August: III Battalion received orders to attack the northwestern part of Elbeuf and occupy positions at the western boundary of the city next to those of the "*Deutschland*" Regiment. This attack cost III Battalion heavy casualties. The civilian population took part in the battle against our units.

Employed as an assault unit, the 11th Company was almost completely wiped out and its commander, Ostuf. Dr. Sembol, was killed. Only a few men succeeded in making their way back to our lines. As a result contact was not made with the "*Deutschland*" Regiment, which also suffered heavy casualties in this action. *Oberjunker* Langanke of the 2nd Panzer Regiment provided excellent support to the panzer-grenadiers, especially those of the "*Deutschland*" Regiment.

As per orders, at 9 PM the "*Der Führer*" Regiment withdrew toward new positions in ravine-filled, complex terrain in the Forét de la Londe, roughly in line with the railway line. The "*Deutschland*" Regiment crossed the Seine in Elbeuf. Regimental command post was in Gd. Essart.

27 August: The "*Der Führer*" Regiment held the clocking position in the Seine loop against several enemy attacks. Meanwhile, in a major operation by the engineers, large numbers of troops and vehicles were brought across the Seine in and near Rouen.

28 August: The bulk of the German units were brought across even

though the enemy air force launched repeated attacks in an effort to disrupt or prevent the crossings. In the early afternoon, from the heights of the bank of the Seine, the "*Der Führer*" Regiment observed enemy tanks crossing the Seine in and around Elbeuf as well as a tank assembly containing approximately 100 vehicles area east of the city. These were reported to the division in the clear.

This assembly of enemy armor lay before the companies like a sand table – a unique opportunity for the artillery. The division commander repeatedly requested artillery fire, however his requests went unheeded. Apparently our artillery was not in position on the other side of the Seine. The regiment had no liaison officer or artillery fire controller. Consequently the enemy was able to mass his tanks without interference.

The attack by the enemy armor began at 2 PM. Radio messages sent to division in the clear were not answered. While the "*Der Führer*" Regiment covered the crossing near Rouen, the battalions' vehicle sections, which had been placed under the command of especially energetic officers, succeeded in forcing the seemingly hopeless crossing. This made it possible to get the combat vehicles, especially the vital armored troop carriers of III Battalion, across the river and thus preserve the regiment.

The regiment was out of contact with the division for hours in the afternoon and it was impossible to determine when the regiment's mission was over and when it could begin sending the companies across. Through the use of special missions officers it was determined that the last elements of the covering units had crossed the railway bridge at the eastern end of Rouen at about 7:30 PM. There were still no orders from division for the regiment to withdraw.

The regiment's neighbor on the right, an army unit, began pulling back. A short time later the regimental commander, acting on his own, likewise gave the order to withdraw from the present positions, with all battalions leaving behind rear guards, and cross the Seine. The regiment crossed the river between 8 and 9 PM, the last unit to cross the Seine, and at 9:20 PM the last of III Battalion's vehicles reached the other side. The regiment initially took up positions in the Roncherolles area northeast of Rouen.

# Retreat toward the Maas – 29 August to 3 September 1944

29 August: The big withdrawal movement to Coullemelle by way of La Feuille, Gourna, Songeons, Marseille and Breteuil began the same night at 2 AM.

30 August: The withdrawal continued through Malpart, Buosi, Court, Guerbigny, Damery, Fresnoy, Etalon, Curchy, Nesle, and Voyennes to Douilly Attilly.

31 August: Further march through Vermand, Secouhard, Bohain, Wassigny, Le Nouvion, La Chapele and Anor. The Belgian border was reached at 2 PM and the march continued via Ochain, Macon and Chimay to Couvin. There the regiment established strongpoint-style security positions in the line Rumigny-Liart-Aubigny. Contact with the battalions was possible only by radio, since terrorist groups had been identified in the forests south of the previous retreat roads. Lone runners and vehicles could not possibly get through.

1 September: At approximately 9 PM the line of security was withdrawn toward Signyle-Petit-Tremblois.

2 September: Withdrawal movement to Yves Gomezee via Marienburg and Philippville began at 1 PM. II Battalion was assigned the security role. At 9 PM the regimental commander was transferred to Neuville.

3 September: At 7 AM the regimental command post was in Merlemont. II Battalion successfully repulsed trong enemy attacks. I Battalion was deployed in Philippville together with 16th Company. III Battalion was positioned in the Olloy-Dourbes sector; there, too, enemy attacks were repulsed. Particularly loathsome were ambushes by terrorists. Beginning at 5 PM withdrawal toward the line Soutour-Sart-Romere-Niverlee. The regimental command post was in Vordeles.

I Battalion received orders to secure and keep open the Maas crossing near Hastière, while a platoon from the 16th Company was ordered to prepare the Maas bridge for demolition.

At about 6 PM the platoon reported that an engineer officer of the army group had received a direct order from *Generaloberst* Model to blow the bridge at 7 PM.

The regimental commander ordered the 16th Company to take whatever steps were necessary in order to prevent the destruction of the bridge, including the use of force, and to take over direct security for the bridge with all of the company's platoons. This order was to be carried out and all contradictory orders were to be ignored, for it was certain that in addition to the companies of the regiment there were at least three divisions west of the Maas. Once the last German units had crossed the regiment withdrew and crossed the Maas near Hastière. The bridge was subsequently blown as per orders. The new line of security was Dinant-Givet. The regimental command post was in Hulsonniaux.

## Defense at the Maas and Fighting Withdrawal to the *Westwall* 4 to 12 September 1944

4 September: The regiment remained in the line of security occupied the previous day. Identity of the adjacent units unknown. The enemy approached the opposite bank slowly and cautiously. In the south, on the Upper Maas, the enemy had already reached the east bank.

5 September: During the night, at 2 PM, the enemy attacked across the Maas and succeeded in establishing a bridgehead roughly at the boundary between I and II Battalions. Both battalions counterattacked at 8 AM and completely destroyed the enemy bridgehead. 209 prisoners were taken, including four officers. Large quantities of weapons and equipment were brought in. Enemy movements on the west bank opposite II Battalion's sector were placed under fire.

6 September: I Battalion of the "*Deutschland*" Regiment was once again placed under the command of the "*Der Führer*" Regiment and was deployed in III Battalion's area. The enemy attacked across the Maas again and once again he succeeded in establishing a bridgehead. This time he even succeeded in getting some tanks across the river.

Such attacks must always succeed given the extremely weakened state of the companies and the thin occupation of the front lines. The battalions had only limited reserves with which to conduct a flexible defense, meaning counterattacks. Consequently, the German situation on the Maas was more of a thin line of security than a defense.

III Battalion "DF" and I Battalion "D" counterattacked once again, and the two battalions succeeded in seriously reducing the bridgehead but were unable to completely eliminate it. We no longer had sufficient forces to do so. Nevertheless, 149 prisoners were taken and the booty in weapons, equipment and vehicles was considerable. There was still no contact with the unit on the left, even though the regiment reconnoitered in the area south of Givet all day.

7 September: At 2 AM the order was received to withdraw by road to Deulin by way of Celles, Haversin, Nettime, Baillonville and Noiseux.

The regiment occupied a line of security at the Ourthe in the Verles-Vailon-Heure-Hogne area. Deployed were: right II Battalion, left III Battalion, 14th Company to secure toward Marche, 16th Company to guard the northern flank.

The unit on the right was probably the 12th SS Panzer Division "*Hitlerjugend*." Meanwhile still no contact on the left.

The fighting withdrawal that followed became more difficult from day to day. Each security sector was almost always twelve to twenty kilometers wide. Only the roads and important features of terrain could be guarded. Contact with the battalion could only be maintained by radio.

Not only did the regiment have to cope with the ever more intensive pursuit by the enemy's armored units, but with growing terrorist activities behind its own lines and the hostility of the civilian population as well. Runners were shot at, and large quantities of iron hooks were strewn on the roads in order to puncture tires. An ambulance was ambushed and shot up by terrorists. The medical officer riding in the vehicle, Ostuf. Dr. Rummler, and his driver were killed even though the vehicle was clearly marked with the red cross. Terrorists also ambushed an armored troop carrier platoon of the 11th Company. The platoon leader was killed in a hail of small arms fire and there were several wounded.

Continuous fighter-bomber attacks resulted in casualties to personnel and vehicles. The nervous strain on the troops was extraordinarily great. Almost always without contact to the left and right and with open flanks, the regiment fought its way back. Several times in the evening there were enemy tanks far behind our lines, threatening to encircle the regiment.

Only the arrival of darkness, in which the enemy almost never fought, enabled all of the elements of the regiment to escape encirclement. The maneuver was repeated each day. Several times the threatening situation forced the regimental commander to order a withdrawal on his own. Fortunately these decisions were confirmed by corresponding orders from the division a short time later. The regimental headquarters and the regimental adjutant Ostuf. Seegerer did outstanding work during this period.

8 September: At 3 PM orders to withdraw via Frenville, Melreux and Fisenne Erezée to Grandmenil. I Battalion rejoined the regiment with its new commander, Hstuf. Kluge. Together with other units of the division it had been employed as Battle Group Kluge.

9 September: At 8 PM withdrawal via Regne, Hebronval and Salmchateau.

10 September: Continued march via Salm and Vielsalm to Goronne. After 11 PM to Petit-Thier.

11 September: No contact or communications with unit on the regiment's left. Reconnaissance revealed that the enemy had broken through there. At 3:30 PM orders to withdraw via Ponteau to Roth (regimental command post: forester's house). At 3:45 PM the regiment crossed the new Reich border. The enemy pursued vigorously and forced the regiment to withdraw via St. Vith and Steinbrück to Elcherat. There it crossed the old Reich border and was now fighting on German soil.

12 September: The regiment was defending the line Maspelt-Sommersweiler-Schlierbach. At about 5 PM the enemy broke through with tanks and mounted infantry and almost reached the regimental command post. All forces were committed and the enemy drive was halted for the time being.

The next sector would be the *Westwall*. There was no division order to occupy the *Westwall* positions. Nevertheless, the regiment had to retreat towards the *Westwall* if it was to prevent the enemy from arriving there first.

On his own decision the commanding officer gave the order to occupy the *Westwall*. In keeping with the regiment's standard combat frontage, the sector Brandscheid-Habscheid-Kesfeld-Leidenborn was occupied. This represented a sector width of sixteen kilometers. It was the commanding officer's intention to have the division assign the regiment a significantly narrower sector, roughly corresponding to the combat strengths of the companies. During the withdrawal the commanding officer drove to the division where his order to occupy the *Westwall* was confirmed. The regiment's defense sector was also confirmed. Due to a shortage of forces there was no way that it could be reduced.

At 6 PM the regiment marched via Winterspelt to Habscheid, where with great difficulty the battalions were directed to their new positions.

# Appendix to Part VII

2nd SS Panzer Division "*Das Reich*"
Ic-426/44 Secret Division Command Post, 21/6/1944

Secret
Enemy Information Sheet No. 10

American units in the strength of ten divisions have been identified north of St. Lô on the Cotentin Peninsula.

A *Fighting style:*

1 *General:*

*Previous experience has shown that the American soldier fights indian-style. He knows how to exploit the divided terrain with its numerous hedgerows. He has been able to achieve some success through the use of concealed snipers even from close range (hidden in trees).*

*Assault operations are usually preceded by massed artillery fire and the use of smoke. Close-support aircraft are also employed to support offensive operations, with the enemy exploiting his command of the air.*

*Just as even lone dispatch riders and cars are harried by fighter-bombers, so to the enemy calls in air support even against single machine-gun nests and isolated resistance.*

*The enemy infantry has tremendous respect for our MG 42 and mortars. In the past it has also shown himself to be extremely sensitive where its rear and flanks are concerned.*

*Naval artillery is also used to combat ground targets and – directed by spotter aircraft – to engage even pinpoint targets far inland.*

*The enemy has achieved his limited success to date only because of his air and artillery superiority, even though he has committed his best elite divisions against weak German security divisions.*

2 *Details:*

*The main line of resistance is laid out strongpoint-style mostly following natural defensive features or villages and is bolstered by artillery and tanks. In general the enemy withdraws before our own forward line.*

*The artillery takes special care to protect its positions with mines.*

*A number of enemy tanks are fitted with "hedge clippers", which when the tank passes through creates a narrow lane and a field of fire for the infantry.*

*While attacking, the enemy infantry can easily be separated from its escorting tanks by well-aimed artillery fire.*

*Hstuf. and Ic* *for the corps headquarters*
*Distributor II* *The 1st General Staff Officer*
*Signed Stückler*

• • •

Extract from the War Diary of Headquarters, 7th Army

26 June 1944: weather conditions rainy.
*Situation in Normandy:*

*In the combat sector east of the Orne strong harassing fire from enemy naval guns fell on the Franceville and Grangues area all day long, while our artillery and rocket batteries engaged ships and disembarkations on the west bank of the Orne Estuary as well as recognized tank assembly areas near Escoville. Enemy assault teams were repulsed by the 346th Infantry Division.*

*After the offensive and defensive battle in the Tilly area had petered out at about 1 AM and there was no activity in I SS Panzer Corps's sector apart from harassing artillery fire and occasional heavy surprise barrages, following heavy artillery preparation at 8:15 AM the enemy once again attacked toward the south near Le Mesnil Patry. After crossing the Caen-Fontenay le Pesnel road, by 10 AM the enemy took the towns of St. Manvieu, Cheux and Rauray and after expanding his breakthrough in the evening reached Crainville sur Odon with his leading elements. Heavy fighting is in progress on both sides of Cheux. In the right sector (west of the Orne), too, the enemy fed in reinforcements and reached our positions. Since 9 PM he has been advancing with tanks in an easterly direction toward Carpiquet. Heavy fighting is in progress there.*

*To support the front and prevent an outflanking in the direction of Caen and south of Tilly, the elements of the 21st Panzer Division on the east bank will subordinate I Battalion of the 22nd Panzer Regiment to the I SS Panzer Corps. As well a panzer battalion of the 2nd SS Panzer Division will be subordinated to the corps for employment with the Panzer-Lehrdivision.*

*Simultaneously, the LXXXIV Army Corps will receive orders to immediately move the entire 7th Rocket Brigade to the west bank of the Orne and place it at the disposal of the I SS Panzer Corps. In order to also prevent an outflanking of the 12th SS Panzer Division and the 21st Panzer Division, at the suggestion of Feldmarschall Rommel the moving-up of a battle group from the 2nd SS Panzer Division ("DF" Regiment) is approved. In order to head off the enemy's drive to the south and southeast as quickly as possible and prevent a breakthrough to the south and a pinching off of Caen, this evening the II SS Panzer Corps will receive orders to expeditiously continue its march northwest across the Orne and after crossing the river to turn northeast.*

*The mission of the LXXXIV Army Corps is to attack the southwards- or eastwards-advancing enemy with the 9th and 10th SS Panzer Divisions and the attached battle group of the 2nd SS Panzer Division ("DF" Regiment).*

*28 June 1944 – weather conditions cloudy, windy.*
*Situation in Normandy:*

*In the afternoon hours of 28 June attacks by enemy tanks from the break-in area toward the northeast, southeast and south were halted by skillfully executed counterattacks carried out by the 12th SS Panzer Division reinforced by elements of the 2nd Panzer Division, the Panzer-*

*Lehrdivision and the 2nd SS Panzer Division ("DF" Regiment). Heavy losses were inflicted upon the enemy and terrain that had temporarily been lost was recovered...fierce fighting by both sides in the break-in area continued into the night.*

*29 June 1944 – weather conditions overcast.*
*Situation in Normandy:*

*...in the II Parachute Corps' sector, following heavy artillery preparation, at 9 AM the enemy launched simultaneous attacks on both sides of the boundary between the 3rd Parachute Division and the 352nd Infantry Division between St. Georges and Villiers-Fossard. The attack, which was made on a broad front with tank support, achieved a minor penetration on both sides of the Moon s. Elle-St. Lô road. The attack was headed off by counterattack, however, and sealed off in the line north end of Bretel-south end of La Forge-La Nicollerie.*

*Following the commitment of the last reserves of the 3rd Parachute Division, the units of the 352nd Infantry Division exhausted by continuous fighting were no longer able to stand up to an attack with its focal point in this sector.*

*The threat of a breakthrough into the deep flank of the LXXXIV Army Corps cannot be disregarded.*

*As a result of this development Panzer Group West received orders to withdraw the battle group of the 2nd SS Panzer Division ("DF" Regiment) taking part in the attack by the II SS Panzer Corps during the night of 29-30 June and 30 June-1 July 1944 and send it to the 2nd SS Panzer Division.*

• • •

Report by the Ia of the 2nd SS Panzer Division to the LXXXIV Army Corps dated 23 July 1944

During the evening hours of 22 July the enemy succeeded in breaking into our main line of resistance under heavy artillery fire and smoke and expanded the penetration by about one kilometer in depth and two kilometers in width.

*A counterattack with tanks restored the main line of resistance to our hands by 10:30 PM.*

*On the morning of 23 July infiltrated enemy forces (one to two companies) were surrounded and destroyed southwest of Le Closet. So far 245 unwounded prisoners, including twelve officers. Number of wounded prisoners not yet determined.*

*At 3 PM thirty enemy fighter-bombers attacked a mortar position in the St. Germain area.*

*At 5:15 PM a platoon-strength enemy patrol supported by eight tanks felt its way toward the sector of II Battalion "DF" and was repulsed. Destructive fire by the artillery caused explosions and fires in Le Canal.*

• • •

Headquarters, LXXXIV Army Corps
Ia Corps Command Post, 14/7/1944

Corps Order of the Day

The withdrawal behind the Lessay river line, the so-called water line, carried out during the night of 13-14 July 1944 marks the beginning of a new chapter in our defensive struggle. In the past twelve days of heavy fighting the corps has frustrated the attempts to break through of an enemy far superior in men and materiel.

*To the officers and men I express my thanks and appreciation for their bravery and their conduct during these difficult, crisis-filled days.*

*The past days have often presented us with crisis situations that could only be mastered through determination, steadfastness and clever measures in command. We have inflicted very heavy casualties on the enemy which have forced him to throw new forces into the battle and repeatedly fill up his depleted ranks.*

*Proud of the defensive success we have achieved, we can look to the future with confidence. The enemy will continue to assault our positions. The present day, which overall has left us in peace, is being used by the enemy to once again mass his artillery and make further preparations for a continuation of his breakthrough attempts.*

*A close-knit fighting team, we stand at a front where every man, depending on the performance of the others, must look with trust at the comrade fighting beside him, always ready to help and take risks on his behalf.*

*The position we are now defending no longer permits us to fight a flexible defensive battle. But it does offer the advantage of favorable terrain, and it is shorter and therefore easier to defend. We must hold it at all costs.*

*We look toward the coming battles conscious of our strength. Our fatherland can expect us to bravely oppose the enemy to the end. Trusting in our comrades and ourselves we will carry out our duty. The enemy will, as he always does when he engages us, meet a tough, determined, unshakable opponent.*

*Distribution:* *The commanding general*
*To the regiment level.*

• • •

Extracts from Telephone Conversations
of Generalfeldmarschall von Kluge

*31 July 1944:*
*9:35 AM – Generalfeldmarschall von Kluge with the chief of Headquarters, 7th Army, Oberst Gersdorff:*

*II Parachute Corps has not been attacked, instead its right flank is threatened. Will withdraw to the directed line during the coming night.*

*Battle Group Pflüger from the 116th Panzer Division with a panzer battalion, a panzer-grenadier battalion, a battalion of self-propelled artillery and elements of the reconnaissance battalion have been subordinated to the LXXXIV Army Corps to intervene in the area north of Avranches. New boundary between the II Parachute Corps and LXXXIV Army Corps near Hamby.*

*Consequently "Das Reich" subordinated to the XXXXVII Panzer Corps (Baron von Funk).*

*The Generalfeldmarschall's greatest concern is Villedieu as key point!*

*Generalfeldmarschall therefore agreed with the plan for "Das Reich" to withdraw toward the line Percy-Villedieu. Obviously the enemy in Avranches has so far been very weak, consisting of armored spearheads. It is planned to move in the 84th and 89th IDD.*

*7 August 1944:*
*9 PM – Generalfeldmarschall von Kluge with commander in chief 7th Army:*

*Description of the situation, not significantly changed, fighter-bomber attacks terrific, losses in tanks considerable. Attack is to be resumed.*

*Generalfeldmarschall: Everyone must give his best in order to force the matter. If we do not make considerable progress tonight and tomorrow morning then the whole business is over. Alencon must remain free since otherwise the troops cannot be fed. Resistance west of Alencon must therefore be such that he (the enemy) can get no farther. I hereby place the rest of the "Leibstandarte" at your disposal.*

*10 PM – Commander in Chief with battle group of the XXXXVII Panzer Corps:*

*Commander in chief: effective immediately "Leibstandarte" at your disposal for continued attack as before; it has twenty assault guns. To where? To St. Clement! The opportunity must be exploited now without regard to risk. We have to get through. Situation demands every possible measure.*

*10:15 PM – Generalfeldmarschall von Kluge with commander in chief 7th Army:*

*Generalfeldmarschall: based on a Führer order I direct that: (a) 10th SS Panzer Division has orders to make its way to you; (b) 12th SS Panzer Division (what is left of it) has orders to advance southwest and reach the ... area. 9th Panzer Division cannot be assigned this mission as it is engaged in battle near Le Mans.*

*Commander in chief: The attack was unsuccessful because of the fighter-bomber attacks and the inability of the 116th Panzer Division to advance. Resistance was stronger than anticipated, but no more than probably two divisions, which are now being steadily reinforced.*

In the book *Waffen-SS in Action*, former *Generaloberst* Paul Hausser wrote the following of the withdrawal movement of 29 July 1944:

> "In mid-July the course of the main line of resistance was basically north of the St. Lô-Perriers-Lessay road. On 17 July, after heavy fighting, the right wing corps (II Parachute Corps) finally lost St. Lô. The subsequent fighting on the army's front, especially that involving the 2nd and 17th Divisions, made it appear that the offensive for the breakthrough to the south was imminent. This decisive breakthrough took place in the battle west of the Vire during the period 25-27 July. Avranches did not bring about the actual breakthrough, instead this success was the result of the fighting from 25 to 27 July. The 2nd and 17th Divisions were fully drawn into this fighting under Baum. Through the Americans drive to the coast, after the breakthrough west of Vire, the western half of the 7th Army was already encircled on 28 July. The breakout from this pocket took place on 29 July behind the armored wedge of the 2nd and 17th SS Divisions from the area of Coutances toward Percy, where in conjunction with the XXXXVII Panzer Corps sent by the 5th Panzer Army (Baron von Funk) it was possible to hold the terrain at first.
>
> *Both SS divisions encountered the strength of the enemy during this breakout. The remaining forces of the LXXXIV Army Corps were insufficient to block the area to the coast (approximately 20 kilometers), consequently Avranches fell to the Americans on 30 July. The tanks of the US 3rd Army under Patton were now able to drive through this breach into Brittany and into the 7th Army's rear toward Le Mans.*
>
> *With approximately eight western divisions and four high-grade (panzer, panzer-grenadier and parachute) divisions, including the 2nd and 17th SS Divisions, the 7th Army fought for 56 days against the entire American invasion force (18 to 19 divisions, including four armored divisions) without support from our air force."*

# In the *Westwall*
## 13 September to 22 October 1944

12 September: While on his way back to the regiment, the regimental commander borrowed a large bunker map from an office behind the front. Every bunker in the regiment's sector was marked on the map. This was the regiment's sole reference during its occupation of the *Westwall* and remained so for some time.

The regimental command post was set up in a large dugout in Habscheid. From there the arriving units were directed to their sectors. Because of the lack of maps the officers and non-commissioned officers had to note the numbers of the bunkers they were to occupy. The regiment had assumed that guide parties would be available for occupation of the bunkers. That was not the case.

Since the combat strengths of the companies had been reduced by the fighting in Normandy and the retreat, in some cases to one fourth of authorized strength, at first only one third or one fourth of the bunkers could be manned.

At dawn the regimental headquarters moved into a headquarters bunker near Nieder-Üttfeld. Since the individual bunkers were extremely well camouflaged, the squads and platoons could only find some of them straight away. Not until the midmorning hours of 13 September were all of the assigned bunkers manned. Many of them were locked and had to be broken open. As we later learned, the keys were in the Bitburg district office! The civilian population was using several bunkers as potato cellars, and in the Leidenborn sector manned by III Battalion they were even being used as bomb shelters or as quarters for bombed-out families. The latter staunchly resisted leaving the bunkers. But as sad as this renewed homelessness for the bombing victims was, in the interest of everyone's safety the bunkers had to be evacuated and manned by the troops.

As these examples show, the *Westwall* was in no way prepared for the defense – at least in the "*Der Führer*" Regiment's sector. Because of the development in the situation on the western front the troops had taken for granted that it would be. No minefields had been laid in the approaches to the *Westwall*, as had originally been anticipated. Some of the "dragon's teeth" anti-tank obstacles had been badly damaged. Therefore the roads leading from the enemy side to the *Westwall* were immediately mined by the 16th Company and additional obstacles were set up.

The field telephone lines to the individual fighting positions, from the companies to the battalion and on to the regiment and division, were likewise unusable as they had not yet been connected together. For days teams of technicians were kept busy at the command posts connecting the appropriate lines.

The bunkers' armor had been rendered obsolete by recently developed armaments. The MG 42 machine-gun and the latest anti-tank guns would not fit in the bunkers designated for these classes of weapons. Consequently they had to be set up next to the combat positions. The 14th Company also went into open firing positions with its 20-mm anti-aircraft guns. The 16th Company was distributed by platoons and helped the battalions organize their defense fields. The 13th Company went into position in the area of the regimental command post.

The bunkers themselves had also not been prepared for a defensive battle. There was neither drinking water, bunker rations nor dressings! The regiment and battalion supply services did outstanding work in the first days and those that followed procuring these vitally needed materials. That the regiment was able to hold the *Westwall* for five weeks under these conditions was in large part due to their efforts.

In the first days the regiment had to wage a defensive battle with no artillery support. Then the II Battalion of the 2nd Artillery Regiment "*Das Reich*" was deployed in the regiment's sector. This battalion, which was almost always in action with the "*Der Führer*" Regiment, initially suffered from a serious ammunition shortage. While forces in the form of replacement battalions were available to occupy the *Westwall* position, as soon as word of an imminent attack was received they left their positions and withdrew.

For these reasons, in the first days the regimental commander was in no way certain whether it was possible to man the sector with his own weak forces to say nothing of holding it! What was expected of the regiment here bordered on the impossible. It therefore seems a miracle that the *Westwall* could be manned and held for a month under these conditions.

It was an almost unbelievable stroke of luck that the Americans, who had constantly been on the heels of the German troops withdrawing toward the *Westwall*, had temporarily halted their attack. For the enemy, who was vastly superior in men and materiel, would have met little resistance and could have broken through the *Westwall* in the first attempt.

One can say that in these first days the *Westwall* was held almost alone by "Goebbels." German propaganda had apparently so convinced the enemy of the *Westwall*'s invincibility that he had great respect for it and did not dare attack it from off the move.

13 September: I Battalion was not available. Sent to the wrong place, it did not go into action until the next day. At dawn the enemy occupied several bunkers in III Battalion's sector. An assault team under the outstanding leadership of Hscha. Peichl attacked these bunkers and retook them after a tough, costly struggle. Given the *Westwall*'s significance to the entire front, this successful operation at this moment was of decisive importance to the regiment in occupying and holding its sector of the *Westwall*. A short time later Hscha. Peichl, a native of Vienna, was awarded the Knight's Cross.

The enemy attacked III Battalion in three places and was beaten off. On 14 September the following units were placed under the regiment's command: a *Luftwaffe* fortress battalion, the 78th Panzer-Grenadier Replacement Battalion (Bonn, *Hauptmann* Zimmermann), and a Russian battalion.

Up to and inclusive of 18 September the 2nd Reconnaissance Battalion was positioned on the regiment's right and had occupied Brandscheid. Beginning on 18 September the Russian battalion, which was under the regiment's command, relieved the 2nd Reconnaissance Battalion.

The Russian battalion was not absolutely reliable. Several bunkers were abandoned with the men taking their weapons with them. According to their comrades they had deserted to the enemy under the command of their group leader.

The 78th Panzer-Grenadier Replacement Battalion was deployed between I and II Battalions "DF" and was absolutely reliable. Cooperation with its commander, *Hauptmann* Zimmermann, was exemplary. The morale of the troops was good.

The *Luftwaffe* fortress battalion was installed between I and III Battalions. Curiously it was composed almost entirely of flight personnel and thus its "human material" was of "outstanding" quality. These men, some of whom had 100 to 150 combat missions to their credit, were hastily assembled into a battalion at a troop training ground when the defense of the *Westwall* became of vital importance. In many cases the men had been assigned to the unit as punishment, for example if a pilot had made a crash-landing, or as a replacement for another punishment.

The battalion had a selection of men and was equipped with the most modern weapons, such as MG 15 aircraft machine-guns and bazookas. It did possess one serious shortcoming, however: the unit's personnel had not the slightest infantry training and had never fired their weapons! They had been told that their first practice firings would take place in the *Westwall* – against the enemy! In the beginning, therefore, this unit's fighting strength was about zero.

An example of this: an important bunker was lost. The regiment had no forces available for an assault team. When the *Luftwaffe* battalion received a clear mission from the regimental commander and exact instructions on how to form an assault team, one of the battalion's companies headed toward the enemy-held bunker in a march column in bright moonlight. The company was pinned down by concentrated enemy fire and sustained several dead and many wounded.

It s only fair, however, to say that this battalion, which was unpracticed in land warfare, later fought splendidly and worked well with I Battalion.

Two navy companies later saw action with III Battalion. The battalion had taken them in shortly before the crossing of the Maas as they had been left leaderless on the west bank of the Maas with no orders to withdraw.

The two companies consisted mainly of seventeen- and eighteen-year-old navy volunteers. Most were high school graduates and had volunteered to serve in one-man submarines. This weapon saw no use during the retreat and so they had been committed at the Maas as alert companies. They were all splendid young men with outstanding fighting spirit and exemplary conduct, surely the best that German youth could still offer the fighting forces.

Since III Battalion had suffered especially heavy casualties in the previous battles, these companies were placed under its command and incorporated into the unit; the young men fit in well there and fought magnificently. The regiment had some difficulty holding onto these two companies, as the navy made repeated inquiries about them via the *Reichsführer-SS* and the division. They stayed only because the regiment replied that removing the companies from III Battalion's sector would result in a very serious weakening of that sector, which might result in an enemy breakthrough and therefore could not be justified.

15 September: Enemy penetrations near Losenseifen, Kesfeld and Spielmannsholz. The situation was still uncertain when darkness fell. There were still some bunkers whose telephone lines to the battalion command posts had not been connected. Patrols were sent out during the night to find out whether it was friend or foe sitting in the bunkers.

In the coming weeks the brunt of the fighting would be borne by III Battalion (Hstuf. Werner), less by the *Luftwaffe* battalion and I Battalion. In general things remained almost peaceful in I Battalion's sector.

During the course of the day an order arrived from *Führer* Headquarters via the Commander in Chief West:

> "1. The Westwall is of decisive importance in the battle for Germany. 2. *Every single combat installation of the Westwall is to be defended to the last round and to the last man.*
>
> *Signed Adolf Hitler"*

This order arrived too late, for a number of bunkers were already in enemy hands as they could not be manned when the line was occupied due to a shortage of forces. Others simply could not be recaptured due to the enemy's fire and tank superiority.

## The End of the 10th Company

16 September: The enemy launched another breakthrough attempt against III Battalion in the area of Kesfeld. During the course of this 10th Company's bunkers were rolled up by tank fire, plow tanks, explosives and assaults by infantry and tanks.

During the battle the regimental commander stayed in touch via III Battalion with the bunkers in the thick of the fighting and spoke to the individual bunker commanders. The only assistance he could provide was a few rounds of artillery fire. There were no tanks, no counterattack reserve, to come to the aid of the hard-pressed men. In this way the commanding officer experienced first-hand the dramatic final struggle for several of the 10th Company's bunkers and heard the last words of their commanders:

> "They're coming with flame-throwers now – terrible heat – dust and smoke – I can't stand it any more..."

One member of 10th Company, who had been taken prisoner a short time before, stated after the war that he had not encountered any members of his company while a prisoner.

17 September: Deep penetrations between II Battalion and the *Luftwaffe* battalion to just short of the regimental command post. Nothing could be done against them. Suddenly the enemy tanks and infantry pulled back. Inexplicable.

During the night III Battalion constantly carried out "telephone reconnaissance." The bunkers were called one after another and thus it was determined whether they were still in our hands. The adjutant of II Battalion used this opportunity to challenge the enemy to a game of soccer.

These measures did allow the situation map to be updated daily. If a bunker was found to be empty it was immediately manned, albeit weakly, by our forces. The experiences after the dramatic end of 110th Company showed that it was impossible to fight effectively in the bunkers given the enemy's expenditure of materiel and fighting methods. They almost always drew the enemy's fire, the enemy tanks concentrated their fire on the embrasures and exits, and very soon the position was put out of action without the weak bunker crew being able to do anything about it. The modern offensive weapons showed themselves to be far superior to the weakly armed and manned bunkers.

Consequently the regiment issued orders for field positions to be dug between the bunkers. In the event of a massed attack by tanks, infantry and flame-thrower tanks the troops were to leave the bunkers and fight from the field positions. This defensive method soon showed good results.

18 September: The Russian battalion relieved the 2nd Reconnaissance Battalion. The battalion remained under the command of II Battalion, and thus the regiment and its attached units manned a width of front of seventeen kilometers.

19 September: Two attacks against II Battalion were frustrated using the new defensive methods.

20 September: The "*Der Führer*" Regiment launched a counterattack with the 16th Company against enemy forces that had broken in on the Heckuscheid-Nieder-Üttfeld road. The leading enemy elements, including an artillery observer, were in a farm approximately 500 meters from the regimental command post. The entire 13th Company, which for the first time had received adequate supplies of ammunition from the supply services, supported the attack with accurate pinpoint fire.

The attack by 16th Company was a complete success. The heavy infantry guns of 13th Company under the command of Ustuf. Böckmann were devastatingly effective and the Americans suffered heavy casualties. The number of field telephone lines underlined the importance the enemy attached to this forward position in the *Westwall.* The enemy was thrown back approximately one kilometer and the widely scattered artillery fire showed that the observation post had been put out of action.

21 September: The II Artillery Battalion "*Das Reich*" finally received sufficient ammunition. One of the battalion's 210-mm howitzers was assigned to work with the regiment and stood ready to fire with effect in front of the regiment's sector. Unfortunately it had only three rounds of ammunition per day. Barbed wire and mines were brought in for the engineers. The armored troop carriers of III Battalion delivered this materiel strictly by night, but they did drive right up to the front lines. Effective immediately the most threatened sector, that of III Battalion, was reinforced every night.

22 September: The enemy air force became very active. During the day it was almost impossible to move about outside the bunkers.

23 and 24 September: No significant enemy attacks. Patrols were beaten back.

25 September: Renewed attack against III Battalion and the *Luftwaffe* battalion was repulsed.

28 September: Strong enemy attacks and heavy barrages on the regiment's entire sector. Immediate counterattacks sealed off minor penetrations and the enemy was driven back.

Enemy maps were captured showing the bunkers in the regiment's sector. Every detail was marked on the maps. The regimental command post was precisely marked, as were the fighting positions of the battalions and companies as well as the underground field telephone net. The regiment had never possessed maps such as these! Renewed enemy attack aimed at the regimental command post. The enemy veered off, however, and once again turned against III Battalion. Our own tank knocked out one enemy tank. This tank had only just reached the regiment was less than 100% serviceable. The enemy attack was smashed in the middle of III Battalion's sector by massed mortar fire. The enemy suffered heavy casualties.

29 September: The regiment was subordinated tactically to the 90th Air Landing Division. At night the flame-thrower tanks of the 12th Company carried out daring counterattacks, and during the day this company's 80-mm and 120-mm mortars proved particularly effective. As before, III Battalion's sector remained the focal point of the defense.

Our fire control was quite outstanding: as soon as a bunker reported an attack, III Battalion had the report confirmed by other positions. All of 12th Company's mortars immediately went into action. There was sufficient ammunition on hand. The artillery battalion was informed via the regimental command post, and the enemy tank concentrations were pounded during the opening phase of the intended attack and forced to turn back by concentrated fire, on our own bunkers if necessary. It was terrific when the 210-mm howitzer fired its shells.

6 October: One motor transport and one bicycle battalion were subordinated to the regiment. The bicycle battalion took over the Leidenborn sector. The motor transport battalion was deployed in the sector held by the battered III Battalion. The new battalion consisted of older and hastily-trained replacements and had almost no combat experience. The average age of the men in the battalion was fifty-five. The tragedy of the situation is reflected in the following incident:

Three flame-thrower tanks of the 12th Company and some panzer-grenadiers of the 11th Company were ordered to carry out a night attack to drive the enemy out of the positions he had captured during the day. One platoon from the motor transport battalion was to take part in the attack. The operation was a success.

Platoon commander *Feldwebel* Maier (sixty years old, veteran of the First World War and wearer of the Iron Cross, First Class) commented to the adjutant of III Battalion: "That went wonderfully, *Herr Oberleutnant.* But could you order your flame-thrower tanks to drive a little slower in future? My men can't keep up. They simply lose their breath when they run fast."

7 to 9 October: No significant enemy attacks. The commander of III Battalion, Hstuf. Heinz Werner, became the thirteenth member of the regiment to receive the Knight's Cross.

10 October: Counterattacks near Losenseifen.

12 October: Orders arrived for the withdrawal of the regiment from the *Westwall.* The 90th Air Landing Division protested vigorously before releasing the regiment. I Battalion had already been pulled out.

16 October: During the night the regiment, minus II Battalion, was pulled out of the line and marched from Pronsfeld via Prüm, Weinheim and Gerolstein to Pelm.

18 October: Memorial day for the Battle of Nations near Leipzig. The Volkssturm was called up, and on the same day 10th Company's battle and its exemplary conduct were made known to the German people by German radio. The company was honored by being named in the *Wehrmacht* communiqué and featured in a special report from the front. A division order of the day issued on the same day declared:

> *"The quiet heroism with which the 10th Company of the SS Panzer-Grenadier Regiment 'Der Führer' defended its sector north of Kresfeld was acknowledged before the entire German people in today's Wehrmacht communiqué: 'In mid-September, immediately after the occupation of the Westwall, the 10th Company fought with fanatical determination against a far superior enemy, especially in tanks, without heavy weapons and without artillery, and held the position entrusted to it to the last breath of every one of its men.'*

*We bow in awe before the greatness of these grenadiers."*

19 October: The regiment was entrained and was transported by rail into the Niedermarsberg area. There the local mayor informed the regimental commander that the defense commissar had forbidden occupation of the city by troops. The commanding officer told him that he only had to listen to the orders of his division and not those of the defense commissar and of course was going to occupy quarters in the city. This brought the matter to a close as far as the regiment was concerned.

22 October: II Battalion rejoined the regiment with the last units. Quartering areas: regimental headquarters and regimental units: Niedermarsberg, I Battalion: Bredelar, II Battalion: Essentho, and III Battalion: Giershagen.

23 October to 11 November: Expedited refurbishment of the regiment.

## Refurbishment in the Niedermarsberg Area

Following the withdrawal of the 4th SS Panzer-Grenadier Regiment "*Der Führer*" from the *Westwall* in the Schnee-Eifel, at the end of October 1944 it was transferred into the Niedermarsberg area in Westphalia for a brief refurbishment of the regiment and the reorganization of I Battalion. At this point in time the regiment had at best forty to fifty percent of its fighting strength. Casualties in the *Westwall* fighting had been exceptionally heavy. All that was left of I Battalion was its supply units. Losses in weapons and equipment as a result of enemy action were considerable.

In the midst of the *Westwall* action, on orders from the division the adjutant of III Battalion, Ostuf. Gerhard Schmager, had taken over a replacement unit consisting of approximately 1,000 enlisted men and noncommissioned officers a few kilometers behind the front. These young soldiers, most of them volunteers, were now sent to the regiment. The amazing enthusiasm of the eighteen- and nineteen-year-old boys could not entirely make up for their abbreviated military training, however.

During the three-week refurbishment the serious losses of trained drivers, the limited allocation of fuel for the driving schools and motorized exercises, the totally inadequate motor pool of I Battalion and the inadequate training of the young replacements were all particularly noticeable. All of these shortcomings would later have negative effects during the Ardennes offensive.

The time available, three weeks, was not nearly sufficient to restore the regiment to its full fighting strength in terms of training and materiel. Following the division's express guidelines, training was limited to purely offensive missions. Officer training consisted of map exercises and training conferences.

Stubaf. Karl August Götsche was transferred to the regiment and took over I Battalion.

The regiment received a very warm welcome from the population of Niedermarsberg.

The members of the regimental band under their band leader Hstuf. Georg Gaul had been made into stretcher bearers and signals men and were sitting around idle in the trains. Contrary to the existing directives, on an order from the regiment they were assembled into a band again began practicing their old, stirring marches daily. The regiment's parade march, the "Prince Eugen March," was also heard again for the first time in a long while.

In addition to combat training, the headquarters company under Ostuf. Hentschel drilled for one hour each day. Soon soldiers were once again marching through the small city to martial music – a scene that had long been absent – much to the joy of the residents of Niedermarsberg. The parades helped pick up their initially somewhat depressed spirits.

The local officials, including the mayor, took part in the ceremonial swearing-in of the recruits, the parade that followed and the awarding of decorations. The population crowded the streets to experience this stirring ceremony and the subsequent military display.

As soon as the division learned of the reformation of the band, the music platoon was requested for numerous functions, which was equivalent to a retroactive approval.

Such was the warm relationship that developed between the troops and the civilian population in these weeks that many men received invitations to private homes. There was plenty of hard work, but also many happy hours.

It was also there that the idea of a rest home for members of the regiment recuperating from wounds or in need of a rest was born. This idea was made reality through the ideal cooperation with Mayor Werpers, who placed the beautifully-situated Diemel castle at the regiment's disposal for this purpose. All of the necessary instructions for the establishment of the home were covered in a regimental order. The specialists of the big reserve hospital generously offered to provide constant medical observation and care to the men staying at the home.

A member of the regiment was placed in charge of the home, and articles from the regiment's stores ensured that the home had sufficient food for a long time.

Unfortunately only once could a shipment of convalescents be sent to the rest home in Niedermarsberg, from Hungary. They experienced the end of the war and the end of the home there. This installation would undoubtedly have had a positive effect on the regiment in the future.

When the time for departure came there were many tears and heartfelt words of farewell and thanks.

It was the regiment's last "home base" and all of the men of the "*Der Führer*" Regiment will always have fond memories of Niedermarsberg.

# The Ardennes Offensive

## Organization of the 4th SS Panzer-Grenadier Regiment "DF" At the Start of the Ardennes Offensive

Regimental headquarters with headquarters company (17th Company), signals and motorcycle scout platoon.

I Battalion: battalion headquarters and signals platoon, 1st, 2nd and 3rd Panzer-Grenadier Companies, 4th (Heavy) Company, supply company.

II Battalion: battalion headquarters and signals platoon, 5th, 6th and 7th Panzer-Grenadier Companies, 8th (Heavy) Company, supply company.

III Battalion (armored troop carrier battalion): battalion headquarters and signals platoon, 9th, 10th and 11th Armored Troop Carrier Companies, 12th (Heavy) Company with self-propelled guns and one platoon of flame-thrower armored troop carriers (three vehicles), supply company.

13th Company (heavy infantry gun company): one platoon of self-propelled guns, two towed platoons.

14th Company (anti-aircraft company): four platoons each with two 20-mm anti-aircraft guns on self-propelled carriages.

16th Company (engineer company): three engineer platoons.

At 11:30 PM on 11 November 1944 completely unexpected transfer orders were received. The "*Der Führer*" Regiment was initially transported via the Lisch reporting center, ten kilometers east of Jülich, into the area northeast of Jülich, with the first transport leaving on 12 November and the last on 15 November. Regimental command post: Mersch, five kilometers north of Jülich. On 18 November the regiment moved into the area east of Rheydt. Regimental headquarters and 13th-16th Companies in Steinhausen, Liedberg, Pesch and Rubbelrath. I Battalion in Büttgen, II Battalion in Kleinenbroich and III Battalion in Giesenkirchen. With the serious fuel shortage in mind, the transport from Niedermarsberg was made by rail and strict camouflage measures were ordered.

Shortly after the units arrived in this area, an order arrived from division to assemble all approaching combat-ready and fully motorized elements of the regiment into a battle group. As part of an operational reserve it was to remain at constant combat and alert readiness at the disposal of the Model Army, in order to meet and seal off a possible breakthrough in the Aachen battle zone.

Under the command of Hstuf. Werner, commander of III Battalion, the battle group's composition was as follows: headquarters and signals platoon III Battalion, two companies from II Battalion, two companies from III Battalion, one platoon (infantry gun) from the 13th Company, two platoons (anti-aircraft) from the 14th Company, one platoon (engineer) from the 16th Company.

As a result of these measures training in the quartering area was extremely limited. The reinforced 16th Company with attached anti-aircraft platoon from the 14th Company and flame-thrower tanks was able to successfully carry out an assault team operation. The 9th Company carried out a similar operation, likewise with live ammunition.

Training was pushed ahead within the realm of what was possible, even though live-fire exercises were for the most part absent out of concern for the civilian population. At the start of the Ardennes offensive the regiment was at about 90% of authorized strength in personnel and weapons, but in vehicles only about 60%.

I Battalion was not yet motorized and at the beginning of December it received bicycles from the division! The condition of these vehicles was extremely poor. I Battalion had no winter clothing, and some of the men had no coats and their footwear was in bad shape.

The regiment's training state at the beginning of December 1944: combat ready for defensive missions, only conditionally combat ready for offensive missions.

At the beginning of December the division issued the first preparatory directives for the rapid assembly of the division in the area west of Cologne. All of the regimental commanders of the II SS Panzer Corps received their first information on the real intentions of the high command from commanding general Bittrich in the form of a conference and a map exercise in which the outlines of the German plan for the Ardennes offensive were sketched out.

According to these, as part of the II SS Panzer Corps the 2nd SS Panzer Division "*Das Reich*" would, depending on how the attack developed, either follow behind the I SS Panzer Corps and later turn north to cover the deep right flank of the army or force a crossing of the Maas (Meuse) south of Liège. The commanding general stressed above all that this offensive was the last great exertion of which the homeland was capable.

The fuel for the operation's movements would for the most part have to be captured by the troops in battle! On account of the tenuous fuel situation no regular supply of fuel could be expected from the 6th SS Panzer Army during the offensive.

The next day the division commander once again swore the regimental commanders to strictest silence about this map exercise. The regiment was issued a full complement of ammunition, but only 2.5 measures of fuel (each sufficient for 100 kilometers). The battalion commanders and the commanders of the regimental units had to swear in writing not to touch these protected stocks.

The regimental commanders repeatedly tried to convince the division to order each vehicle to carry ten to twelve measures of fuel, at least at the start of the offensive, in order to bridge the supply difficulties in the first days of the offensive and place the troops in a position to capture fuel at all! The division had to reject all of these proposals as the required quantities of fuel were obviously not available.

In the last days before the offensive, on instructions from the division orders were issued concerning the collection and reporting of captured stocks of fuel as well as the formation of captured fuel collection detachments.

The regiment remained in its quartering area until 13 December 1944.

## Concentration and Attacks

13 December: After being placed on alert, during the night of 13-14 December the regiment marched via Glehn-Holzheim into Area B. Regimental command post in Fliestedten. I Battalion had difficulties making the move because of a lack of vehicles.

14 December: Night march via Bergheim into Area C. Regimental command post in Lommersum.

15 December: Rest in Area C.

16 December: Rest in Area C. Unit commanders informed of the start of the Ardennes offensive at the division command post.

17 December: Rest in Area C.

18 December: Before daybreak the regiment marched via Euskirchen and Münstereifel into Area D. Regimental command post: two kilometers east of Burr. One kilometer east of the regimental command post was a firing position for the V 1. V 1s were launched all day and night. No noticeable activity on the part of the enemy air force during the first days of the offensive on account of the foggy weather.

19 December: The regiment remained in Area D. Requests to division for fuel were in vain as our fuel trucks were en route, as per orders,

in order to pick up fuel in the Cologne (!) area. These supply vehicles also did not return in the following days.

20 December: In the evening march via Blankenheim, Hillesheim, Oberbettingen and Schönecken into Area E. Regimental command post in Reuland. Fuel ran low. Still no supply.

21 December: Morning continued march via Wayweiler and Dasburg into Area F. No enemy activity in the air. At 11:30 AM the Reich border was crossed near Dasburg. Regimental command post in Binsfeld. The regiment arrived in Area F on the last of its fuel; however, some vehicles ran out prior to reaching the area and, where possible, were towed the rest of the way.

It was announced that the army's 2nd Panzer Division had driven far to the west against little resistance and was already nearing Dinant.

No air activity, the road to the Maas lay open, however the entire division was immobilized for twenty-four hours for lack of fuel. The division could also not be supplied from the air as our air force was in no position to do so.

22 December: Fuel arrived during the course of the midmorning. The regiment received orders to reach the Petits Tailles area with an attached artillery battalion from the division in the afternoon, in order to relieve from there the advance detachment of the 560th Volksgrenadier Division, which was pinned down before the Baraques les Fraitures crossroads. American motorized units and tanks were holding the crossroads.

The regiment marched off in the late afternoon and its first units reached the directed area after darkness had fallen. Contact was immediately made with the commander of the 560th's advance detachment, *Major* Hevel (?), and preparations were made to relieve that unit. Little enemy fire. The advance detachment was relieved during the night, with II Battalion to the right of the road, command post beside the road approximately 700 meters southeast of the crossroads, and III Battalion to the left of the road, command post in a forester's house approximately 500 meters southwest of the crossroads.

Great demands were made of I Battalion. With some on foot and some on bicycles, the companies made only slow progress in the heavy blowing snow. The heavy equipment was transported in vehicles, and each truck had at least two vehicles in tow because of lack of fuel. At times during the night loud tank sounds were heard from the crossroads. Command post: Petits Tailles.

23 December: The 560th's advance detachment left in the morning. The regiment moved its command post to Les Tailles, southwest of the main road. Reconnaissance by both battalions revealed that the Baraques les Fraitures crossroads was strongly held by the enemy. Twelve enemy tanks were counted, enemy artillery fire began for the first time. Previous attempts to seize the crossroads had been frustrated by the strength and watchfulness of the enemy. During the midmorning the regiment was sent a Panther company and an assault gun company; both units were placed under the command of the regiment. The Panther company was instructed to work with II Battalion and the assault gun company with III Battalion.

The "*Der Führer*" Regiment's plan of attack: II Battalion, bolstered by 13th Company and elements of 14th Company, would attack toward the crossroads on both sides of the main road supported by tanks. III Battalion, bolstered by elements of 14th Company, would attack along the road from the west toward the crossroads supported by the assault guns. The artillery battalion would prepare the attack with firing a brief, heavy barrage on the crossroads and then seal off the road northwest of the crossroads. Forward observers assigned to II and III Battalions to ensure close cooperation. Attack to begin at approximately 3 PM.

After bitter fighting, by nightfall the Baraques les Fraitures crossroads was in our hands. The Panther company, whose commander deployed his tanks skillfully and daringly, and the assault guns, which provided outstanding support to III Battalion in its attack, made particularly important contributions to this success. Fifteen enemy tanks were knocked out, and in addition to standard vehicles numerous half-tracked vehicles were captured. The enemy force was obviously an armored battalion that had been hastily sent forward with orders to hold the crossroads at all costs.

New assignments were issued after the attack objective was reached: for II Battalion: continuation of the attack in the direction of Malempré; for III Battalion: advance along the road to the northwest without delay and reach the forest exit northeast of Odeigne.

The first units of I Battalion, its men travelling on foot, on bicycles and in vehicles, arrived during the late afternoon and moved into Petites Tailles. The battalion was completely dispersed.

Attacking across difficult terrain, II Battalion reached the forest north of Baraques les Fraitures during the night of 24 December. There strong enemy resistance initially halted the attack.

III Battalion became involved in heavy forest fighting directly northwest of Baraques les Fraitures and during the night of 24 December was unable to take out the tanks dug in along the road. The battalion suffered heavy casualties, and among those killed was the commander of 11th Company, Ostuf. Rosenstock.

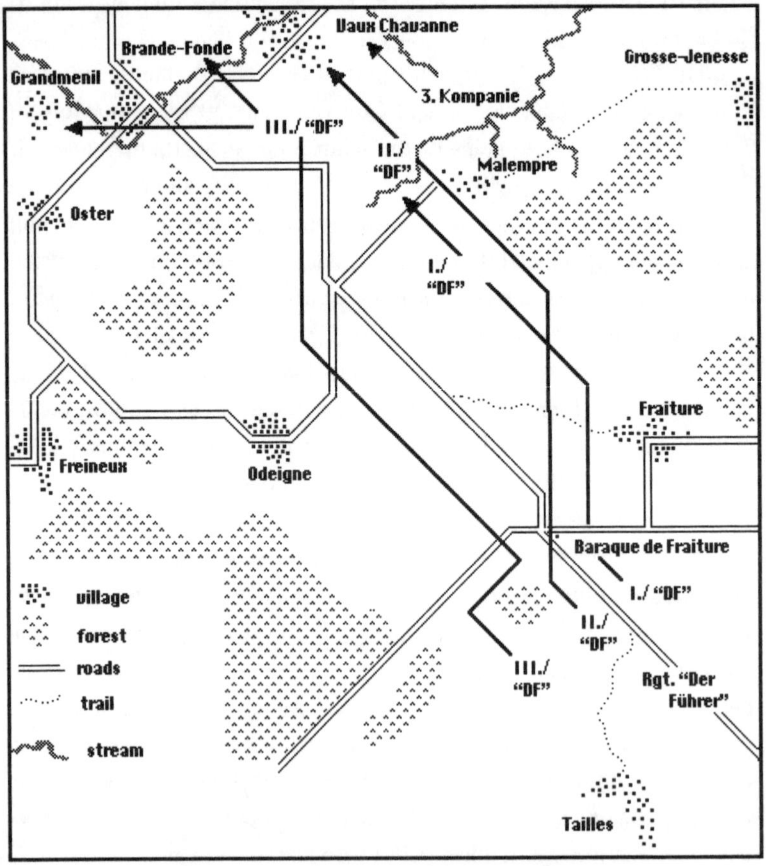


The situation from 23 - 26 December, 1944

24 December: Heavy enemy artillery fire on the crossroads and III Battalion's positions. The commander of the engineer platoon subordinated to III Battalion, Ustuf. Braun, was killed by a direct hit by an artillery round. Hstuf. The commander of III Battalion, Hstuf. Heinz Werner, was wounded. The commander of 12th Company, Ostuf. Heinrich Manz, took over the battalion, which was still feeling the effects of the tough night battle in the forest. In the afternoon III Battalion resumed its attack to the northwest and during the night the bulk of its forces reached the edge of the forest northeast of Odeigne.

The 9th Company under Ustuf. Kurt Cronjäger advanced the farthest and was already in front of Grandmenil. The 1st and 3rd Companies were ordered to advance via the Baraques les Fraitures crossroads and "Pifosse" toward Malempré, clear the woods of enemy troops, and secure the forest edge south of Malempré. In a rapid forest attack the 3rd Company overcame fierce enemy resistance and gained a foothold near "Pifosse" in close combat. The company's losses were considerable. In fact the point platoon was literally wiped out.

During the night orders were received from division to the effect that effective immediately III Battalion was placed under the command of the panzer regiment for an armored thrust toward Grandmenil and was to move its armored troop carriers into position during the night.

25 December: II Battalion reported a 5% incidence of frostbite during the night. The attack terrain was swampy. During the midmorning the regiment took Malempré with I Battalion on the right and II Battalion on the left. Regimental command post in Malempré.

26 December: Continuing the attack, II Battalion only got as far as the hill due west of Malempré, where its advance was halted by a strong enemy defense. II Battalion quickly regrouped and then drove the enemy from his positions, advanced through densely wooded terrain and took the village of Vaux Chavanne. A vigorous counterattack could not be held and the battalion occupied positions at the edge of the forest south of Vaux Chavanne. Heavy artillery fire on our positions.

III Battalion was committed with the panzer regiment in Manhay and Grandmenil. According to information from the division, the 9th SS Panzer Division "*Hohenstaufen*" was on the regiment's right and pushing to take Vaux Chavanne. During the night of 27 December the 3rd Company was sent to II Battalion.

27 December: II Battalion and the attached 3rd Company received orders to attack at 1 AM. Under well-directed artillery and mortar fire the companies of II Battalion were halted before the enemy's strongly fortified positions. The 3rd Company, which was supposed to carry out a flanking attack, ran into extremely heavy defensive fire when it launched its attack and was completely shattered. The division insisted that the attack must be continued. The enemy fire on II Battalion's sector grew heavier, restricting all movement.

On an express order from the division, the commander of 3rd Company, Ostuf. Gerhard Schmager, scraped together what was left of the company (twelve men!) and attacked again. He succeeded in breaking into the enemy positions.

In the early morning hours the enemy fire increased in intensity once again, and the company was forced to withdraw to its starting point, suffering additional casualties.

III Battalion had taken over the Manhay sector. The enemy launched fierce counterattacks toward Grandmenil-Manhay. Liaison officers from the 9th SS Panzer Division arrived at the regiment; however, the gap between the "*Der Führer*" Regiment and the "*Hohenstaufen*" Division remained,. The enemy artillery fire and air activity increased noticeably. During the day an order arrived from division stating that in the coming night the "*Der Führer*" Regiment was to be relieved by elements of the "*Hohenstaufen*" Regiment for use in an offensive operation farther southwest. Since it proved impossible to relieve the relieving "*Hohenstaufen*" units on time, only weak elements of the regiment could be pulled out of the line during the night.

28 December: During the early midmorning the regimental commander was ordered to the division command post, where Sepp Dietrich, the commander in chief of the 6th SS Panzer Army, was waiting. Dietrich presented the Knight's Cross with Oak Leaves to the commanders of the "*Deutschland*" Regiment, Ostubaf. Günther Wisliceny (No. 687), and the "*Der Führer*" Regiment, Otto Weidinger (No. 688), for the outstanding achievements of their regiments on the invasion front. The decisive act by the commander of the "*Der Führer*" Regiment had been the counterattack and opening of the Falaise Pocket, in which the 7th Army was surrounded.

This decoration was special recognition for the countless actions and feats of combat by the battalions, the individual companies and squads, and the individual accomplishments to the most junior panzer-grenadier of the "*Der Führer*" Regiment in the summer and autumn of 1944.

28 December: After Ostuf. Manz was wounded Ostuf. von Eberstein took over III Battalion. The units of I and II Battalions that had remained in the positions were not relieved until midmorning. The "*Der Führer*" Regiment at first moved into the Chabrehez area (west of Les Tailles). According to its orders, it was supposed to be in its new Devantave assembly area (without III Battalion) by evening; all available units were sent there, although the bulk of the panzer-grenadiers were absent on account of the delay in their being relieved.

29 December: Since the regiment was not yet completely assembled and as its present position was especially vulnerable to air attack, it was moved back to Chabrehez on orders from division and with the agreement of the 560th Volksgrenadier Division. In the late afternoon the regiment moved back into the Devantave area – I Battalion once again in a tiring foot march.

The regiment was supposed to take Amonines in a night attack that same evening, however this proved impossible as I Battalion's point unit, the 3rd Company, did not arrive until the early morning hours after a night march in heavy blowing snow.

At the urging of the division, during the night the regiment carried out a raid on Amonines with the 16th Company. The attack was halted by concentrated enemy fire at the southern boundary of Amonines. Company commander Ostuf. Wolf was killed and his loss was sorely felt.

30 December: The regimental command post was moved to Les Prangeleux. The "*Der Führer*" Regiment took over the Wegespinne sector, which extended from 1.7 kilometers southeast of Amonines (on the right the 560th Volksgrenadier Division, contact not yet established) – forest edge southeast of Amonines-Hill 405 (1.5 kilometers south-southwest of the church of Amonines) – to and including Magoster. On the left: the "*Deutschland*" Regiment.

The units were deployed as follows: right, I Battalion; left II Battalion with attached 14th Company; boundary: west end of the Bois de Bave forest. At the regiment's disposal: 16th Company in Hennet Ferme, 13th

Company in the Les Prangeleux area. Instructed to cooperate with the "*Der Führer*" Regiment: II Battalion of the Armored Artillery Regiment "*Das Reich*."

31 December: Enemy artillery extremely active against I Battalion's sector. The commander of the 3rd Company was wounded.

1-2 January 1945: Attack by I Battalion toward Amonines halted by heavy enemy artillery fire. The regiment's entire sector under harassing artillery fire. Much reconnaissance activity by both sides. The place of the regimental adjutant, Ostuf. Seegerer, was temporarily taken by Hstuf. Buch, newly transferred to the division. Hermann Buch was assigned to the "*Der Führer*" Regiment for familiarization (from 1 to 17 January 1945).

3 January: No contact with the unit on the right, the 560th Volksgrenadier Division. The 16th Company was inserted into this gap. Nevertheless, the company, under Hscha. Reinisch, failed to establish contact with the 560th Volksgrenadier Division.

A squad from the motorcycle scout platoon was sent to reconnoiter and ran into strong enemy forces advancing on the Amonines-Dochamps road. The squad leader was wounded and he and some of his men were captured. Only two men made it back to the regiment to report what had happened.

4 January: The enemy artillery fire steadily grew in intensity. The enemy attacked without pause. After heavy artillery preparation Hill 405 was attacked by tanks and had to be abandoned. I Battalion was tied down along the entire width of its sector and was unable to release any units for a counterattack. The division assault company and an assault gun company were sent in and placed under the battalion's command for the attack on Hill 405.

5 January: Hill 405 was retaken by the newly arrived units.

6 January: Enemy pressure on the regiment's entire sector. Particularly heavy pressure on II Battalion's sector under its commander Hstuf. Hannes Schulzer.

7 January: The 7th Company was attacked by superior enemy forces in Magoster. In spite of a determined defense the company was shattered. Only a few grenadiers, led by the company commander, succeeded in fighting their way through in heavy close combat and taking advantage

of friendly mortar fire. Further penetrations against II Battalion.

After the loss of the 7th Company the battalion was forced to withdraw its positions to the northern edge of the wood southeast of Magoster and to the small Les Belles river north of Devantave.

8 January: Enemy attack with strong artillery support on the sector held by I Battalion (because of the heavy casualties suffered in the recent battles, 3rd Company was disbanded as a combat company) and the 16th Company. The enemy achieved a number of penetrations, but in each case these were sealed off after the defenders summoned the last of their strength.

9 January: Extremely heavy enemy artillery fire on Devantave from 7 to 9 AM. At about 9 AM the enemy fired smoke shells. Heavy enemy attack on the "*Der Führer*" Regiment's entire sector. At about 9:30 AM enemy tanks and infantry forced their way into Devantave. Eighty American tanks were counted on the Devantave-Les Prangeleux road.

Contact was lost with III Battalion. Elements of the battalion withdrew toward the edge of the woods south of Devantave. Isolated, I Battalion fought on both sides. The simultaneous enemy attacks from the direction of Devantave and from the northeast (Aisne Valley) threatened to cut off the battalion. Pulled back to the line Dochamps-Le Wate, I Battalion was hit by an enemy tank attack from Devantane. As of 10 AM the regimental command post was at the edge of the woods south of Dochamps. No contact with the 560th Volksgrenadier Division or the "*Deutschland*" Regiment. The Second Battalion of the division's armored artillery battalion was on the hill south of Dochamps in the front line in an open firing position without infantry protection. The "*Der Führer*" Regiment's new positions ran along the edge of the woods south and southeast of Les Prangeleux-Le Wate.

10 January: During the night of 9-10 January the regiment was withdrawn from its previous sector and moved via Berismenil and Wibrez to Dinez. The Third (Armored) Battalion had meanwhile been subordinated to the division's armored reconnaissance battalion and had gone into position in the Baraques les Fraitures area. The adjutant of III Battalion, Ostuf. Wolleweber, was killed.

11 January: The "*Der Führer*" Regiment was placed under the command of the 12th Volksgrenadier Division. During the night of 12 Janu-

ary the regiment was inserted between the 12th Volksgrenadier Division and the "*Deutschland*" Regiment in the area south of a line Bihain-Petites Tailles. Main line of resistance: Fange de Longfat-Rouge Fange-Pisserotte. The First Battalion of the 19th Panzer-Grenadier Regiment remained in position and was subordinated to the "*Der Führer*" Regiment. Regimental command post in Lomre, which was also the site of the 12th Volksgrenadier Division's command post under *Oberstleutnant* Lempke. Excellent cooperation between two regiments.

13 January: The enemy kept up the pressure on the "*Der Führer*" Regiment's entire sector. The enemy failed to achieve any penetrations, although the fighting strengths of the companies had been seriously reduced by combat casualties and numerous cases of frostbite. There were many days when the losses to frostbite were just as high as the other casualties, which were considerable.

Aided by the complex terrain, the enemy succeeded in places in gaining a foothold in our main line of resistance with assault teams and lone tanks. Although the penetrations were sealed off, there was not sufficient strength for a counterattack. In the evening the enemy achieved a deep penetration at the boundary between the "*Der Führer*" and "*Deutschland*" Regiments.

15 January: The enemy attacks were made in greater strength and made progress on both sides of Lomre. The situation was complex. By the afternoon Lomre was almost surrounded and both regimental command posts were now moved out. The "*Der Führer*" Regiment withdrew to new positions along the Sterigny-Cherain-Sommerain road. Regimental command post in Cherain.

New positions were occupied during the night of 16 January. The regimental command post was now located in Renglez. II Battalion went into position near Sommerain, which was also the site of the regiment's forward command post. Hstuf. Schulzer, the commander of II Battalion, was wounded in an enemy attack on Sommerain. The regimental commander temporarily took command of the battalion. In the afternoon the regiment was pulled out of the line on orders from division.

During the night of 17 January the "*Der Führer*" Regiment moved to Weiswampach and assembled in the Krombach area. III Battalion was returned to the regiment's command. Ostuf. Seegerer once again assumed the duties of the regimental adjutant and Hstuf. Buch became division adjutant. Orders arrived from division for the regiment to pull back behind the *Westwall.*

18 January: The regiment marched via Burg-Rauland-Winterspelt into the Bleialf area.

There were serious fuel problems. Elements of the regiment were halted before and in some cases in the *Westwall* line. The march roads were hopelessly clogged. All attempts to obtain the desperately needed fuel were unsuccessful. As many stranded vehicles as possible were taken in tow. The enemy pursued relentlessly and vehicles, even some of the precious armored troop carriers, had to be blown up in order to prevent them falling into enemy hands.

19 to 21 January: The regiment remained in the Bleialf area until the last units had arrived.

21 January: At approximately 5 PM the regiment moved to Pelm via Prüm.

22 January: The regiment's quartering area: Stroheich-Pelm. All train units, which had previously been separated from the regiment, were recalled from the Großbüllesheim area. The regiment remained in this area until 3 February. It was announced that the regiment was being withdrawn from the western front and was to be employed for new missions in the east. Destination unknown. At the beginning of February the division commander, *Brigadeführer* Heinz Lammerding, left the division. *Standartenführer* Karl Kreutz, formerly commander of the 2nd Armored Artillery Regiment, took over command of the "*Das Reich*" Panzer Division.

4 February: The regiment marched via Mayen and Koblenz to Nieder-Bieber and was entrained there on 7 February, destination unknown.

## Observations on the Operations in the Ardennes

Own fighting strength: the "*Der Führer*" Regiment went into the Ardennes offensive with only two relatively combat-ready battalions (II and III). When the attack began I Battalion was not operational. The reorganization, training and motorization of the battalion could not be completed in the time available, approximately two weeks. The replacement personnel were extremely inexperienced and except for a very small percentage lacked vehicles. The attempt to make the companies of I Battalion mobile through the use of bicycles failed on account of their extraordinarily poor condition. Another factor was command difficulties, as the commander of I Battalion lacked combat experience. This difficulty was repeatedly reported to the division.

With the exception of the attack on the Baraques les Fraitures crossroads, the armored III Battalion was under the command of other units during the entire Ardennes offensive. Consequently the "*Der Führer*" Regiment's fighting strength was seriously weakened. Essentially it could only count on II Battalion and the regimental units.

Decisive shortcomings: from the first day on the units were separated on orders from above and for the most part fought under unfamiliar commands, even though in many cases other units of the division were their immediate neighbors. As a result the combined striking power of the division and with it the "*Der Führer*" Regiment was lost.

As a result of completely inadequate supply of fuel, during the decisive twenty-four hours (19 December 1944) the "*Der Führer*" Regiment, like the other units of the "*Das Reich*" Panzer Division, was immobilized, although the road to the Maas was practically open. It appears that this one day was sufficient for the enemy to recover from the shock of surprise and occupy the most important traffic junctions with hastily mobilized armored units. The regiment's inadequate vehicle complement severely restricted its mobility and was in no way equivalent to that of a panzer-grenadier regiment of a panzer division.

The "*Der Führer*" Regiment's combat casualties were extremely heavy and equaled approximately thirty to thirty-five percent of the combat strengths. Added to these were casualties due to frostbite of approximately eight to ten percent caused by damp and inadequate clothing. The regiment's losses in officers were particularly heavy. The 3rd and 7th Companies were particularly hard hit.

Reason for the failure of the offensive in the regimental commander's view:

Inadequate training, equipment and most importantly fuel supply. Splitting up of the units. The absence of promised support from the

*Luftwaffe*. The enemy's materiel superiority, especially in tanks and artillery. The opposing side's determined fighting spirit after recovering from the initial shock of the surprise German offensive, particularly on the defensive (see Baraques les Fraitures). Lack of conviction on the part of the high command of the possibility of an operational success, especially in view of Germany's overall military situation. The offensive troops committed had been exhausted by the year-long defense and fighting withdrawal and at most were still suitable for a defensive role. Scarcely anyone believed that the Ardennes offensive would be a decisive success. The accomplishments of the troops in these battles must therefore be rated all the higher.

Looking back, today it can be said that in view of the overall situation on all fronts even a successful Ardennes offensive could no longer have changed the outcome of the war.

But if it was the high command's intention to use this offensive – successful or not – to gain several months of breathing space for the western front and therefore postpone the inevitable surrender from winter to the spring and thus avoid much heavier human losses – especially in the east – than this offensive cost, then the Ardennes offensive achieved its objective in spite of everything.

## Combat Report on the actions of the 2nd Armored Reconnaissance Battalion "*Das Reich*" with attached units of the "*Der Führer*" Regiment and of the 3rd Engineer Battalion 2 from 1 to 13 January 1944 during the Ardennes offensive

The 12th Volksgrenadier Division was east of the Liège-Houffalize road abreast of Malempré, while west of it at approximately the same level was the 560th Volksgrenadier Division. The enemy launched repeated attacks against the sectors of both divisions but gained little ground. Enemy tank forces pressed south, especially along the road. The threat of a breakthrough was great, since the wings of the 12th and especially the 560th Volksgrenadier Division did not extend to the road. The 2nd Reconnaissance Battalion was ordered to guard the road and especially the strategically important crossroads at Baraques les Fraitures. The 2nd Reconnaissance Battalion was placed under the command of the 12th Volksgrenadier Division.

The 2nd Reconnaissance Battalion's efforts to establish contact between the two divisions failed. Under increasing enemy pressure the wings of the two divisions bent more and more away from the road.

The 2nd Reconnaissance Battalion, with several attached tanks of I Battalion, 2nd Panzer Regiment, remnant units of III Battalion "DF" and the 3rd Company of the 2nd Engineer Battalion, was now at the focal point of the inevitable defensive battle at the Baraques les Fraitures crossroads. The 2nd Reconnaissance Battalion's command post was in Fraitures; also situated there was the regimental command post of *Oberstleutnant* Lemm of the 12th Volksgrenadier Division. *Hauptmann* Remer of the Lemm regiment's II Battalion was deployed near Malempré as battalion leader. The battalion fought very bravely and supported by the weak III Battalion "DF" under Ostuf. Ernst von Eberstein it eliminated penetration after penetration. There followed enemy tank and infantry attacks with very strong air support and intense artillery fire, especially along the road; these were beaten back by the 2nd Reconnaissance Battalion. The enemy's losses were considerable. Seven enemy tanks were destroyed in one attack alone. Prisoner statements revealed that the enemy was attempting to force a breakthrough with roughly two armored divisions. The enemy achieved penetrations on both sides of the 2nd Reconnaissance Battalion but they were partly eliminated by counterattacks.

Twenty degrees below freezing, snow and ice and days-long forest battles ground down even the best units.

On 4 January the enemy took Fraitures. The remaining elements of the Lemm Regiment's II Battalion under *Hauptmann* Remer were taken prisoner.

The 2nd Reconnaissance Battalion continued to hold its positions three kilometers northwest of the Baraques les Fraitures crossroads. After the loss of Fraitures the 2nd Reconnaissance Battalion also guarded to the east with its right wing bent back.

The II SS Panzer Corps's assault company was placed under the 2nd Reconnaissance Battalion's command. Enemy dive-bombers bombed the forest and crossroads. Enemy fighters attacked any rifleman who moved.

The 3rd Company of the 2nd Engineer Battalion attacked an enemy tank that had broken through and put it out of action from close quarters. A shortage of ammunition for our heavy weapons was keenly felt. Field telephone wires were repeatedly severed by artillery fire, radio communication was poor. Our artillery and rocket batteries supported as best they could. Employment of an artillery corps promised tangible relief. But the lack of signals equipment forced the artillery corps to fire by plan only, with the result that entire salvoes fell among the companies of the reinforced 2nd Reconnaissance Battalion. The resulting casualties were considerable and had an adverse effect on morale.

The enemy pressure increased steadily, and the enemy succeeded in infiltrating into the 2nd Reconnaissance Battalion's severely thinned defense lines. The 3rd Company of the 2nd Engineer Battalion did outstanding work here. Felled tree obstacles and mined, very skillfully positioned, delayed the enemy's pursuit and made it possible for our companies to carry out a planned withdrawal to new positions.

The "*Deutschland*" Regiment took over the sector around the Baraques les Fraitures crossroads. The 2nd Armored Reconnaissance Battalion, with the attached III Battalion "DF" and 3rd company, 2nd Engineer Battalion, was deployed in the line one kilometer northwest of Point 611 at the edge of the woods west of Petites Tailles, excluding swampy areas, through Point 614 at the northern exit from Les Tailles, to 500 meters north of Chabrenez.

The 2nd Reconnaissance Battalion repulsed tank supported attacks north of Les Tailles. The enemy then tried to outflank it and applied pressure against the adjacent units, especially the 560th Volksgrenadier Division on the right.

The enemy applied great pressure on 6 January, especially against the 2nd Reconnaissance Battalion. III Battalion "DF" engaged in fierce house fighting in Les Tailles. While it proved possible to drive the enemy back there, the 2nd Reconnaissance Battalion's 3rd Company could no longer bear the pressure. No reserves were available for a counterattack. The enemy tanks entered Les Tailles and neared the 2nd Reconnaissance Battalion's command post. Our assault guns knocked out three enemy tanks in the streets. Observer aircraft skillfully directed the enemy's artillery fire.

The enemy outflanked the 2nd Reconnaissance Battalion from the west and threatened to surround the battalion. The reinforced 2nd Reconnaissance Battalion held its positions until nightfall. Because of the activities of the enemy's air force, disengaging from the enemy during the day would have been tantamount to suicide.

Enemy tanks continued to lurk near the 2nd Reconnaissance Battalion's command post.

When darkness came the reinforced 2nd Reconnaissance Battalion, unhindered by the enemy, disengaged and occupied a new line of security approximately one kilometer south of Les Tailles.

These actions by the 2nd Armored Reconnaissance Battalion were recorded by the commander of the battalion, Stubaf. Krag, from memory. Time differences are possible after 5 January 1945.

## The Battle in Hungary

8 to 13 February 1945: On 8 February the first trains transporting the "*Der Führer*" Regiment departed for an unknown destination. Everyone believed that they were bound for the area east of Berlin or Silesia. Even the railroad personnel only knew their next stopping point. At first the trains traveled only by night. By day they remained hidden in tunnels in order to avoid the constant threat of air attack.

The trains passed through Gießen, Hanau, Würzburg, Treuchtlingen, Donauwörth, Augsburg, Munich, Rosenheim and Salzburg. Between the Main and the Danube the trains also traveled by day, as there was no direct threat from the air there. After the journey continued from Salzburg to Vienna it gradually became a certainty that the destination had to be the Hungarian combat zone.

The first Russian bombers appeared in the Hungarian lowlands. Soviet aircraft attacked crossroads and railway junctions with light bombs. Most missed their targets by several hundred meters. Everyone breathed a sigh of relief to have escaped the deadly threat of American fighter-bomber attacks in the west.

Sent the wrong way, the trains had to backtrack through Raab to Csorna. In beautiful weather the regiment's six transport trains were unloaded and the units took up quarters. Regimental headquarters and regimental units in Farad, I Battalion in Osli, II Battalion in Vitnied, III Battalion in Szarföld.

One of the regiment's trains had been mistakenly directed to the Brenner Pass, making the men think that were about to see action in Italy.

14 February: Personnel replacements for the regiment arrived and were assigned to the battalions and regimental units.

After arriving in its new quartering area, II Battalion received a new commanding officer in place of the wounded Hstuf. Hannes Schulzer. He was Hstuf. Schmelzer, a former company commander in the 2nd Engineer Battalion "*Das Reich.*" At the time III Battalion was being led by the senior company commander, Hstuf. Manz, in place of its regular commanding officer, Stubaf. Heinz Werner, who had been wounded during the Ardennes offensive. Commander of I Battalion was Stubaf. Götsche.

The regiment was badly understrength as a result of the heavy losses suffered in the Ardennes, especially in officers, enlisted men and equipment. Fortunately Stubaf. Werner and Hstuf. Schulzer arrived a few days later, even though their wounds had not had time to fully heal.

The 2nd SS Panzer Division "*Das Reich*" was scattered over an area of 120 kilometers and had adopted extraordinary concealment measures. In Hungary the division went by the name "Training Group North." The "*Der Führer*" Regiment bore the name "Otto North" and the "*Deutschland*" Regiment the name "Günther North" (first names of the regimental commanders). Orders were issued for all vehicles to be carefully camouflaged against being seen from the air. Vehicle traffic was only permitted at night and then only to the degree required. By day only the most important communications personnel were permitted to move about on foot. Troops moving up for training could only proceed one squad at a time. Under no circumstances were foot or vehicle columns permitted.

It gradually became clear that the 6th SS Panzer Army under the command of *Generaloberst* Sepp Dietrich was being assembled for operations in Hungary. According to the directives issued by "Training Group North", the "*Der Führer*" Regiment had approximately four weeks to rest and refit. These days were sorely needed to integrate the young replacements into the regiment's ranks and supplement the stocks of weapons, equipment and vehicles badly decimated in the Ardennes offensive. Extraordinary fuel conservation measures were introduced. Driving schools were restricted to night operations on a severely reduced scale. Once again the training of the new arrivals was found to be badly wanting. As a result a brief but intensive period of training was begun. While the daylight hours were used for firing practice, theoretical instruction, and familiarization with weapons and equipment, the night was used for field training. The squads, platoons and companies were in the field from early evening until early morning. The units were fitted together organizationally. Most training exercises were live fire. Special emphasis was placed on the coordination of all light and heavy infantry weapons. There was one battalion and one regiment level signals exercise. Live-fire battalion exercises were to conclude the training program.

At this time all of the regiment's soldiers noticed many Hungarian troops, usually in company strength and unarmed, but with smoking field kitchens and several train vehicles, marching through the country, apparently with no plan and no destination. It was obviously the intention of the Hungarian command to keep its units from seeing action by constantly issuing new transfer orders. Only *one* Hungarian corps was deployed at the front!

Several map exercises supplemented the training of the officer corps. *Brigadeführer* Werner Ostendorff, who had been the division's first Ia when the motorized SS V Divisions were formed in Pilsen in 1939, took over as commander of the 2nd SS Panzer Division "*Das Reich*" in Hungary. Typical of the strict discipline in the division is the fact that the division judge held "court day" at this time. Old offenses against good conduct and discipline were punished.

I Battalion, which had been reorganized just before the Ardennes offensive and which had gone into action before it was completely equipped, had particular difficulties in training. Once again it was lacking in equipment and vehicles. As well the battalion underwent a change of command: Stubaf. Götsche was transferred, and Hstuf. Engelmann from the *Junkerschule* at Tölz assumed command.

Budapest fell on 12 February. The 8th and 22nd SS Cavalry Divisions and the 13th Panzer Division had gone down fighting in the city. Before the German Army Group South under *Generaloberst* Wöhler stood the Russian shock armies: north of the Danube the Soviets held a bridgehead west of the Gran River. They were at the foot of the Vertes Mountains and held a projecting salient from the Drau River to the western corner of Lake Balaton.

The 6th SS Panzer Army under the chief of staff, *Generalmajor* Krämer, at first consisted of the I and II SS Panzer Corps with the panzer divisions "*Leibstandarte*", "*Hitlerjugend*", "*Das Reich*" and "*Hohenstaufen*." A cavalry corps, the 44th Infantry Division "*Hoch- und Deutschmeister*" and the III Panzer Corps under *General* Breith with the 1st and 3rd Panzer Divisions were placed under its command.

According to the OKH's plan, the 2nd Panzer Army was to advance east south of Lake Balaton, elements of Army Group Balkans (E) were to advance north across the Drau toward the Danube. The task assigned to the 6th SS Panzer Army: attack southeast from the narrows north of Lake Balaton.

The *Wehrmacht* High Command, in agreement with Army Group South, insisted on this offensive plan for the 6th SS Panzer Army in spite of unfavorable weather and terrain conditions. Arguments and counter proposals by the army were unsuccessful. Deadline for the attack was 6 March, and its objective was Dunaföldar on the Danube. The careful concealment of the panzer divisions was probably already rendered invalid when units of the I SS Panzer Corps were committed against the Russian Gran bridgehead as part of the 8th Army from 17 to 22 February 1945.

2 March: The commander of the "*Der Führer*" Regiment had just left with the commander of the "*Deutschland*" Regiment on an inspection when the "*Der Führer*" Regiment was unexpectedly put on alert. Training was therefore ended after just fourteen days. I Battalion, which was still not operational, at first remained in the quartering area, where it pressed ahead with its training, especially by the non-commissioned officer training company.

3 March: As per orders, the "*Der Führer*" Regiment marched off in the morning. As per division order, at first only the day's objective was announced. The companies marched by way of Csorna to Raab.

4 March: Continued march to Hyul.

5 March: At 3 AM the regiment resumed its march to Csösc Pzc via Kirati, Cseteny and Scadar.

6 March: Continued march to Kiskeci and Orhida via Valpalota, Nadasla and Dany.

On 8 March the II SS Panzer Corps under *General* Bittrich was supposed to attack southeast from the narrows between Lake Balaton and Lake Velenser, break through the enemy positions and together with the I SS Panzer Corps, which was deployed farther to the south, reach the Danube south of Budapest on a broad front. As soon as the Danube was reached, a drive to the north was supposed to relieve the nation's capital, Budapest.

7 March: The regiment moved by way of Stuhlweissenburg and the Aba highway across the almost completely open terrain into the assembly area near Bolondvari-Tania. Casualties to heavy air attacks.

As a result of blunder on the part of the high command the troops had been placed on the move much too late to reach the assembly area in time for the start of the attack by the SS panzer corps.

For "reasons of concealment" the vehicles had to be parked many kilometers west of the assembly area. Some battalions had to march up to twenty kilometers in full combat gear before reaching the assembly area and consequently arrived there exhausted and physically worn out. This had to have an adverse affect on the coming attack.

The "*Deutschland*" Regiment was supposed to attack in the front line. The "*Der Führer*" Regiment, together with the Second Battalion of the Panzer Regiment "*Das Reich*" under Stubaf. Dieter Kesten, the Third Armored Battalion under Stubaf. Heinz Werner, and II Battalion under Hstuf. Hannes Schulzer, formed an armored group which was to stand ready to exploit a successful breakthrough, continue the attack through the positions and if possible take up the pursuit of the shattered enemy.

Things were to work out differently.

Late on the afternoon of 7 March the unit commanders were briefed in the open by the division commander, *Gruppenführer* Ostendorff. During the drive into the assembly area the regimental commander was witness to a telephone conversation between the chief of staff of the II SS Panzer Corps, Ostubaf. Baldur Keller, and the 6th SS Panzer Army. Ostubaf. Keller informed the panzer army straight out that the attack could not start the next day because at that very moment the leading elements of the "*Deutschland*" Regiment were just passing the corps command post and still had ten kilometers to march in order to reach the assembly area. However the panzer army referred to the unmistakable order issued by the army group and *Führer* Headquarters and insisted that the attack was to be carried out the next morning no matter what and under no circumstances could it be called off.

Under this bad omen the commander of the "*Der Führer*" Regiment issued his men their orders and the unavoidable happened:

The point unit of the "*Deutschland*" Regiment arrived in the assembly area in the early morning hours, totally exhausted. The corps artillery, already in position, subsequently fired a short but intensive barrage as the signal to attack. The "*Deutschland*" Regiment could not attack, however, because its leading elements had just arrived in the assembly area! The 2nd Artillery Regiment, part of which was still en route, unlimbered from off the move beside the advance road in order to take part in the barrage, which probably came as a complete surprise to the enemy. The available ammunition was soon expended, however the enemy was alerted along the entire front and was surely amazed that no attack followed – the moment of surprise that had been so carefully prepared was lost. As a result the attack had to be repeated at 5 AM the next morning, at the same spot but now without the element of surprise.

9 March: At 5 AM there was another short, but again fierce barrage. The panzer-grenadiers advanced toward Hills 149, 153 and 159, and the companies succeeded in taking Hills 149 and 153. Heavy flanking fire from the north prevented the taking of Hill 159. The attack was supposed to be made along a ridge extending to the east. This had the disadvantage, however, that the attack terrain could be viewed from all sides and an advance made difficult by flanking fire. The attack through the valley was impossible because of the swampy terrain.

During the midmorning the "*Der Führer*" Regiment's armored group was sent to attack Hill 159, while the "*Deutschland*" Regiment remained in the positions it had reached and simultaneously covered the left flank. There was a considerable gap to the south to the I SS Panzer Corps. On the left were units of the 9th SS Panzer Division "*Hohenstaufen*." Command of this armored group by the commander of the "*Der Führer*" Regiment was complicated by the lack of communications equipment (radio). No sooner had the leading tanks driven over Hill 159 when they came under heavy anti-tank fire from the north. Three tanks were knocked out in quick succession. Every tank or armored troop carrier that drove over the hill would surely be knocked out. Going around was impossible, since the rainy period had softened the ground in the valleys and the tanks could not move forward. As a result the attack was stopped and could not be resumed until the flanking anti-tank barricade had been eliminated.

Late in the morning the division commander *Gruppenführer* Ostendorff came to the regimental commander, and together they discussed the further conduct of the attack in the front lines. On the drive back *Gruppenführer* Ostendorff's *Kübelwagen* took a direct hit and he was seriously wounded while his aide was fatally hit. Staf. Karl Kreutz, commander of the Artillery Regiment, initially assumed command of the 2nd SS Panzer Division "*Das Reich.*" *Gruppenführer* Ostendorff refused to allow himself to be evacuated until he had formally transferred command. He died in a hospital in Bad Aussee a few days before the surrender.

On this day an outstanding and unforgettable soldier fulfilled his fate. While serving as commander of the 2nd SS Panzer Division "*Das Reich*", he sustained the serious wound that was to end his soldier's life in the sector of the "*Der Führer*" Regiment, in which he had led a machine-gun company during peacetime.

His desire, his unlimited creativity, his "do it yourself" attitude and his tremendous offensive spirit were borne by the purest idealism. Once he had been shot by covering parties of his young 17th SS Panzer-Grenadier Division "*Götz von Berlichingen*" when he pressed forward at the risk of his own life.

As Ia of the motorized SS V Division "*Reich*", during the fierce defensive battle near Yelnya in the central sector of the Eastern Front in 1941 he had led the division's engineer battalion on a daring raid into the rear of a group of Russian forces that was seriously threatening the division's northern flank and smashed the Soviets at that place. For this feat the then Ostubaf. Werner Ostendorff was awarded the Knight's Cross on 13 September 1941. Following his death on 1 May 1945, on 6 May he was awarded the Knight's Cross with Oak Leaves.

The Russian anti-tank front was eliminated during the afternoon. The flanking cover to the north, effectively established by units of the 9th SS Panzer Division, had a favorable effect.

The "*Der Führer*" Regiment's armored group resumed the offensive at about 9 AM on 11 March. The "*Deutschland*" Regiment assumed responsibility for guarding the right flank of the 2nd SS Panzer Division and carried out this task offensively, meaning through limited attacks to the south. The left flank was guarded as before by the 9th SS Panzer Division.

The regimental commander led the attack in a radio-equipped armored troop carrier, and in beautiful weather the attack by the tanks of the 2nd Panzer Regiment's II Battalion, the armored troop carriers of III Battalion, the gunners of the 2nd Artillery Regiment and the panzer-grenadiers of II Battalion unfolded in classic style. The "*Der Führer*" Regiment's armored group made good progress, and during the afternoon, after heavy fighting, it succeeded in taking the village of Csillag-Major. Enemy resistance stiffened considerably.

Here the leader of the regiment's signals platoon, Ostuf. Hans Hentschel, received the order assigning him to the signals school at Leitmeritz. His departure left a gap that was difficult to fill at that moment.

The Ia of the 2nd SS Panzer Division "*Das Reich*", Ostubaf. Albert Stückler, was slightly wounded in the "*Der Führer*" Regiment's attack area during this battle. The Ic of the division, Hstuf. Aurel Kowatsch, who had accompanied the attack, was fatally wounded.

12 March: Staf. Rudolf Lehmann, the former chief of staff of I SS Panzer Corps, took over the 2nd SS Panzer Division and was immediately briefed on the situation by the commander of the "*Der Führer*" Regiment. Simultaneously Ostubaf. Stückler left the division and became chief of staff of the I SS Panzer Corps. Stubaf. Ralf Tiemann became Ia of the 2nd SS Panzer Division "*Das Reich*."

Meantime the enemy situation had changed significantly. Referring to recent aerial reconnaissance photographs, air liaison officers reported that the enemy had considerably bolstered his forces in the area north of Stuhlweissenburg-Mor. There Soviet tank and motorized forces were facing the weak German defense front and the few Hungarian cavalry screening units. The 6th Panzer Division had bogged down in the face of stiffening resistance; however, attacking south, the cavalry corps under Count Harteneck had succeeded in advancing as far as Fünfkirchen.

In the early morning the "*Der Führer*" Regiment continued the attack in the face of growing enemy resistance and drove toward Kulsö-Püsköp-Myr and further toward Heinrich-Major. II and III Battalions sustained heavy casualties, several tanks and armored troop carriers were put out of action. II Battalion's main responsibility was to secure and screen both flanks in the Kulsö-Püsköp-Myr area. In further costly fighting the regiment reached the village of Heinrich-Major with the tank crews and the panzer-grenadiers of III Battalion. The enemy resistance there was so intense that the seriously weakened armored group had to go over to the defensive. The regiment had conducted the attack in the sector of the II SS Panzer Corps with the Second Panzer Battalion under Stubaf. Dieter Kersten alone (tank commander Hscha. Hans Siebert destroyed his 65th enemy tank there). This attack could neither be supplied by division or by the corps, and the flanking protection by II Battalion alone was insufficient. Furthermore the enemy launched counterattacks.

This was to be the last major offensive action by the "*Der Führer*" Regiment in the war, apart from numerous advances and attacks with limited objectives which were required in the course of subsequent defensive battles and fighting withdrawals.

In his book *The Last Battle*, Erich Kern wrote of the fighting up until 17 March:

> "For the 'DF' Regiment, especially for the Werner armored troop carrier battalion, the days that followed were a severe test. Far to the front, constantly threatened on both wings and in the flanks, this Third Battalion of the 'DF' Regiment, supported only by a few tanks as the majority were out of action, truly fought an heroic struggle. Rations and ammunition were brought forward only by night, as the supply routes passed through completely open terrain and could be seen by the enemy from three sides. Werner's battalion command post was in the cellar of a completely destroyed house in which the wounded, who could also be evacuated only by night, accumulated. Nevertheless, not a day went by that the regimental commander Weidinger did not come to see the endangered Third Battalion's situation for himself and assist Stubaf. Werner in word and deed. In spite of continual requests by the 'Das Reich' Division to the corps and the army

for authorization to abandon this forward post at Heinrich Major, no permission was forthcoming."

The panzer-grenadiers of III Battalion named their position "Alkazar." II Battalion's dashing assistant medical officer was killed by a ricochet at the main dressing station. The regimental commander received news that I Battalion had arrived at Varoslad.

15 March: The regiment received the surprising news that Stuhlweissenburg was being threatened from the north and that it had already had to be evacuated by the entire train.

16 March: The non-commissioned officer training company, formerly with I Battalion, was disbanded and its men, too, were en route to the regiment. At about noon the Russian batteries opened a drum fire on the "*Totenkopf*" and "*Wiking*" Panzer Divisions of the IV SS Panzer Corps positioned in the Stuhlweissenburg-Mor area. The inserted Hungarian units were overrun, only the German units defended themselves with the courage of desperation. The spearheads of the Soviet armored units reached Valpalota and Hajmasker, drove toward Lake Balaton and neared Enying. The overall situation of the front was verging on catastrophic. The entire 6th SS Panzer Army was facing encirclement as a result of the advances by the 3rd Ukrainian Front under Marshall Tolbukhin.

17 March: The brave III Battalion was still in Heinrich-Major, repulsing every attack by the far-superior enemy, sometimes in hand-to-hand combat. The regimental commander made repeated pleas to the division for the withdrawal of his panzer-grenadiers, for the companies of III Battalion were bleeding to death in the truest sense of the word. But all of these requests were obviously turned down on orders from above.

On 18 March, when it was scarcely expected, the order finally came to withdraw the position, meaning a new mission order for the "*Der Führer*" Regiment within the 2nd SS Panzer Division.

The overall situation had meanwhile fundamentally changed:

During the previous night the Hungarian First Army, which was deployed between German corps at the great bend of the Danube, had without warning laid down its weapons, and this morning the Russians had immediately driven into this gap with tanks and advanced west along the Danube. According to the latest reports their armored spearheads were already in the area approximately thirty kilometers east of Raab and thus deep in the rear of the German front.

## Fighting Withdrawal in Hungary to the Reich Defense Position

18 March 1945: On account of the new situation the commander of the "*Der Führer*" Regiment received orders to pull his unit out of its present positions and, together with the rest of the division, after a big night outflanking march halt the Russian advance, if possible in the area east of Raab, and establish a new front.

II Battalion was withdrawn without difficulty. This was more problematic where III Battalion was concerned, since the enemy was still very near to the battalion's positions and the cellar (also the command post) was packed with seriously wounded. Nevertheless III Battalion, with a total effort on the part of all of its officers, non-commissioned officers and enlisted men, but especially by the rations and combat trains, succeeded in disengaging from the enemy undetected and evacuating all of the seriously wounded.

After being pulled out of the line the regiment initially marched to Falu Battyan.

19 March: The regiment was subjected to several air attacks, however there were no casualties or losses.

19 to 20 March: In the evening the regiment marched via Veszprem, Papa, Tet, Menföszanak, Raab and Babolna Puszta to Cse-Merhazy Major. Screening parties were sent out at dawn.

21 March: March to Navyg-Mand, where German flak batteries were already deployed in a ground role to guard against enemy tanks.

III Battalion occupied positions, while II Battalion was sent to attack in the direction of Taly Psz. And quickly reached its objective. The inhabitants of the village were very happy to see German soldiers again after having been under Soviet occupation for one day. It seemed inconceivable to them, and II Battalion sympathized with their tragedy, that the village had to be evacuated again during the night of 22 March as part of the overall situation. Some of the inhabitants voluntarily left the village and headed west toward an unknown destination. During the day II Battalion was cut off by a marauding Soviet point unit. The commander committed a small capable reserve and it succeeded in restoring contact.

22 March: Attacks by enemy infantry were beaten off during the day. At 11 PM the regiment withdrew toward the line Kisicmand-Navigmand-Ordögto. I Battalion rejoined the regiment here and was immediately deployed on the right wing, on the right of II Battalion.

23 March: The enemy pushed especially hard against the regiment's right wing. I Battalion, newly formed and still inexperienced, under the command of Hstuf. Engelmann, suffered heavy casualties on its first day in action.

24 March: The "*Der Führer*" Regiment had to hold a sector fourteen kilometers wide. Once again all of the battalions had to be deployed in the front line: right I Battalion, center II Battalion, left III Battalion. The adjacent unit on the right was the "*Deutschland*" Regiment. Enemy attacks against the entire sector were repulsed.

25 March: The enemy attacked continuously. The "*Der Führer*" Regiment achieved great defensive successes.

26 March: The defensive fighting went on unabated. At 9 PM the regiment withdrew via Babolna-Bscz. And Bönyretelap to Hosaly Bscz.

27 March: At about 1 PM the enemy penetrated III Battalion's weakly-held positions as far as Györszen-Tivan; the defenders only able to partially seal off the penetration. At 8 PM the regiment pulled back to Raab. The regimental command post remained in the city, which had been almost completely evacuated by the civilian population.

28 March: The regiment assembled west of Raab and marched via Csorna to Fadosfa and at about noon reached Beled. New lines of security were occupied. During the afternoon the enemy achieved a penetration against II Battalion on the left in the direction of Kapuvar. At 11 PM the regiment pulled back again.

29 March: Screening parties in the line Himod-Hörey-Vitnye. The regimental command post was in Göbes. Left I Battalion, center III Battalion, right II Battalion. The enemy kept up the pressure, even though all attacks were beaten off. During the night the regiment made another withdrawal.

30 March: heavy enemy attacks near Fer Toszent-Miklos. The regiment pulled back to Esterházy and at 11 PM marched into the area east of Lake Neusiedler.

31 March: After pulling back toward Mexiko Psz., at 8 PM marched in a northeasterly direction. The regiment received orders to occupy positions in the "Reich Defense Position" from which there was to be no withdrawal, allegedly on a "*Führer* order." The few anti-tank ditches were likely to be no obstacle to a massed enemy attack.

1 April: The regimental command post was in Andau. Dangerous enemy breakthrough in the direction of Halbthurn. The regiment set up its command post there at 4 PM and at 10 PM moved to Parndorf.

During the just-described fighting withdrawal the "*Der Führer*" Regiment had had to guard a huge sector at least twenty kilometers wide. All three battalions had to be deployed in the front line and received the most vital assistance from the regimental units. With the large sector and the reduced combat strengths caused by the daily casualties, the regiment had long been unable to husband forces for a reserve.

The lines of security – there could be no defense positions during these battles – could only be manned strongpoint fashion. When there was a penetration, which was the case almost daily, it was sealed off by runners and staff members until nightfall...and the regiment pulled back again.

The physical and mental stresses faced by the panzer-grenadiers were tremendous. It was the hymn of unshakable bravery and comradeship, of unconditional comradeship between officers, non-commissioned officers and enlisted men, which rang out once again here during the final weeks of the war in this last desperate attempt to save the Reich from the onslaught from the east.

With his inexhaustible masses of tanks and infantry the enemy was overpowering. All day long the battalions and companies were almost constantly in battle with the hard-pressing enemy. Often the squads and platoons were overrun by Russian tanks. But again and again the men regrouped and fought their way through to their companies. The next day the battalions were once again in combat with the enemy in their new lines of security – an indication of an outstanding and veteran unit.

The lines of security occupied after 17 March cannot be accurately described, as they were often only held for hours. Therefore often only the location of the regimental command post is given. This also applies for the period to come.

2 April: The retreat roads were completely clogged by columns. At 8 AM the regimental command post was set up in Trautmannsdorf. There the regimental commander received orders that the regiment was no longer to occupy the "Reich Defense Position" as the overall situation had already fundamentally changed: the enemy had already broken through south of Lake Neusiedler near Ödenburg in the direction of the Vienna Woods and was threatening Vienna!

At 2 PM the regimental command post was moved to Moosbrunn and a short time later to Gramat-Neusiedel. Heavy enemy attack on Moosbrunn. II Battalion, deployed to defend the village, suffered heavy casualties. The battalion adjutant, Ostuf. Walter Spriegel, and the commander of 8th Company, Ostuf. Niemüller, were killed when enemy tanks broke through to the battalion command post. As a result of heavy enemy attacks, I Battalion lost contact with the front. III Battalion was able to hold its positions in spite of fierce enemy attacks.

3 April: The regimental command post was moved to Velm. The enemy pursued immediately. After 4 PM the regimental command post was in Kanzlerhof.

"Battle Group Hauser" under Stubaf. Hans Hauser, which the day before had been sent by division into the gap between the "*Deutschland*" and "*Der Führer*" Regiments and had prevented a decisive breakthrough by enemy tanks near Münchdorf, fought its way from the south through to the "*Der Führer*" Regiment and was at first placed under its command. This battle group, made up of convalescents and men separated from their units, without supplies of ammunition, weapons and equipment and without food, was exhausted after this difficult mission. The commander of the "*Der Führer*" Regiment therefore incorporated the men of the battle group into the various battalions, and a few days later Stubaf. Hauser took over command of I Battalion. The 2nd SS Panzer Division approved these moves retroactively. For his actions and those of his men in this important defensive success, on 6 May 1945 Stubaf. Hauser was awarded the Knight's Cross by the commander in chief of the 6th SS Panzer Army.

The day that Battle Group Hauser linked up with the regiment also saw the arrival of further replacements from Vienna. These men on leave, convalescents and stragglers had been organized into companies at the SS Motor Vehicle Technical Institute in Vienna. The regiment had to integrate these replacements – roughly three companies – into its existing companies in the midst of battle. Because of the situation its was not possible to record the names of these men, since the regiment was engaged in a difficult fighting withdrawal day and night and was not given a moments rest.

It is therefore tragic and very painful that not only was it impossible to state the number of casualties from among these replacements in the following battles, but also to list their names. As a result it was also not possible to notify the families of the men who were killed.

It must be said, however, that because of disruptions in communications not all of the death and wounding notices for old members of the regiment reached their destinations, meaning the families.

## The Battle for Vienna

4 April: The "*Der Führer*" Regiment occupied a new defense line east of Leopoldsdorf. Regimental command post in the brick works. Deployment: I Battalion right, III Battalion center, II Battalion left.

5 April: Heavy enemy attacks toward Vienna from the northwest. The Russian plan was clear: to seize the city of Vienna as quickly as possible in a concentric attack. I Battalion under Hstuf. Engelmann achieved a significant defensive success.

The Russian artillery and mortar fire on the regiment's positions steadily grew stronger. A direct artillery hit on the command post seriously wounded ten men and killed four panzer-grenadiers.

Here the regimental commander received an alleged "*Führer* order", the gist of which was that effective immediately there were to be no more withdrawals. The troops were to fight their last battle in their present positions.

The regimental commander argued that because of the use of replacements from outside the regiment and the huge widths of front the unit commanders could not prevent the soldiers from withdrawing on their own during the night. The response: in that case "the headquarters and all available units would have to join the defense and were to go under in the final battle."

Similar orders had arrived in recent days. Since in this situation such "*Führer* orders" seemed absurd, the regimental commander did not feel bound by them and acted according to his conscience.

This view of the regimental commander was apparently also shared by the headquarters of the 2nd SS Panzer Division "*Das Reich*", which was the first to change positions. Subsequently the "*Der Führer*" Regiment also moved its commanding officer to Vösendorf.

What would the consequences have been if the regiments had fought the last battle in their positions and had been destroyed?

The enemy would not have been repeatedly held up by the front fighting a delaying action, as he had so far. Instead, after completely destroying the German defense position, he would have been able to very quickly drive unhindered with his tanks and mounted infantry through Austria into Germany and occupy larger areas of Austria and Germany before the western Allies than he would have been able to do against the very slow and determined withdrawal of the front in Austria. This action surely spared many lives and spared them captivity at the hands of the Russians.

In this confusion of orders of the last days of the war, where the orders of the high command were obviously in stark contradiction to the opinions of the middle and lower levels of command, the unit leaders were increasingly forced to rely on their own consciences and use common sense to act in the best interests of the whole.

The men of the "*Der Führer*" Regiment sensed this conflict. As a result their faith in the regiment and division command remained unshakable to the end.

The order to withdraw came at about 8 PM. For unexplained reasons III Battalion did not receive the order until approximately 10 PM. Meantime the enemy had blocked the Vösendorf-Leopoldsdorf road. III Battalion lost its cohesion as a result of the night withdrawal, however it was able to regroup quickly in the new defense line. II Battalion and I Battalion from Aschau were able to withdraw on time.

6 April: The new defense line was occupied. The enemy attacked without pause and was repulsed. The Soviets drove toward the city of

Vienna from three sides with strong tank and artillery support. The regimental command post was in Erlaa, from 5 PM in Altmannsdorf. Vienna was burning in places and looked abandoned. From 11 PM the regimental command post was in the Rosenhügelgasse north of Schönbrunn Park.

Vienna had been declared a fortress. The city was to be defended at all costs – a completely hopeless undertaking given the open nature of the city.

Understandably the population of the city hoped for the end of the battle and the war. Accounts by their countrymen, who had barely escaped the horrors of Russian occupation, were scarcely believed. If only the beliefs of the residents of Vienna had been true! But the men of the "*Der Führer*" Regiment had seen grisly sights in the villages of the Burgenland and the outskirts of the city during local counterattacks.

7 April: The regiment fought in the center of the city of Vienna. The situation was uncertain. The first Russian tanks appeared in the inner city, there was no contact with the downtown itself.

On his own initiative, *Sturmmann* Lange of the 16th Company blew up a small canal bridge at the moment that the first Soviet tanks and infantry were about to cross. This Soviet advance was aimed directly at the rear of the fighting battalions of the "*Der Führer*" Regiment. The regimental commander recommended the young soldier for the Knight's Cross, which was awarded to him a short time later.

There was no recognizable front within the city. The battalions fought on from strongpoints, defending to all sides. Contact with the division command post by runner was intermittent. The enemy was said to have already occupied the district of Grinzing. The regiment's train was able to withdraw at the last minute. The enemy advanced toward the Danube bridges and threatened to cut off the regiment.

8 April: Attempts by the enemy to break through to the Danube failed. The regiment's situation became more serious by the hour. At 10 PM the "*Der Führer*" Regiment's command post was moved into the Rotmühlgasse. During the night there was an eerie stillness in the city. The next morning units of the 2nd SS Panzer Division were to break through to the Ring and the Danube bridges. In the night guns of the 2nd Artillery Regiment went into direct firing positions at various intersections in order to seal off the breakthrough streets.

9 April: The regiment remained locked in bitter defensive fighting. At first light of dawn the brave tank crews of the 2nd Panzer Regiment achieved a breakthrough to the Ring and the Danube Canal. The regiment withdrew from its positions and followed the units that had broken through. This time the brave gunners took over the rear guard with their guns and covered the division's withdrawal from the inner city. This was a truly magnificent accomplishment by the 2nd Artillery Regiment under the circumspect command of the regimental commander, Staf. Karl Kreutz, who received the Knight's Cross with Oak Leaves for his actions and those of his gunners. At 6 PM the "*Der Führer*" Regiment occupied a command post near the Floridsdorf Bridge.

When his I Battalion pulled back, Hstuf. Engelmann took up position in front in an armored troop carrier; the vehicle was knocked out by a Russian tank on the Uferstraße on the south bank of the Danube. Everyone in the vehicle was killed. Stubaf. Hauser took over I Battalion.

10 April: The main line of resistance ran along the Danube Canal. II Battalion was deployed front right and left I Battalion. III Battalion was temporarily in reserve. Fighting on the "*Der Führer*" Regiment's left was the "*Deutschland*" Regiment and further to the Reich Bridge elements of the 3rd SS Panzer Division "*Totenkopf*."

11 April: Massed enemy attacks and crossing attempts were beaten back with heavy losses to the enemy.

12 April: Repeated heavy attacks were beaten off. The enemy succeeded in capturing small bridgeheads. North of the Danube the enemy was already driving west in the direction of Bisam-Berg. Once again the threat of encirclement loomed. On the 2nd SS Panzer Division's left the 3rd SS Panzer Division withdrew across the Reich Bridge. The bridge subsequently fell into the enemy's hands intact. According to an allegedly express "*Führer* order", the bridge was not to be blown and the installed demolition charges had to be removed from the prepared firing chambers.

At 10 PM the command post was in a school due south of the Floridsdorfer Bridge.

In these days, at the request of the administration of the world-famous Lippizaner stud farm (*General* Wessely), the commander of the 2nd SS Panzer Division "*Das Reich*" ordered the Lippizaner stallions, which were still in Vienna at that time, brought out of the city in the division's trucks and evacuated to St. Pölten, where they were placed in the care of the American General Patton.

Meanwhile *General* von Bünau had arrived with a small staff and had been named battle commander of the city and "fortress" of Vienna. *General* von Bünau had orders to hold Vienna at all costs. By this time more than half of Vienna was already in enemy hands. It was therefore a mission that had been completely overtaken by events.

13 April: Battle commander *General* von Bünau issued the order that all presently held positions were to be held at all costs. Meanwhile events had followed in rapid succession. The enemy attacked with a tremendous materiel superiority. The regimental commander and all of his officers and non-commissioned officers tried to hold the tottering front, however in the face of the enemy's fire superiority they could not succeed in spite of all the efforts of the calmly-fighting panzer-grenadiers. It was impossible to survey the battle in the deafening noise of battle and the dust of the house-to-house fighting.

Fortunately the regimental adjutant, Ostuf. Seegerer, had meanwhile evacuated the regimental command post, which was already in the front lines, on his own initiative and had withdrawn the regimental headquarters valuable radio vehicles to north of the Danube. Without this decision it is unlikely that the command apparatus of the "*Der Führer*" Regiment could have remained intact in the final weeks of the war until the surrender.

The situation deteriorated more and more. The companies were forced back toward the Floridsdorfer Bridge from all sides. Our bridgehead became ever smaller and threatened to collapse at any time. The headquarters and units collected beneath the arches south of the Danube. Battle commander *General* von Bünau, who spent most of his time with the commander of the "*Der Führer*" Regiment, once again unequivocally ordered the division commander, Staf. Lehmann, who was also at the regimental command post with his 1st General Staff Officer *Major* Joachim Schiller, to hold the bridgehead to the last man. The gist of what the *General* said was as follows:

He would never cross the bridge alive, because he did not wish to see his family held responsible for his actions, as had happened to the battle commander of Königsberg after that city was captured.

The regimental commander therefore immediately ordered new bridgehead sectors and a new main line of resistance, which ran around the bridgehead at a distance of about two-hundred meters. The positions were energetically pushed forward again, as a result of which the bridgehead no had a diameter of about 400 meters. The division commander directed the positioning of the heavy weapons, which had gone into position on the north bank of the Danube, in the new main line of resistance and ordered them to lay down concentric fire in front of the bridgehead. An army flak battalion on the far bank supported the division and intervened in the defensive battle with its heavy guns.

Our positions were under almost continuous heavy fire from mortars and machine-guns and later submachine-guns. The men took cover in shell holes and fought grimly from there. Losses were heavy during the late morning, mainly from enemy mortar fire. All of the less seriously wounded who could walk were given permission by the regimental commander to withdraw across the bridge. The seriously wounded were placed beneath the arches right beside the Danube so that they might obtain a degree of protection from the heavy enemy fire and be cared for by the doctors and medics.

The division commander, Staf. Lehmann, and the regimental commander were of the opinion that the regiment could hold the bridgehead until nightfall at best, before pulling back across the Danube to the north. The unit on the left, which was supposed to remain in the bridgehead with the "*Der Führer*" Regiment, had already pulled back across the Danube.

The division and regimental commanders tried to make the battle commander see that it was madness to allow the Reich Bridge to fall into enemy hands intact as per the "*Führer* order", allowing the enemy to cross unhindered, while at the same time the bridgehead at the Floridsdorfer Bridge was supposed to be held "to the last man."

The battle commander could not be influenced. With no steel helmet, wearing only a forage cap, hand grenades in his belt, he stood unmoved in the heaviest fire.

The division commander was wounded in the early afternoon. Two military policemen carried him back. The Ia of the division, *Major* Schiller, accompanied him.

The working relationship between the young division commander and his regiment and independent battalion commanders, which can be characterized as exemplary, thus came to an end for the time being.

Before he was evacuated, Staf. Lehmann issued the commander of the "*Der Führer*" Regiment orders to hold the bridgehead at all costs until nightfall, but then to withdraw across the Danube. But this was contrary to the express order of the battle commander.

The number of seriously wounded beneath the arches had meanwhile climbed to fifty-six.

At noontime *General* von Bünau had sent his Ia to the commander in chief of the 6th SS Panzer Army, *Generaloberst* Dietrich, in order to describe the situation and if possible request new orders. When the battle commander asked the regimental commander what orders he had received from his division commander, he replied that he was under orders to pull back across the bridge at nightfall, but only after all of the seriously wounded had been evacuated. But since it required four bearers to carry each wounded man, this would have required the withdrawal from the front of 224 men, without whom the bridgehead could never be held.

When the Ia returned he reported to the general that the commander in chief of the 6th SS Panzer Army was of the same opinion as the division and regimental commanders.

*General* von Bünau now also bowed to the view of the commander of the "*Der Führer*" Regiment. During the afternoon a tank commanded by Ostuf. Karl-Heinz Boska came racing across the bridge to support the troops holding the bridgehead. The tank was knocked out by the enemy as it drove off the bridge and the crew were wounded.

The regimental commander sent a special missions officer to the division to ask that all available ambulances be readied on the north bank of the Danube by nightfall in order to evacuate the seriously wounded from the fire zone as quickly as possible. Meanwhile preparations were made to evacuate the seriously wounded. Eight ambulances waited on the far bank.

Meantime the regimental adjutant Ostuf. Seegerer had made all the necessary preparations to receive and sort out the troops returning from the bridgehead.

The sound of battle grew louder and louder. Deployed frontally, III Battalion once again suffered heavy casualties, and in the opinion of the acting commander of III Battalion, Hstuf. Wilhelm Bickel, it was unlikely that the weak companies would be able to hold their positions until nightfall. He nevertheless received clear orders from the regimental commander that they must hold. For if the bridgehead collapsed during the day losses would be greater and the chaos complete. And the seemingly impossible succeeded.

Our artillery, supported by the army flak battery, intensified its fire in front of the main line of resistance and provided outstanding help to the regiment.

Here the panzer-grenadiers gave another example of their oft-proven fighting spirit, and the veteran members of the regiment probably realized that it was in their old peacetime garrison that they were now having to fight against this tremendous Russian superiority.

With the onset of darkness individual squads disengaged from the enemy and in a display of natural comradeship helped evacuate the wounded until the improvised dressing station was empty.

The final order to withdraw to the "*Der Führer*" Regiment, which was bolstered by elements of the "*Deutschland*" Regiment, was issued quickly. The last to cross the bridge was III Battalion under the command of Hstuf. Bickel.

Based on the information brought back by his Ia, the battle commander was in agreement with the measures taken by the regimental commander. He formally thanked him for the excellent fighting spirit and determination of his men. The order from the 6th SS Panzer Army, which made the battle commander personally responsible for the blowing up of the bridge, he trustingly handed over to the regimental commander, since he would know best when the last of his men had crossed. Only then did the battle commander leave the bridgehead and make his way to the prepared regimental command post in Floridsdorf.

The regimental commander convinced himself of the organization at the bridge to take in the returning, completely intermixed combat units. Ostuf. Seegerer and the men of the regimental headquarters had done outstanding work. Guides stood ready to meet the battalions and companies and direct them to their quarters.

At the bridge the regimental commander satisfied himself of the preparations by army engineers to blow the structure and waited for the last squads and platoons. All units commanders reported that no wounded had been left behind. Listening sentries were moved up to the bridge to receive stragglers.

By nightfall the noise of battle had almost completely died down. Now and then a shell impacted; however, the night was illuminated by the reflections of numerous fires burning in Vienna. When it was certain by all human measurement that there were no more German soldiers left in the bridgehead or on the other side of the river, the regimental commander gave the engineer *Leutnant* the order to blow the bridge. Ignited electrically, the center span went up. The enemy would not be able to follow here in the morning, and the regiment gained a breathing space as a result.

Only through the outstanding cohesion of all of the squads, platoons and companies and the excellent support provided by the heavy weapons was it possible to end this battle.

But Vienna was in Russian hands!

14 April: The command post was in Jedlersdorf. The regiment was now faced with encirclement north of the Danube, where the enemy was pushing west in the direction of Bisam-Berg. The road along the Danube could be seen by the enemy, the roads north of Bisam-Berg were already in enemy hands. The only possible avenue of retreat, therefore, was the road through Bisam-Berg, part of which was a sunken road.

The "*Der Führer*" Regiment began this march, which was to be one of the most strenuous night marches of the recent months, at 10 PM. Bogged down horse-drawn vehicles of the army and traffic jams caused delays. Every unit commander and officer intervened personally to get the march moving. The headquarters of the "*Der Führer*" Regiment was at the head of the regimental units, which was moving at the end as the last march unit. In spite of all efforts it proved impossible to complete the march before daybreak as the express order from division had specified. The conditions proved stronger.

15 April: At daybreak the enemy drove into the flank of the "*Der Führer*" Regiment and ran into the regimental units, which were forced to take heavy casualties. Nevertheless the march was kept going in order

to avoid even greater losses. Because of the length of the column the regimental commander did not learn about the losses until the march objective. The regiment passed a new defense line and marched via Eggendorf to Eggendorf am Wagram.

The entire regiment assembled in this area, moving in all train units. After weeks of fighting in Hungary and Vienna the companies urgently needed the one-day rest.

17 April: Departure by way of Krems to Gansbach. A message center was set up in Krems.

18 April: The regiment occupied a line of security with front facing east, with II and III Battalions on both sides of Gansbach and I Battalion in Kirchschlag.

19 April: The "*Der Führer*" Regiment was relieved in its positions by the companies of the "*Deutschland*" Regiment.

20 April: Transfer into the Maria-Landegg area. 620 replacements arrived and were assigned to the battalions.

21 April: A planned attack by the regiment for the purpose of reconnaissance in force was called off.

22 April: At about 8 PM the regiment marched into the area south of St. Pölten. In these days the regiment learned by way of division of an event that was beyond the comprehension of the officers and men.

Adolf Hitler had issued instructions that the entire 6th SS Panzer Army under its commander in chief *Generaloberst* Dietrich with the I and II SS Panzer Corps, in which were fighting the oldest and most battle tested divisions of the *Waffen-SS*, the panzer divisions "*Das Reich*", "*Leibstandarte*", "*Totenkopf*", "*Hohenstaufen*" and "*Hitlerjugend*", was to remove its cuff titles. Furthermore a general freeze on promotions was placed on the army. All of this was done because it had not accomplished its mission in Hungary, had abandoned the "Reich Defense Position" southeast of Vienna, and had failed to defend the city of Vienna, which had been declared a fortress, to the last man in spite of his express order to do so.

Adolf Hitler had withdrawn his trust from these extremely battle weary and bloodied units because they had avoided offering the enemy one last battle in a terrain which was neither a prepared defense position nor a fortress.

That these divisions fought a hopeless battle day after day in order to make it as difficult as possible for the Soviets to enter Austria and Germany, making great sacrifices in the process, was not taken into consideration.

*Generaloberst* Guderian was originally supposed to have brought the order to the 6th SS Panzer Army but refused the mission.

Hitler's order was ignored by the commander in chief of the 6th SS Panzer Army, Sepp Dietrich, and the regiments kept their cuff titles.

23 April: The "*Der Führer*" Regiment occupied the so-called "Claudia Position" with its command post in St. Margarethen.

24 April: No enemy contact.

25 April: The "Claudia Position" was rendered invalid. The regiment was put abroad several transport trains for shipment into the Passau area.

From the orders and short-notice transfers it became apparent that the situation and the command conditions were becoming increasingly confused. It was rumored that the regiment was to be deployed on the "Western Front" against the western Allies.

26 April: The transport trains rolled toward Passau. Radio contact was planned between the regimental headquarters and the transport trains during the journey.

The regiment's small operations section drove by way of Melk and Linz to Eferding. Near Oberüttling the regiment's radio station tried to establish contact with the trains. In vain. Thus the whereabouts of the transport trains was uncertain.

Due south of Passau the regimental commander learned from an army corps headquarters that the individual transports had been diverted by "*Führer* order" north across the Danube in the direction of Budweis-Iglau for a planned operation in the Brünn area. The regimental units had already detrained and were driving in the direction of Iglau.

The regimental commander later learned that, acting on a "*Führer* order," general staff officers had stopped the transports, which were then unloaded or redirected toward the north. The transport commanders who refused to carry out these orders because they did not come from the "*Der Führer*" Regiment were threatened with court martial for refusing to obey a "*Führer* order."

As a result of the constant transfers, of orders and counter-orders, some of which did not come via the chain of command as in the incident described above, the regiment had seen no action since the battle for the Floridsdorf Bridge, or for fourteen days, and the 2nd SS Panzer Division "*Das Reich*" was torn apart.

In view of the desperate situation at the fronts, where all forces were urgently needed, it must appear more than curious that a regiment, which though badly bloodied in the previous battles had retained its command structure completely intact and had twice received replacements, went fourteen days without seeing action. The obvious suspicion is that some office used this process to disperse a veteran combat division and keep its battle-tested regiments out of the last round of the war – a suspicion that was subsequently not confirmed but one that can also scarcely be refuted.

The commander of the "*Der Führer*" Regiment made repeated protests to the commanding general that the regiment's transports had been diverted en route without his knowledge. The latter referred to the "*Führer* order" with a shrug of his shoulders and made it clear that he hadn't understood such instructions and orders for a long time.

Meantime the order for action in the Brunn area had once again been superseded, and a special missions officer from the division brought the order for an immediate transfer into the area north of Dresden.

28 April: The regimental units arrived at the command post in Hossau and were entrained immediately.

29 April: At 5 AM the regiment's operations section drove off and at about 11 AM reached Prague, where it remained until 2 PM.

Prague made an absolutely peaceful impression, and all of its inhabitants seemed to be going about their business. According to German authorities, among them the Ia of the commander of Prague, Stubaf. Franz Knebel, there was no threat of unrest or uprisings breaking out in the city in spite of the nearness of the front. The "*Der Führer*" Regiment was to discover how wrong this prognosis was several days later.

During this stop the regimental commander met Princess Stephan zu Schaumburg-Lippe, who had the thankless task of preparing for the possible evacuation of the German population from Prague even though she had no transport available to her. The evacuation had previously been forbidden so as to avoid creating unrest among the Czech inhabitants.

Thanks to the fact that the regimental commander learned of this problem now, he was later able to take appropriate measures to decisively assist in the evacuation of the Germans from Prague with the "*Der Führer*" Regiment.

In Leitmeritz Ostuf. Hentschel, commander of the "*Der Führer*" Regiment's signals platoon, rejoined the regiment. On 30 April the regiment departed for Groß-Röhrsdorf via Tetschen-Bodenbach, Dresden and Bischofswerder. The regiment assembled in this area. The German divisions of the 4th Panzer Army positioned there had achieved a great defensive success and had destroyed a large number of tanks, especially of the 2nd Polish Armored Division which was fighting on the Russian side. The residents of the villages breathed a sigh of relief on seeing German units again.

1 May: The regimental command post was in Dobra. A strong relief attack toward the Reich capital Berlin was planned from there with several tank and motorized divisions.

In the evening German radio announced that it would be broadcasting an important special bulletin. Soon thereafter it was announced that the *Führer* and supreme commander of the German Armed Forces had fallen in the final battle for Berlin and that Grand Admiral Dönitz had taken over command of the Reich government.

The "*Der Führer*" Regiment was gripped by a curious mixture of shock that total defeat had now a certainty, and relief that the unequal and hopeless struggle, which in fact was only a battle for time, would now soon end. Now no one could call upon "*Führer* orders."

During the night the regimental commander assembled all of the officers of the "*Der Führer*" Regiment and informed them of the death of the supreme commander. Included in his remarks, the commanding officer aid that no one was released from his oath since that oath had also been made to the German people. Their only remaining mission now was to see out the end of the war, sparing as many human lives as possible, with honor and decency. Discipline and obedience as well as a strong inner cohesion made it possible for the regiment to get through the coming days and weeks correctly and avoid serious casualties.

Shocked and reflective, the officers returned to their companies to pass their commanding officer's words on to the men.

2 May: The planned preparations for the attack toward Berlin were dropped, and on 3 May the regiment moved into the Wachau area then on 5 May into the Arnsdorf area. The regiment was supposed to be deployed in the direction of Bauzen toward Görlitz. Several times the order was withdrawn and a new one issued.

## Last Action in Prague

6 May: On this day, as we learned later, the commander of the "*Der Führer*" Regiment, Ostubaf. Otto Weidinger, was awarded the Knight's Cross with Oak Leaves and Swords for his regiment's decisive actions in the *Westwall*, in the Ardennes battle, in the fighting in Hungary and in Vienna. Every member of the regiment could be very proud and satisfied that their great efforts in the last months of the war were acknowledged by the awarding of this high decoration to their commanding officer shortly before the end of the war.

After numerous orders and counter-orders the "*Der Führer*" Regiment finally received a clear mission: action in Prague. The "*Der Führer*" Regiment was bolstered into a battle group through the subordination of the 2nd Armored Reconnaissance Battalion's armored car company, an army armored car company (exact designation not known) and the Second Battalion of the division's 2nd Artillery Regiment. The battle group left the formation of the 2nd SS Panzer Division "*Das Reich*" and was placed under the direct command of the army group commanded by *Generalfeldmarschall* Schörner.

The "*Der Führer*" Regiment received orders to march directly to Prague, where contrary to all predictions the uprising had broken out. German units had already been surrounded by the Czechs there. The "*Der Führer*" Regiment had to fight its way through to Prague, help put down the uprising, get through to "*Wehrmacht* Square", establish contact with the *Wehrmacht* commander in Prague, *General* Toussaint, and receive further orders from him.

This was obviously going to be the "*Der Führer*" Regiment's last action. The 2nd SS Panzer Division "*Das Reich*" had ceased to exist as a cohesive unit. The sister regiment "*Deutschland*" was fighting in Austria, the division headquarters and the other division units including the 2nd Panzer Regiment remained in the Dresden area.

Meantime a speech by Grand Admiral Dönitz was broadcast by German radio. In it he said that resistance against the western allies had become senseless, but that all of the divisions on the Eastern Front were to continue resisting the onslaught by Russian forces with all their strength so as to allow the western allies to occupy as much of the German Reich as possible.

Shortly before the "*Der Führer*" Regiment's departure an army group radio station reported in which had direct contact with *Generalfeldmarschall* Schörner. The regiment moved off at 5 AM and marched without incident through Arnsdorf, Dresden and Dippoldiswalde to Leitmeritz.

There the regimental commander learned from the SS Signals School in Leitmeritz that radio reports had announced that Prague had already been occupied by American units or that at least their advance detachments had reached the city. Since no resistance was to be offered against the western powers, the regimental commander sent the following radio message to the army group:

> "According to radio report Americans are already in Prague. How do we behave toward the Americans?"
>
> *The answer: "Do not listen to enemy broadcasts, carry out mission as rapidly as possible!"*

The anti-tank barriers and roadblocks began a few kilometers from Prague. The regiment encountered stragglers from all branches of the service; their weapons had been taken away by the rebels. At first the barricades were unmanned. A short time later the point came under fire. Since mining of the terrain made bypassing the resistance difficult and would have meant lost time, the "*Der Führer*" Regiment fought its way to within four kilometers of the Troja Bridge in Prague. The advance received effective support from the armored cars, which were driving in the point position, and the anti-aircraft guns mounted on self-propelled carriages.

Moving quickly, the army armored car company freed a radio transmitter which was put back in service by the German authorities.

Clearing the badly damaged roads took a great deal of time and effort. An army group liaison officer, whom the commander of the "*Der Führer*" Regiment knew personally, arrived with the express order from *Generalfeldmarschall* Schörner for the battle group to advance into the city as quickly as possible and expeditiously carry out its assigned mission. It was of decisive importance to all of Army Group Schörner that the uprising in Prague be put down as quickly as possible.

The verbally-transmitted order was underlined once again by a direct radio transmission from the *Generalfeldmarschall* to the regimental commander, which was worded as follows:

> "The honor and glory of the 'Der Führer' Regiment is at stake if you fail to reach the inner city of Prague by 7 May.
> *signed Schörner*"

All of the panzer-grenadiers worked to clear away the barricades in the light from the headlamps of the armored cars.

7 May: Resistance stiffened, therefore the "*Der Führer*" Regiment had to prepare to attack. II Battalion under Hstuf. Schulzer was deployed in the front line, and under covering fire from the armored cars and self-propelled anti-aircraft guns it fought its way to the Troja Bridge. The attack cost the "*Der Führer*" Regiment about 25 dead.

The "*Der Führer*" Regiment's command post, situated in a villa high on the slopes of the north bank of the Moldau, offered an outstanding view of the former "Golden City," where only days before the regimental commander had sat together with good friends and which had unexpectedly become the witch's cauldron of the uprising. One of the few cities in Europe largely untouched by war, it was now to be the scene of the most senseless bloodletting of the entire conflict.

An emissary arrived in the form of a Czech lieutenant from the resistance group; his aim was to negotiate a halt to the fighting. The regimental commander promised to do so provided the "*Der Führer*" Regiment met no further resistance. The Czech officer rejected this. He wanted the "*Der Führer*" Regiment to withdraw in the direction of Leitmeritz. Ostubaf. Weidinger's reply was clear and simple:

"That is absolutely out of the question. The purpose of the Czech uprising in the last days of the war is to gain the recognition of the Allies as a power at war against the German Reich. But the rebels alone bear the responsibility for those killed in this battle as they do if this fine city is damaged by fighting at the last minute. The battle group would prefer to carry out its mission without fighting. The Czech resistance is senseless because they know very well that they will achieve their national objective, liberation from the Germans, in a few days even if they don't fight."

8 May: In the early morning the attack was continued across the bridge with support from all heavy weapons and a bridgehead established. The signals officer monitored radio broadcasts in order to keep the commander of the "*Der Führer*" Regiment informed about developments in the overall situation. Radio Prague changed hands several times: the Czechs called for a cessation of the fighting that they themselves had started. Fires broke out in various parts of the city. Negotiations between German authorities and the rebels were said to have been initiated. The radio broadcast a report that the surrender of the German forces on all fronts was to take place during the night of 8-9 May 1945, when a cease-fire was to take effect. Contact had not yet been established with the *Wehrmacht* commander, *General* Toussaint. The army group liaison officer offered to go the rebels as a parlementaire and together with them make contact with the *Wehrmacht* commander.

The regimental commander's clear and unequivocal condition for the cessation of fighting was: "Unopposed and free passage to *Wehrmacht* Square!"

The German parlementaire was supposed to return by 3 PM. A cease-fire began. The army group was kept informed about developments in the "*Der Führer*" Regiment's situation by radio. Communications over 150 kilometers functioned perfectly. When the parlementaire failed to return by 3 PM, and with the army group pressing for the mission to be completed, the regimental commander complained vehemently to the Czech officer about the non-compliance with his conditions. He got the impression that the rebels were just trying to buy time. At 3:30 PM the commander of the "*Der Führer*" Regiment gave the Czech officer one last deadline of 4 PM. If the German emissary was not back by then, the "*Der Führer*" Regiment would resume its attack toward "*Wehrmacht* Square." Preparations for this were completed immediately.

At 4 PM the parlementaire was still not back. The regimental commander gave the order to attack. The heavy weapons had just opened fire when word came from II Battalion that the parlementaire had just reached the battalion's lines. The German officer requested a halt in the firing immediately, as a cease-fire had just been signed by the German commander and the rebels a few minutes earlier. The Czechs were prepared to open the roadblocks and guarantee the battle group free passage to "*Wehrmacht* Square." By 6 PM the streets were passable.

At this moment war operations by the "*Der Führer*" Regiment ended. There in Prague another ring of fate closed for the regiment:

From June to September 1939 the "*Der Führer*" Regiment had been stationed there as the guard regiment of the Reich Protectorate of Bohemia and Moravia. At that time the regiment had arrived a new unit – today, on the last day of the war, the "*Der Führer*" Regiment, now hard-tested and battle-proven in many theaters, ended its battle there.

The parlementaire was of the opinion that with the start of the cease-fire the "*Der Führer*" Regiment had completed its combat mission. There was no need for the regiment to march through Prague, instead it could withdraw to the north.

However the commanding officer recalled his conversation with Princess Stephan zu Schaumburg-Lippe from a few days earlier and remembered that the majority of the German civilian population was still in the city. Thus he made his decision: the regiment would march to "*Wehrmacht* Square" in any case, in order to subsequently transport as many Germans as possible out of the city in the regiment's vehicles. Furthermore the regimental commander felt himself duty-bound to report to the *Wehrmacht* commander in spite of the cease-fire and simultaneously carry out the regiment's last order.

The supply units had used the intervening time to equip the regiment with all the necessities from the well-stocked *Wehrmacht* supply dumps in the city of Prague.

And so on the day of the surrender all three battalions of the "*Der Fuhrer*" Regiment received sufficient replacements to bring them up to full strength, were provided with twelve measures of fuel, were extremely well provisioned with food and received plentiful stocks of ammunition. The existing stores were also supplemented with vehicles and equipment of every kind. Thus at the end of the war the regiment possessed a fighting strength which it had seldom achieved during its last operations.

Shortly after 6 PM the regimental commander issued the following order:

> *"The war is over! This afternoon a cease-fire was concluded between the Wehrmacht commander and the rebels in Prague. This was made easier by the fact that the Czechs were made aware of the great fighting strength of the 'DF' Regiment, which had already reached Prague and was ready to continue the attack at any time.*
>
> *The German Armed Forces will surrender at 12 AM tonight. Effective immediately the guns will fall silent.*
>
> *The 'DF' Regiment and all of its subordinate units will march to Wehrmacht Square to make contact with the armed forces commander, with the leading elements moving out at 7 PM.*
>
> *As many German women and children as possible are to be taken along in the vehicles. Since the 'DF' Regiment is beginning its final march in the direction of Pilsen, the vehicles may and must be loaded to maximum capacity. German soldiers may of course be taken along when there are no civilian passengers.*
>
> *Not another shot will be fired by the 'DF' Battle Group, however all weapons are to be kept ready to fire. Weapons may be used only if the column is stopped by the Czechs or comes under fire.*
>
> *Effective immediately the use of alcohol is banned in the entire 'DF' Battle Group. Anyone who becomes a prisoner under the influence of alcohol seriously damages the prestige of the regiment.*
>
> *Absolute march discipline must obviously be maintained until we reach the Americans. Destination is Pilsen. The march roads have been marked by the motorcycle scout platoon. Departure 7 PM."*

The regimental commander subsequently sent the following radio message to the 2nd SS Panzer Division "*Das Reich*":

"Following the cease-fire the 'DF' Regiment will be marching in the direction of Pilsen into captivity. The 'DF' Regiment signing off. Long live Germany!"

The following radio message was sent to Army Group Schörner by way of the 4th Panzer Army:

*"Mission accomplished. Contact has been made with the Wehrmacht commander in Prague. Following cease-fire the Battle Group 'DF' Regiment will march to Pilsen and surrender to the Americans. Battle Group 'DF' Regiment signing off. Long live Germany!"*

On the other side of the Troja Bridge the commander of the "*Der Führer*" Regiment was met by a Czech officer, who in the last negotiations had striven honorably to put a quick end to the senseless bloodshed. Both agreed that the fighting was senseless. At exactly 7 PM all roadblocks were opened by the Czechs. Guided by Czech officers, the "*Der Führer*" Regiment moved off. The Czech sentries at the barricades saluted the German officers. "*Wehrmacht* Square" was reached without incident.

At approximately 8 PM the commander of the "*Der Führer*" Regiment reported to the *Wehrmacht* commander, *General* Toussaint, who was pleased to have his fighting strength bolstered. Czech officers ran through the headquarters, shouting and demanding provocatively that the various German agencies evacuate their offices.

A squad from III Battalion under Stubaf. Werner quickly restored order and the rebels disappeared without the use of weapons. *General* Toussaint advised the regimental commander to withdraw south toward Austrian territory since the Prague airfield and Prague-Ruzyne were held by Vlasov troops, who as of late had begun shooting at Germans.

The regimental commander stuck to his decision to head for Pilsen, however. For certain there were American units there, and if the regiment was going to march into captivity, then it had to be American.

A short time later State Secretary Frank arrived and expressed great joy at being able to meet the regimental commander in person. The approach of the "*Der Führer*" Regiment battle group had been announced the day before, and the German civilian population had reacted to this news with relief. Inadequately informed as to the overall situation, State Secretary Frank believed that he could remain in Prague for another twenty-four hours, in order mainly to organize the evacuation of the German civilian population.

The regimental commander strenuously advised against this, since the Soviets had launched a major attack south from the Dresden area. In any case the regiment was going to leave Prague that night, or in a few hours, and drive to Pilsen to surrender to the Americans. The order had already been issued to the companies to take as many German civilians on board the vehicles as they could carry. Furthermore, any Germans who wished to go along in their own vehicles could of course place themselves under the protection of the regiment and join the column. These measures would surely go a long way toward solving the evacuation problem from Prague.

Faced with this new – to him – situation, State Secretary Frank decided to leave Prague with the regiment. The garrison of Prague's citadel, the Hradschin Castle, was also preparing to depart and likewise wanted to go along under the protection of the regiment. The regimental commander received word that the wounded in the hospitals of Prague were being evacuated aboard several hospital trains which had been standing under steam at the main railway station since the afternoon.

He issued orders to the leader of the division's armored scout car company to escort State Secretary Frank out of Prague and made him responsible for his safety.

Meantime the regiment's huge column (more than 1,000 vehicles) had picked up every German who could possibly be reached. These people were extremely glad to be given a last-minute opportunity to escape the now hostile city and the hands of the Czechs, who now felt themselves to be "victors", and get to the Americans. All of the vehicles were overfilled and the regimental commander saw to it personally that the men of the regiment provided excellent care, especially to the women and children.

A unit of "female flak auxiliaries" arrived at the last minute before departure, and because of overloading of the trucks they were assigned to the vehicles of the regimental headquarters. As it later turned out, they were SS female auxiliaries; they were wearing blue-gray flak uniforms and were therefore mistaken for flak auxiliaries.[14] Only the runes on the sleeves of their uniforms identified them as members of the SS belonging to the SS Division "*Hitlerjugend*." They all carried SS identification papers and later voluntarily went into a *Waffen-SS* camp even though the Americans wanted to send them on to a camp for members of the *Wehrmacht*. The girls, whose number also included a number of Dutch, all behaved magnificently toward their American captors.

## Account of the Last Days in Prague

The former house leader of the SS Female Auxiliary Corps in Oberehnheim, Princess Stephan zu Schaumburg-Lippe, described the events in Prague in April-May 1945:

*"In mid-April 1945 the course of the war took me to Prague to the staff of the BdW SS (commander of the Waffen-SS), Brigadeführer Count Karl Friedrich Pückler. This beautiful city was in a state of peacetime quiet, which struck me as odd, because I came from war-torn Thuringia. But this quiet was to prove deceptive. Apart from rumors going round of a coming revolt that was to soften up Prague for the entry of the Soviets, reports stated that a stream of refugees was moving toward Prague from Silesia and also from the south. The core consisted of approximately 48 treks with countless wagon columns, horse-draw vehicles and cattle. As was typical in those days, there were other masses of refugees heading in the opposite direction from Saxony, Thuringia and Austria, fleeing before the advancing Americans. They all threatened to completely clog the roads, which had to be kept clear for the advance or retreat of our troops.*

*So far nothing had been done in Prague to get the German women and children in the place to safety, even though the Russian front was moving nearer from the north and east. They expected and hoped that the Americans would occupy the capital city of the Protectorate. They were now outside Pilsen and had taken up position there.*

*After everything that I had experienced and seen while coming from the west, during a conversation with the Brigadeführer on this topic, I forcefully urged him to order the necessary measures as soon as possible.*

*The following day Staf. Dr. Voss, president of the Skoda Works, informed me that the Brigadeführer wanted to entrust me with this task on account of my experience in organization. He would make available to me office space and personnel.*

*I was thoroughly aware of the tremendous responsibility that this would place on my shoulders! I took a deep breath and made my way to Hradschin Castle in order to clarify the situation and if possible coordinate our action with the arrangements made by the civilian administration and the Wehrmacht authorities.*

*I discovered that:*

*First, that the rumors about the stream of refugees did not correspond to the facts and that as they were spread exceeded anything heard.*

*Second, there was no order to evacuate the civilian authorities. On the contrary, no such arrangements had been made, 'in order to avoid a panic.'*

*After a lengthy discussion I declared that the Waffen-SS commander had ordered the immediate evacuation of the families of all members of his agencies. I asked them to take note of this!*

*Count Pückler hoped that this would subsequently stimulate the responsible Protectorate authorities to likewise take action. He was not wrong.*

*I was given an office in the BdW building. An Untersturmführer and his wife, both extremely capable and precise staff members, were assigned to me and were then supplemented by a third person. The first thing we had to do was determine the number of people to be evacuated in order to then decide with the quartermaster, SS-Ostubaf. Harzig, the size and number of trucks required. Furthermore we had to determine to where the families were to be taken to safety and who would escort and protect the transports, which had to drive through the partisan area.*

*In the following days the hallway in front of my office was completely filled with men of every rank, all fathers, who came to report the size and composition of their families. Apparently news of our activities had quickly got around everywhere, for the calls for help from members of other elements of the armed forces also increased by the hour. The telephone rang continuously.*

*Beautiful spring weather once again illuminated the beauty of this historical city with its magnificent old buildings. The lilacs bloomed in the gardens. The Moldau flowed peacefully beneath the magnificent Karls Bridge and past our offices. Everything seemed to be in order.*

*On 29 April the Ia, Stubaf. Knebel, and I took advantage of the good weather and were walking from the apartment of Count Pückler, where we were quartered, down past the foot of Hradschin Castle to the Karl Bridge, when a motorized SS column, apparently units of the 'Das Reich' Division, came toward us. Suddenly a dispatch rider veered out of the column, stopped in front of us and declared, 'the commander of the 'Der Führer' Regiment requests Stubaf. Knebel to salute him as per regulations!' Taken aback at first, Knebel looked around and then gave a shout of joy, for there, standing laughing in his Kübelwagen, was Ostubaf. Weidinger, with whom he had taught at Junkerschule B. He had us climb in and drove us to the office, where Knebel invited him into a snack bar. There we also talked about the situation in Prague. Taking advantage of this favorable moment, I asked Ostubaf. Weidinger to where his regiment was going now. When he answered to Dresden, where the division headquarters was located and where the regiment was supposed to pick up ammunition, the thought went through my head: 'You'll never fire it off!' – 'But in an emergency you could help us get the families out of Prague if our hands were tied here!' So I asked the commander of the 'Der Führer' Regiment to stay in contact, and if news of the outbreak of the uprising reached him to carry out the withdrawal from Prague. Ostubaf. Weidinger promised to do everything that he could.*

*We had placed approximately 500 mothers and children under military protection in the Bavarian Forest, where an emergency camp took them in, but there were still remained far more than three times as may families impatiently waiting to be evacuated, especially since the mood in the city seemed to have changed. One heard a growing number of squabbles between Czechs and Germans in the bars and on the streets. A general nervousness took hold, the first scattered shots were fired.*

*The SS commander conducted very serious negotiations with the commander in chief General Toussaint and representatives of Reich Administrator Frank in order to prevent the premature departure of individual units, to stop the administrative authorities from hindering the recovery of endangered civilians and to maintain a solid front.*

*It was also due to his own initiative alone that needless demolitions were avoided therefore that the artistically-unique Karl Bridge was saved.*

*Things soon began to happen quickly. News of the battle in and around Berlin, of the Führer's death, the rapid advance by the Russians, who had crossed the borders of the Protectorate everywhere, the to us unbelievable halt by the Americans west of Pilsen filled everyone with anxious concern and increased the pace our work.*

*The last truck which we, filled with worry, had allowed to depart 24 hours before the outbreak of the revolt, was personally accompanied by an SS-Ustuf. Employed in the 'family evacuation' office and his wife, since telephone calls had suggested that there were shortcomings in the accommodations in the emergency camp and that supplies were not getting through. They were to create order.*

*On advice the Ustuf. had (very reluctantly) to exchange his uniform for civilian clothes.*

*And then the storm broke! It was 5 May. It was triggered by a completely unexpected but aimed shot from the pistol of the Czech traffic policeman in Wehrmacht Square when Ogruf. Hans Kammler returned his salute as he drove past. (Ogruf. Kammler was on his way to the Führer in Berlin, believing his proper place during the final phase of the war to be at his side, but he got stuck in Prague.) He reacted immediately and his bullet hit its target!*

*What happened then, how Prague was quickly turned into a bubbling witch's cauldron in which cruelty, murder and death reigned, has been described elsewhere.*

*I gathered women and children who were designated for the next transport in the main room of a building on Wehrmacht Square and days before had instructed the SS female auxiliaries to leave their quarters in the cramped old city and likewise make their way there in case they could not find accommodation at their offices. A tank determined that this had happened.*

*Of course we now extended our assistance to all German families which placed themselves under our protection. As a result the quarters grew into a mass camp.*

*6 May: By now Prague was in chaos! And we were in the middle of it! Czech partisans shot at our windows from the opposite houses, indeed even from the other side of the Moldau. Thank God most of the bullets went into the ceiling above us. We had only one or two slightly wounded, who cursed furiously but continued working.*

*Units quartered in the building sent squads of men in an effort to free the surrounding streets and the Luftwaffe hospital opposite; an assault gun positioned in the entrance gave covering fire. Since our four-story house was made of solid concrete and all of the hallways were linked by an open stairway, indescribable noise filled every room. As a result we could often only understand each other by shouting.*

*While the building increasingly transformed itself into a fortress under siege, I received a report by telephone from out Ustuf. that the transport had reached its destination safely. What was going on in Prague anyway? I gave him a situation report, which was given credibility by shots, and warned him against coming back. His answer was typical: 'I'm not going to become a prisoner without my uniform. I'm going to get it!' (He definitely got it!)*

*An increasing number of civilians, who had been surprised by the goings on in the streets, streamed into the house, naked fear and dismay in their eyes. For on the sidewalks lay the dead and wounded, which also included housewives. I myself saw a woman carrying a shopping bag shot on a relatively quiet side-street during a pause in the fighting! And the bullet certainly did not come from a German weapon.*

*Wounded were carried in and brought into a hastily-erected emergency hospital. They included many all too young but brave soldiers of the HJ Division.*

*I had to look after the mass quarters of the civilians. The people had to be calmed and cooked for. Trying to bring a measure of order to this frightened throng was an almost hopeless undertaking. The people of Prague had not experienced nights under bombing. Again and again mothers understandably attempted to rush home to see to their children, but the conditions outside forced them back.*

*Then in the evening it became quieter, night fell and we heard no more shooting. The cellar slowly emptied itself except for a modest group of Germans, but also some Czechs who were afraid of their countrymen.*

*My only hope in these difficult days was the "Der Führer" Regiment.*

*There was no doubt that Ostubaf. Weidinger would think of us – but would he come in time? Or was he pinned down by other orders? If this were the case, would they succeed in sending some other assistance?*

*On 7 May aircraft dropped bombs. At first we did not know whether they were our machines or Russian, but then we learned that they were German fighter-bombers that had bombed free other agencies.*

*On 8-9 May the guns fell silent, and only occasional shots were still heard. Rumors that relief for Prague was at hand caused me to breathe a sigh of relief. Had Ostubaf. Weidinger done it and was he going to keep his word? The rumors intensified and became a certainty.*

*And those are the facts.*

*While I was unable to completely carry out the task assigned to me, to evacuate the German families, the Waffen-SS regiment "Der Führer", at the cost of casualties to itself, saved all of the German women and children it could reach in the approximately 1,000 vehicles available to it, in order to take them with it into captivity, and in doing so saved thousands from the hell of imprisonment, torture, death and beatings at the hands of the Czechs.*

*Following lengthy negotiations with Czech emissaries, Count Pückler succeeded in obtaining our unrestricted departure.*

*The headquarters moved out on 9 May led by parlementaires with white flags. They did little god when we became involved in streetfighting in spite of the cease-fire. We at least succeeded in picking up the wounded, but only after turning around three times were we able to leave Prague via side streets. After numerous delays caused by the retreating Schörner army, we crossed the Moldau after twelve noon. It marked the border between the Russians and the Americans – if one reached it by 11:30 AM! We crossed it one hour too late.*

*On 11 May we were handed over to the Russians together with 40,000 German soldiers who had been put into a 15-kilometer-long camp near Pisek by the Americans.*

*Neither Ogruf. Kammler nor the SS commander Count Pückler and Stubaf. Knebel, who was promoted to Ostubaf., survived this hour."*

## The Regiment's Last Journey

The battle group of the "*Der Führer*" Regiment moved off at approximately 8 PM. Progress was halting because the roads leading out of Prague were completely clogged with vehicles and refugees. All of the regiment's officers worked to stoppages, and it was a nerve-wracking night.

9 May: Not until dawn did the vehicle column pass the suburb of Ruzyne. There was no sign of Vlasov troops. The regiment's march road was well marked, just as if the troops were on a mission. A major accomplishment by the dispatch rider section.

At the city limits the march column was halted by a German general and a Czech colonel. The general ordered the regimental commander to hand over the regiment's weapons there, because the We*hrmacht* commander in chief had promised this to the rebels the day before and the cease-fire was concluded only on this condition.

Ostubaf. Weidinger declared to the officers that he knew nothing about such an agreement and that he had orders to hand over the "D*er Führer*" battle group and its weapons over to the Americans.

The German general (his name is not known) threatened the regimental commander, declaring that he might be brought before an Allied court martial if he did not abide by this cease-fire condition.

Thereupon the regimental commander ordered his troops to render their weapons unusable and then surrender them. The Czech colonel and the German general protested loudly: the weapons had to be surrendered intact and piled on the road. But it was already too late for that! Everywhere in the column the disassembled weapons flew left and right into the ditches. The artillerymen spiked their guns. One gun commander shot himself beside his gun.

Informed in time, the armored car company bypassed this point in the road, and after a brief interval the "Der *Führer*" Regiment's march column moved off again with the two officers still protesting. Only a fraction of the weapons had been rendered unusable. The pistols had not been surrendered, for it was questionable whether the Czechs would abide by the cease-fire.

It seemed very strange that the *Wehrmacht* commander of Prague had not informed the regimental commander of this condition of the cease-fire.

The march proceeded smoothly. On the way the regimental commander ordered the war chests emptied during the next rest stop. Every member of the regiment was paid until the war chests were empty. This was a measure that later proved its value. Later, in prisoner of war camp, the money was used to supplement the men's rations. It was also used to help many refugee families, who were in great distress, from the prisoner of war camp.

In captivity it was learned that the Czechs had fired on the last units in the regiment's column while they were still in the inner city. A number of men were killed. Thus the rebels had clearly broken the terms of the cease-fire and were guilty of a serious breach of the international rules of war. No Czech is known to have been brought before an Allied military court to answer for this.

A company commander later told the regimental commander that during the drive from Prague to Pilsen he had heard battle noise right beside the march road while passing through a village. He and the company entered the village where they found the Czechs in the process of inflicting a real bloodbath on German men, women and children. Unfortunately the company arrived too late to prevent the worst. Again no Czech was ever brought before an Allied military court for this crime.

At about 10 AM the leading elements of the regiment, which were accompanied by commanding officer Ostubaf. Weidinger, were stopped by a picket line from the U.S. 2nd Infantry Division (Indian Division) and ordered to get down from their vehicles by the American soldiers. All weapons had to be handed over. It is odd that the American soldiers should be very interested in the men's wristwatches: these, too, were collected in short order by the soldiers of the "Indian Division." This was something we had previously only seen the Russians do. For the men of the "Der *Führer*" Regiment the next hours were the most depressing in their entire lives as soldiers.

The regimental commander's legitimate hope that he might be able to surrender the regiment to an American regimental commander proved unfounded. No American officer showed himself during the spectacle that followed.

The regimental headquarters was led into a meadow, where the commander, the officers and men were first relieved of their decorations and personal valuables. It goes without saying that this plundering was carried out under a threat of force by the Americans.

Then one of the "Indians" declared that the entire regimental headquarters was now going to be shot. The regimental commander answered icily: "We don't care," and had signals officer Ostuf. Hentschel translate. "Then you are still proud that you are here?" answered the American. Replied Ostuf. Hentschel: "You can bet we are."

During the midmorning the various battalions and units of the "Der *Führer*" Regiment arrived and were taken prisoner by the American 2nd Armored Division in a similar fashion.

Certain sorts of Czechs very quickly turned up there to accuse the men of the regiment of being "body-strippers." These dreary appearances went on for several days until the Americans, after ongoing complaints, remembered their mission of protecting the prisoners of war.

The town in which the regiment went into captivity was called Rokiczany. The SS-V Division had been formed there after the Polish campaign of 1939 and the "Der *Führer*" Regiment was incorporated into the division.

On that 9 May 1945 it was clear to every soldier of the "D*er Führer*" Regiment just what an unconditional surrender meant for a people and its armed services. It was the worst fate and synonymous with the condition of total rightlessness and with being at the absolute mercy of the will of the victor.

## VIII[15]

## The 3rd and 4th Companies from 6 May 1945 until the Surrender

6 May: At approximately 10 AM there was a commanders' conference at the command post of I Battalion, commanding officer Stubaf. Hauser. Subject: revolt in Prague. The Czechs had taken up arms. The "*Der Führer*" Regiment was to march to Prague expeditiously as a battle group and put down the revolt.

As they had no vehicles, the 3rd and 4th Companies marched on foot to the Dresden-Heidenau-Dohna road and were picked up in Nieder-Schlottwitz by vehicles sent back by the regiment. Detailed orders from the officer accompanying the vehicles. The 3rd and 4th Companies moved off at once.

The bridge over the Elbe at Loschwitz was crossed in searing heat and the vehicles quickly passed through the desert of rubble that was Dresden. The city where art and culture had once bloomed had been terribly devastated by American bombing raids. With good order and march discipline Heidenau was reached and after a brief rest the troops settled in to the Dohna area. The men were exhausted. The 4th Company's heavy equipment and most of the ammunition was loaded aboard three trucks.

7 May: Departure at approximately seven in the morning. Roads were crowded and clogged with stragglers from every service branch. Beside the road one saw the great suffering of the civilian population. A few kilometers from Nieder-Schlottwitz there was an attack by American fighter-bombers. They were spotted early and the companies suffered no

losses. The medics helped the injured women and children here. At 9 AM the companies took up positions at the south end of Nieder-Schlottwitz. The St*absscharführer* was sent by car in the direction of Glashütte, destination the town of Bärenstein, in order to guide an expected vehicle column. Further strafing attacks until 2 PM, fortunately without casualties. At 3 PM the *Stabsscharführer* was still not back and the vehicle column had not arrived. The companies set out again on the Glashütte-Zinnwald road, since the vehicle column had to come down this road. The Reich boundary was crossed near Zinnwald at approximately 9 PM. Morale of the platoons and squads good in spite of physical effort. During the night men of 3rd Company discovered an abandoned vehicle park. A selection of vehicles was fueled and loaded.

8 May: Companies moved out at 5 AM; Teplitz-Schönau was reached at about 6:30 AM. Unable to establish contact with local garrison. Hasty departure evidenced by files and bundles of paper. The first rumors appeared: "The German armed forces have surrendered!" Soldiers were seen wearing white armbands with rank badges and nationality emblems removed. One rumor followed on the heels of another. In this chaos the men of the 3rd and 4th Companies demonstrated the old regimental spirit: unshakable in discipline and order. Most of the civilian population behaved correctly. Soldiers separated from their units asked to be taken into the companies, and by 10 PM the platoons and squads were fully motorized. Fighting strength was boosted considerably through the incorporation of an 88-mm anti-aircraft gun and four armored troop carriers. The strength of the companies climbed to 600 men. A M*ajor* from the staff of Army Group Schörner arrived and produced a detailed written order in which the commander of 3rd Company, Ostuf. Schmager, was made personally responsible for getting the two companies to the "*Der Führer*" Regiment in Prague as expeditiously as possible. Ostuf. Schmager placed the 4th Company under his command and the two companies were combined as "Battle Group Schmager."

Patrols sent down the road to the south returned with unpleasant news: main and secondary roads in the direction of Louny and Leitmeritz completely clogged and overfilled with columns from the north. The west road through Aussig appeared more favorable. The battle group intended to reach Aussig and then turn south in the direction of Leitmeritz.

The battle group moved off at 11:30 AM and the first ten kilometers were covered rapidly. During a halt a Russian reconnaissance aircraft flew too low over the column, was fired on, and when it turned away was smoking heavily. The downing of the aircraft could not be confirmed. In front of a village a strong roadblock manned by civilians wearing armbands. Several bursts of machine-gun fire into the air put a quick end to this nonsense. Rifle fire showed that the rebels wanted to fight. Covered by the 4th Company, the 3rd Company broke into the village. Captured German soldiers and women were freed. Only the iron discipline and clear orders of the battle group commander prevented the freed men from taking revenge. The scenes of the tortured German men during the liberation were awful.

During the afternoon forward progress by the battle group was slow. Again and again roadblocks had to be cleared, and chasing away the rebels took time. Fortunately there were no casualties. Aussig was reached at approximately 8 PM. The companies found shelter in a closed building complex. A strong guard was posted. Patrols were sent down the Leitmeritz road.

News reports received by the battle group's own radios repeatedly spoke of the surrender of the German armed services. The road to Leitmeritz was not passable. Ostuf. Schmager personally convinced himself of this. Vehicles of all kinds, horse-drawn and motor, sat abandoned, jumbled together. The chaos was indescribable. A team was assigned to monitor all radio broadcasts and signals and report every thirty minutes. The battle group remained at alert status.

9 May: By about 3 AM the situation had become more confused and uncertain. The leader of the battle group held a conference with all of the officers and non-commissioned officers: the battle group's orders were clear. Prague, and with it the regiment, was to be reached no matter what. The regiment would welcome the augmentation of its strength by the two companies. But was the "*Der Führer*" Regiment still in Prague? The radio reports spoke of surrender.

Decision by the battle group: companies were to move out immediately and head north. Destination: the wooded terrain north of Aussig.

The specified area was reached at about 4 AM, and a favorable spot was chosen in which to establish and fortify an all-round position. The spirits of the panzer-grenadiers were low. The leader of a so-called "Werewolf" unit made contact and proposed that the battle group enter into partisan warfare. Ustuf. Gerhard Schmager rejected this impossible nonsense clearly and emphatically.

The day passed slowly. A series of patrols were sent out and each brought back the same report: everywhere they saw disarrayed Wehr*macht* columns, without weapons and equipment, without vehicles, beaten and harried. Anyone who fell into the hands of the Czechs was brutally treated, whether man, woman or child. The night passed without incident. It was sad to see the woebegone and frightened women and children who had joined up with the battle group in Aussig.

The 10th and 11th of May passed. The battle group remained armed and ready. The first Russian tanks were sighted at noon on 12 May rolling down the Teplitz-Schönau road. Long columns of captured German soldiers were seen. The radio reports repeatedly confirmed that the German armed services had surrendered. Units still under arms were supposed to surrender themselves.

On the evening of 12 May 1945 the battle group formed into an open square and Ostuf. Schmager spoke to the assembled men:

> "Officers, non-commissioned officers and enlisted men of the 3rd and 4th Companies of the 4th SS Panzer-Grenadier Regiment 'Der Führer'!
>
> *After clarifying the situation I have come to the following conclusion: the war is over! The German armed services have surrendered on all fronts! Any further fighting would mean a senseless sacrifice!*
>
> *In the name of the regimental commander, Ostubaf. Weidinger, I thank you all for the great personal risks you have taken in the past difficult years. We can all look back with pride on our regiment's great accomplishments. In this hour we wish to remember our fallen comrades...*
>
> *I hereby give the order to disband the 3rd and 4th Companies. Weapons and vehicles and all equipment are to be rendered totally unusable. All emblems that indicate membership in the Waffen-SS are to be destroyed.*

*We will not let the Czechs separate us from our rank badges and 'Der Führer' cuff bands, instead we will do that ourselves.*

*Men! Keep faith with our poor fatherland in the years that lie before us! Remain decent and sober citizens in civilian clothing as well and do your duty in your future workplaces as was your daily and obvious duty as soldiers in one of the best German regiments in the years at the front.*

*I wish you all a happy return home to your families. All the best!"*

These words sounded incomprehensible. The faces of the men twitched. Even veteran non-commissioned officers did not hide their tears. The ranks of the assembled platoons stood frozen and completely motionless as the officers removed each other's shoulder boards and Ostuf. Schmager and Ustuf. Nau bade each man farewell with a handshake. All of the precious emblems earned over hard years of combat were placed in a pile, soaked in gasoline and set on fire. Over...

In the last issuing of orders that followed the extensive stock of maps was distributed to the squads, and the squad leaders received the last order to first cross the Reich border with their men following a prescribed plan. Once in the homeland, so they hoped, the soldiers of the W*affen-SS* would also find help in getting to their families. No one could suspect how wrong they were, as the next few days would show. A contemporary poster in Heidelberg said: anyone who takes in, helps or fails to report soldiers of the *Waffen-SS* to the responsible authorities will be punished. Forced labor awaits the soldiers of the *Waffen-SS*!

• • •

Thus ended the war service of the 4th SS Panzer-Grenadier Regiment "*Der Führer*", which in its years at the front had developed into an ideal German-Austrian fighting brotherhood and harmoniously united in the Austrian and Prussian-German military tradition. The comradeship that proved itself in the war has lasted through captivity to the present day.

## The Last *Wehrmacht* Communiqué

*9 May 1945*

The Wehrmacht High Command announces:

*In East Prussia on Tuesday the German divisions defended to the utmost the mouth of the Vistula and the western part of the Frische Nehrung. The 7th Infantry Division in particular distinguished itself. For its outstanding conduct the commanding officer, General von Gauchen, was awarded the Knight's Cross with Oak Leaves, Swords and Diamonds.*

*The bulk of our army group in the Courland, which under the command of Generaloberst Günther has for months been opposing greatly superior Soviet tank and infantry formations and has held out through six major battles, has won undying fame. It has rejected every demand for a premature surrender. In perfect order the aircraft flying to the west have evacuated the wounded and heads of families. The officers and staffs have remained with the troops.*

*In keeping with the conditions accepted by us, hostilities and all movement will cease at midnight.*

*After heroic resistance the defenders of Breslau, who foiled every Soviet attack for two months, have succumbed to the enemy superiority at the last minute.*

*On the southern front, too, all staffs of the main units as far as Dresden have received orders to cease fire. The revolt by the Czechs in almost all of Bohemia and Moravia may interfere with our carrying out of the cease-fire conditions and our communications in this area. The high command has so far not received any reports on Army Groups Löhr, Rendulic and Schörner.*

*Far from the Fatherland the defenders of the Atlantic strongpoints, the troops in Norway and the garrisons of the islands in the Aegean have upheld the honor of the German soldier with obedience and discipline.*

*Since midnight now the guns have fallen silent on all fronts. The Wehrmacht has given up the hopeless struggle on order of the Grand Admiral. With this the almost six-year-long heroic struggle has come to an end. It brought us great victories, but also serious defeats. In the end the German armed services honorably succumbed to an overwhelmingly superior force. True to his oath, the German soldier gave his utmost and performed unforgettably for his people. To the end the homeland supported him with all its strength at great cost. The unique accomplishment of home and front will find its ultimate recognition in a later fair judgement of history.*

*The enemy, too, will not fail to acknowledge the accomplishments and sacrifices of the German soldier on land, on water and in the air. Therefore every soldier can lay down his weapon upright and proud and in this most difficult hour in our history bravely and confidently go to work for the eternal life of our people.*

*In this hour the Wehrmacht remembers its fallen comrades. The dead obligate us to show unconditional loyalty, obedience and discipline to our Fatherland, bleeding from countless wounds.*

## The Regiment in Captivity

For the members of the regiment there now began a difficult period as prisoners of war with countless degradations and tricks.

In the meadow camp at Rokyczany some of the men slept in tents, others camped in the open. Abruptly rations were almost cut and consisted solely of gruel. A period of gnawing hunger began.

The prisoners were subjected in turn to arbitrary acts by the victors and by Czech civilians. "Frisking," meaning the taking of all watches, rings and other valuables, was part of the daily routine. After several visits with an American officer by the commanding officer these unworthy proceedings were stopped.

Everyone in this hopeless and depressing camp were grateful for one thing: since the Americans considered all members of the *Waffen-SS* to be war criminals, the regiment remained together and neither the commanding officers nor the other officers were separated from the non-commissioned officers and enlisted men.

The regiment continued to exist as a homogenous unit until the men were transported to their various regions. The outstanding front-line comradeship and the excellent relationship between officers, non-commissioned officers and men that had existed since the regiment's formation proved themselves all over again.

In this and later camps the men of the regiment displayed outstanding conduct and a level of discipline that astonished the Americans.

From the first day on it was clear that the purely front-line and combat divisions of the W*affen-SS* were included among those who were to be made scapegoats for the entire German people. This attitude on the part of the victors only caused us to draw even closer together.

The greatest concern, which bothered us day and night and loomed before us for weeks, was the fear that the Americans would hand the regiment over to the Russians. For at certain intervals Russian officers appeared for talks with the Americans.

At that time we did not yet know that the Allies intended to divide several of the best-known divisions of the W*affen-SS* among themselves and that we had been awarded to the Americans.

23 May 1945: The regiment, less elements of II Battalion, was loaded onto trucks and taken to the police barracks in Klattau. This camp already contained four-thousand members of the army and the police, as well as four-hundred members of the W*affen-SS* in a separate, heavily-guarded enclosure. By 25 May the regiment was moved into this SS camp with a total of 2,000 men, raising the number of prisoners there to 2,400. Our men were forced to squeeze themselves into a few buildings.

While those in the W*ehrmacht* camp had voluntarily removed their rank badges, the regiment continued to wear them as before. The regimental commander took over as camp senior officer from Ostubaf. Kneisel.

On order of the Americans all prisoners had to be grouped immediately according to their region of origin.

A few days later the American camp commander informed us that we could again wear our war decorations, the majority of which had been stolen. Several men subsequently presented the commanding officer with a Knight's Cross with Oak Leaves which they had fashioned themselves from silver and an Iron Cross, Second Class. The commanding officer now wore this decoration (the original had been taken from him by American soldiers when he was taken prisoner) for the entire regiment.

One day during the daily roll call the commander realized that four men had disappeared. When he reported this to the camp commander the AM became furious and threatened to have the senior German officer shot for failing to maintain discipline. The latter answered this rebuke by reminding the camp commander that the American troops were responsible for guarding the prisoners. Furthermore the four had fled only out of fear that the entire camp would be handed over to the Russians. If he could have an assurance that they would not be handed over, then it would be unlikely that there would be any more escape attempts. These considerations had the effect of calming down the American commander.

On 28 May another 1,900 men of the Waff*en-SS* arrived in our camp. The *Wehrmacht* camp was forced to let us have one of its buildings.

The period from 29 May to 8 June passed relatively monotonously. Our rations were totally inadequate. One day the senior officer was told that the prisoners could trade valuables for bread with the American guards at the watch towers. He immediately went to the American camp commander and informed him that forbidden such bartering. He requested that he issue a similar ban for the American guards to avoid a repetition of this mutually unworthy picture. It was therefore all the more important to improve the camp rations. The American agreed; however, the improved rations were a long time coming.

9 June: A new American sentry fired into the camp and hit three men who were sunbathing. One was killed, the other two were wounded. In spite of intervention the reason remained a mystery. Allegedly one man had put a foot across the three-meter boundary, in which the guards shot immediately. Only a very few of the dead man's comrades were permitted to leave the camp for his burial.

A short time later another shot was fired during the noon rest. A few moments later the senior German officer and the camp commander met at the scene. A dead Obe*rscharführer* lay at the outer barbed wire fence. While he had stepped into the three-meter death zone with the permission of the outer sentry in order to trade his watch for bread, the other sentry, who could cover the three-meter zone with his machine-gun from the flank, shot the man down from a distance of about ten meters. The man was buried in the cemetery in Klattau. Neither the senior officer nor another officer were allowed to go to the burial, which was attended only by three or four of the dead man's friends.

From 10 to 16 June the rations were reduced even further. They now allegedly provided just 800 calories per day. We sought diversions to counter depression, boredom and hunger.

17 June to 3 July: As a result of several interventions and after talks with the American commander, we were given permission to supplement our rations ourselves. Money that had been carefully hidden and thus survived the various "friskings" was collected from everyone in the SS camp. We received permission to take a truck under guard and drive to the farms around Klattau to buy potatoes, peas, beans, lentils and bread. From this day on our there was a marked improvement in our rations.

SS Camp
Klattau, 22 June 1945

Menu for 23 June 1945

| | | |
|---|---|---|
| Lunch: | One-pot pea dinner | |
| | Tinned corned beef | 50 g |
| | Peas | 50 g |
| | Fresh potatoes | 300 g |
| | Dried onions | |
| Supper: | Bread soup | |
| | Bread (one loaf for ten men) | 100 g |
| | Clarified butter | 10 g |
| | Sugar | 50 g |

For work details:
One load of bread for each six men and one tin of corned beef for each fourteen men.

The young were especially well taken care of. Their rations were supplemented by with an egg. The worst cases of malnourishment of boys under the age of eighteen, who had faded away to skeletons, were shown by the senior officer to the senior American officers who visited the camp. In each case these occasions were used to request an improvement in the camp rations.

Work details were now permitted to work outside the camp in exchange for better food. A camp theater was put together under the leadership of Ustuf. von Ammon and its presentations provided distractions.

One day the leader of an outside work detail reported that the Czechs had taken away several members of the detail. They emptied their canteens, took away their bread and stood them against the side of a house in the blazing heat. The prisoners were not allowed to move for an entire hour. Another SS man was beaten so badly by the Czechs that his back was covered with red welts.

The senior camp officer protested to the American commander and showed him the men who had been mistreated. He reminded him that the American guards were responsible for the safety of German prisoners of war and asked him to take steps to prevent such incidents. The American, by the way an excellent soldier of Greek origin who soon afterward volunteered to serve in the Far East, was furious at his guards and even more furious at the Czechs. He assured the senior German officer that he would immediately order his guards to open fire should another Czech dare lay hands on a German prisoner.

A short time later he drove out to the work detail with the senior German officer and showed him that his guards had surrounded the work column and that it was impossible to get through the line of guards from the outside. The senior officer expressed his thanks for the American's correct attitude. There were no more incidents after this.

Another 123 Waffen-*SS* men came to the camp from Marienbad.

4 July: Two members of a work detail gave the following account of the mistreatment of German women in the Klattau prison:

> "On 3 July 1945 we were assigned to a work detail for labor service in the Klattau prison. Working with us there were three German women from the Klattau prison. According to them, one German had killed her two children in the cell because of the constant mistreatment. Another woman attempted suicide.
>
> *Furthermore they said that there were also SS men in the prison, one of whom tried to complain to the American guard about the bad treatment. He was later so badly beaten for this that he died.*
>
> *An artist was forced to paint a picture showing SS men mistreating Czech children.*
>
> *The food in the prison was said to be very bad.*

> *According to a woman from Essen their children had been taken away from them.*
>
> *The women said that they had been searched for weapons in the marketplace and stripped naked. They received the same treatment each time they were interrogated.*
>
> *These are the statements as they were made to us by the women."*
> *(Two signatures)*

The report was passed on to the American camp commander with a request to look into it. On it was noted:

> "Since it is possible that the wives of members of the SS are there, there is great anger in the camp over their treatment."

The camp officers never received an answer to their request.

One day the German Protestant minister from Klattau prison visited us in the camp. He was completely starved and emaciated and described the awful conditions in the prison. Men, women and children, wounded, seriously ill and old people lay crowded together in a hall. He described mistreatments, suicide attempts, deaths and a rapid decline in the morale and will to resist of the German prisoners, the majority of whom were women, because of the deplorable conditions. The camp officers invited the minister to supper and shared what little they had with him. The only help the prisoners of war could give him was a large sum of money which would enable him to intervene in the most serious cases.

In other cases the SS camp send help by way of the work party to German families whose plight was especially serious.

The former American camp commander was relieved by Captain Drumheller. As a result of various conversations with the senior officer of the SS camp and the good behavior of the SS men, both camp commanders, front-line officers, came to a more objective disposition toward our problems. Captain Drumheller had faced the "DF" Regiment during the Ardennes campaign and knew the names "Das *Reich*" Division and "*Der Führer*" Regiment very well. When we asked, he confirmed that he knew these units as decent and fair opponents and he was unaware of any war crimes committed by members of this division. There was no "fraternizing" by either the Americans or Germans, however each showed respect and understanding toward the other.

10 July: The former regimental commander and his staff assumed the leadership of the entire camp with 6,150 men.

11 July: The former senior We*hrmacht* officer, *Major* Horn, and the last members of the *Wehrmacht* left the camp. As a result conditions became less crowded and there were easier days.

27-28 July: Another 180 officers and non-commissioned officers arrived from Eipowitz.

The behavior of several members of the penal platoon, which was in the camp, caused the camp leadership serious problems. The penal platoon consisted of former SS men who had been convicted of military or criminal offenses and kicked out of the SS but who nevertheless continued to wear their uniforms without rank badges and were deployed at the front within the SS. Several of them now thought that their time had come and that they could gain advantages at the expense of the camp leadership. They had free access to the CIC at any time and denounced anyone who gave them the least cause to do so.

The senior German officer took the problem to the American camp commander and declared that unless this situation was changed he could no longer be responsible for discipline in the camp and would have to step down as camp leader. Thereupon the American camp commander gave instructions for an order in English and German bearing his signature to be hung at several places in the camp; it stated that no inmate of the camp might go to the CIC without first asking permission of the German and American camp commanders.

An order arrived for transfer to Germany. Everyone breathed a sigh of relief: the danger of a handover to Russian was gone! The camp theater gave farewell performances, the camp inmates were assigned to three different camps.

30 July: At 8 AM the inmates assigned to A Transport for Weiden set off on foot for the loading station Klattau. The 1,954 men were from the regions Anhalt, West Prussia and foreign. The column marched in step, and soon the song "When the Colorful Banners Fly" sprang up from the throats of almost 2,000 men. The American guards also fell into step and obviously enjoyed the lively song. But soon the American camp com-

mand received the first protests from the Czechs and singing was banned even as the march to the station was in progress.

At 2 PM the B Transport bound for Sulzbach-Rosenberg set off for the station. It, too, consisted of 1,954 men, this time from the regions of Salzburg, Upper Danube West, Vorarlberg, Carinthia, Tyrol, Lower Danube, Styria and Brandenburg. Since singing was forbidden, the column whistled their farewell song. But even now the Czechs protested and the whistling had to be stopped – much to the regret of the American guards.

1 August: After a silent march, C Transport bound for Regensburg with 1,490 men from the regions of Bavaria, the rest of Austria, Baden, Württemberg and Brunswick together with the camp leadership boarded at the station and departed at 8 AM. The American camp commander bade farewell to the camp leadership correctly.

At 2 PM D Transport, the last, moved off for Weiden with 497 men from the regions of Rheinpfalz, Hamburg, Bremen, Lübeck, Magdeburg and Halle-Merseburg and the rest of the men in the sick bay. As we later learned, the two transports to Weiden fared worst of all, because they were delivered to the former concentration camp at Flossenburg and there, especially in the beginning, experienced very bad and bullying treatment.

## In Prisoner of War Camp 22 – Regensburg

2 August: Transport C arrived in the camp, which had been set up for approximately 12,000 to 15,000 prisoners. The men from Klattau stood out here in that they still wore rank badges and saluted. The first difficulties soon appeared. The CIC soon forbade the salute.

The shipment of men moved into half-finished barracks with no roofs, as a result of which a large percentage of the men were practically sleeping under the open sky in spite of the already cold nights. Our own specialists soon put roofs on the barracks and more or less finished them.

Rations were meager and the daily routine consisted of slogans, roll calls and checks.

From one place in the camp one could see in the clear, sunny late-summer days the Walhalla, the memorial to great Germans, an uplifting sight in a disconsolate time.

30 August: The 1927-28 age class was registered. There was talk that it would soon be released.

Meanwhile a very good camp theater with an outstanding showmaster (Gert Knabe) became active.

Unexpectedly, in those days all prisoners received American C-rations – as we later learned on General Patton's order. On account of their caloric content they represented a significant and much welcomed improvement in our rations.

A tragic accident suddenly shattered our daily life. One day the block officer was called into one of the barracks, in which three men had suddenly died and three more were experiencing severe cramps. They had celebrated a birthday during the night and brewed a "liquor" from wood alcohol, cocoa and sugar. The block officer immediately had the ambulance summoned and the three men who were fighting for their lives were transported to the hospital. Fortunately they could be saved, only one lost the sight in one eye.

During September our own personnel, organized into work teams, made the barracks ready for winter.

At the beginning of October the men from Klettau were moved from Block 3 to Block 6.

The first "black" visits by family members were secretly carried out at the fence, usually at a distance of about ten meters. The American sentries often looked to the side with silent patience, but sometimes things went wrong. Some wives of camp inmates were suddenly arrested at the fence, sent to the women's prison in Regensburg and brought before a military court. The sentences handed down ranged from eight days to three months.

While on watchtower duty many of the Americans passed the time by shooting sparrows in the camp. Once a bullet entered the infirmary barrack and one of the patients was fatally wounded.

Shots were also occasionally fired at the visitors in order to keep them away from the fence. One young man from Regensburg, who wanted to pass his brother some food through the wire, was forced to pay for this with his life.

# In Prisoner of War Camp 430 – Landshut

17 November 1945: All officers were moved to POW 430 in Landshut together with all the officers from the small Camp Saal near Regensburg. 300 officers were accommodated in Hall 5 in three-level bunk beds.

We found it especially depressing that there had been a total ban on mail since the start of our captivity, or for six months, and many were still in total uncertainty as to the fate of their relatives.

The SS camp formed the third section of the general camp, in which there were approximately 150 generals and general staff officers, some of them well known, under the leadership of the former army commander Ge*neraloberst* Hoth.

The former camp leadership from Klattau and the block leadership from Regensburg also took over the leadership of the SS camp here. From the very first cooperation with the leadership of the general camp was excellent.

3 December: Our comrades from Austria were moved to Ebensee and Glasenbach. The farewell was very heartfelt and we were sad to see them leave. We had shared so may tough, difficult days during the war years and in captivity and endured them in best comradeship.

An extremely varied cultural life soon developed in the camp. Under expert direction a camp orchestra and large camp choir were formed. We enjoyed our own variety stage with its varied program; the Americans liked it too and never missed a performance. There were concerts, poetry readings, morning ceremonies, and courses in English and French as well as in various specialized fields. A well-known female singer gave several song recitals in the camp, a special cultural treat for which we were grateful.

One day we received a visit from Bishop Neuhäußler of Munich, who had come to Landshut for confirmations. We were especially pleased about this visit from outside. After the service the senior officer informed him of his worries and problems, such as inadequate food, inadequate care for the sick, no mail and other things. The bishop was visibly impressed by what he heard and promised to what he could to help within his very modest limits.

Another time a Swedish delegation of the Red Cross came to inspect the camp. The senior officer also informed them of our most pressing problems. A request for sports equipment such as fistballs, boxing gloves, etc, was fulfilled within a short time. The favorite sport in the camp was fistball, and there were many heated competitions.

On Memorial Day 1945 Gener*aloberst* Hoth issued an order of the day containing moving words on the meaning of sacrifice.

And then came our first Christmas in captivity. The hills surrounding the camp lay beneath a deep blanket of snow – a magnificent winter landscape.

On the evening of 21 December there was an outdoor celebration of the winter solstice. The men formed up in an open square around a pile of wood and the senior camp officer reported the assembled company present to Ge*neraloberst* Hoth.

Meanwhile American tanks had driven up around the camp, the muzzles of their cannon and machine-guns pointing menacingly at the camp. Apparently they feared that trouble and escape attempts in these days, which so profoundly spoke to the German soul.

*Generaloberst* Hoth found soldierly, but at the same time consoling and reflective words for the winter solstice in captivity. He said:

> "Today our thoughts wander back to the last years of the war, in which we often had to fight hard instead of celebrate. I myself think with deep emotion of Christmas Day 1942, when 'Wiking' soldiers, in true brotherhood in arms, relieved my army headquarters at Sinoviki south of Stalingrad in bloody street fighting after Red tanks had broken through. With the same gratitude I remember the three oldest SS divisions, 'Leibstandarte', 'Das Reich' and 'Totenkopf', which were under my command in the spring and summer of 1943 for the last great German offensive near Kharkov and which added new glory to their banners there. It will always be one of my proudest memories that the supreme commander had entrusted to me three battle-hardened SS divisions... Our thoughts today go to our families, there are many among us who do not even know where theirs are. I had devoutly wished to at least be able to obtain permission for a Christmas salute for you. My request was not granted in keeping with an unlawful and cruel rule!..."

The camp leader movingly thanked the *Generaloberst* for his touching words and added:

> "We have fought hard and passionately for Germany. Fate has willed it otherwise than we could ever have dreamed. Nevertheless we intend to bear our fate upright and manfully. At the time of the great victories it was east to declare one's faith in one's ideals. Today, when everything has collapsed, when rank and name, money and relationships no longer mean anything, it is endlessly more difficult to stand up for one's opinion and protect one's ideals. In these months we are experiencing the greatest test of character that was ever placed upon us. We want to and will pass it."

When the *Generaloberst*'s speech was over the pile of wood burst into flames, then the men, lost in thought and deeply moved by this unforgettable and unusual solstice celebration, returned to their quarters.

Simple but meaningful celebrations were held in the various quarters on Christmas Eve and New Year's Eve. The old familiar Christmas carols rang out into the winter night. The Christmas and New Year's Eve speeches were given by the camp leader.

The presents that came into the camp for Christmas came from the Bavarian Association of Roman Catholic Charitable Organizations. The camp leader sent a letter to Bishop Dr. Neuhäußler thanking him for the gifts, the collection of which he had organized.

Over New Year's the American tanks standing guard were bolstered by mortars!

The inspiring holidays could not conceal the fact that every single man was having a difficult time bearing his personal fate. This was especially true of the disabled and seriously disabled, whose treatment was lacking in spite of the efforts of our camp doctor. For example they were denied badly needed follow-up amputations and massages. They suffered most from the inadequate quarters and the severe cold. The crushing uncertainty over the fate of their relatives weighed on very many, as there was still a total ban on the exchange of mail seven months after the cessation of hostilities. The ban had been lifted for the general camp some time earlier.

The Landshut camp had one big advantage over the Regensburg camp: visits at the camp wire were officially permitted on Sundays between 1 and 6 PM. It was almost a miracle how many wives learned of our whereabouts in spite of the ban on mail and how many people gathered at the camp wire every Sunday. While the presence of two barbed wire fences prevented physical contact, prisoners and visitors could see and talk to each other. And so every Sunday countless prisoners stood opposite their relatives and called their experiences to them. For many it was their first contact with their loved ones at home. These visiting days resulted in a major boost in camp morale. Sometimes the visitors were permitted to deliver parcels to the camp gate. These were examined closely by the American guards, nevertheless many letters were smuggled into the camp in this way.

On 2 January 1946 the camp leader once again asked in a letter to the American camp commander for the release of the mail that had arrived and for permission for all prisoners of war to write letters, since receiving letters had been permitted in all prisoner of war camps since 1 September 1945 and writing letters since 15 December 1945. Furthermore he made reference to a report by Bavarian radio on 1 January 1946 which stated that effective that day all civilian internees in Bavaria were permitted to send and receive mail.

As a result of the camp leader's petition each prisoner was allowed to send word to his family on a preprinted double-sided postcard and inform them of his address.

Finally, on 26 January 1946, the huge quantity of mail that had collected was released in batches after being censored. Everyone breathed a sigh of relief. This represented a major step forward, for with the receipt of mail the nagging uncertainty about relatives was relieved.

Sadly, many now grieved over the death of relatives. Others were happy that someone thought dead was found to be alive. Many received news that their marriages had broken up. Many others received no mail at all and had to go on living with the uncertainty about the fate of their families.

A fine young Fleming, who had joined the Waffen-SS as a European volunteer, attempted suicide, because he learned through his mail that his family had been tormented and harassed because of him. A few minutes later the camp senior officer was by his bed, comforted him and encouraged him to go on living; fortunately the young man overcame his desperation. The sudden onrush of events had simply been too much for him.

Of the men who received no mail, most were from the eastern parts of Germany, from East and West Prussia, Danzig, Silesia, Pomerania and the Sudetenland. The urge for freedom in these men became ever stronger, and it is not surprising, therefore, that many tried to get out of the camp to search for their families themselves.

In fact many did succeed in getting past the wire. Attempts were made in diverse ways. However, one man who tried at night to crawl to the fence at a poorly-lit spot was shot by the American sentry in the next watchtower.

One especially daring fellow walked past the sentry through the gate in broad daylight with a surveyor's pole over his shoulder and told the sentry that he had to take the pole to a work detail. The bored American said 'Okay' and the prisoner was outside. He calmly walked toward several houses, leaned his pole against the side of a house – and was never seen again!

Others escaped through the drainage system. However escape became more difficult daily. The exits, including those of the drainage system, were closely guarded. Extra foot patrols were employed at night and finally the drainage system was mined!

New fields of work developed in the camp with the manufacture of wallets and slippers from twine in every possible color and style; during the Sunday visits these articles were given to relatives as small presents.

30 January: Because of this day the Americans once again moved in tanks. As on New Year's Eve, there was a "counter-demonstration" with the lusty singing of "Only Freedom Belongs to Our Lives." The next day we heard that the guards had enjoyed the lovely singing of the prisoners.

9 February: One-thousand men arrived from the Plattling camp.

Especially popular were our boxing matches, which were under the direction of a well-known amateur boxer. The boxing gloves had been sent to us by the Red Cross. Our workmen had built a regulation ring.

*General* Beuckemann, who had received permission from the American camp commander to listen to the daily news on a small radio, passed this on to the camp in the form of a brief summary. These accounts of events outside the barbed wire, which took place once a week, were very popular and extremely well attended. Especially closely followed was the Nuremberg Trial, which had already begun and lasted many months.

Another general had built up an extensive camp library which was much used by all of the camp inmates.

29 March: The American authorities demanded that all inmates fill out the large questionnaire for civilian internees with 132 questions. These included very personal questions which could in no way be considered democratic, for example which party one had voted for in 1932.

In agreement with all of the comrades the camp leader rejected this unreasonable demand as it was incompatible with our status as prisoners of war. The American camp commander declared himself to be satisfied with this declaration.

2 April: The camp leader had meanwhile contacted the defender of the SS at Nuremberg, Dr. Babel, by letter. On his advice a defense committee was formed in the camp; it assembled exonerating evidence for the Waff*en-SS* in Nuremberg in the camp, especially sworn statements from generals who had had *Waffen-SS* divisions placed under their command.

All young men were examined for fitness to work with the labor forces in France. Because of the serious malnourishment the insightful and responsible German camp doctor found so few suitable candidates that the matter was dropped.

On 30 April 1946 the SS defense attorney, Dr. Babel, arrived in the camp. The next day there were lengthy discussions between the camp leader and the lawyer.

Before he went on to the Regensburg camp, he spent a social hour with us one evening and was surprised by the artistic standard of the choir and the orchestra and deeply impressed by the devotion with which the men sang and played.

8 May: On the anniversary of the surrender the camp commander Gene*raloberst* Hoth issued the following order of the day:

9 May 1946

*"Today is the first anniversary of the day on which the bulk of the German armed forces laid down their weapons after a fight to*

*the end. Sadly we think of this day and the consequences for our people and every one of us that sprang from it. Driven to the outer frontiers of the Reich by an overwhelming superiority, deprived of the means to wage war, there was no longer any prospect of a successful resistance. Standing erect, conscious of having kept our soldier's honor untarnished, in the firm belief of having fought six years for the good cause of our people, we began the march into captivity.*

*None of us could know that it would go on interminably, that they intended to take from us the last thing we had: our soldierly honor, our own respect for ourselves. What bitter months lie behind us, months of deepest spiritual and physical distress. Today, after a year as prisoners, we can proudly declare: we have not fallen prey to desperation, we are still standing erect, we have recognized the goal worth fighting for: to resist with all our might the intention to defame our German race before the world and burden it with a guilt which we will never acknowledge as justified.*

*It is not possible for us to publicly express our feelings on this day of deep sadness. We intend, however, to cease all work for half an hour and forgo the relaxation in games and conversation which usually takes place at this time.*

*I therefore order:*

*On 9 May 1946, between 6:30 and 7 PM, no one is to enter the streets and open areas of the camp. Everyone will remain quietly in his room.*

*Signed Hoth, Generaloberst"*

We experienced a wonderfully warm spring and early summer. Our workmen built benches at suitable places and everywhere one saw sun worshipers eager to brown themselves in the warm sunshine after the long, cold winter.

16 May: The general camp was disbanded and moved to Garmisch. This meant saying goodbye to our respected camp commander *Generaloberst* Hoth, whose deportment and behavior toward the Americans in the past months had been an example to everyone. During the

farewell ceremony, the setting for which was provided by the choir and the orchestra, those leaving sat mixed in with those who were staying. The *Generaloberst* exchanged manly and moving words with the camp leader. The departing camp commander climaxed his speech by saying: "If I have regained my belief in the German people, then it is only because of the exemplary behavior of the SS men in this camp!"

19 May: Finally there was a happy day for us in the camp, one which gave us all hope for an early release. All SS men, up to the rank of U*nterscharführer*, whose homes were in the American zone, were released. 420 men left the camp!

Everywhere one saw happy, beaming faces. For those staying behind truly celebrated with those being released. Many of them had picked a town at random in the American zone, since they came from the occupied eastern areas, had lost their old home and had to seek a new one. Many of the returnees took a homeless comrade home with him. At first many found no other way out than to work as civilian employees of the American authorities, as they were welcome workers there and were treated decently, while the German authorities knew how to make life especially difficult for newly released prisoners of war of the W*affen-SS*.

For those staying behind, however, there was one regret mixed in with the shared joy of the departure: for on this day we lost our youth, whose carefreeness and joyful light-heartedness had often helped us endure the past difficult times.

At the camp gate the camp leader said goodbye to every man, and they spontaneously gave their former regimental commander a last salute. We who were staying behind waved after them until they had disappeared from our view.

6 June: The camp orchestra gave a farewell concert for the enlisted men and non-commissioned officers who were released into the British zone on this day.

9 June: Release papers were made out for all the remaining inmates of the camp. Each received 80 Rei*chsmarks* discharge pay. But the release papers were not issued to us.

10 June: On this day (Whit Monday), following a generally formal interrogation, everyone was placed in civilian internee status. A so-called Automatic Arrest Report was made out for each of us – and so we had

suddenly become civilian internees. In spite of all protests by the camp inmates and in spite of the absence of any basis in international law, there was nothing we could do about it.

In the very rare cases where comrades clearly placed themselves on the side of the occupying power in order to trick and denounce their comrades, then the entire camp opposed these denouncers with single-minded determination.

At the end of June it was announced that the Landshut camp was being disbanded and that all inmates were to be transferred to the civilian internee at Regensburg.

29 June: The last camp inmates were ready to leave. At 11 AM all were loaded into trucks and at approximately 1 PM arrived in our old camp at Regensburg.

## In the Regensburg Civilian Internee Camp

Our former camp was in the midst of being transformed into a camp for civilian internees. We "Landshuters" occupied Block 9, and the former camp leader now became block senior officer. Here, too, an orchestra and camp choir had been formed in the previous months, performing among others the works of Bruckner, Schumann and Weber.

27 August: 3,600 men arrived from Langwasser near Nuremberg. With them came *Generaloberst* Hausser and *General* Gille, the last German foreign minister Count Schwerin von Kroszigk, several other ministers, state secretaries, senior ministerial officials, *Gauleiters* and other high-ranking personalities from the party and state. In this way we internees learned many interesting facts and incidents, whose contexts would otherwise always have remained unclear and dark.

30 September: After months of negotiations the "Nuremberg Judgement" was rendered. With the exception of the mounted SS, the entire SS was branded a criminal organization. We took the judgement calmly – conscious that this unjust collective judgement could not brand us as criminals. We knew that we had done our duty in the war and as soldiers and that all judgements to the contrary were the products of the most evil propaganda, and that in terms of willingness to serve and courage the

W*affen-SS* could count itself among the bravest units of the German Army. Rarely was there ever such pure idealism as in the ranks of the *Waffen-SS*.

Neither could we take seriously the accusations that we had planned the war and that the *Waffen-SS* had been intentionally created for the purpose of committing crimes. Our present eighteen-year-olds were just six years old when the Nazis came to power! The vast majority of us were still under age in 1933.

So ultimately the Nuremberg judgement achieved something that it surely never intended: it fortified in extraordinary fashion the inner cohesion of the former members of the W*affen-SS*.

12 October: The camp was prepared for the coming winter. For the first time German sentries in green uniforms and armed with rifles patrolled the camp, having relieved the Polish guards. So it had come to this! German soldiers were being guarded by Germans in the middle of Germany!

On one occasion several of the civilian internees witnessed the following scene: an old woman pushing a handcart loaded with manure passed one of the German guards. He called to her: "Granny, that's a dirty job you're doing!" The old woman replied: "My business is still cleaner than yours!"

A large display with amateur handcrafts and works of art by the internees was organized under the motto "By your works shall they know you." The Americans eagerly bought the items on display.

Meantime a democratic camp order was introduced. The direction lay in the hands of three mayors assisted by their district councils and spokesmen. Each block had to select a spokesman in a secret vote. The current senior officer was chosen as spokesman for Block 9.

1 November: Visitor barracks were opened in which daily visits were allowed.

13 November: The camp trial court began to work. For the time being, however, it only viewed material. We believed that we could see the end of captivity lighting up like a silver strip on the horizon.

18 November: All outside parties were cancelled, since with the beginning of trial court proceedings escape attempts were feared.

24 December: We celebrated Christmas Eve reflectively and quietly in our individual barracks. The most important things to us were the pack-

ages and letters from home, which as a Christmas surprise had been kept from us and were now distributed. There was no celebration of the winter solstice.

25 December: At 9 AM the Bishop of Regensburg, Dr. Buchberger, held a solemn Pontifical Mass for the internees in the camp, during which the Regensburg Cathedral Sparrows sang their well-known, familiar Christmas carols. It was a special kind of Christmas present which we accepted with grateful joy. The year 1946 rang out with intimate New Year's Eve celebrations in the individual barracks.

12 January 1947: The men from the different regions were transported to their various homes.

The first to go were the Württembergers, who were moved to Kornwestheim. With them the former regimental commander left the Regensburg camp. For him this was the actual hour of his departure from his regiment, with which he had been allowed so many unforgettable experiences. A number of members of his regiment accompanied him to the camp gate. Generalob*erst* Hausser and *General* Gille had been shipped out shortly before this. They, too, were escorted to the camp exit by us.

15 January: The Hessians left the camp and went to Darmstadt, while the Bavarians from Ludwigsburg and Hohenasperg were moved to Regensburg.

25 January: On orders from high up the first democratic assembly took place in the camp.

7 February: A large scale surprise raid was carried out on the camp by 900 state police, during which a search was made for escape materials. Nothing suspicious was found and the big operation ended without fanfare.

1 April: Finally, after two years imprisonment, the disabled were released.

8 May: The former members of the regiment had been behind barbed wire for two years!

In the second half of 1947 the release of the remaining camp inmates finally began.

## Handover to France
## In Military Pretrial Detention

For about 250 men of the former "*Das Reich*" Division, including approximately 40 to 50 members of the "*Der Führer*" Regiment, captivity was far from over, however. The worst was still before them.

They had been collected from all the camps in the American zone by a French commission under Captain Tretnel and were now gathered in the special camp at Dachau – the former concentration camp.

And so after having "graduated" from Camp 75 at Kornwestheim and Camp 74 at Ludwigsburg, the former regimental commander was taken from Civilian Internee Camp 76 at Hohenasperg and together with several members of the division was transported to Dachau, where he met many old acquaintances. All of the new arrivals were forced to spend the first three days packed six or seven to a one-man cell, then they were directed into the special camp.

From there the members of the "Das *Reich*" Division were delivered to France.

On 12 August 1947 it was approximately sixty men. French military police picked up the truck transport at Dachau. All of the prisoners had to sit on the floor with their knees drawn up, packed tightly together, and they spent the entire four-hour journey to Reutlingen in that uncomfortable position. They were repeatedly harassed and yelled at by their guards. In one truck the prisoners' cigarettes were taken away, and one prisoner was mishandled by a guard with a bayonet and was wounded. There was just one brief rest stop during the entire trip.

Everyone was glad when this awful transport ended in Reutlingen. All of the Germans who were to be taken to France for trial were assembled in the former French prison. The last commander of the "De*utschland*" Regiment, Günther Wisliceny, also arrived there.

19 August: The former division members were transported to the special camp at Lahr-Dinglingen for members of the "D*as Reich*" Division. Above the entrance to this camp stood in large letters: *Camp de Concentration* (concentration camp).

Lahr-Dinglingen was a large civilian internee camp which also included a women's camp. It was guarded by German police. The French authorities decreed that no policeman who had not spent a certain time at the beginning of his career guarding his own countrymen in an internment camp could enter the French zone.

The special camp within the big camp was guarded by heavily-armed Frenchmen carrying machine-guns. Treatment was particularly bad and malicious. Shaving was forbidden – supposedly to prevent suicides. The food was terrible. The total ban on mail, which had been lifted eighteen months earlier in Landshut, was reintroduced. Only now and then was it possible to smuggle out letters through the German guards.

The following incidents are described here in order to illustrate the manner in which the camp was run and the situation at that time: drunken French military policemen often went through the barracks at night, opened the doors, shouted to wake the prisoners and forced them to report present by shouting "Achtung!"

All signs in the camp and the borders around the gardens were painted in the French colors blue-white-red.

The entire big camp, including the women's camp, was forced to turn out each day for the flag parade, and a German civilian internee was forced to lower the tricolor as the Mars*eillaise* was played. Subsequently all of the internees, including the women, had to march past with eyes turned toward the French commandant. A woman was once placed under arrest because she had looked straight ahead instead of looking at the commandant.

The mother of one of the comrades who was in the special camp with us was in the women's camp, while his father was being held in another internment camp. Once his mother was sentenced to three days arrest because she was found with a letter she had written to her husband. The son was arrested at the same time and mother and son ended up in the same arrest barracks.

For security reasons the special camp was not required to take part in the evening flag parade, which was only right to the prisoners. On one occasion during the ceremony things appeared too loud in the SS camp for the French and as soon as the parade was over French military police armed with submachine-guns entered the special camp, rousted the prisoners from their barracks and forced them to run around the barracks for half an hour, the two regimental commanders in the lead, until they collapsed from weakness and exhaustion and could go no farther. An older, white-haired comrade suffered a heart attack and collapsed at the barbed wire. The prisoners were herded back into the barracks, lungs burning.

There was no German camp leader in this special camp, no kind of representation for German interests – only prisoners or to put it better "criminals."

One day the two regimental commanders were questioned by an American officer in the presence of the French camp commander in his office. While the camp commander sat at his desk they quietly described the awful conditions in the camp to the American officer. The latter shrugged his shoulders regretfully: once the prisoners had been turned over there was nothing more that the Americans could do.

Several women tried to visit their husbands in the camp but this was and remained forbidden.

As a special "marking" red SS runes were painted in red on the backs of the inmates uniform jackets. Every conceivable measure was taken to make escape impossible. In September another transport arrived from Germersheim with members of the "Das Re*ich*" Division.

The months spent in the Lahr-Dinglingen special camp were the worst of the entire captivity.

On 16 November the former commander of the "De*r Führer*" Regiment was summoned to the camp commander's office with all his luggage. There he was told that he was being sent to Bordeaux. During the journey he was to speak to no one. In Bordeaux he was brought before the court. Guarded by two gendarmes and in handcuffs, he was driven by car to Strasbourg where he was placed in a reserved compartment of a train for transport to Bordeaux via Paris. The trip took two days. When the policemen saw that their prisoner had not been given any food for the trip, they kindly shared their rations with him.

18 November 1947: Arrival in Bordeaux and delivery to a military jail.

Several members of the "Re*ich*" Division were already there. Some of them had been delivered by the British.

The members of the division were now to be made responsible for all of the actions which the division had to carry out against the m*aquisards*.

In his first interrogation the former commander of the "*Der Führer*" Regiment was accused of being responsible for the actions of a German battalion in Tulle. He appealed this charge as it lacked any basis in fact. He assumed that the trial would soon be called off.

However, almost nothing happened for a year. The investigating judge, Captain Lesieur, was obviously uncertain as to how to go about investigating such a complex case.

In the summer of 1948, however, it appeared that the first members of the division would soon be able to go home with a "no*n lieu*" (dropping of the case). The release was announced by the French lawyer. Expectations were raised sky-high, but nothing happened. The long court vacation began, and for weeks nothing was done.

When the court resumed sitting the prisoners received the depressing news that the collective guilt law, the so-called L*ex Oradour*, had been passed in the meantime and that consequently no one could be released. According to this law anyone could be seen as a perpetrator and punished even if he was only a member at the same time in the same area of a unit accused of crimes by the court.

The anger among the prisoners at this unprecedented law was great. Even in France itself voices were raised in criticism of this retroactive collective law.

Meantime many members of the division had arrived.

Gradually it became apparent according to which fundamentals the investigation was to be carried out.

The members of the division were accused of all "crimes" committed in southern France within a certain radius of the division's quarters. These now had to prove that they were not personally involved. This "reversal of the burden of proof" was the direct result of the fact that the SS had been declared a criminal organization by the Nuremberg judgement.

Regarding the march to Normandy, a strip of land on both sides of the advance road of approximately thirty kilometers was laid down. The same rules as above also applied to this second part of the trial: all combat operations that took place in this area during a certain time were charged to the division as "crimes" and once again each individual had to prove his innocence. The military court considered as "crimes" practically every combat operation against maqui*sard* bases. Every house that caught fire as a result was considered arson, ever dead among the maquisards and the civilian population murder according to civil law. The court ignored, however, the fact that following the Allied declaration, at the time of the march the *maquisards* were already considered regular troops by them, and thus operations against them fell under the heading of normal combat operations.

Two years later, in 1950, the actual interrogations began. The division members came from Periguieux in batches, arranged by unit. Through the paying of the lawyers, which was done by the Central Legal Protection Office in Bonn, the lawyers, who at first were acting as court-appointed counselors, became freely chosen defense attorneys.

Sometimes they expressed their amazement to us prisoners that while the federal German government was supporting the prisoners materially and financially, since its creation it had never demanded that France return the imprisoned Germans, which should have been expected of any government. The prisoners, too, could not understand the federal government's position on this point.

On the other hand, in material things the German prisoners of war in France had been supported by the federal government since 1949; each prisoner received 1,000 Francs each month, equal to about 12 DM. As well, underwear was issued several times and each prisoner received a new civilian suit and a pair of shoes.

The Protestant pastor Friedrich and the Catholic priest Prokop earned special merit in caring for the prisoners. Both did much to ease the suffering of the prisoners and were the only personal link to Germany. We will always owe them our gratitude.

Pastor Friedrich's health deteriorated during these years of tiring work. He returned to Germany a sick man and died in his home parish a few years after completing his mission.

In spring 1951, before the start of the various trials, the first members of the division were finally released after their cases were dropped. Everyone was very happy. The ice had finally been broken – a beginning had been made!

The former regimental commander had to undergo three different trials of inquiry. After the finding of "non lie*u*" for Tulle, he was supposed to be made responsible for all the happenings in the regiment's quartering area in southern France and along the march road into Normandy. Fortunately, however, he was able to prove that he was on leave when the events in southern France took place and that he had not taken over the regiment until after its arrival in Normandy. This case was also dropped. Nevertheless, he and about fifty men of the division, who were in the same situation, were to be brought before the court. The sole remaining charge: voluntary membership in the *Waffen-SS*.

Meanwhile the French side had also taken up the struggle against the inhuman collective guilt law. The former chief French judge at Nuremberg, Donnedieu du Fabre had bluntly characterized the "*Lex Oradour*" as "legalized genocide." So this fateful law was gradually dismantled by France herself and was not used again in practice. The individual trials against the various units of the division began in June.

The legal proceedings against the first fifty men of the division took place on 19 June 1951; among them was the former commander of the "D*er Führer*" Regiment. Through fortunate circumstances it had not taken part in any actions against *maquisards*. The trial lasted all day, and since it was expected that everyone would be found innocent, no spectators were invited. Only two German students and an English woman watched the trial. Dr. Roemer attended as representative of the federal German government.

In his closing statement for the accused the former commander of the "D*er Führer*" Regiment thanked the French attorneys for their defense and for their summation, in which they said everything possible to refute the charges. He said how much every German regretted the sacrifices that the struggle against the *maquisards* had cost both sides and concluded with the words: "In the name of my comrades I would like to state emphatically that we only did our duty for our nation and for our people!"

There was great joy when the court clerk called into the big arrest cell behind the courtroom, in which everyone was tensely awaiting the verdict: "T*ous acquittés*!" (all not guilty).

The very next day everyone traveled via Paris and Kehl to Tuttlingen, where they received their release papers from French captivity. Previously they had stopped for a day in Paris in order to experience the beauty of the city on the Seine and climb the Eiffel Tower. They received all possible support from the German embassy. Otto Weidinger took the opportunity to discuss with the embassy's legal advisor the problems facing the Germans still in Bordeaux and possible measures to help them.

The prisoners had to endure further petty harassment from the French police when they crossed the border. After six and a quarter years as prisoners they finally walked away from Tuttlingen as free men!

The various trials for the individual units of the division were completed in the weeks and months to come. Except for a few, all were found not guilty or (because of their high rank) were given a formal sentence, which was considered served, and returned to Germany. Only the men of the 3rd Company "Der *Führer*" were forced to wait a long time for their trial and were the last members of the division to go free.

• • •

Following his return from captivity the former regimental commander occasionally turned to former regimental comrades and all former members of the *Waffen-SS* in the veteran's bulletin "*Der Freiwillige*" for donations to assist those comrades still being held in France. This relief action was well received and each time large sums of money were received for the comrades in France.

It was several years before these men, too, returned from France. The last former members of the regiment were released on 17 April 1959, fourteen years after the end of the war. On this day the history of the regiment ended.

Through the generosity of his comrades it was possible to present the last returnee with a considerable sum of money to tide him over. Offers of assistance in helping the comrade, who had been in captivity from age twenty-two to thirty-six, get a new start poured in from all parts of the Federal Republic and Austria. He was able to begin this new chapter in his life with a free three-week vacation with another former member of the regiment in Tyrol.

This manifestation of the comradeship and generosity which had spanned the war and captivity is the most fitting conclusion to the history of the regiment. The men of the 2nd SS Panzer Division "Das *Reich*", and particularly the men of the "*Der Führer*" Regiment, had proven not only in the war, but also in the hard years of captivity, that they were what they always wanted to be:

Comrades to the end!

## EPILOGUE

Even after the conclusion of our regiment's history many comrades from peacetime, from life at the front and from captivity have remained in touch and have become friends for life. The best proof of this are the annual reunions of our old regiment, which always become a celebration of memories and which no one wants to miss.

The final chapter on the captivity of the "D*er Führer*" Regiment was not written to open old wounds or to renew hatred, but to bring into the open the long silenced truth about the fate of the *Waffen-SS* in captivity through the example of the "*Der Führer*" Regiment.

In spite of everything that we experienced in French captivity as men of the "*Das Reich*" Division and the "*Der Führer*" Regiment, we returned from France without hate.

In prison we met many excellent Frenchmen who had fought by our side in the east as European volunteers, helped defend the fortress of Kolberg and fought valiantly to the end in the Battle of Berlin. They became our best comrades in prison. They had wanted the same thing that both sides are striving for today – the ultimate reconciliation between France and Germany. Their tragedy was just that they had wanted it twenty years too soon.

The French attorneys exhausted every possibility in defending the Germans before the Standing High Military Court in Bordeaux and many of them did more than their duty.

The end of the Second World War also marked the end of an epoch. It was probably the last war to be fought entirely with conventional weapons. Europe had lost its centuries-old place in the world. It became increasingly clear that the Second World War was lost not only by Germany but by all of Europe. The atomic age was announced loudly and unmistakably by the apocalyptic effects of the two American atomic bombs dropped on Hiroshima and Nagasaki.

It is our hope the last war with all of its harshness and inhumanity forced the peoples of Europe and the world to realize that another conflict between peoples under today's circumstances must inevitably result in the end of humanity and therefore has to be avoided. The enmity between Germany and France appears to have been overcome.

French and Germans have fought each other long enough. The partnership between two peoples is inevitably the actual cornerstone of European unity and the precondition for a true peace.

But there must also be a reconciliation with Russia and with our immediate eastern neighbors Poland and Czechoslovakia if peace in Europe is to finally become a reality.

We will never give hope that a just peace will be realized on the basis of the peaceful reunification of Germany.

# APPENDICES

I

Order of the day to soldiers of the 18th Army, 14 May 1940

Army order (18th Army), 16 May 1940

Extract from division order for continuation of the march on 20 May 1940

Division order for the continuation of the march on 21 May 1940

Extract from division order for 23 May 1940

Extract from division order for 24-25 May 1940

Order of the day XXXXI Army Corps, 26 May 1940

Division order for defense during the night of 26-27 May 1940

Division order for continuation of the attack on 28 May 1940

Radio message from SS-V Division to the "DF" Regiment, 13 June 1940

Extract from division order for the departure of the division on 11 June 1940 (preliminary order)

Extract from division order for 16 June 1940

Radio message from SS-V Division to the "DF" Regiment, 24 June 1940

Order of the day by the commander in chief of Army Group B, 25 June 1940

Extract from division order by special missions officer, 26 June 1940

Division order SS-V Division, 30 June 1940

II

*Generaloberst* Guderian on the *Waffen-SS*

Order of the day "*Reich*" Division, 26 July 1941

Combat report by the SS-V Division "Reich" on operations from 22 June to 28 July 1941

Division order for 29 July 1941

Order of the day "*Reich*" Division, 9 September 1941

Order of the day "*Reich*" Division, 12 September 1941

Order of the day by the commander in chief of Panzer Group 2, *Generaloberst* Guderian, to the soldiers of the SS Division "Reich", 23 September 1941

Order of the day "*Reich*" Division, 23 September 1941

Order of the day by the commander in chief of Panzer Group 4, *Generaloberst* Hoeppner, 2 October 1941
Order of the day "*Reich*" Division, 23 October 1941
Order of the day XXXX Panzer Corps, *General* Stumme, 16 November 1941
Order of the day XXXX Panzer Corps, *General* Stumme, 27 November 1941
Order of the day XXXX Panzer Corps, *General* Stumme, 9 December 1941
Order of the day "*Reich*" Division, 11 December 1941
Order of the day XXXX Panzer Corps, *General* Stumme, 13 December 1941
Order of the day "*Reich*" Division, 21 December 1941
Order of the day "*Reich*" Division, 11 January 1942
Order of the day commander of the "DF" Regiment, 1 January 1942
Extracts from the *Wehrmacht* communiqué concerning the fighting around Kharkov 1943

III
Operations by I Battalion, SS "DF" in January and February 1943 in the Donets bend area

IV
Division order "Das *Reich*" Division No. 30 (extract), 24/8/1943
Division order "*Das Reich*" Division No. 31 (extract), 26/8/1943
Headquarters, XI Army Corps, daily report, 26/8/1943 (extract)
Order of the day "*Das Reich*" Division, 17/9/1943
Division order "*Das Reich*" Division No. 40, 21/9/1943 (extract)

V
The commander of the 75th Infantry Division to the leader of the SS Armored Battle Group "*Das Reich*", 14 April 1944
Order of the day by the 168th Infantry Division on the occasion of the departure of the SS Armored Battle Group "*Das Reich*" from the division formation, 15 April 1944
The *Wehrmacht* communiqué reports...

VI
Enemy intelligence sheet No. 10, secret, the 2nd SS Panzer Division "*Das Reich*", 21 June 1944
Extracts from the war diary of Headquarters, 7th Army, 26 to 29 June 1944
Report by the Ia of the 2nd SS Panzer Division "*Das Reich*" to the LXXXIV Army Corps, 23 July 1944
Corps order of the day by Headquarters, LXXXIV Army Corps, 14 July 1944
Extracts from *Generalfeldmarschall* von Kluge's telephone conversations:
31 July with chief Headquarters, 7th Army, *Oberst* Gersdorf
with *General* Warlimont (*Führer* Headquarters)
7 August with commander in chief 7th Army, *Generaloberst* Hausser
The *Wehrmacht* communiqué reports on 18 October 1944
On 8 May 1945 the armed forces high command announced

## Rank Abbreviations

| Abbreviations: | Waffen-SS Rank | Equivalent Army Rank |
|---|---|---|
| Gren. | Grenadier | Grenadier |
| Strm. | Sturmmann | Gefreiter |
| Rttf. | Rottenführer | Obergefreiter |
| Uscha. | Unterscharführer | Unteroffizier |
| Oscha. | Oberscharführer | Feldwebel |
| Hscha. | Hauptscharführer | Oberfeldwebel |
| Stabsscha. | Stabsscharführer | Hauptfeldwebel |
| (senior NCO) | | |
| Ju. | Junker | Fähnrich |
| Oju. | Oberjunker | Oberfähnrich |
| Ustuf. | Untersturmführer | Leutnant |
| Ostuf. | Obersturmführer | Oberleutnant |
| Hstuf. | Hauptsturmführer | Hauptmann |
| Stubaf. | Sturmbannführer | Major |

| | | |
|---|---|---|
| Ostubaf. | Obersturmbannführer | Oberstleutnant |
| Staf. | Standartenführer | Oberst |
| Brigadeführer | | Generalmajor |
| Gruppenführer | | Generalleutnant |
| Obergruppenführer | | General |
| Oberstgruppenführer | | Generaloberst |

# BIBLIOGRAPHY

"*Waffen-SS im Einsatz*" by Generaloberst Paul Hausser
"*Ritterkreuzträger der Waffen-SS*" by Günther Krätschmer
"*Erinnerungen eines Soldaten*" by Generaloberst Guderian
"*Verlorene Siege*" by Generalfeldmarschall von Manstein
"*Stalingrad...bis zur letzten Patrone*" by Heinz Schröter
"*Ein Mann verliert einen Weltkrieg*" by Karlheinrich Rieker
"*Krieg in Europa*" by Friedo von Senger und Etterlin
"*Der grosse Rausch*" by Erich Kern
"*Die Uhr blieb stehen*" by Erich Kern
"*Sie kommen*" by Carell
"*Der zweite Weltkrieg*" by Fuller
"*Gekämpft, gesiegt, geschlagen*" by Generaloberst Rendulic.
"*Wie das Gesetz es befahl*" from the Welsermühl Verlag
"*Unternehmen Barbarossa*" in the magazine Kristall 1961-62
"*The Battle of Kursk*" by Soviet Colonel I.I. Markin
"*The Great Battle before Moscow*" by A.M. Samsonov
"*West of Voronezh*" by Soviet Colonel V.P. Morosov
"*Die Schlacht bei Rshew*" with the official seal of Headquarters, 2nd Army

The war diary of the "*Deutschland*" Regiment, western campaign 1940

Pages from the war diary of the "DF" Regiment, western campaign 1940

Diaries of the 3rd and 6th Companies "DF", western campaign 1940

Diary of the 9th Company "DF", Kharkov operation 1943

"*Der französische Widerstand und seine Bekämpfung durch die deutsche Besatzungsmacht*" by Dr. Hans Luther, Institute for Occupation Questions, Tubingen

"*Division Das Reich*", Vols I-III, by Otto Weidinger, Munin Verlag

"*Das Gesetz des Handelns*" – "Operation Citadelle" 1943 by Ernst Klink, Deutsche Verlagsanstalt, Stuttgart 1966

**Unpublished Sources**

Solemn declaration by Ostuf. Gerlach

Extracts from the "Tulle File" at the International Military Court Nuremberg

Report: "The Last days in Prague" by Princess Stephan zu Schaumburg-Lippe

Order of the day by *Generaloberst* Hoth, 9 May 1946

## 4th SS Panzer-Grenadier Regiment "DF"
## Recipients of the Knight's Cross
## In the Order Awarded

1 Georg Keppler, born 7/5/1894, died 16/6/1966

Knight's Cross: 15/8/1940 as SS-*Oberführer* and commander SS/"DF", 1945: SS-Ogruf. and Gen. d. W-SS, com.gen. XVIII SS Corps.

2 Ludwig Kepplinger, born 3/12/1911, KIA 6/8/1944

Knight's Cross: 4/9/1940 as Hscharf. and platoon leader 11./"DF", killed as Stubaf. and commander of a panzer battalion in the 17th SS Panzer-Grenadier Division "*Götz von Berlichingen*"

3 Otto Kumm, born 1/10/1909

Knight's Cross: 16/2/1942 as Ostubaf. and commander SS Rgt. "DF"

4 Vinzenz Kaiser, born 28/2/1904, KIA April 1945
Knight's Cross: 6/4/1943 as SS-Hstuf. and leader III (Arm.) SS "DF"

5 Sylvester Stadler, born 30/12/1910
Knight's Cross: 6/4/1943 as Ostubaf. and commander 4th SS Panzer-Grenadier Regiment "DF"

6 Simon Grascher
Knight's Cross: 14/8/1943 as Uscha. and platoon headquarters section leader 9 (Arm.) "DF"

7 Willi Grieme, born 4/10/1914
Knight's Cross: 17/9/1943 as Ostuf. and leader of 4/"DF"

8 Josef Lainer, born 13/3/1920
Knight's Cross 8/10/1943 as Oscha. and platoon leader in 3/"DF"

9 Helmut Kämpfe, born 31/7/1909, KIA June 1944
Knight's Cross: 10/12/1943 as Stubaf. and commander III (Arm.)/"DF"

10 Alfred Lex, born 10/6/1913, KIA 11/3/1944
Knight's Cross: 10/12/1943 as Hstuf. and leader I/"DF"

11 Herbert Schulze, born 1/4/1914
Knight's Cross: 16/12/1943 as Stubaf. and commander II/ "DF"

12 Joachim Krüger, born 30/11/1920, KIA 14/8/1943
Knight's Cross: 24/6/1944 as Ustuf. and leader 10 (Arm.)/ "DF"

13 Heinz Werner, born 2/12/1917
Knight's Cross: 23/8/1944 as Stubaf. and commander III (Arm.)/"DF"

14 Adolf Peichl, born 8/12/1917, died 4/6/1969
Knight's Cross: 16/10/1944 as Hscharf. and platoon leader 12 (Arm.)/"DF"

15 Otto Weidinger, born 27/5/1914
Knight's Cross: 21/4/1944 as Stubaf. and commander 2nd Armored Reconnaissance Battalion "*Das Reich*"

16 Hans Hauser, born 31/1/1916
Knight's Cross: 6/5/1945 as Stubaf. and commander I/ "DF"

17 Lange, (not known)
Knight's Cross: 6/5/1945 as Strm. and squad leader 16/ "DF"

## "*Der Führer*" Regiment
## Recipients of the Knight's Cross with Oak Leaves

1 Otto Kumm, 221st Knight's Cross with Oak Leaves: 6/4/1943 as Staf. and commander 4th SS Panzer-Grenadier Regiment "*Der Führer*"

2 Sylvester Stadler, 303rd Knight's Cross with Oak Leaves: 16/9/1943 as Ostubaf. and commander 4th SS Panzer-Grenadier Regiment "*Der Führer*"

3 Otto Weidinger, 688th Knight's Cross with Oak Leaves: 26/12/1944 as Ostubaf. And commander 4th SS Panzer-Grenadier Regiment "*Der Führer*"

4 Vinzenz Kaiser, 787th Knight's Cross with Oak Leaves: 18/3/1945 as Ostubaf. And commander 38th SS Panzer-Grenadier Regiment

(murdered by US soldiers while prisoner of war along with 300 other men)

5 Heinz Werner, 864th Knight's Cross with Oak Leaves: 6/5/1945 as Stubaf. and commander III (Arm.)/"DF"

## "*Der Führer*" Regiment Recipients of the Knight's Cross with Oak Leaves and Swords

1 Otto Kumm, Knight's Cross with Oak Leaves and Swords (138): 4/4/1945 as Brigf. and Gen. d. *Waffen-SS*, commander 7th SS Volunteer Mountain Division "Prinz Eugen"; last post: commander 1st SS Panzer Division "LSSAH"

2 Sylvester Stadler, Knight's Cross with Oak Leaves and Swords (150): 6/5/1945 as Brigf. and Gen.Maj. d. *Waffen-SS*, commander 9th SS Panzer Division "*Hohenstaufen*"

3 Otto Weidinger, Knight's Cross with Oak Leaves and Swords (148): 6/5/1945 as Ostubaf. and commander 4th SS Panzer-Grenadier Regiment "*Der Führer*"

Altogether members of the regiment were awarded:

| | |
|---|---|
| Knight's Cross | 17 |
| Knight's Cross with Oak Leaves | 5 |
| Knight's Cross with Oak Leaves and Swords | 3 |

## Decorations

It is no longer possible to determined the number of German Crosses in Gold, the extremely high number of Iron Crosses, First and Second Class,

Infantry Assault Badges,
Tank Battle Badges,
Close Combat Clasps in Bronze, Silver and Gold,
Wound Badges in Bronze, Silver and Gold,
War Merit Crosses with Swords

They are, however, proof of the spirit of bravery and of sacrifice which always motivated the men of the "*Der Führer*" Regiment.

But the high-ranking decorations of the Knight's Cross, Knight's Cross with Oak Leaves and Knight's Cross with Oak Leaves and Swords were also special decorations for the entire regiment.

The words spoken by the commanding officer of the SS-Division "*Das Reich*", *SS-Brigadeführer* and *Generalmajor der Waffen-SS* Wilhelm Bittrich (former commander of I Battalion/"*Der Führer*") when he was awarded the Knight's Cross on 21 December 1941 apply to them all:

*Comrades!*

*In a serious hour I have been decorated with the Knight's Cross by the Führer and Supreme Commander.*

*You should know that I do not bear this recognition alone. I see this cross on every fighting man of the division. I wear it for the dead and for you who are still fighting.*

...

*I stand in awe before the dead and your spirit of sacrifice.*

*signed Bittrich*

## Notes:

[1] s written by Georg Keppler based on diary entries and the war diary of the "DF" Regiment and the "*Deutschland*" Regiment.

[2] Himmler first expressed this notion on the occasion of a visit to the troops of the SS-Division in Holland in September 1940 before all the officers of the division. It resulted in much discussion among the division's officer corps.

[3] This section was written by Otto Kumm using personal writings and notes. It was supplemented with combat reports and documentary material as well as verbal and personal statements by former members of the regiment.

[4] The "Ritter-Adler" Assault Gun Brigade.

[5] The enemy units involved were the 6th Guards Cavalry Corps, the 111th Soviet Rifle Division, the 201st Tank Brigade, units of the 180th Rifle Division, elements of the 48th Guards Rifle Division and the 146th Guards Rifle Regiment. Combined under the command of Colonel F.I. Rudkin, the 179th Tank Brigade and the 1245th Anti-Tank Artillery Regiment had established a strong anti-tank defense position taking advantage of the terrain.

[6] This section was compiled and written based on the chronology and diary of Georg Seegerer. Detail information provided by Opificius, Pahnke and Weiß.

[7] This chapter was compiled from the account by Sylvester Stadler and the chronology of Georg Seegerer, supplemented by material provided by Herbert Schulze, Heinz Werner, Günter Werner and Otto Weidinger.

[8] Compiled by Otto Weidinger based on the records of Georg Seegerer.

[9] This section was written by Otto Weidinger, who in these weeks was attached to the regimental headquarters for familiarization purposes and held no official position. This account is therefore not a justification of his own actions rather a factual description of events by a non-participating observer.

[10] This information is taken from the book *Der französische Widerstand gegen die deutsche Besatzungsmacht und seine Bekämpfung* (The French Resistance against the German Occupation and Measures Taken against It), P 74-78, Institute for Occupation Questions, Tübingen.

[11] Dr.jur. Hans Luther: *Der französische Widerstand gegen die deutsche Besatzungsmacht und seine Bekämpfung*, P 76-78, Institute for Occupation Questions, Tübingen.

[12] These declarations are from the files of the French counsel for the prosecution at the International Military Tribunal at Nuremberg.

[13] After evaluating the papers left by *Gruppenführer* Lammerding, Herr Herbert Taege supplemented and expanded the report on Tulle and Oradour with appropriate additions.

[14] This section was written by Otto Weidinger using the timetable and diary of Georg Seegerer. It was reworked and supplemented by evaluating war diaries, original maps and sketches, orders and other documents.

[15] Statement by Frau Herta Püringer, Ridau, on 12/2/1965.

[16] This section was written by Gert Schmager.

[17] Since there are no reports concerning the camps at Sulzbach-Rosenberg, Weiden-Flossenbürg and Saal bei Regensburg, where parts of the regiment were held for a time, the Regensburg and Landshut camps, in which the author was held, were described as representative of the other camps.